Frederick William Puller

The Primitive Saints and the See of Rome

Frederick William Puller

The Primitive Saints and the See of Rome

ISBN/EAN: 9783744776714

Printed in Europe, USA, Canada, Australia, Japan

Cover: Foto ©Lupo / pixelio.de

More available books at **www.hansebooks.com**

THE SEE OF ROME

BY

F. W. PULLER

OF THE SOCIETY OF S. JOHN THE EVANGELIST, COWLEY

WITH A PREFACE BY

EDWARD, LORD BISHOP OF LINCOLN

SECOND EDITION

LONDON

LONGMANS, GREEN, & CO.

AND NEW YORK: 15 EAST 16th STREET

1893

CONTENTS.

LECTURE III.

THE RELATION OF S. PETER TO THE APOSTOLIC COLLEGE AND TO THE CHURCH.

LECTURE IV.

THE GROWTH OF THE PAPAL POWER FROM THE PEACE OF THE CHURCH TO THE END OF THE PONTIFICATE OF DAMASUS.

LECTURE V.

The Growth of the Papal Power during the Sixty Years which followed the Death of Damasus.

PART II.

COMMUNION WITH THE ROMAN SEE IS NOT THE NECESSARY CONDITION OF MEMBERSHIP IN THE CATHOLIC CHURCH.

LECTURE VI.

The Unity of the Church.—I.

LECTURE VII.

THE UNITY OF THE CHURCH.—II.

The Acacian Troubles.

APPENDIX.

PREFACE

I remember seeing, some few years ago, in Dr. Pusey's own handwriting, a letter written in answer to a friend who had asked him to recommend the most important works in refutation of the Socinian heresy.

Dr. Pusey's answer was to this effect—that such a question would indeed admit of an answer of considerable length, but for himself he had always considered the first fourteen verses of the first chapter of S. John's Gospel to be quite sufficient.

The title of this book, *The Primitive Saints and the See of Rome*, has reminded me of this incident.

The way of the truth is one: the paths of error are many, and in many of them there is much to be seen that is attractive, and for a time pleasant; but in the end they do not satisfy, not leading us to that perfect rest of head and heart which is only to be found in the way of truth.

In the writings of the Primitive Church, we do not

see at once how many possible errors are excluded
and refuted by them until we have the later dis-
tortions and confusions of the faith brought before us.
When these later errors are placed beside the rule of
the one faith, the fact of their variation, and the
degree of it, becomes apparent.

Hence, as new forms of error spring up, it is necessary to look again at the one rule of the faith, that
we may not be deceived. This is the object of the
present book. The Fathers of the first four centuries
are so unconscious of the claims made by the Roman
Church at the present time, and in the Middle Ages,
in the matter of jurisdiction, that a reader of those
early writings would not think of collecting the accu-
mulative evidence on the subject which they afford until
the modern claims had been pressed upon him. For
this reason Father Puller at once states the position
which he holds to be inconsistent with the teaching
of the great writers of the earlier centuries, by quotations of Roman documents of the highest authority.
He begins with the dogmatic definition of Pope Boniface VIII. in his bull, *Unam Sanctam:*[1]—" We therefore declare, assert, and define that for every human
creature it is altogether necessary to salvation that
he be subject to the Roman pontiff." Afterwards [2]

---

[1] p. 2.   [2] pp. 5, 6.

he cites from the decrees of the Vatican Council of the year 1870 that "the Roman Church, by the appointment of the Lord, holds the chief authority of ordinary power over all other churches, and that this power of jurisdiction belonging to the Roman pontiff is a truly episcopal power," and "an immediate power." Further, that all the pastors and all the faithful, whether taken separately or taken altogether, are bound to the authority of the pope "by the obligation of true obedience, not only in things which pertain to faith and morals, but also in things pertaining to discipline and government of the Church throughout the world." It is added that "this is the teaching of the Catholic faith, and that no one can deviate from it without the loss of faith and salvation."

Such assumptions are so contradictory to the honest interpretation of the writings and acts of the Church of the first centuries, that it is difficult to see how they could ever be made, except through ignorance or the blinding influence of ambition

Bishop Butler has remarked that "people are too apt inconsiderately to take for granted that things are really questionable, because they hear them often disputed. This, he says, is so far from being a consequence, that we know demonstrated truths have been disputed, and even matters of fact, the objects of our senses." [1]

It would seem as if the converse of this principle were also true, and that people are to apt inconsiderately to take for granted that what is confidently asserted must necessarily be true. Some false principle of this kind has, we feel sure, unconsciously it may be, induced many minds to yield assent to the constant repetition of the groundless assumptions of the modern Roman claims with regard to jurisdiction. We have long been convinced that the modern Roman Church has unduly magnified the question of jurisdiction, and has endeavoured to clothe it with a degree of mystery and terror which it does not possess.

The chief practical factor in jurisdiction is really negative, and is based on human considerations with a view to the preservation of order, and as a safeguard against the human infirmities of ambition and the love of power, in the exercise of the truly mysterious powers conveyed by ordination and consecration. So Bishop Wordsworth says, " The episcopal office is of divine institution, and cannot, in its spiritual nature and ministrations, be affected by any

---

[1] *Charge to the Clergy of Durham,* 1751, p. 310. Oxford Edition, 1830.

human laws; the actual *exercise* of *authority* of bishops as diocesans, metropolitans, and patriarchs, may depend for its distribution and apportionment upon secular circumstances, and be subject to modifications from civil authority after ecclesiastical consultation."[1] And so Father Puller has expressed his own belief. "To sum up this part of our subject. By divine right all bishops were inherently equal, but by custom and ecclesiastical legislation the bishops of the metropolitical sees acquired certain rights which were delegated to them by their brother bishops. Moreover, among the most important Churches a certain order of precedence grew up, which corresponded with the civil dignity of the cities in which those Churches existed; and, finally, the Churches which were founded by the apostles were treated with peculiar reverence."[2]

In his Epistle to the Romans, S. Paul, more than once, leaves the particular point in dispute, and recalls those to whom he is writing to the consideration of some first principle, or generally accepted truth, by which in reality the point at issue was governed. "God forbid: for theh how shall God judge the world?"[3] or, "Nay; but, O man, who art thou that repliest against God?"[4]

---

[1] *Theophilus Anglicanus*, pt. i. ch. xii., p. 117, 2nd edit.
[2] p. 18.   [3] iii. 6.   [4] ix. 20.

Some method of this kind is what is wanted in dealing with the modern Roman claims. Instead of allowing the mind to be unduly biassed by the supposed interpretation of particular passages, it should be recalled to make an honest judgment on the general object and meaning of the writer from whose works the passage in question is taken. Is it possible, we would ask, that the great Fathers of the early centuries could have commented as they did upon the great Petrine texts, "On this rock I will build My Church," and "Feed My sheep," if they had seen in them authority for asserting the vital necessity of obedience to S. Peter and to his successors in the particular see of Rome?

Can we conceive that S. Irenæus or S. Cyprian could have written and acted as they did if they had regarded the Bishop of Rome as the infallible and supreme authority over the whole Church?

Could the Fathers of the Council of Nicæa have passed the canons which we know they passed if they had recognized the papal supremacy? We need to bring our minds to the consideration of such words as Dr. Bright has given us in his notes on the sixth canon of Nicæa: "The omission (of a saving clause acknowledging the unique and sovereign position of the Bishop of Rome) is a proof, if proof were wanted, that the First Œcumenical Council knew nothing of the doctrine of papal supremacy." [1]

These simple primary facts are of great importance, for we must remember that the last word has by no means yet been spoken with regard to the mediæval and modern claims of Rome.

Only, alas! about one-third of the world is as yet Christian, even in name. The great world of India and China, as it becomes acquainted with the history of the Church, must make up its mind upon these assumptions. It is of the utmost importance that we should present the truth to the independently educated Heathen mind in the most exact and strongest form possible. The great Eastern Church rejects those claims with unshaken confidence. The intellectual Protestant world in Europe resents them. With ourselves in England, the increased knowledge of history is enabling us to see with increasing clearness the human origin out of which many of those ecclesiastical claims have sprung, and the human infirmities which have supported and developed them. The increased study of history in our universities is a marked feature of the last fifty years. Formerly, the requirements of candidates for ordination, with

---

[1] *Notes on the Canons of the First Four General Councils*, by W. Bright, D.D., p. 21. Oxford: 1882.

regard to Church history, were limited, almost exclusively, to a knowledge of the first three or four centuries, and of the Reformation, which left them in blank ignorance of the very thousand years in which the claims of the papacy grew up. This ignorance on our part gave a great opportunity for the strong assertions of the advocates of the Roman claims. Now the study of mediæval history has enabled us to appreciate more fully the truth of the quotation with which the late learned Archbishop of Dublin concludes his lecture on " The papacy at its height " in the time of Innocent III., when he speaks of it as " the grandest and most magnificent failure in human history."[1] Father Puller has brought out very clearly[2] how much in the Roman claims to jurisdiction may be traced to the merely human source of the Rescript of Gratian, towards the close of the fourth century. Yet " the new system," he adds, " applies only to the West." " There is not a word in the Rescript about the Eastern empire." " It is limited, local ;" " patriarchal, not papal." And the patriarchal jurisdiction over Gaul, Britain, Spain, and Africa " was the creation of the State, not of the Church."[3] The same is true of the Rescript of

[1] *Mediæval Church History*, by Archbishop Trench, p. 162. 1877.
[2] pp. 155–160.   [3] pp. 158, 159.

Valentinian III., which formed a new starting-point in the development of the papal power.[1]

Viewed in connection with the persistency of the Roman assumptions generally, the failure of the repeated attacks of Roman writers upon the validity of Anglican orders is very encouraging. Nothing could have been stronger than the assertions which have been made. The historical facts of the consecration of Parker and of Barlow have been disputed, but no candid weigher of historical evidence would now doubt them. The validity of the form used in ordination and consecration has been denied, but the better liturgiologists of the Roman communion have shown that such denial would be suicidal. Attempts have been made to hang the weight of the validity of our orders upon the subtle thread of *intention*, but here in truth we agree; "*Intentio faciendi id quod facit Ecclesia, quod Christus instituit,*" we heartily accept.[2] Indeed, one of the latest

---

[1] pp. 212–215.

[2] Cf. Hooker (*Eccles. Pol.* v. lviii. 3) : "Inasmuch as sacraments are actions religious and mystical, which nature they have not unless they proceed from a serious meaning, and what every man's private mind is, as we cannot know, so neither are we bound to examine, therefore always in these cases the known intent of the Church generally doth suffice, and where the contrary is not manifest, we may presume that he which outwardly doth the work, hath inwardly the purpose of the Church of God." And *Elementa Theol. Dogm.,*

writers against Anglican orders has honestly admitted that " it is very unfortunate that the Nag's Head story was ever seriously put forward; for it is so absurd, on the face of it, that it has led to the suspicion of Catholic theologians not being sincere in the objections they make to Anglican orders." [1] Quite so. And this compels us to mention what we would willingly, if sorrowfully, pass over in silence—the worse than merely human element on which much of the Roman claims are based; the false documents, the forgeries; and the unaccountable false use of true documents, such as the quotation of the fifth canon of the Council of Sardica by the Roman legates at the Council of Carthage as a canon of the Œcumenical Council of Nicæa. " The Council of Nicæa was venerated in Africa, as elsewhere, and its canons received as authoritative." But " when the legates quoted the Sardican canon as if it were Nicene, the African bishops at Carthage must have been thoroughly puzzled. They thought that they knew the Nicene canons well, and this canon quoted

vol. vii. p. 135. Schouppe, S.J. 1870. " Non requiritur intentio faciendi id quod facit Ecclesia Romana; sed sufficit intentio generalis faciendi quod facit Ecclesia."

[1] *The Question of Anglican Orders Discussed,* by the very Reverend T. H. Estcourt, M.A., F.S.A., Canon of St. Chad's, Birmingham, p. 154. 1873.

by the legates which allowed appeals to Rome, was
completely new to them."[1]   The whole case of
Apiarius is most instructive.   We may compare with
it the false quotation, as from the sixth canon of
Nicæa, which was made by the Roman legate Pas-
chasinus at the Council of Chalcedon.[2]

There is perhaps an element of comfort to be
derived from the recognition of the existence of these
forgeries.   On the one hand, it frees us from the
necessity of any longer straining our minds to
account for facts which appear in all honesty so
unaccountable.   On the other, it may mitigate the
moral responsibility of those who have honestly
based their words and actions upon them, believing
them to be genuine.   It is, for example, hard to
understand how any one familiar with the writings
of S. Irenæus, could speak of S. Peter as the sole
founder of the Roman see.   The anti-Pauline Clementine romance may explain the source from which
this invention was derived.[3]   The interpolations in
the writings of S. Cyprian, the supposed decretals
of the early popes, given in Isidore's decretals, and
woven into the decretum of Gratian and the later
canon law, and into the theological system of the

---

[1] See pp. 188, 189.   [2] See Dr. Bright's *Notes* (as before), p. 198.
[3] See pp. 48, 49.

schoolmen,—all these, and other like inventions, have had much to do with building·up the papal system, and have given confidence to the modern assumption of universal jurisdiction.

It is much to be wished that the writings of the schoolmen, as a whole, should be seriously taken in hand by a competent body of scholars, so that they might be thoroughly edited, and the statements contained in them tested by the knowledge which we now possess. A valuable residuum would, I have no doubt, remain in all the branches of scientific knowledge; but it would be a *residuum*. Not all their assertions could be accepted. The same is to be wished with regard to canon law. The contributions which have been made by Von Schulte[1] and others ought to be attended to and followed up.

Hitherto Roman writers have too often made their assertions, and then retired into the dark places of the schoolmen and the canon law, as into a wood; and we, from ignorance, have been afraid to follow them. The whole ground wants clearing, and sowing with the good seed of the truth.

But this is perhaps travelling beyond the limits

---

[1] *Die Geschichte der Quellen und Literatur des Canonischen Rechts, . . . von Dr. Joh. F. von Schulte.* 1875.

of the present volume, *The Primitive Saints and the See of Rome.*

The book should be studied carefully, in order that the contrast between the modern Roman claims and the teaching of the primitive saints may be seen in detail, and the importance of the contrast may be fully appreciated.

The latter part is chiefly occupied with the contravention of the Roman position, as expressed by Cardinal Wiseman : "According to the doctrine of the ancient Fathers, it is easy at once to ascertain who are the Church Catholic, and who are in a state of schism, by simply discovering who are in communion with the see of Rome and who are not." [1]

The impossibility of accepting this statement is very fully and ably shown from the history of S. Meletius, S. Flavian, S. Chrysostom, and many others, who during their lifetime were the recognized leaders and champions of the Church, and who were reckoned among the saints after their death, though their lives were lived, in part or altogether, out of communion with the see of Rome. [2]

While the historical force of the book cannot be

---

[1] pp. 220, 221.

[2] " S. Meletius, even while president of this second General Council, was still out of communion with the West " (*The Councils of*

felt without a careful study of its contents, there is one element of power which it possesses for which I cannot refrain from expressing my most sincere thanks: I mean the brilliancy of the Christian spirit which runs through it all. This is in a measure a new and a most powerful factor in our controversy with Rome. The self-devotion and zeal of many in the Roman communion have been a great weight in the scale when the mind has become weary of arguing. The $\dot{\eta}\theta\iota\kappa\dot{\eta}\ \pi\acute{\iota}\sigma\tau\iota\varsigma$ has a persuasive force of great and deserved value. It partakes of the mysterious power of personal influence, and is the result, not of mere intellectual cleverness, but of character and life.

A light of new brilliancy seems to be thrown on these old records, as they are represented to us by one who has voluntarily renounced those worldly comforts and advantages which most of us in the Church of England have claimed it to be our rightful liberty to enjoy. Nothing but the pure desire to state the truth, that so the light and life and love which

the *Church from A.D.* 51 *to A.D.* 381, by the Rev. E. B. Pusey, D.D., p. 306. J. H. Parker. 1857).

"S. Hilary died on May 5, at the age of forty-eight. He was, like Meletius, a man of acknowledged sanctity outside the Roman communion" (*History of the Church from A.D.* 313 to 451, by W. Bright, p. 389. Parker. 1860).

belong to the Body of Christ, by virtue of her union with her Divine Head, might be with us in their fullest perfection, could have induced this author to write a book of controversy.

It is this perfect charity and chivalrous confidence in the truth, through the power of the Holy Spirit, which gives us new hope that, in God's good time, Wisdom will be justified of her children; and that, as we are each and all indwelt by the Holy Spirit in greater fulness, we shall be taught by the same Spirit to speak the truth in love, and to "grow up into Him in all things, which is the Head, even Christ: from whom the whole body fitly joined together and compacted by that which every joint supplieth, according to the effectual working in the measure of every part, maketh increase of the body unto the edifying of itself in love."[1]

So may the Saviour's prayer be fulfilled, "that they may be one even as We are One."[2]

EDWARD LINCOLN.

[1] Eph. iv. 15, 16.   [2] S. John xvii. 22.

AUTHOR'S PREFACE

THE first five lectures printed in this volume were
delivered in the Church of All Hallows-on-the-Wall,
in the city of London, to an audience consisting of
clergymen, working for the most part in the parishes
of London and its suburbs. They were delivered at
the request of an association of East End incumbents,
which is known by the name of "Our Society," on
five consecutive Thursday mornings in Lent, 1892.
These five lectures deal with the claim to a supremacy
or primacy of jurisdiction, as of divine right, which is
made on behalf of the Roman pontiffs. The two
remaining lectures have been written subsequently,
and deal with the theory that communion with the
see of Rome is the necessary condition of communion
with the Catholic Church.

I have not thought it necessary to devote any
lecture to the consideration of the crowning claim of
the papacy to doctrinal infallibility, because, if I am
not mistaken, this claim to infallibility is usually set
forth as a consequence logically involved in the
doctrine that the pope has a primacy of jurisdiction,

(a)

and that he is the necessary centre of communion.[1] I have preferred to deal with these two more fundamental claims. If they can be shown to be unwarranted, it will evidently follow that the logical superstructure, which has been built upon them, is baseless.

I wish particularly to call attention to the fact that, in dealing with the historical argument against the papal claims, I have not attempted to cover the whole ground, even within the limits of the first six centuries, beyond which period I do not profess to go. If I had made any such attempt, this book would have become so voluminous, that it would probably have secured very few readers, and the object which I had in view, when I undertook to prepare it, would be defeated. I have been obliged to make a selection among the historical episodes and passages from the writings of the saints, which throw light on my general subject, in order that I might be able to treat the episodes and passages so selected with some fulness of detailed statement and discussion. I particularly regret that I have been unable to discuss the history of the Roman pontificate in relation to the four great heresies connected with the names of Arius, Pelagius, Nestorius, and Eutyches, and also that I have been able to say so very little about the third, fourth and fifth of the Ecumenical Councils, and less than I could have wished about the first and second.

In the third lecture and in the earlier part of the

---

[1] Compare Bottalla, *The Infallibility of the Pope*, pp. 3, 4.

sixth lecture I have discussed the witness of Holy
Scripture in regard to the two fundamental papal
claims. The rest of the book is mainly taken up
with an appeal in regard to those claims to the acts
and writings of the great saints of the Primitive
Church. It was the fact that such an appeal con-
stitutes the main argument of the book, which decided
me in the choice of its title. I do not think that it is
necessary for me to vindicate the importance of such
an appeal. The genuine sons of the Church of
England have always professed themselves to be
ready to abide by it, and the traditional theology
of the Roman communion has been accustomed to
assign a very high place to the witness of the Fathers.
If there are any Roman Catholics in the present day
who shrink from the appeal to the saints of the
Primitive Church, it is desirable that they should be
encouraged to declare their opinions openly. While
we shall sincerely grieve at the declension from the
Catholic standard which such a change of front would
betoken, the explicit abandonment of the traditional
argument of the Church's defenders will at any rate
show how hopeless it is to defend the modern claims of
the papacy by an appeal to the witness of the Primitive
Church. New doctrines need new theological methods
to uphold them. As for us, we are content to stand
upon the old paths.

As I have said, my appeal is mainly to the acts and
writings of the saints of the Primitive Church; and
for the purposes of this argument I acknowledge none

as saints except those whose sanctity the Church has recognized in some formal way. [It was not until the twelfth century that in the West the canonization of saints was reserved to the pope. In the earlier times the right of decreeing the recognition of the sanctity of this or that servant of God appertained, in the first place, to the bishop of the diocese to which he belonged. Such a decree would, when first promulgated, be authoritative only within the bishop's own sphere of jurisdiction; but, if it was approved and accepted by other bishops, it would gradually acquire a wider and in many cases an ecumenical authority. In later times, before the twelfth century, the decrees of canonization usually emanated from the Provincial Synods.[1] In the great patriarchal sees there was sometimes a tendency to canonize patriarchs who can hardly be said to have deserved the honour. The Bollandists have noted this tendency in regard to some of the occupants of the see of Constantinople, but the same thing might be said with truth concerning some Roman popes. In dealing with the bishops of Rome and Constantinople, I have not felt bound to use the title of saint in every case in which the name

---

[1] Mabillon, *Acta SS. ord. S. Bened.*, tom. vii. pp. lix., lx., *Præfat. in sæc decim.*, §§ 91, 92; cf. Benedict. XIV., *De serv. Dei beatif. et beat. canoniz.*, lib. i. cap. vi. § 9, *Opp.* tom. i. p. 17, ed. 1767. The saints, to whose testimony appeal is made in this book, are for the most part venerated throughout the Church, both in the East and in the West. In some few cases the veneration of this or that saint may, according to circumstances, be confined to the East or to the West. Where the veneration is purely local, as in the case of the ten saintly bishops of Como (p. 319), attention is called to the fact.

of this or that bishop has found a place in the local calendar.

Although these lectures were originally addressed to a clerical audience, I hope that they may be found to have some interest for that large and increasing body of laymen who recognize the importance of these questions. Having this object in view, and feeling sure that in any case some of those whom I should most wish to interest in the main argument of my book, would be repelled by the frequent occurrence of quotations in the Latin and Greek languages, I have tried to keep Latin and Greek as much as possible out of the *text* of the lectures, and to relegate quotations in those languages to the notes. I have not scrupled to lighten my own labour by using any accessible translations of patristic passages which I wished to quote in English. I do not think that I have ever done so without carefully comparing the translation with the original, and without correcting any expression occurring in the translation which seemed to need correction.

I hope that I have not anywhere transgressed the rules of Christian courtesy. The nature of my argument is of such a character that I have been compelled at times to criticize and controvert the statements and arguments of others; but I should be extremely sorry if there was a single word which might seem to be either uncharitable or consciously unfair.

I had written thus far, when I received a copy of the Preface with which the Bishop of Lincoln has enriched my book. I wish to express my gratitude to him for the Preface itself, and for his kindness in finding time to write it in the midst of his unceasing pastoral labours. Perhaps I ought to have foreseen that his affection would lead him to speak of me in a way that I do not deserve. May our Lord reward him, both now and in the world to come, for the manifold ways in which he has poured out his goodness upon me, ever since the old Cuddesdon days, more than a quarter of a century ago.

I desire also to thank Dr. Bright for taking the trouble to read over the proof-sheets of the fifth lecture, and for making several helpful suggestions in regard to the treatment of the case of Apiarius.

My thanks are also due to other kind friends, who have been good enough to answer questions, and who have in that way put me in the right track, and enabled me to solve various problems. But I must specially record my gratitude to my friend the Rev. V. S. S. Coles, of the Pusey House, who read carefully through the manuscript of this book, and whose remarks have led me to add here and there notes which will, I think, strengthen the general argument.

Lastly, I must thank my friend and brother, the Rev. P. N. Waggett, for his careful correction of the proof-sheets of the whole book, and for the help which he has given me in the work of making the index, and in other ways.

F. W. P.

The Mission House, Cowley S. John
Feast of S. Patrick, 1893.

NOTE TO SECOND EDITION

This second edition is practically a reprint from the
first with a very few corrections, mostly verbal.

I had not expected that the first edition would
have been exhausted so soon, and I have been too
much occupied with other work to take advantage
of the reviews of my book which have appeared. I
hope, however, that, if a third edition is called for,
I shall be able to prepare for it by carefully considering what my critics, whether favourable or
adverse, have written. I am very grateful to some
of them for their very helpful reviews, and for the
kind words which they have used about myself and
my book.

F. W. P.

The Mission House, Cowley S. John,
  September 2, 1893.

LECTURE I.

I AM to speak to you, my dear brothers, in these lectures about the controversy which we, who belong to the English branch of the Catholic Church, have continually to carry on with the upholders of the claims of the Roman papacy. I suppose that most of us would very much prefer to keep aloof from controversy; or, if we must have it, we should wish to spend our time and labour in doing battle with the materialists and positivists and agnostics who set themselves to undermine the very foundation of the Christian faith. If it were possible, we should like to treat our Roman Catholic neighbours as brethren, differing from us in certain matters of more or less importance, but whose work, taken as a whole, we could accept as a substantial aid in the struggle with sin and unbelief. Now, undoubtedly there are English Roman Catholic writers and workers whom we *can* regard in this more favourable light. We thank God for their writings and for their work, and we desire to profit by their wholesome teaching and by their good Christian example. Unfortunately, when we consider the Roman

B

communion in England as a whole, we are obliged to
admit that there is another side to the matter.   One
very prominent aspect of that communion is the
controversial position which she takes up in regard to
the spiritual *status* and spiritual claims of our Mother,
the Church of England.   I do not complain of this
controversial attitude.   If a man sincerely believes
that the Roman pope is infallible, and that communion with him is one of the divinely ordained
conditions of salvation; if he adheres to the dogmatic
definition of Pope Boniface VIII. in his Bull *Unam
Sanctam,* in which occurs the following passage:
"We therefore declare, assert, and define that for
every human creature it is altogether necessary to
salvation that he be subject to the Roman pontiff;"[1]—
I say that, if a man holds with sincerity such a faith
as that, he is bound to do what he can, as opportunity
may offer, to bring his neighbours and fellow-country-
men to the same belief with himself; and here, in
England, he will almost necessarily have to take up
a position of controversial antagonism to the claims
of the English Church.   But then, on the other hand,
we, who repudiate these papal theories; we, who hold

---

[1] "Porro subesse Romano Pontifici, omni humane creature declara-
mus, dicimus, et diffinimus omnino esse de necessitate salutis."   This
bull is in the *Regestum* of Boniface VIII., in the Vatican library.   A
heliotype copy of it was published in 1888, in a work entitled *Speci-
mina palæographica Regestorum Romanorum Pontificum ab Innocentio
III. usque ad Urbanum V.* (see the *Revue des Questions Historiques*
for July, 1889, tome xlvi. pp. 253-257).   The bull is also to be found
among the *Extravagantes Communes* of the *Corpus Juris Canonici,*
lib. i. tit. viii. cap. i. (ed. Friedberg ii. 1245, 1246).

that those theories were the offspring of ambition and ignorance, and that they have been spread by violence and forgery, and who with all our hearts accept the Church of England as historically the authentic representative of the Catholic Church of Christ in this country ;—we, I say, are forced almost against our will to do battle from time to time on behalf of our spiritual mother; and we are, therefore, bound to equip ourselves with some sufficient knowledge of the controversy between England and Rome, so that whether in public or in private we may be able to strengthen our people against those who would undermine their faith in the Catholicity of the Church to which they belong.   Moreover, for the sake of our own peace of mind, it is of the highest importance that we should become solidly convinced that in our controversy with Rome about the papal claims, the truth is substantially on our side.

It was the sense of the importance of helping my brethren to have clear and true views on this matter, which led me to accede to your secretary's invitation to give this course of lectures.   I confess that I enter on them with fear and trembling; not from any doubt as to the side on which the truth lies, but from my consciousness of the very imperfect way in which I shall be able to handle the subject, and from the dread that I may do more harm than good by my treatment of it.   I will ask your prayers that I may be helped and guided to say what shall tend to promote God's glory, and the Church's well-being, and the good of souls. I will do my utmost to be fair and accurate. If I make slips, as may very easily happen, I shall gladly correct them, when they are pointed out; I do not want to win a victory by any assertions or arguments which will not stand the test of investigation. I hope sincerely that no mistakes will be made, the exposure of which would endanger the solidity of the proof of those central facts on which the argument really hinges.

And now to come more directly to our subject. I cannot, of course, attempt in five lectures to cover the whole ground of this far-reaching controversy. I must make a selection; and I select the papal claim to a primacy of jurisdiction,[1] because the discussion of that claim will take us into the very heart of the matter. I propose, if I have time, to deal with the following divisions of the subject :—

1. The position of the see of Rome during the first three centuries.

2. The relation of S. Peter to the Apostolic College and to the Church.

3. The origin and growth of the papal jurisdiction.

4. The truth about the unity of the Church.[2]

My purpose is to deal with these different points

---

[1] In the sixth and seventh lectures, which were not delivered with the others, I have discussed the cognate but not identical claim which is made on behalf of the pope, when it is asserted that he is the necessary centre of communion for the whole Church.

[2] The fourth heading is dealt with in the two lectures (the sixth and the seventh) which constitute the second part of this book (see pp. 219–324).

with special reference to their bearing on the modern Roman claims, and it will therefore be well to set those claims before you in their most authentic form. We could not have them in a more authentic form than in the decrees of the Vatican Council of the year 1870. That Council is accepted by the pope and by the Roman Catholic hierarchy and by the whole Roman Catholic Church as an Ecumenical Council. It was in their view an Ecumenical Council, *over which the pope himself presided.* The decrees were promulgated by Pope Pius IX. from his presidential throne. There were 535 votes registered, of which 533 were in favour of the decrees with which we are dealing, and two only were adverse.[1] After the suspension of the Council, the decrees were accepted by all the other bishops of the Roman communion. In quoting the Vatican decrees, I am quoting an authority which cannot be gainsaid by any member of the Roman Catholic Church. What, then, do these decrees say in reference to the jurisdiction of the Roman pontiff? They say, or rather the pope and the Council say in them, that "the Roman Church, by the appointment of the Lord, holds the chief authority of ordinary power over all other Churches, and that this power of jurisdiction belonging to the Roman pontiff is a truly episcopal power," and that "it is an immediate

---

[1] After the voting, the pope, rising from his seat, said, "Decreta et Canones, qui in Constitutione modo lectâ continentur, placuerunt Patribus omnibus, duobus exceptis: Nosque sacro approbante Concilio, illa et illos, ut lecta sunt, definimus et Apostolicâ auctoritate confirmamus" (*Collectio Lacensis,* tom. vii. coll. 487, 488).

power." They go on to say that all the pastors and all the faithful, whether taken separately or taken all together, are bound to the authority of the pope "by the obligation of true obedience, not only in things which pertain to faith and morals, but also in things pertaining to the discipline and government of the Church throughout the world." They add that "this is the teaching of the Catholic truth, and that no one can deviate from it without the loss of his faith and salvation." They further teach that, in consequence of the apostolic primacy which the Roman pontiff enjoys *jure divino,* "he is the supreme judge of the faithful, and that recourse may be had to his judgment in all causes which appertain to the jurisdiction of the Church ; " "that the judgment of the apostolic see cannot be revised by any one, and that no one may pass judgment on its decisions ; wherefore those who affirm that it is allowable to appeal from the judgments of the Roman pontiffs to an Ecumenical Council as to an authority higher than the pope, are wandering from the straight pathway of truth." They pronounce an anathema on "any one who asserts that the Roman pontiff has only an office of inspection or direction, but not full and supreme power of jurisdiction over the universal Church ; " or "that he has only the chief part, and not the total plenitude, of that supreme power."[1]

Assuredly, if these decrees truly represent the

---

[1] These passages are quoted from the *Constitutio Dogmatica Prima de Ecclesiâ Christi,* which was passed by the Council and confirmed

mind of our Lord, we must accept the view commonly attributed to Cardinal Cajetan, namely, that "the Church is the born handmaid of the pope."[1]

And we are not to suppose that it is the theory of the Roman Church that this teaching about the power of the pontiff is some late development unknown to antiquity. On the contrary, the pope, when he promulgated the decree from which I have been quoting, expressly stated, in his own name and in the name of the Council, that he rested his teaching on the plain testimony of Holy Scripture, and that in this definition he was adhering to the clear and perspicuous decrees of his predecessors, the Roman pontiffs, and of the general Councils.

This, then, is the teaching, the truth of which we are to investigate. And we are to begin this morning by considering the position of the see of Rome during the first three centuries.

The local Church of Rome was organized in early times in precisely the same way as the local churches in other cities.[2] Each local Church was governed by

by the pope at the fourth session, on July 18, 1870 (cf. *Collect. Lacens.*, vii. 482–487).

[1] Cf. *Apol. Tractat. de Comparat. Auctorit. Papæ et Concil.*, cap. i. I must confess that I have some doubts as to whether this passage, when taken with its context, bears out the common idea about its meaning.

[2] Some modern Protestant writers suppose that the episcopate did not exist at Rome until the second century. Bishop Lightfoot, on the other hand, says concerning the names of S. Linus and S. Anencletus, the two bishops of Rome who, according to tradition, immediately followed the apostles and preceded S. Clement, "I see no reason to question that they not only represent historical persons, but that they were bishops in the sense of monarchical rulers of the Roman

a bishop, who had his priests and deacons to assist him. When the bishop of any Church died, his successor was normally chosen from among the priests or deacons who formed the clergy of that Church. This was the rule at Rome, as it was the rule elsewhere. The bishops of the various Churches looked on each other as brothers and colleagues. When Cornelius, Bishop of Rome, writes to Cyprian, Bishop of Carthage, he begins his letter as follows: "Cornelius to Cyprian, his brother, greeting;" and he concludes with the words, "Fare thee well, dearest brother."[1] And when Cyprian replies, he writes in the same strain: "Cyprian to Cornelius, his brother, greeting;" and he goes on, "You have acted, dearest brother, with diligence and affection, in dispatching to us in haste Nicephorus the acolyte."[2] We have various letters written by S. Cyprian to other Roman bishops besides Cornelius, as, for example, to Lucius and to Stephen, and they are all written in the same tone of perfect equality. Similarly, when S. Cyprian writes to another African bishop about the Roman pope, he alludes to him, not as a superior, but as an equal. To Pompeius, Bishop of Sabrata, Cyprian says, "Since you have desired to be informed what answer our brother Stephen returned to my letter, I have sent you a copy of that answer; on reading

Church, though their monarchy may have been much less autocratic than the episcopate even of the succeeding century" (*S. Clement of Rome*, ed. 1890, i. 340; compare i. 68).

[1] S. Cypriani *Ep.* xlviii., *Opp.* ed. Ben., p. 62.

[2] *Ep.* xlix., p. 63.

which you will more and more discover his error." [1]
Stephen is, of course, the pope.

All the bishops, wherever their sees might be, were held to be successors of the apostles, both as regards order and as regards jurisdiction; so that, as the great Belgian canonist, Van Espen, says, "The bishops receive by succession the very authority of the apostles, so that whatever the apostles had of episcopal power—that is, of power concerned with the government of the Church—has been transferred by them into the bishops, as their successors in the Church's administration and government." [2] It is important to notice that Van Espen, following the early writers, teaches that the bishops succeed to the apostles, not only in matters connected with order, such as the power of confirming and ordaining, but also in matters connected with jurisdiction, such as the administration and government of the Church. Moreover, he says that in their governing authority the bishops succeed not merely to this or that apostle, but to all of them in common; in other words, each bishop inherits the whole episcopal jurisdiction of the apostolic college. [3] To use the words of S. Cyprian:

---

[1] *Ep.* lxxiv., p. 138. One may also notice that S. Cyprian, writing (*Ep.* lii., p. 66) to the Bishop Antonianus, speaks of "our colleague Cornelius" ("Cornelium collegam nostrum"), and of "our brother bishop Cornelius" ("Cornelio co-episcopo nostro"); and writing (*Ep.* iii., p. 8) to the priests and deacons of Rome about Pope Fabian, he calls him "that good man my colleague" ("boni viri collegæ mei").

[2] *Jus Eccl. Univ.*, i. xvi. 1, 7. Dr. Neale describes Van Espen as "the first canonist of his own or of any age" (*History of the Church of Holland*, p. 175). He was born in 1646, and died in 1728.

[3] By what may be called the by-laws of the Church, the bishops

"The episcopate is one; it is a whole in which each enjoys full possession" ("Episcopatus unus est, cujus a singulis in solidum pars tenetur").[1] And the result of this primitive teaching, as Van Espen points out, is that "essentially, and setting aside later legislation, all bishops are equal in their power and authority in governing the Church."[2]

Having laid down the doctrine of the essential equality of all bishops, not only as regards order, but also as regards jurisdiction, as a foundation, we go on to notice two cross-principles, which came in afterwards, and which in practice modified that equality. The first cross-principle is the special authority which gradually grew up in the Church of the principal city of each of the geographical regions which

are, under ordinary circumstances, restrained from exercising their jurisdiction outside of their own particular diocese; but in a Provincial Synod they legislate for the province, and in an Ecumenical Synod for the Church at large.

[1] S. Cypr. *De Unit. Eccl., Opp.* ed. Ben., p. 195. The translation is from the English version of S. Cyprian's treatises in the Library of the Fathers, edited by Newman. Archbishop Benson (Smith and Wace, i. 745), describing S. Cyprian's teaching in this passage, says, "The apostleship, continued for ever in the episcopate, is thus universal, yet one; each bishop's authority perfect and independent, yet not forming with the others a mere agglomerate, but being a full tenure on a totality, like that of a shareholder in a joint-stock property." Mr. Rivington (*Authority*, p. 102) translates the passage, as I have done. The expression "in solidum" is a technical legal phrase. Examples of its use may be found under the second title of the 45th book of the Digest (vol. ii. pp. 677–680, ed. Mommsen, 1870). To give one instance—Priscus Javolenus says, "Cum duo eandem pecuniam aut promiserint aut stipulati sunt, ipso jure et singuli *in solidum* debentur et singuli debent: ideoquo petitione acceptilatione[ve] unius tota solvitur obligatio."

[2] *Suppl. in Jus Univ. Eccl.,* i. xvi. i. 7.

collectively made up the Roman empire.[1] As a rule, Christianity would get a footing first in the metropolis of each region. The other lesser cities would be evangelized by missions sent forth from thence; and so the suffragan sees would look on themselves as daughters of the metropolitical see. The metropolitan bishop was the natural centre of unity for the bishops of the province. When a see became vacant, it would be the metropolitan who would call together his brother bishops to consult about the appointment of a worthy pastor to succeed to the empty throne; and the metropolitan would naturally preside at the preliminary meetings for consultation and election, as well as at the consecration service itself. If troubles arose among the bishops, whether heresies or schisms or quarrels or other wrong-doings, or if new and difficult questions emerged, concerning which it seemed desirable that the neighbouring bishops should act together, it would be natural for the bishops to meet in synod, and it would also be natural that the metropolitan should take the initiative and summon his brethren; and the metropolis would normally be the obvious place of meeting. Under such circumstances the metropolitan would of course preside, and in most cases he would be

---

[1] In some cases the limits of the ecclesiastical province did not coincide with the limits of the civil province. Geographical facilities of access made themselves more felt than the provincial boundaries, as laid down by the imperial government; *e.g.* the Bishops of Tyre and Ptolemais, in the province of Syria, attended a synod at Cæsarea, in Palestine, in the latter part of the second century (cf. Duchesne *Origines du Culte Chrétien*, pp. 18, 19).

entrusted by the synod with the duty of seeing that its decisions were carried out. Thus by the natural course of events, and by the free action of the essentially co-equal prelates, a certain precedence and pre-eminence, and, more than that, a certain right of initiative and of inspection and of administration, would by common consent be lodged in the occupant of the metropolitical see.[1] But the very fact that what we may call the provincial system grew up naturally, and adapted itself to the varying geographical and ethnographical and political circumstances of the different regions, would necessarily result in a great want of uniformity. In some places the ecclesiastical provinces would be very small. In other places they would be very much larger. The bishops of the great cities of the empire, such as Rome, Alexandria, Antioch, Carthage, would naturally extend their influence over a far wider area than would the bishops of places like Thessalonica or Corinth. Thus there would be large provinces and small provinces, and the metropolitan of a large province would normally be a more important person than the metropolitan of a small province. And again, while the

---

[1] Compare Möhler, *On the Unity of the Church*, part ii. chap. ii. §§ 57–60 (French translation, pp. 189–198, ed. Bruxelles, 1839). Möhler's summary of this chapter is worth noting: "Les communautés voisines se réunissent, et leurs évêques forment un tout uni ensemble qui se crée un organe et un centre dans la personne du métropolitain," etc. There is an admirable paragraph describing the natural process by which the office of the metropolitan grew up, in an article by Father de Smedt, S.J., the President of the Bollandists, in the *Revue des Questions Historiques* for October, 1891, pp. 424, 425. The title of the article is *L'organisation des Églises Chrétiennes au iii* siècle.

system was growing up, there would be no necessary uniformity in regard to the measure of power which was delegated by the bishops of the province to the metropolitan. In a small province containing several flourishing churches, the suffragan bishops would maintain a very independent position, delegating only the *minimum* of initiative and direction to the metropolitan. In a large province containing one very important central Church and a great number of relatively weak Churches, there would be a strong centralizing tendency, and the metropolitan bishop would be entrusted with very large powers over his suffragans. Such was eminently the case with the Churches in the two chief cities of the empire, Rome and Alexandria. The Bishop of Rome presided, as metropolitan, over the bishops throughout Central and Southern Italy; and ultimately the three islands of Sicily, Sardinia, and Corsica were aggregated to his province.[1] Similarly, the Bishop of Alexandria was the ecclesiastical centre, not only for Egypt, but also for Libya and the Pentapolis; and both at Rome and Alexandria the metropolitan bishops exerted an authority over their suffragans which was quite abnormal, and which tended to obscure the inherent equality of the various members of the episcopal body. Doubtless this tendency did not show itself fully during the first three centuries, and perhaps during those centuries there was nothing actually unhealthy; but un-

---

[1] Cf. Duchesne, *Origines du Culte Chrétien,* p. 30.

doubtedly the great concentration of authority which gradually grew up in those sees constituted a germ, which might easily develop into a source of danger.[1]

I hope that I have now made it clear, that the civil importance of the city in which an episcopal see was erected very often reacted on the ecclesiastical relations of the bishop of that see to the bishops of the cities round about. Moreover, in the case of the leading cities of the empire, such as Rome, Alexandria, Antioch, Carthage, Ephesus, their relative civil precedence was reproduced in the hierarchy of the Church. Thus the city of Rome was the capital of the empire; and as a result the Bishop of Rome took precedence of the other bishops in the Church. Alexandria was the second city in the empire, and the Bishop of Alexandria ranked next to the Bishop of Rome in the order of the Catholic episcopate; and so on with the rest. And this precedence carried with it

[1] Cf. Duchesne, *Origines du Culte Chrétien*, p. 375, n. 2, as regards the relations of the Bishop of Rome to his suburbicarian suffragans. In illustration of the statement in the text, so far as it deals with Alexandria, I would refer to the article on "Synesius" in Smith and Wace (iv. 779). The writer of the article says, "Equally noticeable is the unqualified obedience which Synesius, though himself Metropolitan of Pentapolis, cheerfully yielded to the 'apostolic throne' of Alexandria. 'It is at once my wish and my duty to consider whatever decree comes from that throne binding upon me,' he writes, to [the patriarch] Theophilus. The unquestionable superiority of Alexandria to all the cities of Eastern Africa had given to the Patriarch of Alexandria an authority over the bishops of those cities unsurpassed, even if it was rivalled, by the supremacy of Rome in that day over the bishoprics of Central and Southern Italy." See also Dr. Bright's *Notes on the Canons of the First Four General Councils*, pp. 17, 18, 207–209.

influence.   In all organized bodies the highest person is most often made a referee or arbitrator, simply because he is highest.   People naturally consult the one who stands first.   Under normal circumstances, he is the natural spokesman and representative of the whole body on occasions when some spokesman or representative is needed.   And what takes place in other organized bodies necessarily took place and still takes place in the Church.   We have only to look at our own English branch of the Church, and we see it taking place on a large scale there.   The *jurisdiction of the Archbishop of Canterbury* is confined to the province of Canterbury;[1] but just because he is, by the consent of all, acknowledged to be the first bishop on the roll of the Anglican episcopate, therefore his *influence extends* throughout the whole Anglican communion.   He naturally presides in the Lambeth Conference; he has the chief share in deciding what subjects shall be discussed there; his advice is continually asked in regard to matters occurring in the colonial Churches; in a very true sense the care of all the Churches is upon him; and all this comes to him simply because he is first.   No canon gives him the influence, no pretence of a primacy, by divine right.   He wields this influence simply because, in the providence of God, he stands

---

[1] There are a few scattered colonial and missionary dioceses which belong to no colonial province, and which look to the Archbishop of Canterbury as their quasi-metropolitan; but they may be considered to be appendages of the province of Canterbury. Their position is abnormal, and in time they will doubtless get more into line.

first on the list. And we may see in him a picture of what, in early days, took place in regard to the Bishop of Rome, and also in their measure in regard to the Bishops of Alexandria, Antioch, and the rest.

Thus the principle of inherent equality, without being in any way abrogated, was modified by the first cross-principle of metropolitical authority and of civil precedence.

The second of the cross-principles which modified the inherent equality of all bishops was the special influence which attached to those sees which had been founded by the apostles. (These sees were called the apostolic sees, and the Churches in which they were erected were called the apostolic Churches. They were the original mother Churches which had received their instruction in the faith directly from the apostles, and had been ordered by them in all matters of discipline, and had had their first bishops consecrated by them. Other Churches, whether near or far away, had in their first beginnings received the light of the gospel either immediately or mediately from one or other of them. And a certain halo of reverence and of special influence distinguished them from the Churches which could not boast of an apostolic founder. When disputes arose in regard to matters of faith or discipline, and the question to be answered was, What was the teaching of the apostles? What was the custom of the apostles? it was a very common practice to consult the nearest apostolic Church, not as if it were infallible, but as having received the apostolic deposit of faith and discipline at first hand from one or more of the apostles, and as therefore being more likely to have retained that deposit free from all alloy. Without pretending to give an exhaustive list of the apostolic Churches, one might name the following in the order of the dates of their apostolic foundation: First, Jerusalem, "the mother of all Churches," as the Fathers of the great Council of Constantinople, of the year 382, style it in their letter to Pope Damasus and the other Western bishops; then Antioch, that "most ancient and truly apostolical Church," as the same Council describes it; then Philippi, then Thessalonica, then Corinth, then Ephesus, then Rome, then Alexandria, then Smyrna. We cannot say for certain that any apostle was ever at Alexandria, but it was considered to be an apostolic see because its first bishop—S. Mark—had received his mission, and probably his consecration, from S. Peter, whose catechist and interpreter he had been. And similarly Smyrna was apostolical because S. Polycarp was constituted bishop of that see by S. John.[1] This is how Tertullian, arguing with heretics, speaks about the apostolic Churches: "Come, now," he says, "thou that wilt exercise thy curiosity to better purpose in the business of thy salvation, go through the apostolic Churches, in which the very seats of the apostles, at this very day, preside over their own places; in which their own authentic writings are

______

[1] Tertullian, *De Præscr. Hær.,* xxxii.

read, speaking with the voice of each, and making the face of each present to the eye. Is Achaia near to thee? thou hast Corinth. If thou art not far from Macedonia, thou hast Philippi, thou hast the Thessalonians. If thou canst travel into Asia, thou hast Ephesus. But if thou art near to Italy, thou hast Rome, where we also (*i.e.* we in Africa) have an authority close at hand."[1] No one ever suggested that the special influence which attached to the apostolic sees, and the reverence which was yielded to them, was a matter of positive divine appointment. It was the natural reverence of Christians for the holy apostles, and for everything which seemed in a special way to have come in contact with the apostles.

So, to sum up this part of our subject, by divine right all bishops were inherently equal, but by custom and ecclesiastical legislation the bishops of the metropolitical sees acquired certain rights which were delegated to them by their brother bishops. Moreover, among the most important Churches a certain order of precedence grew up, which corresponded with the civil dignity of the cities in which those Churches existed; and, finally, the Churches which were founded by the apostles were treated with peculiar reverence.

If we now confine our attention to the more powerful Churches which took the lead in ecclesiastical matters, it will be worth while to ask the question whether their influence mainly rested on

[1] *De Præscr. Hær.*, xxxvi.

the civil dignity of the city, or on the apostolical character of the see. I think that there can be no doubt that their influence mainly resulted from the civil dignity of the city. For example, during the greater part of the first three centuries the see of Jerusalem, which in the apostolic days had been the most influential of all sees, exerted very little influence on the general course of Church affairs. The city had been destroyed by Hadrian, and the new city was comparatively feeble and uninfluential. So, again, Philippi and Corinth, which were apostolical, had much less influence than Carthage, the capital of Africa, which made no pretence to an apostolical foundation. If we compare Antioch with Alexandria, we find that both S. Peter and S. Paul had spent some time in Antioch, whereas Alexandria could only trace back to S. Mark the Evangelist, and through him indirectly to S. Peter. Judged by apostolical pretensions, Antioch ought to have ranked before Alexandria; but Alexandria was the second city of the empire, and Antioch was the third,[1] and the order of civil dignity governed the situation. The Church of Alexandria, though only quasi-apostolical, ranked second, and "the truly apostolical Church" of Antioch ranked third. And doubtless as it was with all the other Churches, so it was with Rome. If we ask

---

[1] Tillemont (ii. 92) speaks of Alexandria as being "cette grande ville qui estoit la première de l'Empire après Rome." Josephus (*De Bello Jud.*, iii. 2, *Opp.* ed. Havercamp, 1726, ii. 221, 222), speaking of Antioch, says that "in size and other advantages it indisputably held the third place in the Roman world."

why the Church of Rome ranked first, the true answer undoubtedly is that Rome was the imperial city, the capital of the civilized world. The primacy hinged on that. The fact that S. Peter and S. Paul had been the apostolical founders of the Roman Church, and had been martyred there, would never by itself have resulted in the primacy of that Church, any more than the fact of Jerusalem being the place where the Saviour died and rose again, and where the Church had come fully into existence on the day of Pentecost, availed in default of civil dignity to secure any commanding position for the Church of the holy city. The apostolicity of the Roman Church immensely added to its influence and helped to attract to it the reverence of Christians all over the world, but the imperial position of the city of Rome was the determining factor which secured for it the primacy. Undoubtedly the Ecumenical Council of Chalcedon was historically right, when in its twenty-eighth canon it defined that "the Fathers properly gave the privileges to the throne of the elder Rome, *because that was the imperial city.*"[1]

---

[1] The truth of the statement in the text does not in any way depend on the twenty-eighth canon of Chalcedon, being a canon of ecumenical authority. S. Leo, and the West following S. Leo, rejected the canon. But it still remains the fact that the Council as a whole passed it, and that the East in practice obeyed it; and there can be no doubt that, whether the decree was or was not ecumenically binding, its statement about the origin of the privileges of the Roman see was historically correct. The divine origin of the jurisdiction claimed by the popes is a fundamental dogma among modern Roman Catholics, or rather it is, in their view, *the* fundamental dogma. One would think that Roman Catholic students of the canons must be somewhat

The position could not be more accurately stated. The primatial privileges of the Roman see were not of divine institution; they were *"given by the Fathers,"* and they were given on the ground of the imperial authority and dignity of the city.

To sum up what has been said in regard to the Roman Church. After the destruction of Jeru-

puzzled to find a great Ecumenical Council, in which all manner of circumstances combined to give a most commanding position to the pope, passing a canon which lays down as an obvious undeniable truth that the privileges of the Roman see were given to it " by the Fathers," because Rome " was the imperial city." For a good account of the enacting of the twenty-eighth canon, and of the way in which, notwithstanding the pope's protests, the canon practically held its ground, see a powerful article in the *Church Quarterly* for October, 1889, entitled, *A Roman Proselyte on Ancient Church History*, pp. 131–133. The Abbé Duchesne, one of the most learned, if not *the* most learned, of living French ecclesiastics, and who, in everything that he writes, is refreshingly fair and straightforward, describes (*Origines du Culte Chrétien*, p. 24) how the popes refused to accept the canons of Constantinople and Chalcedon, which regulated the precedence and jurisdiction of the see of Constantinople; but he candidly adds, "Mais leur voix fut peu écoutée; on leur accorda sans doute des satisfactions, *mais de pure cérémonie*." In ante-Nicene times even ceremonial satisfactions would have been refused, as the histories of Popes Victor and Stephen show. Mr. Richardson (*What are the Catholic Claims ?* p. 93) attempts to reply to the Fathers of Chalcedon by asking the question, " Can any one point to a human grant of the primacy to Rome ?" The inconclusiveness of the argument implied in that question may be shown by asking another, Can any one point to a human grant of the primacy over Africa to Carthage? or of the primacy over Palestine to Cæsarea? Yet who supposes that the jurisdiction of those sees was secured to them by the *jus divinum ?* Compare the remarks of Möhler and of Father de Smedt, to which reference is made in the note on p. 12. It ought to be observed that, when the Fathers of Chalcedon attributed the privileges of the Roman see to the fact that it was the imperial city, they were merely repeating what the second Ecumenical Council had implied in its third canon, seventy years before (see Dr. Bright's *Notes on the Canons of the First Four General Councils*, p. 93, 1st edit.).

salem, which during the first forty years after Pentecost had been the natural metropolis of Christendom,
the Churches which had been constituted in the
great cities of the empire took the lead in the order
of their civil precedence, with the Church of Rome
necessarily in the first place. The mere fact of holding the first place was a cause of growing influence.
One result of the pre-eminent influence of the Roman
see was that the ecclesiastical province over which
it acquired metropolitical jurisdiction was much
larger than any other province in the Church, except the province over which the see of Alexandria,
which ranked next to Rome in honour, presided.
The see of Rome had also the glory of having been
founded by the two great apostles, S. Peter and
S. Paul, who were martyred outside the walls, and
whose bodies were reverently treasured and had in
honour by the Roman Church. The Roman see was,
therefore, very eminently an apostolic see, and it
was the only apostolic see in the Western or Latin-
speaking portion of the Church. In the East apostolic sees in some sense abounded. In the West there
was but one, and that one was the primatial see of
the whole Church. No wonder that the Bishop of
Rome was held in high honour, and was the natural
person to take the initiative in movements affecting
the whole body. But we must be careful not to
exaggerate in this matter. There was a marked
primacy of honour and influence, but there was no
primacy of jurisdiction. The inherent jurisdiction of

the Roman see was exactly the same as the inherent jurisdiction of every other see in Christendom. Its acquired or delegated jurisdiction was limited to the suburbicarian provinces of Central and Southern Italy with the adjacent islands. Outside those provinces throughout the Church, but specially in the West, Rome had influence, but no jurisdiction. Similarly the Bishop of Alexandria's acquired jurisdiction was limited to Egypt, Libya, and the Pentapolis, but his influence extended over the whole Church, and specially over the East.

In the preceding statement I have tried to set before you a true view of the relations of the various sees to each other, and specially of the relation of the Bishop of Rome to his brothers and colleagues in the episcopate during the first three centuries. The justification of that statement will be perceived if the facts of early Church history and the writings of the early Fathers are studied. As I am giving a lecture, and not writing an exhaustive treatise, I can only discuss a small selection of facts and passages, but I honestly think that the selection which I shall make will be a fair selection. I propose, then, to consider—

1. The Paschal controversy in the time of Pope Victor :

2. The famous passage of S. Irenæus about the Roman Church :

3. The history of S. Cyprian of Carthage.

1. The bishops of Proconsular Asia, whose metropolis was Ephesus, had been accustomed ever since

the time of the apostles to keep the feast of Easter on the day of the Paschal full moon, whether that day fell on a Sunday or on any other day of the week. The bishops in all the other provinces of the Church, both in the East and in the West, kept Easter on the Sunday following the Paschal full moon. The bishops of the province of Ephesus asserted that they had received their custom by tradition from S. John; and one can hardly doubt that that assertion of theirs was true, because S. Polycarp assured the Roman pope Anicetus that he had always kept the feast so "with John, the disciple of our Lord, and the other apostles with whom he had lived."[1] However, the Churches, which kept Easter on Sunday, also claimed that they had received their custom by tradition from the apostles. During the greater part of the second century the two customs went on side by side, and yet the Church was not disturbed by any serious dissension in connection with this matter. On the contrary, when the Christians from Asia came to Rome, they were allowed to keep the feast on their own Asiatic day, although the Roman Church itself kept the feast always on the Sunday. This large-hearted tolerance was exhibited by the five Roman bishops, Xystus, Telesphorus, Hyginus, Pius, and Anicetus,[2] whose pontificates lasted from about A.D. 118 to about A.D. 165. It seems probable that Pope Soter, the successor of Anicetus, forbade the Asiatic Christians who came to Rome to keep their Asiatic

<hr>

[1] Euseb., *H. E.*, v. 24.   [2] Tillemont, iii. 103

Easter in Rome itself... He appears to have required all Catholic Christians living in Rome to keep the feast together on the Sunday after the full moon; but he remained in peace and fellowship with the bishops of Asia, who in their own province of Asia went on celebrating the festival on the day of the full moon. Soter's successor, Eleutherus, followed on the same lines. But Victor, who succeeded Eleutherus, and who governed the Roman Church from about A.D. 188 to about A.D. 198, determined to make an effort to establish uniformity, and to suppress altogether the Asiatic custom. He appears to have written letters in the name of his Church to the various metropolitans, begging them to summon their Provincial Synods, and to discuss in them the question of the proper day for the celebration of the Easter festival. It is important to notice exactly what the pope's action was at this initial stage. He was the first bishop in the Church, and it was most fitting that he should take the initiative. What he did was to *ask* the other metropolitans to summon their synods. He did not command them to do so; he *asked* them. Polycrates, the Bishop of Ephesus, writing later on to Victor and to the Roman Church, says: "I could also mention the bishops that were present [at the synod in Ephesus], whom you requested (ἠξιώσατε) me to summon."[1] The word ἀξιόω seems to be the right

---

[1] Euseb., *H. E.*, v. 24. Tillemont (iii. 633) expresses Polycrates' meaning thus: "Polycrate dit que Victor l'avait *prié* d'assembler les Evêques de l'Asie."

word to express requests made by one Church to
another Church. Thus, after the death of S. Polycarp, the Church of Smyrna wrote a short account of
his martyrdom to the little Church of Philomelium,
in Phrygia. Towards the conclusion of the letter
the Smyrnæans say, " Ye indeed *requested* ($\dot{\eta}\xi\iota\dot{\omega}\sigma\alpha\tau\epsilon$)
that the things which happened should be shown
unto you at greater length." [1] S. Clement of Rome
uses the word $\dot{\alpha}\xi\iota\dot{o}\omega$ three times of *entreating* or
beseeching God. [2] So Pope Victor, who had no juris-
diction in the province of Asia, *requested* Polycrates
the metropolitan to exercise the authority which he
possessed, and to convoke ($\mu\epsilon\tau\alpha\kappa\alpha\lambda\epsilon\tilde{\iota}\nu$) the bishops of
his province. In compliance with the request of the
Roman Church, synods were held in many provinces,
as, for example, in Palestine, in Pontus, in Gaul, [3] in
Osrhoene, and elsewhere. There was a unanimous
determination throughout the Church, except in Asia,
that Easter should be celebrated on Sunday. Victor
held his own local synod in Rome ; and in communicating its decision to Polycrates he appears to have
threatened that if the Asiatics persisted in their
custom, they would be cut off from the communion
of the Roman Church. Polycrates, with the consent

---

[1] *Mart. Pol.*, xx.   [2] S. Clem. Rom. *ad Cor.*, li. liii. and lv.

[3] Perhaps in Gaul the synod was diocesan rather than provincial.
It seems probable that in the time of Victor there was only one
bishopric in Gaul, the seat of which was at Lyons. See an article by
the Abbé Duchesne, entitled *L'origine des diocèses épiscopaux dans
l'ancienne Gaule*, which appeared in the *Bulletin et Mémoires de
la Société Nationale des Antiquaires de France*, tome l. pp. 387–390
(Paris : 1889).

of the Asiatic bishops, replied in a letter full of interesting details, addressed, not to Victor only, but to the whole Roman Church, in which he says, "I am not scared by those who terrify us [with threats], for they, who are greater than I, have said, 'We ought to obey God rather than men.'"[1] "Upon this," Eusebius says, "Victor, the Bishop of the Church of the Romans, forthwith endeavours to cut off the Churches of all Asia, together with the neighbouring Churches, as heterodox, from the common unity; and he proscribes them by letters, and proclaims that all the brethren there *are utterly* (ἄρδην) *separated from communion.*   However, these measures did not please all the bishops.   They exhort him, therefore, on the other side to pursue peace and unity and love towards his neighbours.   Their writings too are extant, very severely upbraiding (πληκτικώτερον καθαπτομένων) Victor.   Among these also was Irenæus, who, in the name of those brethren in Gaul over whom he presided, maintains indeed that the mystery of the Lord's resurrection should be celebrated only on the Lord's day; but he also becomingly admonishes Victor[2] not to cut off whole Churches of God, which preserve the tradition of an ancient custom. . . . And this same Irenæus, bearing out his

---

[1] Euseb., *H. E.*, v. 24. S. Jerome (*De illustribus viris*, cap. xlv., *Opp.* ed. Vallars., 1735, ii. 874) translates Polycrates' words as follows: "Non formidabo eos qui nobis minantur."

[2] The historian Socrates (*H. E.*, v. 22. 16, ed. Hussey, 1853, ii. 626) says that S. Irenæus "strongly inveighed against (γενναίως κατέδραμεν) Victor" on this occasion.

name, and a peacemaker in temper, exhorted and
mediated in ways like these for the peace of the
Church. He also wrote, not to Victor alone, but to
very] many other rulers of Churches respecting the
question which was agitated." [1] We learn from
S. Anatolius of Laodicea, who wrote about eighty
years after the event, that S. Irenæus appeased the
whole quarrel, and that both sides continued to observe their traditional custom. S. Anatolius mentions
that in his day the Asiatic Churches still continued to
celebrate Easter on the day of the full moon.[2]

There are various points in this narrative to which
it may be well to call your attention. Polycrates
was a man whose orthodoxy, as Eusebius tells us,[3]
was notorious, and he is described in the *Synodicon*
as a very holy person; [4] and yet when Pope Victor
required him to alter his day for keeping Easter, and
threatened him with excommunication if he refused,
he replied that he was not scared by Victor's threats.
He evidently had not been brought up in the teaching
which was so clearly set forth by the Vatican Council.
Polycrates, though he must have been educated
among those who knew S. John, had not been taught
that all the pastors and all the faithful are bound to
the authority of. the pope "by the obligation of true
obedience, not only in things which pertain to faith
and morals, but also in things pertaining to the
discipline and government of the Church." Still less

---

[1] Euseb., *H. E.*, v. 24.　　　[3] Tillemont, iii. 109, 110.
[2] *H. E.*, v. 22.　　　[4] Tillemont, iii. 107.

did he know that "none can deviate from this teaching without the loss of his faith and salvation." From the point of view of the Vatican Council, Polycrates' letter was a wicked act of rebellion, and all the bishops of Asia, by consenting to that act of rebellion, became partakers in their metropolitan's guilt. But the Fathers of the Church were wholly unconscious of that view of the matter. When S. Jerome writes a short life of Polycrates, he says nothing about rebellion or any other wrong-doing, but quotes the most important part of Polycrates' letter, including his refusal to conform himself to Victor's decision, as a proof of the ability and weight of the man.[1] Moreover, S. Irenæus, and numbers of other Catholic bishops, took the same view. No doubt they thought that there had been wrong-doing; but in their view, not Polycrates, but Victor was the culprit. They "very severely upbraided" Victor. As far as we know, they said nothing to Polycrates. But perhaps for our purpose the most important point to notice is that nobody seems to have supposed that communion with the Catholic Church depended on communion with the Roman see. Victor wrote letters, in which he announced that all the Asiatic brethren were "*utterly* separated from communion." It was, of course, in the Roman bishop's power to exclude them from the communion of the Roman Church. In those days it was in the power of every bishop to decide who was to be in the com-

---

[1] S. Hieron., *De Viris Illustribus*, cap. xlv.

munion of his Church, and who was to be excluded. But exclusion from the communion of the Roman Church, though it might *lead* to exclusion from the communion of the Catholic Church, did not necessarily involve such exclusion. Therefore Eusebius tells us that, while Victor, speaking for his own Church, announced that the Asiatics were "utterly separated from communion," he at the same time "*endeavoured* to cut them off, as heterodox, *from the common unity.*" He *endeavoured*, but he failed in his endeavour. The other bishops objected to Victor's proceeding. They refused to withdraw their communion from Polycrates. He therefore remained united to the common unity of the Catholic Church, although cut off from the communion of the Roman Church. (A very important principle underlies this fact. Evidently, in the second century the Church was in no way the born handmaid of the Roman pontiff. The theory set forth in the Vatican decrees was unknown. The Roman Church was not held to be the necessary centre of unity. We may also gather from this whole history that it is a very dangerous thing to attempt to learn the rightful authority of the Roman popes from the claims which they make. The Roman popes, with very few exceptions, have been much too fond of putting forth baseless claims. But the right way of dealing with such claims, if we may judge by the example of S. Irenæus and other holy bishops of his time, is to inveigh against the claimant strongly, and to upbraid him severely, and to refuse to give in to his claims. That was how the Catholic Church dealt with Pope Victor in the closing decade of the second century. He evidently learnt a salutary lesson, and withdrew his abortive excommunication; and after that everything went on as if nothing had happened.

2. I now pass from the Paschal controversy, in which S. Irenæus took such a prominent part by opposing the unchristian action of the Roman pope, and I proceed to consider the famous passage in that same Father's treatise, *Against all Heresies*, which Roman Catholics are very fond of quoting, but which, if it is properly considered, is seen to be wholly irreconcilable with the papal claims. S. Irenæus, in his controversy with the various Gnostic sects, is appealing to the tradition of the true faith which has been handed down from the apostles. He says, "It is within the power of all, who may wish to see the truth, to contemplate clearly the tradition of the apostles manifested throughout the whole world in every Church: and we are able to enumerate those whom the apostles appointed to be bishops in the Churches, and their successors, quite down to our own time; who neither taught nor knew anything like what these [heretics] rave about. . . . But because it would be too long in such a volume as this to enumerate the successions in all the Churches, we point to the tradition of that very great and very ancient and universally known Church, which was founded and established at Rome by the two most

glorious apostles, Peter and Paul;—we point, I say, to the tradition which this Church has from the apostles, and to her faith proclaimed to men, which comes down to our time through the succession of her bishops, and so we put to confusion all those who, in whatever manner, either on account of self-pleasing, or of vain glory, or of blindness and perverse opinion, assemble in unauthorized meetings. For to this Church, *propter potentiorem principalitatem,* it is necessary that every Church should resort —that is to say, the faithful, who are from all quarters; in which [Church] the tradition which is from the apostles has ever been preserved by those who are from all quarters."[1] I have left the words " *propter potentiorem principalitatem* " untranslated, because their interpretation is disputed; and it will be desirable to study carefully the closing sentence in which they occur, and thus to arrive at their probable meaning. I had better read this closing sentence in the Latin. S. Irenæus, of course, wrote it in Greek, but unfortunately the Greek of this passage is not extant, and we must make what we can of the ancient Latin translation. That translation runs as follows: "Ad hanc enim ecclesiam propter potentiorem principalitatem necesse est omnem convenire ecclesiam, hoc est, eos qui sunt undique fideles, in quâ semper ab his, qui sunt undique, conservata est ea quæ est ab Apostolis traditio." The first point to be discussed is the meaning of the phrase, "convenire ad."

----

[1] *Contra Omnes Hæreses,* iii. 3. 1, 2.

Does S. Irenæus mean to say that it is necessary that
every Church should *agree with* the Church of Rome ?
or that every Church should *resort to* the Church of
Rome ?   The Italian Jesuit Perrone, quoting and
adopting the comment of Dom Massuet, rejects the
second of these two interpretations as *absurdissi-
mum ;*[1] and with Perrone and Massuet agree the
greater number of Ultramontane writers and some
Gallicans.[2]   I hope to show you that this rejected
interpretation is not only not absurd, but is almost
certainly the true explanation.   I find that the
word *convenire* is used in the Vulgate one hundred
and eleven times.   In ninety-seven places it means
"resort to " or "assemble ; " and in ten places it is
translated,[3] "agree with," usually in the sense of
making a bargain or agreement with another person.
It is clear that the more usual meaning of *convenire*
is to "resort to."   But the point can be pressed more
closely home.   I find that in twenty-six passages the
verb *convenire* is followed by the preposition *ad*, and
in every one of these passages "convenire ad " *means*
" *to resort to* " *or* " *come together to.*"[4]   It would per-

---

[1] *Prælectiones Theologicæ*, edit. 1841, ii. 425.

[2] As instances of Roman writers who translate the expression *convenire ad*, "resort to," one might mention R. I. Wilberforce, in his
Principles of Church Authority (p. 134), written when he was passing
from the Anglican into the Roman communion ; and Thomassinus, in
his *Traité des Edits, et des autres moiens pour maintenir l'Unité de
l'Eglise Catholique*, tom. i. p. 37, edit. 1703.

[3] In the Douay Version.

[4] It has been suggested that the original Greek expression used by
S. Irenæus, which has been translated "convenire ad," was συμβαίνειν
πρός : but can any instance be cited from ancient Latin translations of

haps be rash to lay down a universal negative, and to say that "convenire ad" never means "agree with;" but undoubtedly its normal meaning is "resort to," and the *onus probandi* lies on those who teach that in this passage of S. Irenæus it ought to be understood in an abnormal meaning. Passages in Latin authors could, no doubt, be found in which "convenire *cum*" is to be understood in the sense of "agree with;" but we have to do here with the expression "convenire *ad*," and not with the expression "convenire *cum*." It is amusing and instructive to notice that Perrone, on one occasion, makes a slip in quoting this passage of S. Irenæus, and substitutes *cum* for *ad*.[1]

There are several touches in the wording of the passage which we are considering, which corroborate the view of the meaning of "convenire ad" which I am urging. When S. Irenæus says that it is necessary that every Church should resort to the Church of Rome, he feels that some explanation is needed, because it is physically impossible for one Church to resort to another Church, and absolutely impossible that every Church in the world should assemble in one city, however great.

Greek authors in which *convenire ad* is given as the translation of συμβαίνειν πρός? Certainly no instance of such a rendering occurs in the Bible. In twelve passages *convenire ad* in the Vulgate corresponds with συνάγεσθαι or ἐπισυνάγεσθαι, usually followed by πρός, once by ἐπί. In other cases various Greek expressions, such as ἔρχεσθαι πρός, συνέρχεσθαι πρός, ἔρχεσθαι εἰς, συνπορεύεσθαι πρός, κ.τ.λ., are the Greek equivalents of *convenire ad*.

[1] *Prælectt. Theoll.*, ii. 408.

S. Irenæus therefore glosses the expression, " omnem ecclesiam," and adds, " hoc est eos qui sunt undique fideles."   This gloss would have been quite superfluous if " convenire ad " had meant " agree with." It is easy to see how every Church can *agree with* another Church; there is need of an interpretation when we are told that it is necessary that every Church should *resort to* another Church, and accordingly an interpretation is given.   S. Irenæus tells us that when he says " every Church," he means the faithful from all quarters.   They are in the habit of resorting to Rome, and in them the local Churches to which they belong may be said to resort thither. Again, if S. Irenæus had meant to say that it is necessary that other Churches should *agree with* the Church of Rome, he would never have used the word ἀνάγκη, which was, no doubt, the Greek word corresponding to " necesse est."   He would have used some word like δεῖ (*oportet*), implying moral obligation.   When the faithful from all quarters came to Rome, they were not pressed by any moral obligation to come there.   Doubtless the necessities of their business compelled them to come to the great metropolis.   Again, if S. Irenæus had meant to say that it is necessary that the whole Church should *agree with* the Church of Rome, he would, when he came to explain what he meant by the whole Church, have used the word *ubique*, and not *undique*. *Agreement with* the Church at Rome in no way implies any need to journey thither.   Christians could *agree* remaining where they were, scattered everywhere (*ubique*). But S. Irenæus uses *undique*, which seems to denote the normal situation of their various homes, with an implied contrast with their present place of sojourning. *Undique* would appear to stand here for the ablative, which can be used of the place from which a person comes. Its *primâ facie* meaning is *"from all quarters,"* not *"every-where."* It is most natural that the idea conveyed by *undique* should occur in a sentence in which *con-venire ad* also occurs;[1] for the true meaning of *con-venire ad* implies a journey, and so a change of location. The faithful from all quarters came to Rome on their business ; and they necessarily brought with them, written on their hearts and memories, the apostolic tradition of the faith, which each had learnt in his own local Church. Thus in Rome the tradi-tion of the faith was preserved not merely by the local Church—that is, by the Roman clergy and the Roman laity—but there was an inflow of Christians from all the other Churches in the world, and the tradition of the faith was found to be everywhere one, and so the apostolic tradition was preserved with great security in Rome by those who came thither

---

[1] As illustrating this combination of *undique* with *convenire ad* in the same sentence, one may compare S. Mark i. 45, where we are told (R. V.) that " Jesus could no more openly enter into a city, but was without in desert places : and they came to him from every quarter " (" et conveniebant ad eum undique "—Vulg.). However, it is fair to point out that in this verse of S. Mark *undique* is more closely combined with *convenire ad*, than is the case in the passage from S. Irenæus. -

from all quarters.[1] Local exaggeration or one-sided-
ness was warded off by the fact that all Churches
were present there in the persons of those of their
members who had occasion to resort thither. But
the faithful *everywhere* (*ubique*) scattered over the
world could not preserve the apostolic tradition *in
the Roman Church* (*in quâ*).[2] They could preserve it
in their own Churches. But S. Irenæus says that

[1] It is worth noting that Roman controversialists, in quoting the
Irenæan passage, sometimes omit the words "ab his qui sunt undique."
For example, F. Lockhart omits them in *The Old Religion*, pp.
30, 31 (3rd edit.). No one would accuse F. Lockhart of omitting
important words intentionally, but one may fairly suppose that he
habitually thought of the passage apart from those words.

[2] Messrs. Addis and Arnold (*Catholic Dictionary*, p. 673, note 3,
s.v. "Pope"), translate the Irenæan passage thus: "For with this
Church, because of its more powerful principality, every Church must
agree—that is, the faithful everywhere—in which (*i.e.* in communion
with the Roman Church) the tradition of the apostles has ever been
preserved by those everywhere." This interpretation is open to many
objections. It deserts the natural interpretation of *convenire ad*, and
gives to that phrase a meaning, which is either impossible or highly
improbable. It also deserts the natural meaning of *undique*; and,
finally, it deserts the natural meaning of *in quâ*. The writer of the
article in a note says, "'In qua,' 'in which'—*i.e.* 'in union with
which,' or 'in the unity of which.'" This is surely a very strained
explanation. The writer feels the necessity of justifying his suggestion, and quotes three passages in order to do so. He says, "Cf. 'Sa-
lutem in eo dedit' (iii. 12. 4); 'Quod perdideramus in Adam'
(iii. 18. 1); and 'In qua una cathedra [sc. Petri] unitas ab omnibus
servaretur' (Optat. *Schism. Don.* ii. 2)." In the two passages cited
from S. Irenæus the preposition " in " preserves its natural meaning.
God gave salvation *in* Christ; and we lost *in* Adam the image of God.
But the faithful everywhere are not *in* the local Church of Rome,
except so far as they resort thither. The passages quoted from
S. Irenæus do not justify the proposed meaning of " in." The passage
from S. Optatus is more to the writer's purpose, but it supplies an
example of a most unusual meaning of " in," a meaning not to be
adopted in other passages except under the stress of absolute necessity.

they preserved it *in the Roman Church*, and *that*
they could only do by resorting thither; he therefore
uses the term *undique*, and not *ubique*.

That Christians from all parts of the world did
come to Rome for business purposes in the time of
S. Irenæus is certain. We have already seen that
eight Popes in succession had to make arrangements
of one sort or another as to when the Asiatic
Christians, who might happen to be in Rome, should
keep their Easter; and if they came from Asia, no
doubt they also came from Antioch, and Alexandria,
and Carthage, and Greece, and Gaul. The Abbé
Duchesne, a first-rate authority, speaking of the
Quarto-deciman Asiatic Christians, says that they
came to Rome on secular business.[1] He says this
incidentally, without any reference to the passage in
S. Irenæus. But the matter is too plain to require
any laboured proof.

It was not only at Rome that the influence and
authority of the local Church was increased by the
conflux of Christians who flocked to the capital for
business purposes. We find the same thing taking
place in a less accentuated form in the metropolis of
each province. The famous Council of Antioch, of
the year 341, says, in its ninth canon, "It is right
that the bishops in each province should know that
the bishop who presides in the metropolis receives

---

[1] "Il y avait toujours à Rome des fidèles Asiatiques de passage,
appelés dans la capitale par leurs affaires, commerciales et autres"
(*Revue des Questions Historiques*, tom. xxviii. p. 13. 1880).

also the care of the whole province, *because all who have business resort to the metropolis from all quarters;* wherefore it seemed good that *he* should enjoy precedence in dignity."[1] The reason given— that "all who have business resort to the metropolis from all quarters"—seems like an echo of the passage in S. Irenæus. The old Latin translation of the canon by Dionysius Exiguus recalls the Latin of the Irenæan translator. Dionysius says, "Propter quod *ad* metropolim *omnes undique,* qui negotia videntur habere, *concurrant.*"[2]

The principle comes out still more clearly in regard to Constantinople, after the imperial court had been moved thither from Rome. S. Gregory Nazianzen, in the touching farewell oration which he delivered in the great church of Saint Sophia in the presence of the second Ecumenical Council, when he was resigning the bishopric of Constantinople, describes the imperial city thus : he calls it "the eye of the world, . . . the bond of union between the East and the West, *to* which the extremities of the earth *resort from all quarters* ($\pi\alpha\nu\tau\alpha\chi\delta\theta\epsilon\nu$ $\sigma\upsilon\nu\tau\rho\acute{\epsilon}\chi\epsilon\iota$, i.e. *undique concurrunt*), and from whence they start afresh ($\mathring{\alpha}\rho\chi\epsilon\tau\alpha\iota$), *as from the common emporium of the faith.*"[3] The same causes which in 381 gave the proud title of "the common emporium of the faith"

---

[1] *Concilia,* tom. ii. col. 589, ed. Coleti, Venet., 1728.

[2] Coleti, ii. 599, 600.

[3] S. Greg. Naz. *Orat.* xlii. cap. 10, *Opp.* ed. Ben., i. 755. The word $\mathring{\alpha}\rho\chi\epsilon\tau\alpha\iota$, as used here, is somewhat difficult of interpretation. The Benedictine editors translate it, *incipiunt*

to Constantinople, the new Rome on the Bosphorus, operated with similar results in regard to old Rome in the time of S. Irenæus.

If we now return to the Irenæan passage, we see that the whole wording of the passage from beginning to end, and the analogous passages in regard to the chief cities of other provinces, and specially in regard to Constantinople, compel us to interpret S. Irenæus' words of the influx of Christians to Rome as the metropolis of the empire. They came to that great metropolis on account of their secular business, but their presence powerfully reacted on the preservation of the apostolic tradition of the faith in the local Church of Rome, which thus became "the common emporium of the faith." The context, therefore, imperatively demands that we should interpret the *propter potentiorem principalitatem* of the secular dignity and imperial authority of the *city* of Rome, rather than of any world-wide spiritual jurisdiction in the *Church* of Rome. The flocking in of men bent on business was produced by the *principalitas* of the *city*, not by the *principalitas* of the *Church*,[1] though no doubt the ultimate result was to give a primacy of influence to that Church. S. Irenæus does not here allude to that result. His eye is fixed on the conservative action in regard to the preservation of the

---

[1] Doubtless some few, such as Hegesippus or S. Justin Martyr or S. Irenæus, might come to Rome to investigate the Christian tradition in the greatest of the apostolic Churches, but they would be the exception. To limit S. Irenæus' words to them would be evidently absurd.

faith in the Church of Rome, which resulted from the
perpetual presence within it of the representatives of
all the other local Churches of the world, who necessarily had to resort to the city, impelled thither by
the pressure of their affairs.

Even if, for the sake of argument, we allowed that
the *potentior principalitas* was to be understood
of the Church, and not of the city,[1] all the more
wonderful would be the absence of all reference to
the infallible authority of the Pope as the security
for the preservation of the apostolic tradition of the
faith. That is the point on which S. Irenæus has his
eye. He is giving reasons why he enumerates the
succession of the Roman bishops rather than the
succession of the bishops of other Churches, as guaran-
teeing that the apostolic teaching has been con-
tinuously handed down. His reasons must seem very
tame to those who believe in the Vatican decrees.
They would say that by a divine promise the see
of S. Peter remains always unharmed by any error,
and that the definitions of the Roman pontiff are
irreformable of themselves, and not through any
consent of the Church.[2] They would therefore point

---

[1] I think that every one must, in fairness, concede two things : (1)
that, apart from the context, the disputed words would very naturally be referred to the Church, which had just been mentioned;
and (2), that no one can say that they *must* refer to the Church. In
order that that interpretation should be the only possible one, it
would have been necessary that S. Irenæus should have written,
" propter *ejus* potentiorem principalitatem." It is the context which
really settles the matter in favour of the reference to the city.

[2] " Omnes venerabiles Patres . . et sancti Doctores orthodoxi

the poor gnostic wanderer to that infallible fountain of truth which God has established in the see of Rome. But S. Irenæus is able to offer no such comfort. He refers first to the various Churches all over the world as manifesting the apostolic tradition. Then he mentions specially the very great and very ancient Roman Church, and he says that to it, because of the *potentior principalitas*, the faithful come flocking in from all quarters, and that the apostolic tradition is preserved in the Roman Church—by whom? by the infallible Pope? No! by these Christians who have come to Rome from the other local Churches. From an Ultramontane point of view, this is truly a tame ending; so tame that we may be quite certain that S. Irenæus knew nothing about papal infallibility. And if he knew nothing about it, that means that S. Polycarp had taught him nothing about it; and that, again, means that S. Polycarp had learnt nothing about it from S. John. It thus appears that, even on the hypothesis that the *potentior principalitas* is to be understood of the *Church* of Rome rather than of the *city* of Rome, the whole passage witnesses against the modern Roman claims; but I have no shadow of doubt myself that S. Irenæus, when he wrote the words,

. . . plenissimo scientes hanc Sancti Petri sedem ab omni semper errore illibatam permanere, secundum Domini Salvatoris nostri pollicitationem." "Docemus et divinitus revelatum dogma esse definimus . . . Romani Pontificis definitiones ex sese, non autem ex consensu Ecclesiæ, irreformabiles esse" (*Constit. Dogmat. Prim. de Ecclesiâ Christi*, cap. iv.; *Collectio Lacensis*, vii. 486, 487).

intended to describe the imperial authority of the
city, and consequently that the passage is silent, not
only about the infallibility, but also about the primacy
and supremacy of the Roman see.[1] I must apologize
for having treated this passage at such great length,
but it is a passage of extreme importance in our controversy with Rome,[2] and I humbly think that the
time which has been spent on it has not been wasted.

[1] Dr. Pusey, in an appended note to his sermon on *The Rule of
Faith*, p. 64, evidently accepts the Benedictine reading "propter
potiorem principalitatem," and translates it, "on account of its higher
original;" applying the words to the Church, and not to the city.
But, writing in all humility, as befits me, when venturing to differ
from so profound a scholar, I am bound to say that the context seems
to me to be decisive in favour of applying the words to the city; and,
when the words are so applied, the more generally received reading
"potentiorem," makes excellent sense, though "potiorem" would do
as well, or almost as well. I see that Dr. Salmon (*Infallibility of the
Church*, 2nd edit., pp. 381–383) explains the passage exactly as I have
explained it; and Bishop Pearson (*De Success. Prim. Rom. Episc.*,
i. xiii. iv., *Minor Theological Works*, ii. 429, edit. Churton) does the
same, and so does Bishop Stillingfleet (*Rational Account*, Part II.
chap. vi., *Works*, edit. 1709, vol. iv. pp. 423–426); to whom may be
added Dr. Cyriacus, a learned ecclesiastical historian belonging to
the orthodox Church of Greece (see the *Church Quarterly* for July,
1882, p. 313); and Döllinger, in his *Considerations for the Bishops of
the [Vatican] Council respecting the question of Papal Infallibility*,
published in October, 1869 (*Declarations and Letters*, pp. 15, 16); and
the Abbé Guettée (*La Papauté Schismatique*, pp. 37–45).

[2] The author of the article "Pope," in Addis and Arnold's *Catholic Dictionary*, says (p. 672), "The most important testimony to the
authority of Rome in the first ages of the Church is that of Irenæus;"
and then he proceeds to quote the passage which we have been considering, and he quotes no other.

LECTURE II.

The Clementine Romance, and S. Cyprian.

I OUGHT now to pass on to the history of S. Cyprian; but it will be well, in the first place, to allude to an event which probably intervened between the time of the writing of S. Irenæus' treatise and the time of S. Cyprian, and which had a very far-reaching and a very evil effect on the later fortunes of the Church of Rome. It seemed but a little seed, but it has borne abundant fruit, and that not of a wholesome kind. Towards the end of the second century, a book found its way to Rome which purported to be written by S. Clement of Rome. It was really a heretical romance, written by some unknown author in the interests of the Ebionitish sect. It has come down to our time in two principal forms—the one called *The Clementine Homilies;* the other, *The Clementine Recognitions.* But there seems to have been a form older than either of these, which was known as *The Circuits of Peter.*[1] To one or more of these editions of the romance was prefixed a spurious epistle, purporting to have been addressed, after the death of

---

[1] There are also still extant two shorter and probably later forms, commonly called *The Epitomes.*

S. Peter, by S. Clement to S. James, the first Bishop of Jerusalem, and describing how S. Peter, before his death, consecrated S. Clement to be his successor, as Bishop of Rome. In this spurious letter S. Peter is represented as speaking a good deal about his chair; but it is not the throne of government of the universal Church, but "the chair of discourse,"[1] or, as we should say, the pulpit in the local community at Rome.[2] S. Peter is represented as saying, shortly

[1] τὴν ἐμὴν τῶν λόγων καθέδραν.

[2] According to the Clementine romance, there is a chief ruler of the universal Church; but the holder of that office is not S. Peter, nor his Roman successor, S. Clement, but S. James, the Lord's brother, "*the bishop of bishops*, who rules Jerusalem, the holy Church of the Hebrews, and the Churches *everywhere* excellently founded by the Providence of God" (*Epistle of Clement to James*, in the salutation). S. Peter receives a charge from S. James to send to him his discourses and his acts year by year (see *Homilies*, i. 20, and *Recognitions*, i. 72). Apostles, teachers, and prophets, who do not first accurately compare their preaching with that of James, are to be shunned (see *Homilies*, xi. 35). They are not to be believed "unless they bring from Jerusalem the testimonial of James, the Lord's brother, *or of whosoever may come after him*" (*Recognitions*, iv. 35). James is styled "the archbishop" (*Recognitions*, i. 73). S. Peter says, "While we abode in Jericho . . . James the bishop sent for me, and sent me here to Cæsarea" (*Recognitions*, i. 72). Altogether, S. Peter is represented as quite subordinate to S. James. Before S. Peter leaves Cæsarea to start on his missionary circuits, he consecrates Zacchæus to be his successor at Cæsarea, compelling him "to sit down in his own chair" (*Homilies*, iii. 63). The account of Zacchæus' nomination and consecration to the bishopric of Cæsarea (*Homilies*, iii. 60–72) is curiously like the account of the consecration of Clement to the bishopric of Rome, as given in the letter to James. In both cases it is a consecration to a local bishopric, and not to a monarchy over the universal Church. Taken as a whole, the Clementine romance is entirely un-Petrine and un-Roman. Nevertheless, there are two points in it, on which the Roman Church fastened. It teaches that S. Peter was the local Bishop of Rome; and it teaches that S. Clement and therefore also the other popes were S. Peter's successors in his Roman chair.

before his death, to the assembly of Roman Christians, "Hear me, brethren and fellow-servants. Since . . . the day of my death is approaching, I lay hands on this Clement as your bishop; and to him I entrust my chair of discourse," etc.[1] Then Clement is represented as kneeling before S. Peter, and entreating him, declining the honour and the authority of the chair.[2] However, S. Peter insists; and, after giving a somewhat lengthy charge, he lays his hands on Clement, and compels him "to sit in his own chair."[3]

All this is, of course, pure romance. No one now dreams of attaching the smallest importance to the story as being in any way historically true; but in the third and fourth and following centuries it was accepted as true. Even when the discourses and teaching attributed to S. Peter were perceived to be heretical, and were rejected, yet the framework of the story was supposed to be a true account of what had actually happened.

Now, it appears that one great object of the author of the romance was to depreciate S. Paul. S. Peter is represented as speaking of S. Paul as "the man who is my enemy," who leads the Gentiles to reject "my preaching of the law."[4] S. Paul's

---

[1] See *The Epistle of Clement to James* (prefixed to *The Clementine Homilies*), cap. ii., Clem. Rom. *Homiliæ*, ed. Dressel, p. 11.

[2] Cf. cap. iii., p. 12.

[3] εἰς τὴν αὐτοῦ καθέδραν. Cf. cap. xix., p. 23.

[4] See *The Epistle of Peter to James*, prefixed to *The Clementine Homilies* (*Hom.*, ed. Dressel, p. 4); and compare Dr. Salmon's article on *Clementine Literature*, in Smith and Wace, i. 576.

labours among tho heathen aro ignored, and S. Peter
is substituted for him as the Apostle of the Gentiles.
S. Peter, we are told, "as being fittest of all, was commanded to enlighten the darker part of the world,
namely, the West, and was enabled to accomplish it."[1]

It naturally results from this anti-Pauline tendency,
that when S. Peter is represented as consecrating
Clement to be his successor, he makes him to sit in
his own chair. From the nature of the case, S. Paul's
relation to the Church of Rome is passed over in
silence. The episcopal chair at Rome is described as
the chair of Peter.

It seems to be generally admitted that this
Clementine romance was written in the East shortly
after the middle of the second century.[2] Bishop
Lightfoot says of it, that its "glorification of Rome
and the Roman bishop obtained for it an early and
wide circulation in the West. Accordingly, even
Tertullian [in his treatise, *De Prœscriptione Hœre-
ticorum*[3]] speaks of Clement as the immediate
successor of S. Peter,"[4] and Tertullian ascribes this
view to the Roman Church of his day.[5] But the
older Roman tradition, which is preserved for us by
S. Irenæus,[6] and which is also preserved in the Canon

---

[1] *Epistle of Clement to James*, cap. i., p. 10.
[2] See Bishop Lightfoot's *S. Clement of Rome*, edit. 1890, i. 55.
[3] Tertull. *De Præscript. Hær.*, cap. xxxii.   [4] i. 64.
[5] In the time of S. Jerome (A.D. 392), "plerique Latinorum" supposed that S. Clement was the immediate successor of S. Peter
(*De Viris Illustribus*, 15).
[6] *Contra Omnes Hæreses*, iii. iii. 3.

of the Roman Mass, gives the order of the earliest
Roman bishops thus :—Linus, Anencletus, Clement.[1]
There is much reason for supposing that the notion
that S. Peter himself consecrated Clement to the
Roman see is wholly due to the Clementine romance,
and therefore that romance must have established its
influence in Rome some time during the last twenty
years of the second century, between the year 180,
which is the approximate date of the treatise of
S. Irenæus, and the year 200, which is the approximate date of the treatise of Tertullian.

Now, S. Irenæus,[2] following the older and truer
tradition, represents the Church of Rome as having
been founded "by the *two* most glorious apostles,
Peter and Paul;" and then he goes on to say that
"the blessed apostles, having founded and builded
the Church, committed the ministry of the episcopate
to Linus." Linus is here described as the *first*
Bishop, and as having received his office from the
two Apostles, who were the joint founders of the
Roman Church.[3] But Tertullian, writing twenty

---

[1] Mr. Allnatt, an Ultramontane writer, speaking of the order of the
Roman bishops, as given by S. Irenæus, says with truth, "This is the
order given also by Hegesippus, Eusebius, and Epiphanius, as well as
in the ancient Canon of the Roman Mass, which expresses *the earliest
traditions of the Roman Church*" (*Cathedra Petri*, p. 85, n., 2nd edit.).

[2] *Loc. cit.*

[3] Döllinger (*Considerations for the Bishops of the* [*Vatican*] *Council
respecting the question of Papal Infallibility*, of which an English
translation is printed in *Declarations and Letters on the Vatican
Decrees*, p. 16) says, "Irenæus knows nothing of a special privilege
accorded to this [the Roman] Church or her bishop as a successor
of Peter."

years later, describes how the apostolic Churches reckon their origin; and he says that "as the Church of Smyrna recounteth that Polycarp was placed there by John," so "that of Rome doth that Clement was in like manner ordained by Peter."[1] Here S. Paul has disappeared, and it is evident that the Clementine romance is already exerting its baleful influence. According to that romance, Clement was placed by S. Peter in *his own* chair; Peter was the first Bishop of Rome, and Clement was the second. The real inventor of the story of S. Peter's Roman episcopate appears to have been the unknown heretic who wrote the romance.[2] When we pass from the

---

[1] *De Præscript. Hær.*, cap. xxxii. The next writer after Tertullian, who mentions S. Peter's name without the name of S. Paul as the starting-point from which to number the Roman bishops, appears to be the anonymous author of the treatise called *The Little Labyrinth*, quoted by Eusebius (*H. E.*, v. 28). Bishop Lightfoot (*S. Clement of Rome*, i. 271; ii. 378–380, ed. 1890) is much inclined to identify this author with S. Hippolytus. Dr. Salmon (Smith and Wace, iii. 98) argues against the Hippolytan authorship, and ascribes the treatise to Caius, who was a contemporary of S. Hippolytus. In their time the popular acceptance of the Clementine myth at Rome had resulted in the omission of S. Paul's name, when the succession of the Roman bishops was being traced up to its source.   .

[2] Dr. Cyriacus, Professor in the University of Athens, in his *Ecclesiastical History* (1881), takes the same view (see *Church Quarterly* for July, 1882, p. 312); so also does Dr. Salmon (*Infallibility*, p. 360, 2nd edit.; and *Introduction to the New Testament*, p. 15, 4th edit. 1889); and apparently Bishop Lightfoot agrees. He says, "The Eastern Romance of the Clementines, however, made him [Clement] the immediate successor of S. Peter, and so *first* on the list. . . . This story was so flattering to the corporate pride of the Roman Christians in the unique position which it assigned to Clement, that it rapidly spread and largely influenced popular opinion in Rome" (*S. Clement of Rome*, i. 344; and compare ii. 501, 502, ed. 1890).

second century into the third, we must be on the watch for references to the chair or see of Peter. No one had any suspicion that the Clementine romance was a lie invented by a heretic. The story was accepted on all sides. Some like S. Cyprian accepted it, but without allowing it to modify to any appreciable degree the traditional teaching of the Church. Others, more closely connected with the Church of Rome, fastened on the notion of the chair of Peter, and used that notion to provide an apostolic basis for the growing claims of the Roman see. I do not wish to be misunderstood; I firmly believe, on what seems to me conclusive evidence, that the Roman Church was founded by the two great apostles, S. Peter and S. Paul, who also were martyred there, and whose bodies remain there to this day. But it is one thing for two apostles jointly to found a Church, and it is another thing for one of them to be its first local bishop. S. Peter and S. Paul were the apostolic founders; S. Linus was the first local bishop; and, as S. Irenæus says, the ministry of the episcopate was committed to him by the *two* apostles If the author of the Clementine romance had not been an Ebionitish heretic, with an inherited hatred of the memory of S. Paul, the world would never have heard of the chair of Peter. It is strange how, from the very first, the Roman claims have been based upon forgeries.[1]

[1] It is worth noticing that the spurious Epistle of Clement to James, which so misled Western Christians in the early centuries, was

I now invite your attention to the history of
S. Cyprian, Bishop of Carthage, and I hope to make
clear to you how, from beginning to end, his whole
action is absolutely inconsistent with the teaching
about the papacy set forth in the Vatican decrees.
I have already pointed out the way in which
S. Cyprian corresponds with the various popes with
whom he was contemporary, on terms of complete
equality. He speaks of them and addresses them
as his brothers and his colleagues. And it must not
be supposed that this familiar style of address was
due to the primitive simplicity of the Christians of
that age. On the contrary, when the priests and
deacons of Rome have occasion to write to S. Cyprian,
they conclude their letter thus: "Most blessed and
most glorious Pope, we bid you ever heartily farewell
in the Lord."[1] And again, when the same priests
and deacons of Rome, writing to the clergy of
Carthage, have occasion to refer to S. Cyprian, they
say: "We have learnt . . . that the blessed Pope
Cyprian has, for a certain reason, retired."[2] It is
clear, therefore, that, whatever may have been the
simplicity of Christians in the third century, it did
not preclude the use of respectful titles in letters to

by no means forgotten in the Middle Ages. The pseudo-Isidore set
it in the fore-front of his collection of papal decretals: cf. *Decretales
Pseudo-Isidor.*, ed. Hinsch., 1863, pp. 30-36.

[1] "Beatissime et gloriosissime Papa." *Ep. cler. Romani ad Cyprianum, inter Cyprianicas* xxxi., *Opp.* ed. Ben., p. 45.

[2] "Benedictum Papam Cyprianum." *Ep. cler. Rom. ad cler. Car-
thag., inter Cyprianicas* ii., *Opp.* ed. Ben., p. 7.

persons in authority; and we may safely draw the
conclusion that when S. Cyprian, writing to the
Roman bishop, calls him his dear brother and
colleague, he so writes because he naturally thinks
of the Roman pope as an equal; whereas the priests
and deacons of Rome, the body of officials, which
is now known as the College of cardinals, realized
that S. Cyprian, as a bishop, was exceedingly
superior to themselves in rank, and that it was their
duty to address him with words of reverential respect,
such as " most blessed Pope," " most glorious Pope,"
and the like.

The episode in S. Cyprian's life which throws
most light on his view of the relation of the Roman
see to the rest of the Church, is undoubtedly his
controversy with Pope Stephen about the validity
of heretical baptism. But it will be well to refer
first of all to some other incidents in his career,
which took place at an earlier stage, and were un-
connected with the heat of controversy, so that we
may be in a position to judge whether his action in
regard to Stephen was a new departure, or whether
it was not rather the carrying out of his normal
principles.

We will take first a passage from one of his letters
to Pope Cornelius, part of which is usually quoted by
Roman Catholics as decidedly in their favour. Their
view proceeds from a misconception as to the meaning
of certain words which S. Cyprian uses. The passage,
taken as a whole, is irreconcilable with the papal

system. S. Cyprian is writing to the pope to warn him against a ringleader of schism named Fortunatus, who had been consecrated to be an opposition Bishop of Carthage by an excommunicated heretic bishop named Privatus. These schismatics had already been condemned by a large council of Catholic bishops held at Carthage under S. Cyprian's presidency. But now, having secured the consecration of their ring-leader, they sent legates to Rome to try and induce Cornelius to recognize them as the true Church of North Africa. A short time before a similar schism had broken out in Rome. Cornelius had been con-secrated pope, and the schismatics had consecrated Novatian to be opposition pope; and both pope and anti-pope had sent legates to Carthage to induce Cyprian to declare himself on their side, and to grant them his communion. *Now* the parts were reversed, and Carthage was the scene of the schism. As soon as Cyprian heard that the schismatics of Carthage had sent legates to Rome, he wrote to Cornelius, his "dearest brother," to put him on his guard. He says, "Having had a pseudo-bishop ordained for them by heretics, they dare to set sail, and to carry letters from schismatic and profane persons to the chair of Peter, *atque ad ecclesiam principalem, unde unitas sacer-dotalis exorta est.*"[1] I need say nothing about the expression, "chair of Peter," as applied to the see of

---

[1] "And to the mother-Church [of the West], whence the united body of [Western] bishops sprang." *Ep.* lv., *ad Cornelium, Opp.* ed. Ben., p. 86.

Rome.   By the time of S. Cyprian Western Christians
had learnt from the Clementine romance to apply the
title to the Roman see.   But what does S. Cyprian
exactly mean, when he describes the Roman Church
as the "ecclesia principalis, unde unitas sacerdotalis
exorta est"?   I have no doubt that he means that
the Roman Church is the mother-Church of Italy
and Africa, whence the whole episcopate of those
countries was derived.   The word "principalis" is
used by African writers in the sense of *ancient* or
primæval.   So Tertullian, wishing to state that
truth comes *first* and falsehood afterwards, contrasts the "*principalitas* veritatis" with the "*poste-
ritas* mendacitatis;"[1] in other words, the "*antiquity
of truth*" with the "*lateness* of falsehood."[2]   The
"ecclesia principalis" is the *primæval* Church, the
mother-Church; in the words of S. Irenæus, "that
very ancient Church, founded at Rome."[3]   Not, of
course, that S. Cyprian thought that the Church of
Rome was the mother-Church of the world.   Obviously that would not be true.   The Church of
Jerusalem is necessarily the mother-Church of the
whole world.   To use the words of S. Irenæus,[4] the
Church of Jerusalem is "that Church from which

---

[1] Tert. *De Præscr.,* xxxi.

[2] Compare S. Augustine's use of the word *principale* in a passage
quoted on p. 102, and see the ancient Latin translation of S. Irenæus,
Contra omnes Hæreses, v. xiv. 1, 2; v. xxi. 1.   Du Cange, in his
Glossarium, s.v. "Principalis," interprets the word to mean "Primus,
primævus, antiquior" (tom. v. p. 447, edit. 1815).

[3] *Contra omnes Hæreses,* iii. iii. 2.   [4] iii. xii. 5.

every Church had its origin :" it is "the metropolis,
the mother-city of the citizens of the new covenant."
But, though the Church of Rome is not the mother-
Church of the world, yet it is the mother-Church
of Italy and of Africa and of the greater part of
the West. The original bishops who evangelized
Africa were no doubt consecrated at Rome.[1] The
episcopate of Italy and Africa issued out from Rome.
S. Cyprian often calls the united episcopate, either
of the whole Church or of some notable part of it,
by such terms as these, "collegium sacerdotale," "collegium sacerdotum;" here he uses the expression,
"unitas sacerdotalis."[2] He means by all these expressions *the episcopal body*, considered as forming

[1] Cf. S. Greg. Magn., *Registr. Epistt.* lib. viii., *Ep.* xxxiii. *ad
Dominicum, Opp.* ed. Ben., 1705, tom. ii. col. 921.

[2] Cf. *Ep.* lii. *ad Antonianum, Opp.* ed. Ben., pp. 66–76. Compare
Hincmar (*De divortio Hl. et Theut*), quoted by Milman (*Latin
Christianity*, ii. 292, note, 2nd edit., 1857): "Nostrâ ætate Hludovicum
Augustum a regno dejectum, post satisfactionem, *episcopalis unani-
mitas*, saniore concilio, cum populi consensu, et ecclesiæ et regno
restituit." Compare also the letter of the bishops of (Northern) Italy
to the bishops of Illyricum, preserved in the 12th *Hilarian Fragment* (*Opp.* S. Hilar. Pictav., ed. Ben., 1693, col. 1359); they say,
"Quicumque igitur *nostræ unanimitatis* optat habere consortium . . .
quæ sunt nostræ sententiæ comprobare festinet." I am not aware
that the genuineness of this letter has been questioned; but, whether
genuine or not, it illustrates S. Cyprian's expression, "*unitas sacerdotalis*." A still better illustration may perhaps be found in S. Augustine's statement about the promise of the keys to S. Peter. In his
295th Sermon (*Opp.* ed. Ben., 1683, v. 1194) he says, "Has enim
claves non homo unus, sed *unitas* accepit *Ecclesiæ*." Here "unitas
Ecclesiæ" evidently means, not the unity of the Church in the abstract, but the united society or body of the Church. It was the
society which received the keys, not an attribute of the society.
Similarly, S. Cyprian's "*unitas sacerdotalis*" means the united body
of the bishops.

a *unity*. Some Roman Catholic writers have supposed that S. Cyprian is intending to teach that the Roman see is the perennial fountain of unity. But the original Latin will not bear that interpretation. S. Cyprian does not say, "unde unitas sacerdotalis *exoritur*," but "unde unitas sacerdotalis *exorta est.*" He is referring to a historical fact which took place long before, namely, the original derivation of the true canonical episcopate of North Africa from the mother-Church of the West.[1]

But to return to S. Cyprian's letter to Cornelius. After referring to S. Paul's commendation (in his Epistle to the Romans)[2] of the faith of the Roman Christians, he goes on, "But what is the occasion of the schismatics going to you, and of their announcing that a pseudo-bishop has been set up against the true bishops? for either they are well pleased with what they have done, and persevere in their wickedness; or, if it displeases them and they desist [from their schism], they know whither they should return."[3] He meant to say, "What is the good of their going to Rome? If they want to be restored to the unity of the Church, they ought to know that they must come to me and my colleagues here in Africa." He shows that this is

---

[1] Mr. Gore (*The Church and the Ministry*, 1st edit. p. 169, n.), speaking of the words "unde unitas sacerdotalis exorta est," says, "These last words mean, I suppose, simply that Peter's priesthood was the first given." Such an interpretation harmonizes thoroughly with S. Cyprian's general teaching, but I feel a difficulty about referring the word "unde" to "Petri;" it seems more natural to refer it to the whole phrase, "Petri cathedram atque . . . ecclesiam principalem."

[2] Rom. i. 8. [3] *Ep.* lv. *ad Cornelium, Opp.* ed. Ben., p 86.

his meaning by the words which follow. He says,
" For since it has been decreed by our whole body,
and is alike equitable and just, that every cause
should be there heard where the offence has been
committed; and a portion of the flock has been
assigned to the several shepherds, which each is to
rule and govern, having hereafter to give account of
his administration to the Lord; it therefore behoves
those over whom we are set, not to run about from
place to place, nor, by their crafty and deceitful boldness, break the harmonious concord of bishops, but
there to plead their cause, where they will have both
accusers and witnesses of their crime; *unless perhaps
some few desperate and abandoned men count as
inferior the authority of the bishops appointed in
Africa,* who have already given judgment concerning
them, and have lately, by the weight of their decision,
condemned those persons' consciences, entangled in
the bonds of many sins. Already has their cause
been heard; already has sentence been given concerning them." In this passage S. Cyprian says that
African Christians have no right " to run about from
place to place," and appeal from the judgment of the
African bishops to the Roman pope. He thus flatly
contradicts the decree of the Vatican Council, which
declares that " in all causes which appertain to the
jurisdiction of the Church," " recourse may be had to
the judgment of the Roman pontiff;" and we must
observe that the Council bases this declaration on the
fact that the pope " presides over the universal

Church " " by the *divine right* of the apostolic primacy."[1] If the theory about the papacy set forth by the Vatican Council is right, S. Cyprian was guilty of repudiating one of the prerogatives of "the true vicar of Christ," which flows immediately from his divinely given primacy of jurisdiction. Nay, S. Cyprian goes further; he implies that no Christians are likely to consider the Roman pope to have a better right than the African bishops to deal finally with the case of these African schismatics, except " some few desperate and abandoned men."[2] It is for Ultramontanes, who profess to venerate S. Cyprian and the early Church, to consider whether they are prepared to accept his teaching on this point; and if not, why not. From the Ultramontane point of view, S. Cyprian is dealing with no minor matter, but with the fundamental question of the relation of the divinely appointed head of the Church to the subordinate members. And then consider, To whom did S. Cyprian write these clear statements of truth? He wrote them to S. Cornelius, the pope; and he begs the pope to read this letter of his to the clergy and people of the local Church of Rome. He says, "Though I am aware, dearest brother, that by reason of the mutual love which we owe and manifest towards each other, you always read my epistles to

---

[1] See p. 6.

[2] The principle laid down by S. Cyprian in the passage discussed in the text was still in full force in the African Church 170 years later, in the time of S. Aurelius and S. Augustine. Compare the letter of the Council of Carthage to Pope Celestine, quoted on p. 199.

the very eminent clergy who there preside with you, and to your most holy and flourishing people; yet now I both exhort and beg of you, to do at my request, what on other occasions you do of your own accord and of courtesy, and read this my epistle."[1] Evidently S. Cyprian knew perfectly well that there was nothing in his letter which would give pain to S. Cornelius. The Catholic teaching concerning the true method of the Church's government was held at Rome in those days, no less clearly than at Carthage.[2]

---

[1] *Ep. cit., Opp.,* p. 89. If S. Cyprian had thought that he was bound to the authority of the pope "by the obligation of true obedience," why does he speak *only* of "the *mutual love,* which we owe and manifest *towards each other*"? It would seem more natural for a fallible subordinate, writing to his infallible superior, to allude in some way to the great condescension shown by that superior in making a practice of reading publicly the subordinate's letters in the assemblies of his local Church. S. Cyprian's words are perfectly appropriate, if he was writing to an equal; they seem very inappropriate, if he was writing to the vicar of Christ, the monarch of the militant Church.

[2] An incidental proof of the fact that the Cyprianic principles of Church government were held at Rome in that age, is supplied by a letter addressed by the Roman clergy to S. Cyprian during a vacancy of the Roman see. S. Cyprian had written to them, giving an account of his resolutions about the treatment of the lapsed. In their reply they say, "To Pope Cyprian, the priests and deacons abiding at Rome send greeting. Although a mind conscious to itself of uprightness, and relying on the vigour of evangelical discipline, and made a true witness to itself in regard to [its fulfilment of] the divine commandments, is accustomed to be satisfied with God as its only Judge, and neither seeks the praises nor fears the charges of any other; yet they are worthy of double praise, who, *knowing that their conscience is subject to God as its only Judge,* do yet desire that their acts should have their brethren's approval" (*Ep.* cleri Romani *ad Cyprianum, inter Cyprianicas* xxxi., *Opp.* ed. Ben., p. 42). If the Archbishop of Paris were to write to the authorities at Rome in the present day during a vacancy in the papal see, reporting the arrangements made

The whole Church would have agreed in repudiating the false theories set forth by the Vatican Council.

I am not professing to write an exhaustive monograph on S. Cyprian's teaching about the government of the Church; and it is impossible for me, within the limits assigned to me, to attempt to deal with the various misrepresentations of his sentiments which have been from time to time devised by Roman Catholic controversialists.[1] A careful consideration of the context, or of parallel passages in other writings of his, will generally suffice to make his meaning clear. Any one who wishes to go more fully into the subject will find much to help him in Archbishop Laud's *Conference with Fisher*, and also in a review of *Wilberforce on the Supremacy*, which appeared in the *Christian Remembrancer* for April, 1855.

I proceed to give an account of an incident in S. Cyprian's life, which has been represented as bearing witness to the supreme jurisdiction of the Roman see.[2] The facts of the case are these :—Marcianus, Bishop of Arles, had joined himself to the Novatian schism,

by him in regard to an important question of discipline, they would hardly return the answer which their predecessors in the third century returned to S. Cyprian. There would probably be some reference to the fact that a pope would soon be elected, who would be able to ratify what the archbishop had done; and there would assuredly be no stress laid on the principle that the judgment of the archbishop is subject to God only, nor surprise expressed at his having reported to Rome the determinations at which he had arrived.

[1] In the Appendix to these Lectures I have dealt with those Cyprianic passages which have been twisted into a Roman sense (see Note B, with its *Addendum*, pp. 334-363).

[2] Our knowledge of this incident is entirely derived from S. Cyprian's *Ep.* lxvii. *ad Stephanum, Opp.* ed. Ben., pp. 115-117.

but still retained his position as chief pastor of the Church in Arles. It appears that metropolitans were not instituted in Gaul until the end of the fourth century or the beginning of the fifth.[1] There was, therefore, no leading bishop in Gaul to take the initiative in proceeding against Marcianus. No doubt in such a case any bishop would have the right to take steps for bringing about the assembly of a council. But, as often happens on similar occasions, what is everybody's business is no one's business. People are shy of putting themselves forward. More- over, Tillemont[2] thinks that possibly the bishops of Gaul had never had occasion to depose a bishop before, and that they would, therefore, wish to be supported by the authority of the leading prelates of the Church in other countries before they girded themselves for their task. Anyhow, the bishops of Gaul, and amongst them Faustinus, Bishop of Lyons, wrote to Pope Stephen, the second successor of S. Cornelius, asking him, apparently, to give them advice and guidance in their difficulty. The Bishop of Rome was the natural person for the bishops of Gaul to write to. He was not only the first bishop in the whole Church, but he was also the nearest metropolitan to Gaul, and his see was the nearest

---

[1] Duchesne, *Origines du Culte Chrétien*, p. 31. See also the re- marks of the Ballerini in their *Observationes in Dissert. v. Quesnell.*, part. ii. cap. v. (*Opp.* S. Leon., tom. ii. coll. 607, et seq., ed. Migne), and in their disquisition, *De Antiq. collection. et collector. canonum*, part i. cap. v. § 4 (*Opp.* S. Leon., iii. 43, 44).

[2] iv. 132.

apostolical see to them, and, in fact, the only apostolical see in the West. If any help was to be got from outside, Rome was the obvious place for the Gallican bishops to apply to. Doubtless if Gaul had been situated near Egypt, the bishops of Gaul would, under similar circumstances, have applied for help and counsel to the Bishop of Alexandria.[1] Or if it had been near Syria, they would have gone to the Bishop of Antioch. It would seem as if Stephen had been somewhat remiss in giving the advice for which he had been asked. The Bishop of Lyons, therefore, wrote more than one letter to S. Cyprian at Carthage, who was the second great metropolitan in the Latin-speaking portion of the Church; and S. Cyprian came to the conclusion that he would write to Stephen to urge him to help the afflicted Church of Gaul. No doubt S. Cyprian held that he had a perfect right to help that Church himself. But as he was living far away, and had only heard from Faustinus, whereas Stephen was near at hand, and had had an application from *all* the Gallican bishops, it was more fitting that the answer should come from Stephen. In his letter to Stephen, S. Cyprian begins by laying down the principle that it is the duty of the bishops generally to give their help in such a case: ' It is *ours*, dearest brother, to advise and come in aid. . . . Wherefore it behoves you to write a very full letter to our fellow-bishops established in Gaul, that they no longer suffer the froward and proud Marcianus . . . to

---

[1] See note on p. 14.

insult over our college (*i.e.* the Catholic episcopate),
because he seemeth as yet not to be excommunicated
by us, who this long while boasts and publishes
that . . . he has separated himself from our communion. . . . How idle were it, dearest brother, when
Novatian has been lately repulsed and cast back and
excommunicated by the priests of God throughout
the world, were we now to suffer his flatterers still
to mock us, and to judge respecting the majesty and
dignity of the Church! Let letters be addressed from
thee to the Province [*i.e.* the region of Gaul in which
Arles is situated], and to the people dwelling at Arles,
whereby, when Marcianus has been excommunicated,
another may be substituted in his room, and the flock
of Christ . . . be again collected together."[1] Thus
S. Cyprian presses on Stephen the duty of writing
a letter of counsel and help to those who had begged
to be advised and helped. It was not the case of a
new heresy or schism arising; that could hardly have
been settled without a council of bishops. Nor was
it a case in which the facts were doubtful. Marcianus himself boasted that he had separated himself
from the Catholic communion. All that was needed
was that the bishops of Gaul should be encouraged
to do their duty and excommunicate their erring
brother, and that then a new bishop should be
elected, and consecrated, and be peaceably accepted
by the Church people of Arles. But again I must
point out that, while S. Cyprian thought that, under

[1] *Ep. cit., Opp.,* pp. 115, 116.

the circumstances, Stephen was the appropriate person to convey the counsel of the Church at large to the Gallican brethren, he takes good care to make it clear that essentially the duty was one which might have been discharged by any other bishop, whose advice might have been asked. He does not write to Stephen in the style of the Vatican decrees. He does not say, " You have the ' full and supreme power of jurisdiction over the universal Church,' and this your ' power is ordinary and immediate over all and each of the Churches, and over all and each of the pastors and of the faithful;'" [1] but he says, "For therefore, dearest brother, is the body of bishops so large, united together by the glue of mutual concord and the bond of unity, that if any of our college should attempt to introduce heresy . . . the rest may come in aid, and as good and merciful shepherds gather the Lord's sheep into the fold. . . . For what greater or better office have bishops, than by diligent solicitude and wholesome remedies to provide for cherishing and preserving the sheep ? . . . For although we are many shepherds, yet we feed one flock, and ought to gather together and cherish all the sheep which Christ has acquired by His own Blood and Passion. . . . Signify plainly to us who has been substituted at Arles in the room of Marcianus, that we may know to whom we should direct our brethren, and to whom write. I bid you, dearest brother, ever heartily farewell." [2] It seems almost

---

[1] *Collectio Lacensis,* vii. 485.   [2] *Ep. cit., Opp.,* pp. 116, 117.

incredible that any one should have discovered in
this letter of S. Cyprian an argument for the modern
Roman claims. Every sentence in it, almost, is a
contradiction of the papal theory. The pope is urged,
no doubt, to write and give his advice; but it is
carefully pressed upon him that he is to write as one
of the College of bishops, to all of whom it belongs
to provide for the. cherishing and preserving of the
sheep. *He* is to write, because application has been
specially made to *him*. If the application had been
made to S. Cyprian by the bishops of Gaul, undoubtedly he would have felt that he was fully
entitled to do all that was necessary. About the
same time he did receive a similar application from
some of the Churches in Spain, and he wrote very
vigorously to them, bidding them abide by the action
of the bishops of their province, and pay no attention to a mistaken *dictum* of Pope Stephen. But in
the present instance the application of the Gallican
episcopate had been made to Stephen, and therefore
S. Cyprian had no *locus standi* for directly inter-
fering.

Rather more than a hundred years afterwards,
in A.D. 390, we find the bishops of Gaul again
in need of external help and counsel. They were
still without the full metropolitical system. But by
that time Milan had become the metropolitical see of
North Italy, and Milan was nearer to Gaul than
Rome. The Gallican bishops, therefore, applied for
advice and help to S. Ambrose of Milan, as well as

to Siricius of Rome; and they got what they needed
from the two great prelates to whom they wrote.
The trouble which was then disturbing them was
very similar to the trouble about Marcianus. It
had to do with the schism of the Ithacians. Eleven
years later the Ithacian question came again to the
front, and the Gallican bishops applied this time to
S. Venerius, the second successor of S. Ambrose, and
to him only.[1] The council of the bishops of the
province of Milan was held at Turin, and in its sixth
canon it decreed as follows: "If any should wish to
separate themselves from the communion of Felix
[the friend of the Ithacians], they shall be received
into the fellowship of our peace, in accordance with
the former letters of Ambrose of blessed memory,
and of the bishop of the Roman Church."[2] Here we
notice that Milan is put first, and Rome second.
Doubtless this order would have been unusual outside
the province of Milan; but in that province it was
the natural order to use, so long as the Catholic
system of Church government prevailed. The bishops
of Milan and Rome were brother-metropolitans, and
the Milanese prelate was more to the bishops of the
Milanese province than the Bishop of Rome was.
They therefore naturally gave him precedence in
their own province. Of course, if the Fathers of the

---

[1] Hefele gives A.D. 401 as the date of the Council of Turin. Sir-
mondus (ap. *Colet.*, ii. 1387), Tillemont (x. 679), and Duchesne
(*Origines*, p. 34) agree that it was a Provincial Council of the
province of Milan.

[2] *Concilia*, ii. 1383, ed. Colet.

Council had supposed that the Bishop of Rome was the infallible vicar of Christ, having immediate episcopal jurisdiction in Milan, Turin, and everywhere else, they would certainly have given a different turn to the wording of their canon. But those dreams had not then been invented. Let us now return to S. Cyprian.

We have a letter written by him in the name of a Council of African bishops to certain Churches in Spain, which needed comfort and help.[1] Two Spanish bishops, Basilides and Martialis, had in the course of the Decian persecution become what was technically called "libellatics;" in other words, they had made an unworthy and sinful compromise with idolatry. S. Cyprian tells us that in the public proceedings before the ducenary procurator Martialis had appeared, and had put in a declaration that he had denied Christ and had conformed to idolatrous worship. Basilides must have made some compromise of a similar kind, for they had both "been contaminated with the profane *libellus* of idolatry." Martialis had also joined himself to one of the heathen *collegia* or guilds, and had in connection with this guild frequented for a long while "the foul and filthy feasts of the Gentiles;" while Basilides, when lying sick, had blasphemed against God; and there were many other heinous sins in which both had become implicated. Basilides, pricked by his

---

[1] *Ep.* lxviii., *ad clerum et plebes in Hispaniâ consistentes, Opp.* ed. Ben., pp. 117–121.

conscience, had confessed his blasphemy, and had voluntarily laid down his bishopric, and had betaken himself to do penance, accounting himself most happy if he might hope to be admitted some day to lay communion. It appears that Basilides' resignation was accepted by the bishops of the province, and that Martialis was by them deposed and excommunicated; and the vacant sees were soon filled by the consecration of Sabinus as successor to Basilides, and of Felix as successor to Martialis. Afterwards Basilides went to Rome and deceived Pope Stephen, who was ignorant of the true state of the case, and admitted him to communion as a bishop of the Church;[1] and Basilides, furnished with letters of communion from the pope, returned to Spain and canvassed to be restored to the see which he had resigned. Martialis seems to have followed the same course. At any rate, in some way, not fully described, he tried by

---

[1] A question may be raised as to the precise character of the pope's action in this case; whether, that is, he simply admitted the deposed bishops to his communion, notwithstanding the sentence of the Spanish bishops, which would be bad enough; or whether he attempted in any way to declare authoritatively that they were restored to their bishoprics, which would be far worse. The learned French Roman Catholic theologian, Dupin, in the appendix to the 5th (al. 6th) volume of the *Nouvelle Bibliothèque des Auteurs Ecclesiastiques* (pp. 185–188), argues in favour of the first of these explanations. Whatever it was that the pope did, S. Cyprian and the African bishops held that it was wrong, and advised the Spanish bishops to ignore it. In the text I have preferred to take the more charitable view of Stephen's action. On pp. 70, 71 will be found a short account of a similar application made by the " Tall Brothers " to S. Chrysostom, whose action was much more in accordance with the canons than was that of Stephen

"deceit" to get put back into his bishopric.   Certain
bishops, following the pope's bad example, admitted
both Basilides and Martialis to their communion.
The result of all this was that the Churches in Spain
were thrown into confusion; and in their trouble
they wrote to S. Cyprian for his advice and aid.
Their application was discussed in a synod, consisting of thirty-seven African bishops, over whom S.
Cyprian presided.   It is interesting to observe what
action S. Cyprian and the African synod took.   Did
they say with the Vatican Council that "the judgment
of the apostolic see cannot be revised by any one, and
that no one may pass judgment on its decisions"?
Did they say that "all the pastors and all the
faithful are bound to the pope by the obligation of
true obedience"?   Did they therefore exhort the
Spanish Catholics to restore the deposed bishops to
communion, and to take counsel with the pope as to
their being reinstated in their sees? or, if that
seemed impossible, did they suggest that a humble
petition should be sent to Rome, begging that the
case might be reheard?   They say nothing of the
kind.   They say that Felix and Sabinus are in full
canonical possession of their sees; and that the
mistaken action of the pope "cannot rescind an
ordination rightly performed."   They say that the
effect of what took place at Rome was not to efface
but to increase the crimes of Basilides.   They say
that, although some of the bishops (and the pope was
one of them) think that the heavenly discipline of

the Church is to be neglected, and rashly communicate with Basilides and Martialis, this ought not to disturb our faith, since the Holy Spirit threatens such bishops in the Psalms, saying, " But thou hatest to be reformed, and hast cast My words behind thee : when thou sawest a thief, thou consentedst unto him, and hast been partaker with the adulterers." They express their belief that these bishops, who are mingled in unlawful communion with sinners who abstain from doing penance, are polluted with the commerce of the guilty, and being joined in the guilt are not separate in the punishment. Finally, they exhort the Spanish Catholics to pay no heed to the action of the pope, and to refuse to communicate with the two profane and polluted bishops, who had been deposed.

The whole incident illustrates admirably the Catholic system of Church government. The sentence of the synod of the province is held to be final. The pope's decision in regard to a matter which had taken place outside his jurisdiction, is considered to have no force in itself. It is neither able to reverse nor suspend the decision of the province. The Spanish Churches are exhorted to ignore it ; and all who act upon it are warned that they will share in the guilt and in the punishment of the miserable men whose actions had caused all the trouble. We learn also from this incident that when any Church was in trouble, it could apply for help to any foreign Church which it might select.[1] It might apply to Rome, if it

[1] Church history is full of the records of such applications, made

chose, as the bishops of Gaul did in the case of Marcianus; but it might apply also to Carthage, if it preferred that course, as the Catholics of Spain did in the present instance. The African bishops had normally no right to exercise jurisdiction in Spain, any more than the Bishop of Rome had either in Spain or in Gaul; but they 'could give advice and comfort, and could help to strengthen the Spanish Churches in maintaining the wholesome discipline of the gospel.

S. Cyprian's action in this Spanish dispute is an admirable illustration of what S. Gregory Nazianzen meant, when he said that Cyprian "presided not only over the Church of Carthage and over Africa, . . . but also over all the countries of the West, and over nearly all the regions of the East and of the South and of the North."[1] It is scarcely necessary to add that this presidency which S. Cyprian exercised was not (outside of Africa) a presidency of *jurisdiction*, but a presidency of *love* and *honour*, and, as a consequence, of *influence*.

either by Churches or by individuals. To name one celebrated case, which occurred about a century and a half later. When the "Tall Brothers" had been most unjustly excommunicated by Theophilus of Alexandria, they took refuge with S. Chrysostom at Constantinople, who very rightly refused to admit them to the participation of the Mysteries, until their case had been judicially investigated; but he permitted them to be present at the Holy Sacrifice among the *consistentes*; and he wrote to Theophilus, "desiring him to receive them back into communion, as their sentiments concerning the Divine Nature were orthodox" (cf. Sozomen., *H. E.*, viii. 13). It need hardly be said that S. Chrysostom had no jurisdiction over Theophilus.

[1] *Orat.*, xxiv. 12, *Opp.* ed. Ben., i. 445.

Hitherto I have been speaking about acts and words of S. Cyprian, which are generally held to have preceded the breaking out of the quarrel between Carthage and Rome on the subject of the validity of heretical baptism.[1] Let us now proceed to consider the light which that quarrel throws on the position of the see of Rome in the Cyprianic age. I shall not attempt to go fully into the controversy, but shall confine myself strictly to that which has a bearing on our general subject. The rough outline of the dispute must be familiar to every one here. S. Cyprian, and the African bishops generally, rebaptized converts from the sects, whether they had been previously baptized in the name of the Holy Trinity or not. The Africans considered that all baptism administered by persons living in heresy or schism was invalid. With the Africans agreed the bishops of Asia Minor, under which term I include Phrygia, Cappadocia, Cilicia, and other neighbouring provinces. The Roman Church accepted the baptism of heretics and schismatics as valid when the right form was used, and refused to rebaptize converts from heresy or schism, but admitted them into the Church, after proof of repentance and faith, by confirmation. Both sides appealed confidently to ancient tradition and custom. S. Firmilian, Bishop of Cæsarea in Cappadocia, says that the custom of rebaptizing heretics, which was maintained in Asia Minor, was

---

[1] Possibly, however, the case of the Spanish bishops may have occurred during the baptismal controversy.

based on that which had been "delivered by Christ and His apostles."[1] "Nor do we," he says, "remember that this ever had a beginning among us, since it has ever been observed here." On the other hand, the very able author of the treatise *De Rebaptismate* speaks of the usage upheld by Stephen as agreeing with "most ancient custom, and with the tradition of the Church," and as being "an old and memorable and most established observance of all the veteran saints and believers," and which has in its favour "the authority of all the Churches."[2] Both sides had a great deal to say for themselves. We in England at the present day follow the practice which was upheld by Stephen, but we have no right to say that it is the only allowable practice. The controversy has never been decided by an authority which binds the whole Church. It is very commonly supposed that the Council of Nicæa settled the matter in favour of the custom of Pope Stephen, but that is a mistake, S. Athanasius, who must have known if any such action had been taken, says, "How should not the baptism which the Arians administer be wholly vain and profitless, having a semblance but nothing real as an aid to holiness;"[3]

[1] *Ep.* S. Firmil., *inter Cyprianicas* lxxv., *Opp.* ed. Ben., p. 149.

[2] *Lib. de Rebapt.* ap. S. Cyprian, *Opp.* ed. Ben., p. 353. Dr. Mason, speaking of the authorship of this treatise, says, "It seems safe to consider" it "as the production of one of the prelates in the entourage of Stephen" (*Relation of Confirmation to Baptism*, p. 124).

[3] Cf. *Orat.* ii., *contr. Ariann.*, §§ 42, 43. See Dr. Pusey's *Note G* on *Tertullian* (*Lib. Fath. tr.*, pp. 286, 287), and Dr. Bright's *Notes on the Canons of the First Four General Councils*, pp. 67, 68

and the post-Nicene Eastern Fathers for the most
part teach that baptism administered by heretics is
invalid, even though the right formula be used; but
they also hold that the Church can, by a high exercise
of its authority, validate that which of itself would
be invalid.　This seems to be the view of the Eastern
Church up to the present time.[1]　However, our business is with the controversy between S. Cyprian and
Pope Stephen.　The question had been discussed for
more than a year in Africa before it was brought to
the knowledge of Stephen.　But in A.D. 256 a council
was held at Carthage, at which seventy-one bishops
were present.　S. Cyprian presided; and in the name
of the council he wrote to Stephen, reporting the
decision at which the assembled bishops had arrived.[2]
He informs the pope that the council had determined
that those "who have been baptized without the
Church, and have among heretics and schismatics
been tainted by the defilement of profane water,
when they come ... to the Church ... ought to
be baptized;" and he concludes his letter thus:
"These things, dearest brother, by reason of our
mutual respect and single-hearted affection, we have
brought to thy knowledge, believing that what is
alike religious and true will, according to the truth

(Nicæa, xix.).　On the whole subject see *The Minister of Baptism*,
by the Rev. W. Elwin, a very learned and thorough book; but Mr.
Elwin hardly does justice, as it seems to me, to the strength of the
argument in favour of the validity of heretical baptism.

[1] See Elwin, pp. 80, 86, 132, 267, 268; compare Gore's *Church and
the Ministry* (1st edit., p. 194, n. 2).

[2] *Ep.* lxxii, *ad Stephanum, Opp.* ed. Ben., pp. 128, 129.

of thy religion and faith, be approved by thee also."
We must observe that S. Cyprian hardly seems to
realize that he is writing to one on whom had " been
divinely conferred the gift of never-failing truth
and faith,"[1] as was the case if the Vatican decrees
are true. He does not submit the decision of his
province to the pope's infallible correction. He tells
his correspondent that the African decision is " alike
religious and true," and he expresses his belief that,
as the pope is also a religious man, he will agree with
what has been decided. No doubt he had a shrewd
suspicion that the pope would disagree, and he therefore adds, " But we know that some will not lay
aside what they have once imbibed, nor easily change
their resolves, but, without interruption to the bonds
of peace and concord with their colleagues, retain
certain peculiarities which have once grown into
usage among themselves." He then proceeds to add
that he does not propose to enforce the African view
by cutting off the pope from his communion if he
disagrees; he considers that this is a matter in which
the two views may co-exist side by side in the Church.
His words are : " In this matter we neither do violence
nor give the law to any one, since each bishop hath,
in the administration of the Church, his own choice
and will free, hereafter to give an account of his
conduct to the Lord. We bid you, dearest brother,
ever heartily, farewell." How is it possible to suppose that S. Cyprian could have written in this strain,

---

[1] *Collectio Lacensis,* vii. 486, 487,

if he had believed the pope to be the infallible monarch of the Church ? His words breathe throughout the spirit of brotherly equality.

To this letter Pope Stephen wrote a harsh reply, which unfortunately has not been preserved, although small fragments of it may be found embedded in the letters of S. Cyprian and S. Firmilian. S. Cyprian, when referring to it, speaks of the "proud," "impertinent," "inconsistent remarks," which Stephen had written "rashly and improvidently." He asks, "Why has the harsh obstinacy of our brother Stephen burst forth to such a degree?" He asks again, "Does he [Stephen] give honour to God, who, the friend of heretics and the enemy of Christians, deems the priests of God, maintaining the truth of Christ and the unity of the Church, worthy of excommunication?"[1] It is evident from these words that the pope had threatened to excommunicate the African Church if the bishops of that Church continued to maintain their practice in regard to the rebaptism of

---

[1] *Ep.* lxxiv. *ad Pompeium contra epistolam Stephani, Opp.* ed. Ben., pp. 138-140. S. Augustine was referring to S. Cyprian's indignant remarks about Stephen in this letter to Pompeius, when he said (*De Bapt.*, v. 25, *Opp.* ed. Ben., ix. 158), "I will not review what he poured out against Stephen under irritation, because there is no need to do so." S. Augustine, who was arguing against the Donatists, had been reviewing the principal points in this letter of S. Cyprian, but the latter's personal remarks about Stephen had no bearing on S. Augustine's controversy with the Donatists, though they have a bearing on our controversy with Rome. S. Augustine adds that "although S. Cyprian was very much moved by his indignation, yet it was in a brotherly way" (quamvis commotius, sed tamen fraterne indignaretur).

heretics.   Stephen was therefore attempting to issue
a command, and to enforce it by every weapon that
he had at his disposal.   If it be indeed true, as the
Vatican Council teaches, that "all the pastors and all
the faithful . . . are bound to the authority of the
pope by the obligation of true obedience, not only in
things which pertain to faith and morals, but also in
things pertaining to the discipline and government
of the Church throughout the world,"[1] now was the
time for S. Cyprian and the African bishops to show
that they realized their obligation.   What actually
happened was this: S. Cyprian convoked another
Council, at which eighty-five bishops were present.
At its first meeting, in his opening speech, he said,
"It remains for us each to deliver our sentiments
on this matter, judging no one, nor removing any
one, if he be of a different opinion, from the right
of communion.   *For no one of us sets himself up
to be a bishop of bishops, or by tyrannical terror
compels his colleagues to the necessity of obedience,*
since every bishop, according to the absolute independence of his liberty and power,[2] possesses a free

---

[1] See p. 6.

[2] "Pro *licentiâ* libertatis et potestatis suæ."   On the meaning of
the word *licentia*, as an attribute of the episcopal authority, see
Bishop Sage's *Vindication of the Principles of the Cyprianic Age*,
chap. v., sections xl.–xliv. (Works, vol. iii. pp. 244–250, edit. 1846).
It should be observed that "S. Cyprian uses the singular throughout.
No *one* can judge or be judged by any other *one*.   He does not say,
no one can be judged by all, as though he were independent of the
college collectively as well as individually, but the only One (*unus et
solus*) who can judge a bishop is Christ Himself" (see an article on
Jurisdiction, by John Walter Lea, *Union Review* for 1866, p. 363, n.).

choice, and can no more be judged by another than
he himself can judge another. But let us all await
the judgment of our Lord Jesus Christ, who singly
and alone has the power both of setting us up in the
government of His Church, and of judging our proceedings."[1] Obviously, when S. Cyprian says, "No
one of us sets himself up to be a bishop of bishops,
or by tyrannical terror compels his colleagues to the
necessity of obedience," he is alluding to Stephen's
haughty attitude and to his threats of excommunication. So plain is the reference, that even Cardinal
Baronius admits it.[2] But if the pope be by divine
appointment all that the Vatican Council has declared him to be, what words could be too strong
to denounce S. Cyprian's attitude towards Stephen ?
On that hypothesis he was an insolent rebel; and his
eighty-four colleagues, who made no protest, were
sharers in his sin. Now, it so happens that S. Au-

---

[1] *Concilium Carthaginense, Opp.* S. Cypr. ed. Ben., pp. 329, 330.

[2] Cf. Baron., *Annall.*, s.a. 258, § 42, ed. Antverp., 1617, ii. 521. In
his own suburbicarian region the pope was practically a bishop of
bishops, as his brother of Alexandria was in Egypt and Lybia (see note
on p. 14). There is no reason to suppose that either of these prelates
ever called themselves by that proud title. Tertullian, after he had
become a rigid Montanist, applied the title *"bishop of bishops"* in bitter
irony either to Zephyrinus (A.D. 198–217) or to Callistus (A.D. 217–
222), who had been modifying the antique rigour of the penitential
discipline of the Roman and of the suburbicarian Churches (see
Tertull., *De Pudicit.*, cap. i., and compare S. Hippol., *Philosophum.*,
ix. 7). S. Cyprian implies that Stephen, by his arrogant threats,
"constituted himself (se constituit) a bishop of bishops " outside his
own province. But the Africans would not give place in the least
degree to these threats, or to the baseless claim which, either
consciously or unconsciously, was implied in them.

gustine has quoted these very words of S. Cyprian, and it is interesting to observe the impression which they made on him.   Does he reprobate them as being rebellious? or does he try and excuse them by some charitable interpretation only half concealing his disapproval?   He does neither of these things.   He expresses his unqualified admiration.[1]   He says, "Quid mansuetius? quid humilius?"   "What can be more gentle?   What more humble?"   What fills him with admiration is that S. Cyprian[2] does not retort on Stephen the threats of anathema which the latter had so lavishly poured forth.[3]   S. Augustine quotes S. Cyprian's words again further on, and he there remarks that they prove that S. Cyprian's "soul was peace-making and overflowing with the milk of charity."[4]   S. Augustine makes these laudatory remarks because he is absolutely unconscious of any taint of rebellion or of impropriety in S. Cyprian's attitude, when he uttered these words.   S. Augustine equally with S. Cyprian accepted the Catholic system of Church government, and knew nothing of the theories which the Vatican Council afterwards for-

---

[1] S. Aug., *De Bapt.*, lib. iii. cap. 3 (*Opp.* ed. Ben., 1688, tom. ix. col. 110).

[2] S. Jerome also dwells on the fact that S. Cyprian had put forth his views on the rebaptizing of heretics, without anathematizing those who disagreed with him; and he specially quotes S. Cyprian's letters to Stephen and Jubaianus, to show that he did not propose to enforce his views either on the pope or on other bishops, by separating them from his communion (cf. *Dial. adv. Lucif.*, 25, *Opp.* ed. Vallars., ii. 198, 199).   [3] Cf. S. Aug., *De Bapt.*, v. 25, *Opp.*, ix. 158.

[4] *De Bapt.*, vi. 6, *Opp.*, tom. ix. col. 164.

mulated and imposed under pain of anathema. S.
Cyprian's words produced the same impression on
him as they do on us, because his view and our
view, in regard to the government of the Church,
are substantially the same; whereas his view and
the Ultramontane view are separated by an impas-
sable gulf. S. Augustine's favourable judgment of S.
Cyprian's general attitude is the more remarkable,
because on the particular point in dispute he agreed
absolutely with Stephen, and was therefore in dis-
agreement with S. Cyprian. But he agreed with
Stephen, not because he thought that Stephen was
infallible, but because he considered that the doctrine
and practice which Stephen maintained had been
afterwards accepted by the Church. He never once
suggests that S. Cyprian was wrong in having held
to his own opinion in defiance of the pope's definition.
He says that "without doubt holy Cyprian would
have yielded, if the truth of this question had been
thoroughly sifted, and declared, and established by
a plenary council."[1] But why should Cyprian need
to wait for a plenary council, when the infallible
pope had spoken, and had threatened to excommunicate those who differed from him? The answer,
of course, is that nobody dreamed that obedience was
due to the pope.[2] Assuredly the eighty-five bishops
who sat in council at Carthage took this view. They

---

[1] *De Bapt.*, ii. 4, *Opp.*, tom. ix. col. 98.

[2] Archbishop Benson says (Smith and Wace, i. 755), "Cyprian is
totally unconscious of any claims made by the [Roman] see, and
resists Stephen purely as an arrogant individual."

unanimously upheld the invalidity of heretical baptism, and repudiated the view put forth by Stephen, disregarding his threat of excommunication.

Having come to this decision, the council sent certain bishops[1] of their number as legates to the pope, to announce to him what they had decided. When these legates reached Rome, Stephen "would not admit them even to the common intercourse of speech;"[2] and "he commanded the whole brotherhood, that no one should admit them into his house; so that not only peace and communion, but shelter and hospitality were denied them."[3] These facts we learn from S. Firmilian's letter to S. Cyprian; a letter written in Greek, but translated by S. Cyprian into Latin,[4] and forming part of the Cyprianic correspondence, which happily still remains. S. Firmilian also tells us that Stephen carried out what he had threatened, and cut off the Church of North Africa from his communion.[5]

[1] "Legatos episcopos" (*Ep. S. Firmil., inter Cyprianicas* lxxv., *Opp.* ed. Ben., p. 150).

[2] *Ep.* S. Firmil., *ut supra.*

[3] *Loc. cit.*, pp. 150, 151.

[4] Bossuet (*Gallia Orthodoxa*, cap. lxx.) says, "Consensit ei [sc. Firmiliano] Cyprianus, ejusque epistolam Latinam fecit, et ad ecclesias edidit." Compare Tillemont, iv. 158. The Bollandist Father Bossue (*Acta SS.*, tom. xii. Octobr. p. 491), after mentioning that Rigaltius and Dom Maran were of opinion that S. Firmilian's letter was translated into Latin by S. Cyprian, says, "Similiter sentiunt Tillemontius *aliique passim.*" Compare Archbishop Benson's note x., in Smith and Wace, i. 751.

[5] "Te a tot gregibus scidisti. Excidisti enim te ipsum." "Quid enim humilius aut lenius quam cum tot episcopis per totum mundum dissensisse, pacem cum singulis vario discordiæ genere rumpentem, modo cum Orientalibus .·. . modo vobiscum, qui in meridie estis" (*Ep.* S. Firmil., *inter Cyprianicas* lxxv., *Opp.*, p. 150).

Moreover, the pope, either at the same time or shortly
before, excommunicated the Churches of Cappadocia,
Cilicia, Galatia, and the neighbouring provinces,
because they agreed with the Church of North
Africa in the matter of the rebaptizing of heretics.
The excommunication of the Asiatics is mentioned
not only by S. Firmilian, but also by S. Denys the
Great of Alexandria,[1] who, though agreeing with
Stephen on the disputed question of heretical
baptism, strongly disapproved of the high-handed
way in which he was trying to enforce his views.
The excommunication of the Africans is not only
distinctly mentioned by S. Firmilian, but is implied
in the way in which the pope treated the African
bishops who came to Rome as legates from the
Carthaginian council.[2]   It must have been after
Stephen had separated S. Cyprian from his communion[3] that the latter sent a letter to S. Firmilian

[1] Euseb., *H. E.*, vii. 7.   To avoid confusion between S. Dionysius
the Great of Alexandria and his contemporary S. Dionysius of Rome,
I have used the English form, Denys, when speaking of the
Alexandrian saint.

[2] According to primitive practice, even ordinary Christian laymen,
when travelling, if they brought letters of communion from their own
bishop, were received in hospitality, and diligently cared for, as well-
known and dear friends (cf. Sozom., v. 16).   This was the *con-
tesseratio hospitalitatis* spoken of by Tertullian as a mark of communion between different Churches (*De Præscript. hæret.*, xx.).
When the pope forbade hospitality to be shown to the bishops sent as
legates by the North African Church, he was manifesting in the most
public fashion that the Roman see had completely separated herself
from the communion of that Church.   Tillemont (iv. 155) rightly
says, "Cette action paroist une rupture entiere."   The whole of
Tillemont's 49th article on S. Cyprian should be studied.

[3] For further proof that Stephen not merely wrote threats, but

of Cæsarea. This prelate was himself a saint, and was the friend of saints. S. Denys the Great speaks of him as one of the most illustrious bishops of his time.[1] He was closely united in brotherly love with S. Gregory the Wonder-worker. The great Council of Antioch,[2] which condemned Paul of Samosata, and which was held shortly after the deaths of S. Denys and of S. Firmilian, couples them together, describing them as "men of blessed memory" (τοὺς μακαρίτας). S. Basil quotes S. Firmilian as an authority on doctrine.[3] S. Gregory of Nyssa, preaching a panegyric on S. Gregory the Wonder-worker, compares the virtue of S. Firmilian to the virtue of S. Gregory. The Church has been accustomed to celebrate his festival on the 28th of October. Even Cardinal Baronius, who for very obvious reasons excluded his name from the Roman Martyrology, is obliged to admit that " scarcely any of his contemporaries appeared to surpass him in learning and sanctity."[4] It was natural that the glorious S. Cyprian, when in trouble, should write to his brother saint of Cappadocia. I have already

actually separated S. Cyprian and S. Firmilian from his communion, see note A. in the Appendix, pp. 325–333.

[1] Euseb., *H. E.*, vii. 5.

[2] "Le plus celebre Concile qui ait été tenu dans l'Église avant celui de Nicée" (Tillemont, iv. 308). Cardinal Newman, in an article which appeared in the *Atlantis* in July, 1858, and which its author republished in 1871, as note iv., appended to the third edition of the *History of the Arians* (p. 443), speaks of the Fathers of this council as being "bishops of the highest authority."

[3] Tillemont, *loc. cit.*

[4] Baron. *Annall.*, s.a. 258, § 47.

referred to S. Firmilian's reply; but it will be well to make one or two quotations from it, as illustrating the view which great saints of the third century took of Stephen's action. S. Firmilian says that, though in past times there have been in different provinces much variety in the way in which the sacramental ordinances have been celebrated, yet hitherto there had not been on that account any " departure from the peace and unity of the Catholic Church. This Stephen has now dared to make, breaking the peace with you [Cyprian], which his predecessors ever maintained with you in mutual affection and respect."[1]   From another passage we learn that Stephen had laid stress on the fact that he was the successor of S. Peter in S. Peter's own chair.   This is the first occasion on which history records the production of the story, which had its roots in the Clementine romance, as a ground for papal claims.   Would that it had been the last as well as the first!   This is how S. Firmilian alludes to Stephen's boast.   He says, " I am justly indignant at such open and manifest folly in Stephen, that he who so boasts of the seat of his episcopate, and contends that he holds the succession from Peter, on whom the foundations of the Church were laid, introduces many other rocks, and buildeth anew many Churches. . . ."   " Stephen, who proclaims that he occupies by succession the chair of Peter, is roused by no zeal against heretics."[2]   Further on

---

[1] *Ep.* S. Firmil., *inter Cyprianicas* lxxv., *Opp.*, p. 144.
[2] *Ep. cit., Opp.* S. Cypr., p. 148.

S. Firmilian apostrophizes Stephen indignantly. He
says, " What strifes and dissensions hast thou stirred
up through the Churches of the whole world ! And
how great a sin hast thou heaped up against thyself,
when thou didst cut thyself off from so many flocks
For thou didst cut thyself off; deceive not thyself;
for he is truly the schismatic who has made himself
an apostate from the communion of the unity of the
Church. For while thou thinkest that all may be
excommunicated by thee, thou hast excommunicated
thyself alone from all. . . ." [1] " This is to have kept
the unity of the Spirit in the bond of peace, to cut
himself off from the unity of charity, and in all
things to make himself an alien to the brethren, and
with the fury of contumacious discord to rebel
against the Sacrament and the faith." [2] These are
doubtless strong words. They are the fervent utterances of a saint indignant at the schismatic course
which was being taken by the bishop of the first
see in the Church.[3] Stephen had no right to complain. He had dared to call the blessed S. Cyprian
a " false Christ," a " false apostle," a " deceitful
worker," [4] and it was quite time that the prelates of

---

[1] *Opp. S. Cypr.*, p. 150.

[2] *Ibid.*, p. 151.

[3] Dom Maran, the Benedictine editor of S. Cyprian's works, rightly
says that " the love of unity breathes through the whole of Firmilian's
Epistle " (*Vit. S. Cypr.*, cap. xxxii., *Opp.* S. Cypr. ed. Ben., col.
cxx.). Baluzius makes a similar observation (*Opp.* S. Cypr. ed.
Ben., p. 513).

[4] S. Firmilian, in his letter to S. Cyprian, quotes these reviling
words of Stephen (p. 151); Dom Maran points out that we have also

the Church should speak out in no faltering terms
of his arrogant attitude and action. This task
S. Firmilian undertook; and we may be sure that
S. Cyprian approved, because there is no doubt that
it was he who translated S. Firmilian's letter into
Latin, that it might edify and instruct the Western
portion of the Church.[1]

Shortly afterwards, under the Emperor Valerian,
the persecution broke out afresh, and Stephen is said
to have died a martyr's death. If he did so die, we
may hope that he purged away in that second baptism whatever was amiss in his life.[2] The dispute
about baptism still went on in the time of his suc-

S. Cyprian's own witness that the words were actually used by
Stephen, because Cyprian "translated Firmilian's epistle into Latin,
or at least authorized its publication" (*Vita S. Cypr.*, cap. xxx.,
Opp. S. Cypr. ed. Ben., col. cxii.). It is obvious that Stephen
would never have used, in a public document, such words about a
great prelate like the Bishop of Carthage, if he had been still in
communion with him.

[1] See note on p. 81.

[2] The Roman Church invokes him as a saint. But it must be
observed that Bishop Pearson throws doubt on the alleged martyrdom
of Stephen. He says (*Annal. Cypr.*, s.a. 257, § v., p. 60), "Pontii
tamen verba prætereunda non sunt: 'Jam de Xysto bono et pacifico
sacerdote, ac propterea beatissimo martyre, ab urbe nuntius venerat,'
quibus Stephanum videtur perstringere, eumque negare, aut omnino
martyrium subiisse, aut si subierit, verum et beatum martyrem
fuisse." The Abbé Duchesne evidently takes the same view as Pearson.
He says (*Liber Pontificalis*, p. 154, note 1), "Il semble donc que
l'ancienne tradition liturgique, antérieure à la *Passio Stephani* ait
été muette sur son martyre. Et ceci s'explique d'autant mieux que
Saint Augustin ne parait en avoir rien su (*vide* Tillemont, *Hist. Eccl.*,
iv. 594), et que le diacre Pontius, biographe de S. Cyprien, se sert en
parlant de Xystus ii., d'une expression qui semble exclure le martyre
de son prédécesseur (c. 14., p. cv., Hartel)." Compare also *Lib. Pont.*,
p. xcvii.

cessor, S. Xystus;[1] but Xystus was "a good and peace-making bishop,"[2] and he seems to have undone the harsh acts of his predecessor, and thus to have brought back the Roman Church into full unity with the Churches of the East and of the South.[3] As it

---

[1] This is clear from the letters of S. Denys the Great, parts of which are preserved by Eusebius (*H. E.*, vii. 5, 7, 9).

[2] " Bonus et pacificus Sacerdos." As has been already pointed out, they are the words which are used concerning Xystus by S. Cyprian's deacon and biographer, S. Pontius (*Vita S. Cypr. per* Pont. Diac., ap. *Opp.* S. Cypr. ed. Ben., col. cxlii.).

[3] There is clear proof that S. Dionysius, the successor of S. Xystus, was in full communion with S. Firmilian (cf. S. Basil., *Ep.* lxx. *ad Damasum, Opp.* ed. Ben., 1730, iii. 164). I am inclined to think that " the good and peace-making " Xystus may have annulled the acts of his predecessor, or, at any rate, may have receded from them, in consequence of the letters of S. Denys of Alexandria (cf. Tillemont, iv. 160, 161). S. Denys wrote first to Stephen on the very grave difficulties which would arise out of his harsh action, and " entreated him " to follow a gentler course; but on Stephen he seems to have produced no effect. If Stephen had yielded, the controversy would have come to an end. S. Denys then wrote twice to two Roman priests, namely, Dionysius, afterwards pope, and Philemon, and he seems to have led them to change their views, so that they were more inclined to peace. Speaking of the way in which Stephen had thrown the Asiatic Churches "into strife and contention," he says in one of his letters to Philemon, "I cannot endure" it. Then he wrote two letters, still on the same subject, to Pope S. Xystus, in one of which he recounts his previous efforts on behalf of peace We may well believe that the "peace-making" propensities of the "good" Xystus prompted him to accede to the entreaties of his brother-saint of Alexandria, and to recede from the separatist position which Stephen had taken up. There was a final letter on baptism addressed by S. Denys and the whole Church of Alexandria to S. Xystus and the whole Church of Rome. This may well have been a letter of congratulation on the restoration of peace to the Church. Eusebius implies that in this final letter the whole subject of the rebaptism of heretics and of the toleration of variations of discipline in connection with that matter was reviewed at length. The preceding summary of S. Denys' action is based on Euseb., *H. E.*, vii. 5, 7, 9.

was in the Paschal controversy, so it was in the Baptismal controversy; it was Rome that was compelled to give way, as it was Rome that had advanced unjustifiable claims. Africa and Asia Minor retained their baptismal discipline unchanged, and had the joy of welcoming back the Roman Church after its wanderings into the straight path of Catholic peace and charity. This happened before the martyrdom of S. Cyprian. Perhaps it was to make some atonement for the outrageous way in which he had been treated by Stephen, that the Roman Church has paid such special honour to S. Cyprian ever since his glorious death. His name is apparently the name of the only man, neither martyred at Rome nor belonging to the local Church of Rome, which finds a place in the canon of the Mass, as used to this day in the Roman Church.[1] It seems to me probable that his name was inserted in the canon by Pope S. Dionysius, the successor of S. Xystus. This latter died five or six weeks before S. Cyprian, and S. Dionysius was consecrated to the Roman see a few months after S. Cyprian's martyrdom, that see having remained vacant during the interval; so that, if S. Cyprian's name was inserted at the time when his death was still fresh in the minds of all Catholics, the insertion would have taken place by S. Dionysius' authority. It is interesting to notice that S. Denys the Great speaks in one of his letters of his namesake of Rome,

---

[1] The names of the apostles and of other saints mentioned in Holy Scripture must of course be excepted.

as having "*formerly* held the same opinion as Stephen"[1] in regard to that pope's high-handed policy of excommunication. The words seem to imply that S. Dionysius had changed his mind, and had been led to favour a more Christian mode of action. Following up this clue, it is worthy of observation that S. Dionysius, during his pontificate, wrote to the Church of Cæsarea in Cappadocia,[2] while S. Firmilian was still its bishop, to console it for the sufferings inflicted on it by the barbarians. He even sent agents into Cappadocia to ransom Christians of S. Firmilian's diocese, who had been carried away into captivity. I like to think of this great pope making some reparation for the treatment which S. Cyprian and S. Firmilian had received at the hands of his predecessor Stephen.

On the whole I submit that, whether we look at the history of the Paschal controversy in the time of Pope Victor, or to the celebrated passage about the Roman Church in the great treatise of S. Irenæus, or to the line of action which S. Cyprian pursued in his dealings with the popes of his day,[3] we find that

---

[1] Euseb., *H. E.*, vii. 5.

[2] S. Basil., *Ep.* lxx. *ad Damasum, Opp.* ed. Ben., 1730, iii. 164. S. Firmilian was Bishop of Cæsarea during the whole of the pontificate of Dionysius, with the exception of the last two months. They both died in the year 269; S. Firmilian in October, and S. Dionysius in December.

[3] I have discussed certain passages in S. Cyprian's writings, which are quoted by Ultramontanes as if they favoured the papal claims, in note B, with its *Addendum*, in the Appendix, pp. 334–363, to which the reader is referred.

the witness of the first three centuries is entirely
adverse to the papal theory set forth in the Vatican
decrees, and that it bears out that view of the position of the Roman see which I attempted to sketch in
my first lecture.

LECTURE III.

THE RELATION OF S. PETER TO THE APOSTOLIC COLLEGE AND TO THE CHURCH.

IN my two previous lectures I adduced various historical facts and various passages from the writings of the Fathers, which seemed to me to prove that the view of the papal authority laid down in the Vatican decrees was not accepted by the Church during the first three centuries of our era. The conditions under which these lectures are given prevent my attempting any exhaustive treatment of the question, but I have not consciously kept back any facts or passages belonging to those centuries which would in my opinion avail to rebut or qualify the general conclusion at which we arrived.[1] I believe that that conclusion is in complete agreement with

[1] A friend has suggested that it would be well that I should refer to the genuine epistle of S. Clement of Rome to the Corinthian Church, in which he, suppressing his own name, and writing in the name of his Church, uses an urgent tone in remonstrating with the Corinthian Christians on the subject of their impious rebellion against their duly appointed presbyters. I can see no expression in that epistle in any way implying a claim on the part of S. Clement to exercise jurisdiction as pope over the Corinthian Church. As Dr.

the truth. The Church at large, during the ages of persecution, did not recognize in the Roman see any primacy of jurisdiction outside the suburbicarian provinces, and still less did it recognize in that see any gift of infallibility.

We may, therefore, enter on the consideration of the scriptural evidence with the expectation of finding that the papal claims find no solid support in the Bible. It would be strange indeed if the New Testament pointed plainly to the pope as the infallible monarch of the Church, and yet that the great saints and martyrs of the first three centuries should ignore such a fundamentally important principle of Church polity. Such an argument might be inapplicable, if we were dealing with some very abstract question of theology. But if a great body like the Church had been subjected by its Divine Founder to an infallible king, it could hardly exist for three centuries without there being very evident proofs that the rule of such infallible king was one of the chief factors in its life. Government is not an abstract theory, but a practical fact.

Let us, however, approach the study of the scriptural evidence in a teachable and dispassionate spirit, desiring to perceive, and having perceived to accept, whatever our Lord and His apostles intended to teach.

Salmon observes (*Infallibility*, p. 379, 2nd edit.), The tone " is only that of the loving remonstrance which any Christian is justified in offering to an erring brother." The reader is referred to Dr. Salmon's treatment of the whole subject of this remonstrance (*Infallibility*, pp. 377–379, 2nd edit.).

I suppose that all will agree that, if the doctrine of the papal monarchy is taught anywhere in Holy Scripture, it is taught in the promise made by our Lord to S. Peter at Cæsarea Philippi, as we find that promise recorded in S. Matt. xvi. 17–19. The Vatican decree quotes this passage and also the passage in the last chapter of S. John's Gospel, in which our Lord is recorded to have said to S. Peter, " Feed My lambs," " Feed My sheep," and it deduces, from what it calls " this plain teaching of Holy Scripture," the conclusion that " a primacy of jurisdiction over the universal Church of God was promised and given immediately and directly to blessed Peter the apostle by Christ the Lord." Following the guidance of the Council, let us proceed to consider the first of these two passages,[1] which, if I am not mistaken, is allowed by every one to be the fundamental passage.

It will be well, I think, to quote the whole passage together with the verses which immediately precede it ; and I will read them first of all as they stand in the Revised Version. S. Matthew says, " Now when Jesus came into the parts of Cæsarea Philippi, He asked His disciples, saying, Who do men say that the Son of man is ? And they said, Some *say* John the Baptist ; some Elijah : and others, Jeremiah, or one of the prophets. He saith unto them, But who say ye that I am ? And Simon Peter answered and said, Thou art the Christ, the Son of the living God. And

---

[1] The other passage, contained in S. John xxi. 15–17, is discussed in Note D. in the Appendix, pp. 371–391.

Jesus answered and said unto him, Blessed art thou, Simon Bar-Jonah : for flesh and blood hath not revealed it unto thee, but My Father which is in heaven. And I also say unto thee, that thou art Peter, and upon this rock I will build my Church; and the gates of Hades shall not prevail against it. I will give unto thee the keys of the kingdom of heaven: and whatsoever thou shalt bind on earth shall be bound in heaven : and whatsoever thou shalt loose on earth shall be loosed in heaven." The Authorized Version and the Douay Version have "the gates of hell" instead of "the gates of Hades;" but of course those two expressions, as used here, are identical in meaning, and in other respects the Authorized Version and the Douay Version agree substantially with the Revised Version in their translation of the promise to S. Peter. The question before us is, What does that promise mean? If the view taken by the Vatican Council is correct, we have here the creation, or at any rate the promise of the creation, of a permanent institution of the most transcendantly important kind. Christ is creating, or at any rate is promising to create, an office, the holder of which shall be His sole vicar and representative in the supreme government of His Church. Dr. Murray of Maynooth, referring to this passage, says that " Peter was thus established by our Lord as the means of imparting to the Church indefectibility and unity, and of permanently securing these properties to her. Peter was invested with supreme spiritual authority to legislate for the whole

Church; to teach, to inspect, to judge, to proscribe
erroneous doctrine, or whatever would tend to the
destruction of the Church; to appoint to offices or
remove therefrom, or limit or extend the jurisdiction
thereof, as the safety or welfare of the Church would
require: in one word, to exercise as supreme head,
and ruler, and teacher, and pastor all spiritual functions whatever that are necessary for the well-being
or existence of the Church."[1]   This is how a learned
professor at Maynooth describes the office which he
considers to have been promised to S. Peter by the
words recorded in S. Matthew, and afterwards to
have been conferred on *him*, and from time to time,
as occasion has arisen, to have been conferred also on
his successors in the see of Rome.   Now, if this really
was our Lord's meaning, this passage is a passage of
the most tremendous importance.   On that hypothesis, one could not but agree with Cardinal Bellarmine when he first puts the question,[2] " What are we
dealing with, when we deal with the papal primacy ? "
and then proceeds to answer his own question thus:
" We are dealing with the principal matter of Christianity" (*de summa rei Christianæ*).   Similarly the
Jesuit Perrone says, " When we are treating about
the head of the Church, we are treating about the
principal point of the matter on which the existence
and safety of the Church herself altogether depends."[3]

[1] Quoted from the *Irish Annual Miscellany*, iii. 300, by Dr. Salmon
(*Infallibility of the Church*, 2nd edit., p. 333).

[2] Quoted by Perrone, *Prælectt. Theoll.*, edit. 1841, tom. ii. pars i.,
p. 308, n.   [3] Perrone, *loc. cit.*

Similarly, M. de Maistre says, "The sovereign pontiff is the necessary, only, and exclusive foundation of Christianity. To him belong the promises, with him disappears unity, that is the Church;" and again, "The supremacy of the pope is the capital dogma without which Christianity cannot subsist."[1] I say once more, If our Lord, by His promise to S. Peter, meant to declare that He would create a permanent representative of Himself to be the infallible monarch of His Church on earth, as the Vatican Council teaches, then I think that we should all agree with Bellarmine, Perrone, and De Maistre, and we should hold that in this passage of S. Matthew we have delivered to us a dogma of the most fundamental character. Surely, therefore, if this view be the true view, when we come to examine the comments of the holy Fathers on this passage, we shall find them unanimously agreeing in the interpretation which they give. Even if they differed about some minor points, yet they will be in complete accord as to the substance. But when we proceed to investigate the comments of the Fathers, we do not find that unanimity which on the Romanist hypothesis would have been anticipated. The Fathers are by no means agreed in holding that the rock was S. Peter himself. It is true that that is decidedly the more common opinion and the oldest; but, nevertheless, some hold that the rock is Christ, and others that it is the doctrine of our Lord's God-

---

[1] *Du Pape, Discours Prelim.*, i. 13, and iv. 5, quoted by Allies, *Church of England cleared from Schism*, 2nd edit., p. 358, n.

head, which S. Peter had confessed, when he said,
"Thou art the Christ, the Son of the living God."[1]

But any candid Roman Catholic who looks carefully into the matter will be astonished when he examines those passages in which the "rock" is interpreted of S. Peter himself. He will be amazed to find that hardly any of them connect the building of the Church on S. Peter with any successors to S. Peter in the see of Rome. It is true that a fair number of such passages might probably be found in the writings of the popes or of papal legates and other similar officials, from the time of Pope Damasus (*circa* A.D. 370) onwards.[2] But, apart from the popes and

[1] In the Liturgy of S. James, at the point in the service where the consecration of the Gifts has just been consummated by the Epiklesis, the priest prays that the Body and Blood of our Lord "may be to those who communicate of them, for remission of sins and for life everlasting, ... for the strengthening of Thy holy Catholic Church, *which Thou didst found upon the rock of the faith*, that the gates of Hades should not prevail against it." These words occur both in the Greek and in the Syriac forms of the Liturgy, and therefore belong to its more ancient portion (see Hammond's *Ancient Liturgies*, pp. 43, 72). In the Roman Missal, the collect for the Vigil of S. Peter and S. Paul runs as follows : "Grant, we beseech Thee, Almighty God, that we whom Thou hast established *on the rock of the apostolic confession* (quos in apostolicæ confessionis petra solidasti) may be shaken by no disturbances." I quote these two Liturgical interpretations of "the rock," partly because of their great interest, and partly because I have not noticed them in the ordinary catenas illustrating the patristic interpretation of our Lord's promise to S. Peter.

[2] Quotations from such sources will not count for much in a controversy of this kind. Our contention is that the idea of a divinely appointed supremacy over the whole Church, as a prerogative of the Roman see, arose very largely out of the exorbitant claims made by the popes. It follows that exaggerated claims in favour of the papacy when they occur in the writings of the popes or of other persons living, so to speak, in a papal atmosphere, and when they stand in

their *entourage*, I only know of two such passages anterior to the age of S. Leo (*circa* A.D. 450). One of these occurs in a certain letter written by S. Jerome when he was a young man, about which letter I hope to be able to say something in my next lecture;[1] and the other occurs in a popular controversial ballad written by S. Augustine for the benefit of the Donatists in the early portion of his ecclesiastical career, about two years after he had been ordained priest. In that ballad, the argument of which appears to be mainly taken from the writings of S. Optatus of Milevis,[2] S. Augustine says, "Number the bishops even *from* the very seat of Peter, and see every succession in that line of Fathers : that [seat] is the rock against which the proud gates of hell prevail not."[3] At first sight S. Augustine, in this passage, appears to identify the Roman see with the "rock." But it is worthy of notice that S. Augustine does not say, "Number the bishops *in* the very see of Peter," but "Number them even *from* the very seat of Peter." The "seat of Peter" seems to be the

marked contrast with the general teaching of the Fathers and Doctors of the Church, cannot be quoted, at any rate controversially, on the papal side. *We* regard them as the proofs of papal ambition. In connection with this subject, it is surely permissible to refer in all reverence to our Lord's own words : "If I bear witness of Myself, My witness is not true" (S. John v. 31).

[1] See pp. 167–176.
[2] Tillemont, xiii. 197.
[3] S. Aug. *Opp.*, ed. Ben., 1688, ix. 8 :—

"Numerate sacerdotes vel ab ipsa Petri sede,
    Et in ordine illo patrum quis cui succedit videte :
    Ipsa est petra, quam non vincunt superbæ inferorum portæ."

starting-point of the succession, not the succession itself; and, if so, it would have to be understood as equivalent to the apostolate of Peter (cf. S. Aug., *Contr. Epist. Manich.*, cap. iv., *Opp.*, viii. 153, where there is a very similar passage); so that the "rock" would be, not the long succession of Roman bishops, but S. Peter in his apostolical office, and in his primacy of order among the apostles, in consequence of which, as S. Augustine would add, he was the symbol of the whole Church. If this was what S. Augustine meant, the passage in the anti-Donatist ballad will fall into line with a few passages in other early writings of his. Otherwise it stands alone. On this interpretation S. Augustine's argument may be thus paraphrased: You Donatists are a comparatively new body; we Catholics can trace up the succession of our bishops to the very apostles themselves, and in particular in the great apostolical see of the West we can give the whole line of names reaching up to the primate apostle, the rock of the Church. This is exactly the argument which S. Augustine does use in his epistle to Generosus (*Ep.* liii., *Opp.* ed. Ben., 1688, ii. 120, 121). In that case there was a special reason for dwelling on the succession of names reaching up to the apostles, because the Donatist priest, to whom the saint is replying, had been boasting to Generosus of the succession of Donatist bishops in the Donatist see of Cirta. But S. Augustine, while tracing the line of Roman bishops up to S. Peter, avoids any identification of them with the " rock." S. Peter, he says, was called the " rock " because he symbolized " the whole Church." Of course the notion of S. Peter having been the first local Bishop of Rome, is the direct or indirect outcome of the Clementine romance.

It will be inferred from these remarks that I do not myself think that in his ballad S. Augustine intended to identify the Roman see with the "rock;" but let us give our opponents the benefit of the doubt—if there be a doubt. Then I say, Is it not very remarkable that S. Augustine, who in his later life wrote many anti-Donatist treatises, never once recurs to this argument, and never once brings in the idea of S. Peter's successors in the see of Rome as included in the rock? S. Augustine often refers to our Lord's promise to S. Peter. In his earlier writings he occasionally interprets[1] the " rock " as meaning S. Peter; and, following S. Cyprian, he thinks that S. Peter, as the leading apostle, was the representative and symbol of the whole Church Militant, just as he also thinks that S. John[2] was the symbol of the whole Church Triumphant. But in his later writings he always takes the view that the "rock" was Christ, *and not S. Peter,* though he still continues to hold that S. Peter is the symbol of the Church. It is important to notice that according to this later view S. Augus-

---

[1] *In Psalm. xxx. Enarr.,* iii. § 5 (*Opp.* ed. Ben., 1691, iv. 156); *In Psalm. lxix.* § 4 (iv. 714).

[2] *In Johann. Evang.* cap. 21, *Tractat.* cxxiv. (*Opp.* ed. Ben., 1690, tom. iii. pars 2, coll. 822–824).

tine not only affirms that the "rock" meant our Lord, but he at the same time denies that it meant S. Peter. This precludes the notion that he was suggesting a secondary meaning, which might be accepted as true, side by side with the primary meaning. The later interpretation excludes the earlier. I will quote one example of this later method of interpretation. S. Augustine, in a sermon on our Lord walking on the water, and on S. Peter sinking, says, "The gospel just read . . . teaches us to consider . . . the Apostle Peter as the type of the one only Church. For this Peter, first in the order of the apostles, most ready in the love of Christ, often answers singly for all. He it was, at the question of the Lord Jesus Christ as to whom men said that He was, when the disciples gave in answer the various opinions of men, and the Lord again inquired and said, 'But whom say ye that I am?'—Peter it was who answered, 'Thou art the Christ, the Son of the living God. One for many he gave the answer, being the oneness in the many.[1] Then the Lord said unto him, 'Blessed art thou, Simon Bar-Jonah, because flesh and blood hath not revealed it unto thee, but My

[1] "Unitas in multis;" that means, I suppose, that S. Peter as leader had a certain uniqueness of position among the many apostles, which qualified him to be the fitting spokesman for the rest; or perhaps it may more probably mean that S. Peter, being one apostle, gave the answer on behalf of the many apostles, because he symbolized the unity of the Church, which is made up of many members. The great terseness of S. Augustine's phrase makes it difficult to say with certainty what his meaning was; but one test of a true interpretation must be its harmony with the saint's general line of teaching in regard to S. Peter's position.

Father which is in heaven.' Then He added, 'And I say unto thee'—as if He would say, ' Because thou hast said unto Me, Thou art the Christ, the Son of the living God '—'I also say unto thee, Thou art Peter.' Simon he was called before; but this name of Peter was given him by the Lord, and that in figure to signify the Church. For because Christ is the Rock (*Petra*), Peter (*Petrus*) is the Christian people. For the Rock (*Petra*) is the mother-word or root-word (*Petra enim principale nomen est*).[1] Therefore Peter (*Petrus*) is from *Petra*, not *Petra* from *Petrus:* as Christ is not called from the Christian, but the Christian from Christ. ' Thou art, therefore,' saith He, ' Peter; and upon this Rock which thou hast confessed, upon this Rock which thou hast recognized, saying, "Thou art the Christ, the Son of the living God," I will build My Church. *Upon Me I will build thee, not Me upon thee.'* "[2] S. Augustine, at the end of his career, when he was seventy-four years old, wrote his two books of Retractations, and in the first of them he calls attention to the fact that in his later writings he had given an interpretation of the " Rock " differing from that which he had given in his earlier years.

---

[1] Notice the word *principale* as used here. It illustrates the meaning of a passage from S. Cyprian, which I discussed in my second lecture (see p. 54).

[2] *Serm. lxxvi. de verbb. Evang. Matth.* 14, [*Opp.* ed. Ben., 1683, v. 415. The teaching of this homily was very familiar to our forefathers in the middle ages. From it are taken the 7th, 8th, and 9th lessons at Mattins on the feast of S. Peter's chains (August 1), in the Sarum Breviary (*Brev. Sar.*, fasc. iii. coll. 572-574, ed. Cantab. 1886).

The passage is interesting, and is very pertinent to our subject, so I will quote it. S. Augustine says, " While I was still a presbyter, I wrote a book against the Epistle of Donatus,[1] . . . in which I said, in a certain place concerning the Apostle Peter, that the Church is founded on him as on a rock: which meaning is also sung by the mouth of many in the verses of the most blessed Ambrose, where he says of the cock—

> ' Repentance once the crowing cock
> Brought to the Church's promised rock.' [2]

But I know that I have afterwards in very many places so expounded the Lord's saying, ' Thou art Peter, and upon this rock I will build My Church,' as to be understood of Him whom Peter confessed, saying, ' Thou art the Christ, the Son of the living God.' And so Peter, named from this Rock (viz. Christ), would typify the person of the Church, which is built upon this Rock, and hath received the keys of the kingdom of heaven. For it was not said to him, ' Thou art the Rock ' (*Petra*), but ' Thou art Peter' (*Petrus*). But Christ was the Rock, whom Simon confessing, as the whole Church confesses Him, was called Peter. But of these two meanings let the reader choose the more probable." [3] There can be no question which

---

[1] The book is, unfortunately, not extant.

[2] S. Ambrose's hymn is, in most Western breviaries, appointed to be sung at Lauds on Sundays after Epiphany and on the three Sundays which precede Lent. In some breviaries it is also appointed to be used on the Sundays after Trinity.

[3] *Retractt.*, lib. i. cap. xxi., *Opp.* ed. Ben., 1689, i. 32. It should

of these two S. Augustine thought the more probable, when he wrote his books of Retractations, and in fact during the whole of the latter part of his life. But the important point for us to notice is the fact that S. Augustine appears to be completely unconscious that he is dealing with a dogmatic passage of high importance. In his early days as a priest he put forth a view which might perhaps be twisted into some likeness to the Ultramontane interpretation which now prevails in the Roman communion; not that S. Augustine had ever really conceived of the Ultramontane theory in its entirety; but still, so far as words go, he wrote three lines in his anti-Donatist ballad which Ultramontanes are very glad to quote. As far as we know, in all his voluminous writings he never again, even in appearance, identified the "rock" with the Roman see. Two or three times—I hardly think more—he identified the "rock" with S. Peter. Afterwards he almost always explains the "rock" as meaning Christ. He could not possibly have

be noticed that S. Augustine does not say, "The reader should accept both of these meanings, the one as the primary, the other as the secondary interpretation; especially he should be careful to hold in any case that the 'rock' means S. Peter, because on that interpretation mainly depends the scriptural proof of 'the principal matter of Christianity.'" But he says, "Let the reader choose the more probable." In S. Augustine's view the two meanings are mutually exclusive. As during the whole of S. Augustine's later life he adhered to the view that the "rock" means Christ, it must be said that he gave up his earlier view that the "rock" means Peter. He did implicitly "retract" and "contradict" and "withdraw" what he had said in his anti-Donatist ballad; although he certainly never intended to express in that ballad the modern papal theory. I make these remarks in reply to Mr. Rivington's words in *Authority*, p. 33.

changed his view on any matter of dogmatic importance without explaining the *rationale* of his change. If he did it nowhere else, he would have done it in his Retractations. The fact that he made the change without making any such explanation, shows conclusively that in his opinion no important dogma depends for its scriptural proof on our Lord's promise to S. Peter; and he therefore certainly did not hold the view of the Vatican Council, that in that promise of our Lord the Holy Scripture plainly teaches us that Christ promised to S. Peter a primacy of jurisdiction over the universal Church, and that that primacy, by Christ's appointment, was to be perpetuated in S. Peter's successors in the Roman see.[1] Even if, for the sake of argument, we granted that he held that view when he was a newly ordained priest, it is quite certain that he must have given it up after he had become a bishop. We may, therefore, set aside the lines from the ballad. Understood as Roman Catholic controversialists profess to understand them, they do not really represent S. Augustine's mature teaching.

As I have already observed, if we except the popes and their belongings from the time of Damasus onwards, the other Fathers, before the time of S. Leo, who interpret the " rock " of S. Peter, in no way connect the passage with S. Peter's supposed successors

---

[1] The Council anathematizes all who deny that " ex ipsius Christi Domini institutione " S. Peter is to have a perpetual line of successors in his primacy, and that the Roman pontiff is such successor.

in the Roman see.   Some, like Tertullian, think that the promise was fulfilled by S. Peter's having taken the lead in founding the Church on the day of Pentecost, and in having admitted the Gentiles into the Church when he commanded that Cornelius the centurion should be baptized.   Others, like S. Cyprian and S. Firmilian, hold that all bishops inherit the promise made to S. Peter, and that therefore the Church is founded on the bishops.   The one view about which, outside Rome and its surroundings, there seems to be a conspiracy of silence among the Fathers anterior to S. Leo, is the view set forth by the Vatican Council.   Such a conspiracy of silence is simply inconceivable, if the Vatican teaching truly expresses the doctrine originally delivered to the Church by the apostles.   It is what we should naturally expect to find if the Vatican teaching is "a fond thing vainly invented," and foisted into the Church at a later date by ambition and ignorance.

I hope that I have made it clear that there is no one authoritative tradition in regard to the true interpretation of the promise to S. Peter.   One might, indeed, fairly say that there *is* a *consensus patrum* excluding the Vatican interpretation.   But setting the Vatican view aside as out of the question, a Catholic will find himself in good company, whether he interpret the "rock" as meaning the true faith in our Lord's Messiahship and Godhead, or as meaning Christ, or as meaning S. Peter.   All these various interpretations are perfectly consonant with the Church's teaching about herself; but, of course, only one of them can be the true meaning which our Lord intended to express when He first uttered the words.[1] Dogmatically they are all admissible, but exegetically one of them is right, and the others are wrong. Let us, therefore, now proceed to consider the passage with the view of determining, so far as we can, what our Lord really meant to promise to S. Peter. I shall confine myself for the present to that part of the promise which is contained in the words, " Thou art Peter, and upon this rock I will build My Church."

To my mind it appears most probable that our Lord intended, when He used the expression " this rock," to signify by it S. Peter. The apostle had been confessing his faith in the Messiahship and in the divine Sonship of the Lord Jesus. It was the first open confession of faith in those great facts, which had been made by any of the apostles since the Lord had gathered the twelve together into one band, and

---

[1] Though the various interpretations are all dogmatically admissible, they cannot all be held together as the true interpretation of our Lord's words. To build the Church on the ever-living Christ is one thing; to build on S. Peter's evangelizing labours wrought long ago is another thing; to build on the universal episcopate is a third thing; to build on the true faith is a fourth thing. In these different connections the expression " build upon " is used in varying shades of meaning, and our Lord, when He spoke to S. Peter, cannot have intended us to understand the word " rock," as used by Him, to denote at the same time a living divine Person, a doctrine, the work of a man who died eighteen centuries ago, and an order of men living all over the world and sharing in an office which is perpetuated from generation to generation.

had given them their preliminary mission to the lost sheep of the house of Israel.[1] This confession of the true faith by S. Peter was a great moment in the progress of the events which were preparing the way for the manifestation of the kingdom of God. The truth had been inwardly revealed to him, and his loyal heart enabled by preventing grace, had grasped the great verity which the Father set before him; and so he answered our Lord's inquiry and said, " Thou art the Christ, the Son of the living God." It was fitting that our Lord should reward His servant's faith by some signal token of His approval; and so the Lord answers, " Blessed art thou, Simon Bar-Jonah : for flesh and blood hath not revealed it unto thee, but My Father which is in heaven. And I also say unto thee, that thou art Peter, and upon this rock I will build My Church : and the gates of Hades shall not prevail against it," etc. Our Lord's words evidently convey a promise to *S. Peter.* One feels that if our Lord had said, " Thou art *Peter,* and upon *Myself* I will build My Church," such a promise would hardly seem suitable to the situation. Moreover, Christ is here the *Builder,* and it seems awkward to have the Builder and the Foundation one. It must also be remembered that our Lord spoke in Aramaic, and that in that language the word for Peter and the word for rock are identical. Our Lord's words may be represented thus: " Thou art Cepha, and upon this Cepha I will build My Church." If no tolerable sense

---

[1] S. Matt. x. 5, 6.

could be assigned to the passage when Cepha the figurative rock is identified with Cepha the person, it might then seem permissible to search for other interpretations; but, if the *primâ facie* interpretation yields a good meaning, it ought to be given precedence. And surely in this case the *primâ facie* interpretation does yield an excellent meaning, which is borne out by parallel passages in the New Testament. We nowhere read in the New Testament of the Church being built upon the true faith, but we do find that S. Paul, writing to the Gentile Christians at Ephesus, says, " Ye are fellow-citizens with the saints, and of the household of God, being built upon the foundation of the apostles and prophets;"[1] and we do find that S. John in the Apocalypse, describing the Church triumphant, the holy city, the new Jerusalem, says that " the wall of the city had twelve foundations, and on them twelve names of the twelve apostles of the Lamb."[2] It is clear, therefore, that the notion of the Church being built upon apostles is a scriptural notion. (Let us try and discover what is exactly conveyed by that notion.) And, first of all, we must observe that in the passage from the Epistle to the Ephesians prophets are joined with the apostles—" Built upon the foundation of the apostles *and prophets.*" Who are these prophets? It seems evident, from two other passages in this same Epistle, that S. Paul is alluding, not to the Old Testament prophets, but to the New Testament prophets, who in

---

[1] Eph. ii. 19, 20. [2] Rev. xxi. 14.

the earliest days, while the Church was being founded, constituted a degree of the sacred ministry inferior only to that of the apostles; as it is written, " He gave some to be apostles; and some, prophets: and some, evangelists." [1] And so, in the First Epistle to the Corinthians, S. Paul says, "God hath set some in the Church, first apostles, secondly prophets." [2] The apostles and prophets, therefore, on whom the Church is founded, are the leaders and chiefs of those evangelical labourers who, by their preaching and teaching, brought the first generation of Christians to the knowledge of Christ, and gathered them into the Church. They organized and took the lead in the work of foundation, and so to them has been granted the high honour of being called the foundation of the Church. It is thus that the admirable Roman Catholic commentator Estius explains the passage. He says that the apostles and prophets constitute the foundation of the Church, "through their ministry, in so far as they announced to men the doctrine of salvation through Christ only, which they had received from God." [3] With Estius agrees the Jesuit commentator, Cornelius a Lapide. [4] And so Bishop Barry, in his note on the passage, says, " The apostles and prophets are the foundation . . . as setting forth in word and grace Him who is the Corner-stone." [5] I have not come across any commentators, either ancient or modern, either Romanist,

---

[1] Eph. iv. 11; cf. iii. 5.   [2] 1 Cor. xii. 28.
[3] Estius, *in Eph.* ii. 19, 20.   [4] A Lapide, *in loc.*
[5] Bishop Barry, *in loc.*, in the *New Testament Commentary for English Readers*, edited by Bishop Ellicott.

Anglican, or Protestant, who suppose that either in the passage in the Epistle to the Ephesians or in the passage in the Apocalypse, the bishops, as successors of the apostles, are to be joined with them as sharing in the glory of being the foundation of the Church. To the bishops is committed the duty of building the upper stories of the temple; the apostles laid the foundation, and by their founding labours have merited to be themselves styled the foundation. As Cornelius a Lapide says, The apostles "are the Church's foundations and founders (for these two expressions come back to the same meaning)." [1]

These parallel passages seem to suggest the true interpretation of our Lord's promise to S. Peter. We know that S. Peter and the other apostles are the foundations of the Church, because he and they are co-founders of the Church.[2] What is there to make us suppose that he is also a foundation of the Church in some totally different sense, of which we have no trace elsewhere in the Bible? If we look to the last clause of the promise, we shall find a signal confirmation of this view, that what was promised to S. Peter was to be actually conferred on all the apostles equally. The last clause of our Lord's promise to S. Peter runs thus: "Whatsoever *thou* shalt bind on earth shall be bound in heaven : and whatsoever *thou*

---

[1] A Lapide, *in Apoc. S. Joh.,* xxi. 14.

[2] Father Bottalla (*Supreme Authority of the Pope,* p. 60) says very truly, "The apostleship had only one definite task to perform—that of laying the foundations of the Church. Those once laid, the apostleship gave way to the ordinary and regular government."

shalt loose on earth shall be loosed in heaven."[1]   But
shortly afterwards, as is recorded in S. Matt. xviii.,
our Lord made this very same promise to all the
apostles.   He said, "Verily I say unto *you*, What
things soever *ye* shall bind on earth shall be bound
in heaven : and what things soever *ye* shall loose on
earth shall be loosed in heaven."[2]   If all the apostles
were intended to share in the power promised to S.
Peter in the last clause, there seems no reason why
they should not share in the honour promised to him
in the first clause.[3]   What, then, was the special
reward which he received?   Why, this—that as he
was the first to confess publicly the Messiahship and
divine Sonship of the Master, so *to him first* were
promised the honours and labours and powers of the
apostolic office.   Up to the time of his confession our
Lord had revealed nothing plainly concerning His
Church.   He had never hitherto used the word
"Church."   Now for the first time He speaks of His
Church, and He makes known to S. Peter that he
is to be a foundation of it, and a ruler over it.
Whether the others are to share with S. Peter, is for

---

[1] S. Matt. xvi. 19.   [2] S. Matt. xviii. 18.

[3] After what has been said in the text about the first and last
clauses of the promise to S. Peter, it seems unnecessary to set out at
length an elaborate proof that the middle clause of the promise—"I
will give unto thee the keys of the kingdom of heaven "—belongs to
all the apostles, and not to S. Peter only.   The reader is referred to
Dr. Pusey's Note R on *The keys given to the Church in the person
of S. Peter*, in the Oxford translation of Tertullian, pp. 514, 515 ; and
to Launoy's Epistle to Hadrianus Vallantius (Lib. ii., Ep. v., *Opp.*
ed. 1731, tom. v. pars ii. pp. 213-242).

the present kept back.   Surely this precedence in
designation was a fitting reward for S. Peter's prompt-
ness in confession.   Moreover, other results flowed
out of this precedence.   It was not the first time that
he had been singled out as the leader.   When our
Lord originally separated the twelve, we are told that
" He called unto Him His twelve disciples;"[1] and the
evangelist goes on to say that " the names of the
twelve apostles are these: *The first*, Simon, who is
called Peter, and Andrew, his brother;"[2] and then
the rest are enumerated.   Evidently on that earlier
occasion, our Lord named S. Peter's name first.
So that not once, but twice, the Lord seemed to
sanction the view that S. Peter was to be the
leader.   All the apostles were peers and equals; all
were to be founders and foundations of the Church;
all were to have the power of binding and loosing;
all after the Resurrection received authority to
remit and retain sins; all were commissioned to
go into all the world to preach, and to disciple, and
to baptize.   But among these equals S. Peter was
singled out by our Lord to be the leader — the
first.[3]   He was *primus inter pares*.   And accordingly in everything connected with the foundation
of the Church he took the lead.   It was he who
proposed that steps should be taken to fill up the
gap in the apostolic college caused by the death of

---

[1] S. Matt. x. 1.   [2] S. Matt. x. 2.

[3] See Note C. in the Appendix, pp. 364–370, for the teaching of
representative Anglican divines on the subject of S. Peter's primacy
of order among the apostles.

the traitor Judas. It was he, standing up with the
eleven, who preached the great Pentecostal sermon
on the Church's Pentecostal birthday. He took the
initiative and was the chief agent in the first miracle
that was wrought—on the lame man at the beautiful
gate of the temple, though S. John was associated
with him. He was the spokesman, when the first
punishment was inflicted on members of the Church
who had sinned, as appears from the history of
Ananias and Sapphira. He with S. John went to
confirm the newly baptized Samaritans, and so was
the principal agent for conveying the sanction of the
apostolic college to the extension of the Church into
that border-land between Judaism and heathenism.
He with S. John confronted Simon Magus, the first
heretic. Above all, as he himself pointed out to the
other apostles, "God made choice among them, that
by his mouth the Gentiles should hear the word of
the gospel and should believe;"[1] in other words, he
first opened the door of the Church to uncircumcised
Gentiles by the instruction and baptism of Cornelius
and his friends. Thus were the foundations of the
Church laid by the combined action of all the
apostles, but in that founding work S. Peter had the
leadership, and took the initiative. I do not doubt
that this recognized leadership resulted from the precedence in designation to the apostolic office, which
came to him as a reward for his priority in confessing
the full truth about our Lord. The reward was most

---

[1] Acts xv. 7.

real and most marked, though it did not involve any primacy of jurisdiction over the other apostles, nor was it ever intended that either the primacy of honour which S. Peter did enjoy, or the supposed primacy of jurisdiction of which there is no trace in Scripture,[1] should be perpetuated for all time in a divinely instituted monarchy over the Church of God, to be inherited by the supposed successors of S. Peter in the Roman see.

Surely it must be allowed to be most significant that the New Testament, which is so clear on the subject of S. Peter's *leadership* in the foundation of the Church, is so absolutely silent in regard to any jurisdiction over the other apostles being vested in him, or exercised by him. But the papal theory, if it is to establish for itself a scriptural basis, must bring forward scriptural proofs of the exercise of *supreme jurisdiction* over the Church by S. Peter. No amount of leadership avails for proving jurisdiction. When S. Paul and S. Barnabas were carrying out their first missionary journey, S. Paul's superior gifts soon established him in the position of leader. He was the " chief speaker."[2] The members of the expedition, of whom S. Barnabas was one, are described as " Paul and his company."[3] But will any one maintain that S. Paul had any primacy of jurisdiction over S. Barnabas ? The idea is, of course,

---

[1] On the meaning of our Lord's words, " Feed My sheep," see Note D. in the Appendix, pp. 371-391.

[2] Acts xiv. 12.   [3] Acts xiii. 13.

absurd. (Leadership) and jurisdiction are two wholly different things. The distinction is quite understood at Rome. The Vatican Council strikes with its anathema any one who says that S. Peter received from our Lord " only a primacy of honour "—that is, a leadership, "but not a primacy of true and proper jurisdiction."

But we go further in this matter. As we deny that there are any passages of Holy Scripture which prove that supreme jurisdiction over the other apostles was ever exercised by S. Peter, so we are also prepared to assert that the general tenor of Scripture is adverse to the claim which is made on his behalf.

If S. Peter had a divinely given primacy of jurisdiction over the other apostles, it seems very strange that they, when they heard that Samaria had received the Word of God, should "*send* to them Peter and John." [1] One could understand a vassal kingdom, not exactly sending, but petitioning, its king to undertake the office of pleading the cause of his kingdom in the court of the suzerain. If a king did undertake such an office, it would be inconceivable that other nobles should be joined with him as members of the delegation. They might accompany him as part of his *suite;* they would never share with him in the duty which he had undertaken to fulfil. But if even a vassal king would never be *sent* by his subjects to represent them in the higher court of the

---

[1] Acts viii. 14.

suzerain, how much less would a wholly independent sovereign be sent by the lesser rulers of his people to carry out some plan on which they had decided. The fact that the apostles sent S. Peter and S. John to confirm the Samaritans, is proof positive that S. Peter was not the supreme ruler of the others. That two equal apostles should be sent by the college of apostles—that is natural. That the subject apostles should send their supreme pontiff and also one of their fellow-subjects on a joint mission—that is incredible.

Again, if S. Peter occupied in the apostolic Church the position which is claimed for the pope by the Vatican Council, how is it conceivable that S. Paul, writing to the Galatians and describing his third visit to Jerusalem, should say that, " when they perceived the grace that was given unto me, James and Cephas and John, they who were reputed to be pillars, gave to me and Barnabas the right hands of fellowship, that we should go unto the Gentiles, and they unto the circumcision." [1] How could he possibly put S. James before S. Peter in an enumeration of the leading apostles? [2] and how could he possibly say of

---

[1] Gal. ii. 9.

[2] It is no answer to this to say that in other Epistles S. Paul gives Cephas priority over all other apostles. Supposing that he does, it will only show that S. Peter had a primacy of order among the twelve. But the fact that in this place, where S. Paul is speaking of Jerusalem, he puts the local bishop before S. Peter, proves clearly to my mind that S. Peter's position was quite different from the position of the pope. The pope would never be named second by any Roman Catholic in such an enumeration. In connection with this

S. Peter, if he was the foundation of the Church in a special sense—in a sense, that is, in which the other apostles were not the foundation,—how could he possibly say of such a one that he along with two other apostles " were *reputed* to be pillars " ? Let us try and imagine a parallel case in modern times. Suppose that two distinguished Roman Catholic missionary bishops, whose line of action had been called in question, should have come to Rome during the Vatican Council, and should there have been granted an audience by the pope; and suppose that there should have been present at the audience two other prelates, leading members of the council; let us say, the Archbishop of Paris and the so-called Archbishop of Westminster. Can we imagine one of the two missionary bishops writing afterwards to his accusers, and describing his interview at the Vatican in such terms as the following? Can we imagine his saying, "When they perceived the grace that was given unto me, Archbishop Manning,[1] Pope Pius IX.,

matter, it may be well to warn the reader that in 1 Cor. xv. 5 no precedence is given by S. Paul to S. Peter, because he is narrating the historical order of events. Nor can 1 Cor. i. 12 be referred to; because S. Paul's natural courtesy would make him give precedence to the senior apostle over himself, and Apollos was not of apostolic rank. It is, I think, fair to quote 1 Cor. ix. 5 in favour of S. Peter's primacy of order.

[1] Perhaps it will be said that Archbishops Manning and Darboy had not that gift of apostolic infallibility which belonged to S. James and S. John, and that therefore the disparity of position which separated the archbishops from the pope is greater than that which separated the two subject-apostles from S. Peter. But such an argument goes only a very little way towards getting over the difficulty. If S. Peter had a divinely given primacy of supreme

and Archbishop Darboy, who are reputed to be pillars, gave to me and my companion the right hands of fellowship"? Such a statement coming from a devout Roman Catholic, who accepts the doctrine set forth in the Vatican decrees, would be absolutely impossible. Why, then, was it not only possible but natural to S. Paul to use such language? Because he did not hold the doctrine of the papal primacy which was set forth in the Vatican decrees. Because it had never entered his mind that such a doctrine would ever be devised and propagated by Christian men.

But perhaps some one will reply that, if any primacy, even if it be only of honour and influence, is granted to S. Peter, there is a difficulty in accounting for his being named after S. James. I see no difficulty whatsoever within S. James' own city and diocese. Outside the jurisdiction of the Church of Jerusalem, S. Peter would certainly, I should suppose have been named before S. James. And if he had had immediate actual jurisdiction over all the pastors and all the faithful throughout the universal Church, he would have been named before S. James in Jerusalem as well as elsewhere. But if he only had a primacy of honour, then as soon as Jerusalem had been erected into a diocese, and an apostle like S. James[1] had become its local bishop, S. James alone

jurisdiction over the other apostles, he could never have been named second, and it could never have been said of him that he with others "were *reputed* to be pillars."

[1] Although S. James was probably not one of the twelve, yet it

would have ordinary jurisdiction within the city, and therefore, according to every principle of Catholic order, S. James, being himself an apostle, ought of right to take precedence.[1] In a previous lecture I pointed out an analogous case.[2] Within the province

seems clear that, like S. Paul and S. Barnabas, he was ranked among the apostles. In Acts ix. 27, S. Luke says that Barnabas took Paul "and brought him to *the apostles*" (πρὸς τοὺς ἀποστόλους). But S. Paul himself, describing the same event in Gal. i. 18, 19, says, "I went up to Jerusalem to visit Cephas. . . . But other of the apostles saw I none, save James the Lord's brother." Bishop Lightfoot, commenting on Gal. i. 19, expresses his opinion that the plural word ἀποστόλους in Acts ix. 27 is "in favour of" the view that S. James was an apostle. But it is fair to add that he holds [why, I know not] that "this argument must not be pressed." However, after a careful discussion of the exact meaning of Gal. i. 19, he arrives at the result that "it seems . . . that S. James is here called an apostle." Estius (*in loc.*), says that there is "no one who denies that James, the brother of the Lord, was an apostle." Compare also 1 Cor. xv. 7.

[1] It should perhaps be mentioned that there are traces in the early Church of an idea that the bishopric of the Church of Jerusalem, the mother-Church of Christendom, was a higher dignity than the apostolate. Thus S. Clement of Alexandria [A.D. 190–203], in his Ὑποτυπώσεις (quoted by Eusebius, *H. E.*, ii. 1), writes, "They say that after the ascension of the Saviour, Peter and James and John, as being those who received the chief honour from our Lord, *strove not after glory* (μὴ ἐπιδικάζεσθαι δόξης), but chose James the Just Bishop of Jerusalem." So Rufinus (*H. E.*, lib. ii. cap. i., ed. Basil., 1535, p. 24), giving the sense rather than literally translating the passage of S. Clement just quoted, speaks of S. James as "the bishop of the apostles;" and S. Hesychius "the Theologian" (Migne's *Patrol. Græc.*, xciii. 1480) calls him "the exarch of the apostles" (but concerning S. Hesychius, see p. 122). However, it is quite possible that this notion of the bishopric of Jerusalem being the highest dignity in the Church may have been derived from the Clementine romance, in which S. James is represented as a sort of hyper-apostolic pope (see p. 45, n. 2). The grain of truth which lay at the bottom of these fancies was undoubtedly the fact that *in Jerusalem* S. James, after his elevation to the episcopal throne, took precedence of S. Peter and the other apostles.

[2] See pp. 66, 67.

of Milan, the Council of Turin (A.D. 401) naturally names S. Ambrose of Milan before the pope. That could not be done now, because the pope is supposed to have ordinary jurisdiction *jure divino* at Milan and at Turin and everywhere else. But in the fifth century it was otherwise; and it was also otherwise in the age of the apostles. S. Peter, when in Jerusalem, was ecclesiastically S. James' guest; and in his own house the host naturally takes precedence of the guests. S. Paul therefore adopts the natural and right order, if rightness and naturalness in such a matter are to be determined by Catholic principles of jurisdiction. He adopted an order which is indefensible and inexplicable, if the teaching of the Vatican decrees is accepted as true and apostolic.

These observations will help us to understand why S. James apparently presided at the Council of Jerusalem. It will be allowed on all hands that, if any one presided at that Council—and one hardly sees how such an assembly could be carried on without a president—it was either S. James or S. Peter who occupied that post. Now, the order of proceedings in the Council, as set forth by S. Luke in Acts xv., was as follows. There was first of all "much disputation."[1] Then there was a speech by S. Peter, who recalled what had happened to Cornelius and his friends at the time of their conversion; how God had given them the Holy Ghost, even as He had given

---

[1] So Liddell and Scott translate the word συζήτησις, referring specially to Acts xv. 7.

Him to the apostles and to the Jewish Christians.
Then S. Peter appeals to the Council not to put an
unbearable yoke on the neck of the new Gentile
Christians; and he expresses his view that the whole
Council believes that all Christians, whether Jewish
or Gentile, are equally saved by the grace of Christ
and he implies that consequently circumcision and
the keeping of the Mosaic law cannot be set forth as
conditions of salvation.[1]   Then followed speeches
from S. Paul and S. Barnabas, rehearsing the miraculous attestations of their work among the Gentiles,
showing that it had God's approval.[2]   Then finally
S. James, after recalling what S. Peter had said about
God's dealings with Cornelius, and after showing that
all this work among the Gentiles had been predicted
long before by the prophets,[3] proceeds to formulate a
decision, which he sets forth for the Council to adopt.
"Wherefore," he says, "*my judgment is* ($\delta\iota\grave{o}$ $\grave{\epsilon}\gamma\grave{\omega}$
$\kappa\rho\acute{\iota}\nu\omega$), that we trouble not them which from among
the Gentiles turn to God, but that we write unto
them that they abstain from the pollutions of idols,
and from fornication, and from what is strangled,
and from blood."[4] Such was the order of proceedings

---

[1] Acts xv. 7-11.   [2] Acts xv. 12.   [3] Acts xv. 14-18.

[4] Acts xv. 19, 20.   S. Hesychius, "the Theologian" ($\acute{o}$ $\theta\epsilon o\lambda\acute{o}\gamma os$),
an illustrious doctor of the Church, who flourished A.D. 412-438, hits
the nail on the head when he says (Migne's *Patrol Græc.*, xciii.
1480), "Peter makes a speech in the assembly, but James *legislates*"
($\Pi\acute{\epsilon}\tau\rho os$ $\delta\eta\mu\eta\gamma o\rho\epsilon\hat{\iota}$, $\grave{a}\lambda\lambda'$ '$I\acute{a}\kappa\omega\beta os$ $\nu o\mu o\theta\epsilon\tau\epsilon\hat{\iota}$). In these words S. Hesychius
expresses accurately and tersely the relative positions of S. James and
S. Peter at the Council, as they are set forth in S. Luke's narrative.
Nevertheless, though the passage expresses the truth, I should not
lay stress on it in controversy, because S. Hesychius was a priest of

at that Council; and in regard to them I observe, first, that S. Peter spoke neither first nor last; nor did he formulate any decision for the Council's acceptance; nor did he promulgate his own authoritative judgment as settling the matter. After much previous debating (συνζητήσεως), he, as a member of the Council, spoke, and recalled certain important events in which he had borne an important part, and which ought to be taken into account in arriving at a decision. His speech is, of course, a weighty speech, but neither in the time when it was delivered nor in its substance is it the speech of a president.[1] When S. Peter had finished, S. Paul and S. Barnabas went on with the debate, and contributed additional facts which would help to bring the Council to a right decision. Then S. James speaks last, just as in the great Council of Carthage, about the baptism of heretics, S. Cyprian, the president, gives his own

the Church of *Jerusalem.* No candid person will press statements about S. Peter written by Roman popes or by Antiochene Fathers; and, similarly, it is unsafe to go to the Church of Jerusalem to learn about S. James.

[1] Bishop Lightfoot (*S. Clement of Rome,* ed. 1890, ii. 490), contrasting S. Peter's marked primacy in the early days of the Church, as recorded in the first twelve chapters of the book of the Acts of the Apostles, with the silence about him in the later apostolic history, says, "In the first part he is everything; in the subsequent record he is nowhere at all. He is only once again mentioned in the Acts (xv. 7), *and even here he does not bear the chief part.* Where the Church at large, as an expansive missionary Church, is concerned, Paul, not Peter, is the prominent personage; where the Church of Jerusalem appears as the visible centre of unity, *James, not Peter, is the chief agent* (Acts xii. 17, xv. 13, xxi. 18; Gal. ii. 9, 12). Peter retains the first place as missionary evangelist to the Hebrew Christians [and to their unconverted Hebrew brethren], but nothing more."

opinion last.[1]   And S. James' speech is eminently the speech of a president.   It formulates the decision.   It introduces the authoritative word κρίνω.   It immediately prepares the way for that unanimous act of the whole Council to which they allude in their synodical letter, when they say, "It seemed good to the Holy Ghost and to us to lay upon you (Gentiles) no greater burden than these necessary things," and then they enumerate the things which S. James had mentioned in his presidential summing up.   That final synodical act appears to be based on S. James' speech.   Altogether it seems quite clear that S. James presided on this occasion, as we should naturally expect would be the case.   No wonder that S. Chrysostom, in his homily on this passage in the book of Acts, says, "This James was bishop, as they say, and therefore he speaks last;" and a little further on he adds, "Peter indeed spoke more strongly, but he [James] here more mildly; for thus it behoves one in high authority to leave what is unpleasant for others to say, while he himself appears in the milder part."[2]

[1] S. Cyprian, as president, had also made an opening speech, in which he referred to the opinion on rebaptism which he had expressed in his letter to Jubaianus; but his synodical judgment was reserved to the end, and was delivered after his eighty-four colleagues had spoken.   So in the third and fourth sessions of the Vatican Council, the Fathers of the Council first of all expressed their judgment on the decrees and canons which had been proposed, and finally Pius IX., who presided, concluded the matter by declaring his own supreme sentence.

[2] The English rendering is taken from the Oxford translation of S. Chrysostom's Thirty-third Homily on the Acts (p. 456).   That translation agrees accurately with the Greek text in the New College

Evidently, in the opinion of S. Chrysostom, S. James, who was an apostle equally with S. Peter, took precedence of him in this council, as being bishop of the city where the council was held, and therefore president thereof. Such a view is irreconcilable with the papal theory as set forth in the Vatican decrees.

I might go on to refer to other passages of the New Testament, as, for example, to S. Paul's rebuke of S. Peter at Antioch, to the way in which he deals with the parties at Corinth, who named themselves

Manuscript (tom. ii. fol. 102), except that the Oxford translator has substituted "James" for "he." I have replaced the "he," but have retained the Oxford "James" within brackets. The Greek text has οὗτος. The New College *codex* is one of the four manuscripts that give what is called "*the old text*," which, as the Oxford translators say in their Preface to Part II. (p. ix), is "incomparably better," as well as "older" than the text given in the Benedictine edition. Mr. Rivington, in *Dependence* (pp. 24, 25), makes what must be called a desperate attempt to make out that "the antithesis is between James and the Judaizers, not James and Peter." The only answer that need be given, is to refer the reader to the Oxford translation of the whole passage, with its context. The interpretation suggested by Mr. Rivington is simply impossible. Mr. Gore has replied to some other remarks of Mr. Rivington, in which the latter deals with an earlier sentence of the same homily, and in which he relies on the unfortunate Benedictine text. See the Preface to the third edition of Mr. Gore's *Roman Catholic Claims*, which is reprinted in the *fourth edition* (pp. xiv, xv.). Second thoughts are not always best. Mr. Rivington says that in his controversy with Bishop Meurin he " was misled" by the Oxford translation. The real fact is that the Oxford translators have accurately given the meaning of the genuine text. Afterwards Mr. Rivington was really "misled" by the Benedictine editors. Mr. Rivington "reprehends" the Oxford translators for putting "James" as the translation of ἐκεῖνος in the earlier passage. That rendering accurately gives the meaning; and the translators gave fair warning in their Preface to Part II. (p. xiii.), that they proposed "to give faithfully, *though not always literally*, the sense." They have certainly, in this case, fulfilled their promise.

after himself, and Apollos, and Cephas, and Christ;
to the tone of absolute independence of any superior
human authority which pervades S. Paul's writings;
to the whole tone of S. Peter's own epistles; but I
think that I have said enough to justify the assertion
which I made that the general tenor of Scripture is
adverse to the claim which is made on S. Peter's
behalf.

I would add that, if S. Peter's connection with the
see of Rome is a fact of such fundamental importance, as would be the case if the theory set forth by
the Vatican Council were true, it is most extraordinary that there is no *clear* allusion in the New
Testament to that connection. / Believing, as I do,
that the words of S. Peter in 1 S. Pet. v. 13, "She
that is in Babylon, elect together with you," refer to
the Church in Rome, I grant that there is in that
passage an *obscure* allusion to a connection between
S. Peter and the Church of Rome. He was evidently
at Rome when he wrote his first Epistle, and in
friendly relations with the Roman Church, whose
salutation he sends to the Christians in various provinces of Asia Minor. But the New Testament nowhere certifies to us that S. Peter shared in the work
of founding the Church of Rome, nor that he joined
with his brother apostle in the consecration of Linus,
its first bishop, however true those facts may be.
Still less does it give any sanction to the fable of his
having been himself the first bishop of Rome, nor to
the groundless theory that he transmitted to his

supposed successors in that see a primacy of jurisdiction over the universal Church, which he never claimed for himself. If, as De Maistre thought, " the supremacy of the pope is the capital dogma without which Christianity cannot subsist," why is there nothing about it in the Scriptures of truth ?

LECTURE IV.

THE GROWTH OF THE PAPAL POWER FROM THE PEACE OF THE CHURCH TO THE END OF THE PONTIFICATE OF DAMASUS.

IN my last lecture I tried to show you how Holy Scripture bears witness against the notion that S. Peter received from our Lord any primacy of jurisdiction over the whole Church.

We have seen also in previous lectures how the great saints and rulers of the Church during the first three centuries repudiated the idea that the bishops generally were subject to the pope. On the other hand, we have seen how various causes combined to give to the Roman see a leadership in the early ages; not a divinely instituted leadership, but a leadership growing up out of the circumstances of the time, and gladly accepted by the Church, as being for the time a useful arrangement.

We have also seen how the Clementine romance seemed to provide a connecting link between S. Peter's primacy of honour and influence, which was naturally recognized in him in virtue of his having been the first to be designated by Christ to the apostolic office, and that later primacy of honour and influence which, as the Council of Chalcedon said, was properly given by the Fathers to the throne of the elder Rome, because that was the imperial city.

We have seen how, on at least two occasions during the first three centuries, the Roman popes advanced unjustifiable claims, and attempted to meddle authoritatively with Churches not subject to their jurisdiction; and how on the last of these two occasions the unhistoric theory that the see of Rome was the see of Peter, and that it inherited S. Peter's privileges, whether real or supposed, was pleaded as a justification of the wrongful claim.

We went on to notice how the Church, led by its great saints, resisted those attempts, and how in consequence the Roman bishops had to give way, and to content themselves with the primacy of honour which had been conferred upon them.

We have also seen to what portentous lengths the popes have gone, as time went on; and what enormous authority they now claim, as of divine right, over the universal Church.

Now, of course the development of this claim had a history;[1] and it will be my object in this lecture

---

[1] It may be well, in a note, to point out that the attempt to transform uncanonically privileges of precedence and honour into a far-reaching jurisdiction is by no means peculiar to the see of Rome. Other sees, which enjoyed from one cause or another a special pre-eminence of honour, did exactly the same thing. Fallen human

and in the next to set before you some of the stages
in that development, and some of the historical circumstances, out of which the growth in the papal
power became possible.   I can only deal with the
matter in a very imperfect way, owing to the

nature is the same all the world over.   Thus the second Ecumenical
Council, by its third canon, gave to the Bishop of Constantinople " the
prerogative of honour next after the Bishop of Rome."   This was a
grant of precedence not of jurisdiction.   Seventy years later the fourth
Ecumenical Council, held at Chalcedon, gave by its twenty-eighth
canon patriarchal *jurisdiction* to the see of Constantinople in Pontus,
Asia, and Thrace.   The way had been prepared for this new
departure by a series of uncanonical acts of interference on the part
of the Constantinopolitan prelates in the Church affairs of those three
exarchates.   Dr. Bright gives a summary account of these acts in his
note on the ninth canon of Chalcedon (*Notes on the Canons of the First
Four General Councils*, pp. 157–160).   Similarly the Council of Nicæa,
in its seventh canon, gave or rather confirmed to the see of Jerusalem
a certain right of precedence, reserving, however, to the Palestinian
Cæsarea its metropolitical dignity.   As time went on, the bishops of
Jerusalem endeavoured to make themselves independent of Cæsarea.
"Immediately after the Council of Nicæa, the Bishop of Jerusalem,
Maximus, convoked, without any reference to the Bishop of Cæsarea,
a synod of Palestine, . . . and proceeded further to the consecration of
bishops" (Hefele, i. 407, E. T.).   There was a "contest about precedency"
between Acacius of Cæsarea and S. Cyril of Jerusalem.   Nevertheless
as late as 415 John of Jerusalem obeyed the summons of Eulogius of
Cæsarea and attended a Provincial Council at Diospolis.   At the
Council of Ephesus in 431, Juvenal of Jerusalem put forward a
monstrous claim, asserting that the Bishop of Antioch, who had
patriarchal rights over all the provinces of Palestine, ought himself
"to be subject to the apostolic see of Jerusalem" (Bright's *Notes*, pp.
23, 24).   There followed a long contest between this Juvenal and
Maximus of Antioch.   At last the latter, weary of the controversy,
agreed that the three provinces of Palestine should be released from
their subjection to his see, and should constitute a now patriarchate,
of which the Bishop of Jerusalem should be the head; and this
arrangement was finally sanctioned by the Council of Chalcedon.   It
is only fair to the popes that the uncanonical aggressions of their
brother patriarchs should be chronicled.

limitations of time which necessarily restrict the length of a lecture; and I propose to dwell specially on the earlier rather than on the later stages of the growth. I intend to point out from time to time indications of the continuance of the earlier and truer teaching, which has never died out, and which we can have no doubt that God will preserve and guard in His Church unto the end.

But, in passing from the Church of the first three centuries to the Church of the fourth and subsequent centuries, we must bear in mind the great change which took place in the whole condition of the Church in consequence of the conversion of Constantine to Christianity, and all that followed therefrom. I cannot attempt to describe that change, but its magnitude can hardly be exaggerated. One may say with S. Jerome that "the Church under the emperors was greater in power and wealth, but she was less in virtues:" (potentia et divitiis major, sed virtutibus minor.[1]) Or, perhaps, still more accurately, one may say with the late Bishop Wordsworth of Lincoln, "In the ante-Nicene age the world had been arrayed *against* the Church; but in the next period the World worked *in* the Church; and it caused more injury to the faith [and, one may add, to Christian life] than when arrayed against it."[2] To put plainly what is implied in Bishop Wordsworth's statement, the world broke into the Church

---

[1] *In vitâ Malchi, Opp.* ed. Vallars, ii. 41.
[2] *Church History*, ed. 1882, ii. 3.

and established itself there, and has remained there ever since. No doubt there were all along tares mingled with the wheat. The Church of the first three centuries was never, except perhaps on the day of Pentecost, in an absolutely ideal condition. But yet during the ages of persecution, the Church as a whole was visibly an unworldly institution. It was a spiritual empire in recognized antagonism with the world-empire. But from the time of the conversion of Constantine, A.D. 312, and still more completely from the time of Theodosius the Great, A.D. 379, the Church and the world seemed, in some respects at any rate, to have made terms with each other. The world, without ceasing to be the world, was no longer *outside*, but had been admitted *within* the sacred enclosure. And that Roman world of the fourth century, what a detestable world it was! On this point Christian writers of every school seem to be agreed. The fervent and eloquent Roman Catholic Montalembert quotes and adopts the words of the Protestant Guizot, who says, "The sovereigns and the immense majority of the people had embraced Christianity; but at bottom civil society was pagan; it retained the institutions, the laws, and the manners of paganism. It was a society which paganism, and not Christianity, had made."[1] Montalembert adds that "this paganism . . . was paganism under its most degenerate form . . . Nothing," he says, " has

---

[1] Guizot, *Histoire de la Civilization en France*, lect. ii., quoted in Montalembert's *Monks of the West* (English trans., 1861, i. 263).

ever equalled the abject condition of the Romans of the empire. . . . With the ancient freedom, all virtue, all manliness disappeared. There remained only a society of officials, without strength, without honour, and without rights. . . . We must acknowledge that in this so-called Christian society, the moral poverty is a thousand times greater than the material, and that servitude has crushed souls more than bodies. Everything is enervated, attenuated, and decrepit. Not a single great man, nor illustrious individual rises to the surface of that mire. Eunuchs and sophists of the court govern the state without control, experiencing no resistance but from the Church." These last words guard Montalembert's meaning.[1] He is speaking of *civil society,* which was now nominally inside the Church; but, side by side with this Christianized paganism, the Church still handed on the glorious traditions which had been bequeathed to her by the age of the martyrs. Though it may be true that the civil society of the fourth and fifth centuries produced no great men, yet the hierarchy of the Church produced a galaxy of heroes. Let me name only five, S. Athanasius, S. Basil, S. Ambrose, S. Chrysostom, and S. Augustine. A religious institution which can produce such splendid names is undoubtedly still full of life; but nevertheless the Church which had admitted the world within her precincts, was in a very different condition from the Church during the first three centuries of her

---

[1] Montalembert, *op. cit.,* pp. 264, 269, 271, 272.

existence.   Speaking of the great saints of the post-Nicene epoch, Montalembert says, " That long cry of grief, which echoes through all the pages which Christian writers and saints have left to us, strikes us at once with an intensity which has never been surpassed in the succession of time.   They felt themselves attacked and swallowed up by pagan corruption.   Listen to Jerome, Chrysostom, Augustine, Salvian especially; listen to them all! They denounced the precocious decay and disgraceful downfall of the Christian people, who had become a prey to vice. They saw with despair the majority of the faithful precipitate themselves into the voluptuousness of paganism.   The frightful taste for bloody or obscene spectacles, for the games of the circus, the combats of the gladiators, all the shameful frivolities, all the prostitutions of persecuting Rome, came to assail the new converts, and to subjugate the sons of the martyrs. . . . However great a margin we may leave for exaggeration in these unanimous complaints, they undoubtedly prove that the political victory of Christianity, far from having assured the definite triumph of Christian principles in the world, had provoked a revival of all the vices which the Christian faith ought to have annihilated." [1]

It was impossible for the effects of this decay of Christian life to be confined to the ranks of the laity. That decay necessarily also affected many of the clergy, and even of the bishops.   There were, no

[1] Montalembert, *op. cit.*, pp. 255, 256.

doubt, in that age many saintly bishops, priests, and deacons. But there were also time-serving bishops, worldly bishops, courtier bishops, heretical bishops, ambitious and haughty bishops. The emperors set the example of giving immense donations of lands and money to the various Churches, especially to the great Churches in the principal cities of the empire; and, most of all, these gifts were lavished on the primatial Church in Rome, the capital city of the civilized world. And the example of the emperors was followed by all classes of society. The property of each Church, or at any rate the income, was at the disposal of the bishop for the time being; and so it came to pass that, especially in the more important Churches, the office of bishop became an object of ambition for worldly-minded men. A pagan historian, Ammianus Marcellinus, speaks of the great wealth which the Roman bishops owed to the donations of the matrons; and he says that it ought not to be wondered at, that the candidates for the Roman episcopate were ready to sacrifice everything to obtain it. The popes, he tells us, ride in chariots splendidly attired, and sit at a profuse, more than imperial table. He goes on to say that it had been happy for them if they had followed the example of many of the bishops in the provinces, who, by their frugal and simple mode of life, commended their pure and modest virtue to the Deity and to all His true worshippers. Ammianus Marcellinus makes these remarks with special reference to the contests, and even bloodshed, which disgraced the Roman Church on the occasion of the election of Pope Damasus in A.D. 366.[1] Another pagan, Vettius Prætextatus, who was generally esteemed for the integrity of his life, and who occupied the high post of prefect of the city, used to say laughingly to Pope Damasus, "Make me Bishop of Rome, and I will become a Christian to-morrow." It is S. Jerome who mentions this fact.[2] We have a startling proof of the worldliness which had crept into the very sanctuary of the Church, in an edict of the Emperor Valentinian I. addressed to Pope Damasus, and which had to be publicly read in the churches of Rome. The emperor "admonished the ecclesiastics and monks not to frequent the houses of widows and virgins; and he menaced their disobedience with the animadversion of the civil judge. The director was no longer permitted to receive any gift, or legacy, or inheritance, from the liberality of his spiritual daughter: every testament contrary to this edict was declared null and void, and the illegal donation was confiscated for the use of the treasury. By a subsequent regulation, it would seem," so Gibbon tells us, "that the same provisions were extended to nuns and bishops; and that all persons of the ecclesiastical order were rendered incapable of receiving any testamentary gifts, and strictly confined to the natural and legal rights of inheritance."[3]

---

[1] De Broglie, *L'Église et l'Empire Romain au ive Siècle*, Part iii. i. 40.

[2] *Lib. contra Joann. Jerosol.*, § 8, *Opp.* ed. Vallars., 1735, ii. 415.

[3] See Gibbon's *Decline and Fall of the Roman Empire*, chap. xxv. Murray's edit., 1862, iii. 253.

Perhaps it will be said that this was an unfair and tyrannical enactment of the civil power. Let us, then, hear how S. Jerome comments on it. He says, in a letter to the priest Nepotianus, "The priests of idols, players, charioteers of the circus, harlots even, can freely receive legacies and donations, and it has been necessary to make a law excluding clerics and monks from this right. Who has made such a law ? the persecuting emperors ? No; but Christian emperors. I do not complain of it. I do not complain of the law, but I complain bitterly that we should have deserved it. Cautery is good; it is the wound which requires the cautery which is to be regretted. The prudent severity of the law ought to be a protection, but our avarice has not been restrained by it. We laugh at it, and evade it by setting up trustees."[1] S. Ambrose also refers to the law in terms, which imply that it was needed.[2] I think that I have said enough to show that the nominal conversion of the empire lowered the spiritual tone of the Church at large, and of the clergy no less than of the laity; and undoubtedly it was in large cities like Rome that the poison of worldliness worked the chief harm.

No doubt, in the earlier decades of the fourth century, the bishops who succeeded one another in the Roman see, as in other great sees, had received

---

[1] *Ep.* lii., *Opp.* ed. Vallars, 1734, i. 258, 259. Compare *S. Jerome,* by the Rev. E. L. Cutts, chap. xi.

[2] S. Ambros., *Ep.* xviii., *ad Valentinianum,* § 13.

their training during the ages of persecution; but as
time went on the Church was more and more
governed by bishops who had been brought up amid
the full sunshine of worldly prosperity. The bishops
were elected by the clergy and people, and if the
tone of the clergy and people gradually deteriorated,
such deterioration would be sure in the end to show
itself in the character of those who were chosen to
fill the episcopal thrones. It is obvious that the process of deterioration would not go on with the same
rapidity in all the different leading centres of Church
life. Some would be more sheltered from evil influences; others would be more exposed to them. It
will, I think, be well to fix our attention specially on
the Church of Rome, and to consider the characters
of three popes who succeeded each other in that sec,
occupying it during the half century which intervened between A.D. 337 and A.D. 385. The names
of these three pontiffs were Pope S. Julius, Pope
Liberius, and Pope Damasus.

All that we know of Pope S. Julius, his steady
support of S. Athanasius, and the friendship of that
great man which he enjoyed, his letter to the Arianizing bishops of the East, his letter to the Church of
Alexandria, his reputation throughout the Church in
the East as well as in the West, the absence of any
charges against him, all combine to set him before us
as worthy of the high position which he held.

Pope Liberius comes before us with a less satis-
factory record. There must have been something

noble about the man, otherwise he could never have held his ground so heroically when he withstood the Emperor Constantius face to face, and, declining all gifts of money from his persecutor, went into exile at Berœa for two years, remaining firm in the confession of his faith in the Consubstantial, and in his fellowship with S. Athanasius. It seems, moreover, quite clear that Liberius was much beloved by his flock in Rome. But then afterwards, as we all know, he failed. He yearned to get back to his beloved people. He withdrew his communion from S. Athanasius. He put his signature to some document, whatever it was, which compromised the faith. Cardinal Baronius, whose opinion may safely be accepted in such a matter, conjectures that his envy of the fortune of the anti-pope Felix, and his longing for the adulation to which he had been used at Rome, were the Delilah that deprived this Samson of his courage and strength.[1] After his return to Rome Liberius recovered himself, and stood firm in his profession of the Nicene faith. But I think that Ammianus Marcellinus, who was a contemporary, implies that Liberius[2] must have

---

[1] See the article on *Liberius* in Smith and Wace's *Dictionary of Christian Biography*. iii. 722.

[2] If we are to believe what S. Jerome tells us in his *Chronicon*, the clergy of the Roman Church, in the time of Liberius, was in a very unsatisfactory condition. Among the entries in the *Chronicon*, for the year 352. occurs the following statement: " When Liberius was driven into exile on account of the faith, all the members of the Roman clergy swore that they would acknowledge no other bishop. But when Felix was intruded into the episcopate by the Arians. most of the *clerici* perjured themselves " (*Opp.* S. Hieron, ed. Vallars., viii. 395, 396).

sanctioned and used the grandeur and luxury which he, the historian, attributes to the Roman bishops, because it was, in his opinion, the desire for such things which led the two competitors for the Roman see, when it was rendered vacant by the death of Liberius, to proceed to such disgraceful extremities of tumult and bloodshed. The pontificate of Liberius coincided with a very critical time in the history of the Church, and it cannot be said that, taken as a whole, his pontificate was worthy of the exalted position which he occupied.[1]

Damasus, the successor of Liberius, began his episcopate most unhappily. In the riots between his partisans and the supporters of his rival Ursinus, 137 persons were killed in one day, and others died afterwards of their wounds. We cannot say for certain that Damasus was responsible in whole or in part for this terrible scandal, although, according to the statement of his opponents, he led his followers on to the attack. It seems in any case clear that the slaughter was committed by his supporters, even if he in no way sanctioned it. It was surely a terrible thing to mount an episcopal throne through streams of human blood. One cannot help feeling that a saint, even if personally innocent, would have resigned all claim to the see under the circumstances. Ammianus Marcellinus divides the blame equally

---

[1] The Abbé Duchesne (*Liber Pontificalis*, p. cxxiii) attributes to Liberius " une ambition déplacée et uue grande faiblesse de caractère,"

between the two competitors.[1]   Passing on from this unhappy commencement, there can, I think, be no doubt that Damasus was accustomed to use a great deal of worldly pomp and luxury.   The words of Ammianus Marcellinus and of Prætextatus have been already quoted, and their witness harmonizes with certain observations of S. Basil.   That great saint, writing about a projected visit of his brother, S. Gregory Nyssen, to Rome, says, " For my part I do not see who are to accompany him, and I know that he is entirely without experience in ecclesiastical matters; and, while he would be sure to meet with respect and to be valued by a *considerate person*, I know not what advantage could arise to the whole Church from the intercourse of such a one as he, who has no mean adulation in his nature, *with one high and lifted up*" (he, of course, means Damasus),[2] "*sitting on I know not how lofty a seat, and so not able to catch the voice of those who tell him the truth on the ground.*"[3] S. Basil here describes Pope Damasus as a haughty, inconsiderate person, who expected to be addressed in a tone of flattery.   S. Jerome, speaking of the Roman clergy in the time of Damasus, paints in vivid colours the pride of the deacons, and

---

[1] Mr. Barmby (Smith and Wace, iv. 1069), speaking of Ammianus Marcellinus, says that "though not a Christian," he "writes of the Christians in a friendly spirit, and shows no bias on the one side or the other of the contest between Damasus and Ursinus."

[2] Tillemont (ix. 225) says, " C'est à dire visiblement avec le Pape Damase, dont S. Basile parle ici."

[3] *Ep.* ccxv. *Dorotheo Presbytero, Opp.* S. Basil., ed. Ben., 1730, tom iii. p. 323.

the foppishness and avarice of some of the priests.
Altogether one feels that, however it may have been
before, a spirit of worldliness had got hold of a large
number of the Roman clergy of all orders in the time
of Damasus. It is easy to see that a worldly clergy
presiding over a very wealthy Church, which, by the
consent of all, enjoyed a primacy of honour in relation
to the whole Church, which not long before had had
its jurisdiction enlarged by the action of the Council
of Sardica,[1] and which even in ante-Nicene times
had made unwarrantable claims, would be likely to
exaggerate their own pre-eminence, and to initiate
a policy of aggression on other Churches less favour-
ably situated. This is exactly what happened. But
before we proceed to consider that policy and the
various ways in which it showed itself, it will be
desirable to recall certain events which took place
earlier in this fourth century, and which throw light
on our general subject.

In the year of our Lord 325, the first Ecumenical
Council was summoned to meet at Nicæa by the
Emperor Constantine. It is important that we should
realize what were the relations in which S. Silvester,
the Bishop of Rome, stood to that great gathering,
which represented the whole Catholic Church. If
S. Silvester was the infallible monarch of the Church,
and was so recognized, his sovereign position ought
to come out clearly in the history of the Council.
But, as a matter of fact, it does not appear that S.

____
[1] See pp. 148–154.

Silvester had anything to do with the convoking of the Council. It was convoked by the emperor, and there is no particle of proof that he consulted S. Silvester before doing so. Nobody attributed any share in the convocation of the Council to the pope until the end of the seventh century—three centuries and a half after the event. Neither is there any reason to suppose that S. Silvester presided in the Council, either personally or by his legates. Eusebius, speaking of Silvester, says, "The bishop of the imperial city was absent on account of his old age, but his presbyters were present and filled his place."[1] These presbyters were two in number, Vincentius and Vito, but they neither signed first nor were they the chief presidents. To quote Cardinal Newman's words, "Hosius, one of the most eminent men of an age of saints, was president."[2] He was·Bishop of Cordova, in Spain, and was the prelate who had the greatest influence with the emperor, and he was probably appointed by the emperor to preside.[3] Some Ultramontanes suppose that he presided as the chief legate of the pope; but none of the early historians speak of him as holding any such position.[4] Vincentius and Vito are the only legates whom they mention. Gelasius of Cyzicus, at the end of the fifth

---

[1] *De Vit. Const.*, iii. 7.

[2] *The Arians of the Fourth Century*, 3rd edit., 1871, p. 257.

[3] Even the Ultramontane Ballerini consider that it is most probable that Marinus of Arles presided at the Council of Arles (A.D. 314) by the emperor's orders (cf. Ballerinn. *obss. in dissert.* v. *Quesnell.*, pars. ii. cap. v. § 4).

[4] *E.g.* Eusebius, Theodoret, Socrates, and Sozomen.

century, is the first person who suggests the idea that Hosius was also a legate; but Gelasius' authority is of the weakest kind.[1] We may safely say that Silvester neither convoked the Council, nor did he preside in it by his legates, nor was the Council confirmed by him in any special way. In one sense, of course, each bishop who was absent from the Council, and who accepted its decisions, confirmed it by that acceptance. But the decision of the Council was enforced on the Arian heretics without anybody waiting to find out whether the pope agreed or disagreed with what had been done.[2] If Silvester was the infallible monarch of the Church, he certainly adopted the strangest methods for asserting his infallibility and his sovereign authority. He simply said nothing about either of them, but he behaved just as he ought to have behaved if he was the first bishop in the Church and nothing more.

But the Council of Nicæa throws light in other ways on the position of the Roman see. In the sixth

---

[1] Dupin calls him "a sorry compiler, who gathered all he met with relating to his subject, both bad and good, without examining whether it was true or false." Mr. Precentor Venables says that "his work is little more than a compilation from the ecclesiastical histories of Eusebius, Socrates, Sozomen, and Theodoret, to which he has added little but what is very doubtful or manifestly untrue:" see Smith and Wace, s.v. *Gelasius* (13), ii. 622; and compare Mansi, ii. 753.

[2] See Bossuet's *Defensio*, pars iii. lib. vii. cap. vii. Bossuet says concerning the dogmatic decree of the Nicene Council, "Facto Patrum decreto, adeo res transacta putabatur, ut nullâ morâ interpositâ, *nullo expectato sedis apostolicæ speciali decreto*, omnes ubique terrarum episcopi, Christiani omnes, atque ipse imperator, ipsi etiam Ariani, tamquam divino judicio cederent."

canon there is a reference to the Church of Rome. In that canon the Council decreed as follows: "Let the ancient customs prevail, namely, those in Egypt, Libya. and Pentapolis: that the Bishop of Alexandria have power over all these, since the same is customary for the Bishop of Rome. Likewise, in Antioch and other provinces, that the privileges be secured to the Churches,"[1] etc. This canon ratifies the ancient custom that the Bishop of Alexandria should retain his fulness of jurisdiction over the various provinces of Egypt, Libya, and Pentapolis. That jurisdiction was very great, as I observed in a previous lecture. But the canon goes on to cite the case of the Roman see as parallel to the case of the Alexandrian see. It says, "since the same is customary for the Bishop of Rome." Rufinus explains that Rome had the care of the suburbicarian Churches, as Alexandria had of the Egyptian and Libyan Churches. The Council says not a word about any Roman primacy of jurisdiction over the whole Church. It puts side by side the privileges of the second see and the privileges of the first see. The bishops of both sees were powerful bishops,—powerful metropolitans,—if you will, powerful patriarchs, though it is practically certain that in the Nicene age they were neither of them, strictly speaking, patriarchs with subject metropolitans.[2] But whatever they were, the nature of their authority

---

[1] On the spurious addition to this canon, in which it is said that the Roman Church always had the primacy, see pp. 277, 278.

[2] Cf. Tillemont, x. 790.

was identically the same.   The canon implies a
certain primacy in Rome, because it proposes Rome
as, in a sort of way, the model; but the primacy
implied by the canon is obviously a primacy of
honour, not a universal supremacy of jurisdiction.
If that had been thought of, it would have been
safe-guarded.   Moreover, if that had been thought
of, Rome would hardly have been mentioned as a
precedent for the limited jurisdiction of Alexandria.
If you are discussing the privileges of this or that
peer, you are hardly likely to illustrate your argument by referring to the prerogative of the king.

But again the Council of Nicæa throws light on
the question whether the see of Rome had a primacy
of jurisdiction over all Churches, by its decree in regard to appeals.   The fifth canon allows persons who
think that they have been unjustly excommunicated
by their bishop to complain to the Provincial Synod,
and the synod is to determine whether the complaint
is a just one, and to make some decree in accordance
with its determination.   Not a word is said about
any appeal from the decision of the Provincial Synod,
either to some greater synod, or to a patriarch, or to
Rome.   The Provincial Synod is set forth as the
final authority for each province.   Now, the Vatican
Council decrees that because the Roman pontiff presides over the universal Church *by the divine right*
of his apostolic primacy, *therefore* "he is the supreme
judge of the faithful, and recourse may be had to his
judgment in all causes which pertain to the jurisdic-

tion of the Church." Why did not the Council of Nicæa safeguard this divine right of its infallible monarch? Is it not marvellous that on the very first occasion when the whole Church has an opportunity of meeting together by representation in an Ecumenical Synod, the one matter in which it seems to take no interest is the divinely given prerogatives of its head? If it alludes to the Roman see in a casual way in its sixth canon, it is only to speak of its minor rights as the local metropolitan see of Central and Southern Italy. Concerning any general powers belonging to Rome as the court of appeal for the whole Catholic Church, it preserves an absolute and, I must add, a significant silence. It is silent, not because it consciously repudiates, but because the idea had not crossed the minds of the Saints and Fathers who composed the Council. Undoubtedly, if the idea had been presented to the synod, and if any claim on behalf of the pope had been urged as a matter of divine right, there can be no question that a repudiation of such claim would have been made in unmistakable terms. But as a matter of fact the claim was not made, and therefore the whole conception which underlies the Vatican decrees was ignored. From whatever point of view we regard that wonderful assembly, the first Ecumenical Council we find in it a perpetual witness against the theory that modern papalism has any foothold in primitive tradition and practice. The Nicene Council set the seal of its ecumenical approval on that system of

Church government which was in use during the first three centuries, and for which the Church of England contends at the present day.

We now pass from the Council of Nicæa to the Council of Sardica, which was held eighteen or nineteen years later, in A.D. 343 or 344. This Council is of very great importance in its bearing on our subject, because it really did give to the pope a certain measure of jurisdiction outside the limits of the suburbicarian Churches. The Council was intended to be an Ecumenical Council, and when it passed the canons to which I am alluding, it intended to give to the pope the right of receiving appeals from all parts of the Church, from the East no less than from the West. As things turned out, the Council was not accepted by the Church as ecumenical, and at the present day no one attributes to it that character.[1] Almost all the Eastern bishops, who had been summoned, withdrew in a body, and the Council, as it was actually held, consisted of about ninety-five Western bishops and only six Easterns. Some of its acts were accepted by the whole Church, as, for example, its declaration that S. Athanasius, Marcellus of Ancyra, and Asclepas of Gaza, were innocent of the charges brought against them; and also its deposition and excommunication of the principal revivers of Arianism; but the disciplinary canons

---

[1] Natalis Alexander, in the seventeenth century, argued in favour of the ecumenicity of the Sardican Council, but his assertion was condemned by the Roman censors (see Hefele's *History of the Church Councils*, vol. ii. p. 176, English trans.).

passed by the Council were not received in the East until the end of the seventh century, and even then many of their provisions were considered as applying only to the Churches of the West.[1] But even in the West itself the canons were by no means universally received. In Africa they were not known in the fifth century. However, although these canons were by no means universally accepted, they are of very great importance in the history of the growth of the papal power. During the years which had elapsed since the Council of Nicæa, there had been a great deal of confusion in the Church. As we have seen, the Council of Nicæa decreed that the affairs of each province should be administered by the synod of that province; no provision was made for any appeal to a higher authority than the Provincial Synod. But, as a matter of fact, appeals had from time to time been made to the emperors, and they had committed the hearing of some of those appeals to such synods as they chose to convoke. Much trouble had arisen in consequence. The great S. Athanasius had been condemned on the most frivolous grounds by a Synod of Tyre, which had no sort of jurisdiction over him, except what it got from the emperor, and twice he had been banished from his see by the imperial authority. He had been supported by Pope S. Julius of Rome, who had recognized the ecclesiastical nullity of the proceedings of his opponents, and the futility of the charges made against him, and

---

[1] See the note on pp. 153, 154.

had granted to him the communion of the Church of Rome. In fact, during all these eighteen years the Church of Rome had played a very good part. It had maintained loyally the Catholic faith as defined at Nicæa, and it had supported the orthodox bishops who were suffering persecution at the hands of the Arianizing emperors and of the Arianizing cabal of Eastern bishops who looked to Eusebius of Nicomedia as their ringleader. When compared with the confusion which reigned in the East, Rome and the West seemed a quiet haven of refuge. We need not wonder that a great Western council, such as the Council of Sardica was, should think that the time had come for providing some canonical method of appeal from the decisions of Provincial Councils which should take the place of the uncanonical appeals to the emperor, which had become frequent. And what could be more natural than to substitute an appeal to the Bishop of Rome, who enjoyed a primacy of honour which was recognized by the whole Church? Not that the Council of Sardica intended that the Bishop of Rome should personally hear the appeal, but they proposed that, if, on being appealed to, he thought that a rehearing ought to be granted, he should have the right to appoint bishops who should hear the appeal. The Council of Sardica only proposed to grant this right of appeal to Rome in the case of a bishop who should have been deposed by the synod of the province to which he belonged; and part of their arrangement was that, if the pope chose to grant a rehearing and to appoint judges, he should be bound to nominate bishops from the neighbourhood of the province in which the case had arisen; although he was also to have the power, if he chose to use it, of sending legates of his own to preside in his name over the court of appeal. There was no thought of giving to the pope any right of evoking the cause to Rome. The appeal was to be heard out in the provinces, in the neighbourhood of the place where the cause had arisen. Such were the main provisions of the famous canons of Sardica,[1] which conferred an appellate jurisdiction of a strictly limited kind on the Roman pope. Before discussing the light which they throw on our general subject, it will be well to quote some of the clauses of one of these canons. In the third canon, "Hosius the bishop said . . . if any of the bishops shall have been condemned in any matter, and thinks that he has right on his side, and wishes that a new council should be convoked; if it please you, let us honour the memory of S. Peter the apostle, and let the bishops who have judged the case [in the Provincial Synod] write to Julius, the Roman bishop, and if he shall determine in favour of a new trial, let there be a new trial, and let him appoint judges," etc. It seems most strange that Roman Catholics should refer with any pleasure to these canons of Sardica. According to the view laid down by the Vatican

---

[1] According to Hefele's numbering, they are the third, fourth, and fifth canons.

Council, the supremacy of the pope belongs to him *jure divino*, and as a consequence of that supremacy every member of the Church, whether he belongs to the clergy or to the laity, has an inherent right of appealing to his judgment in any matter appertaining to the jurisdiction of the Church.   But here we have the fathers of the Council of Sardica carrying a resolution, so to speak, in favour of the Roman see, and determining that, in honour of the memory of S. Peter, they will in certain rare cases give to the pope a very restricted right of determining whether there shall be a rehearing, and of appointing bishops who shall form the court of appeal, and of deputing one or more legates to preside in that court.   And all this is proposed by Bishop Hosius tentatively—"si vobis placet"—"if it please you."   On the papalist theory, the whole proceeding must appear insufferably impertinent.   It did not so appear to S. Athanasius and to the other Fathers of the synod, because they knew nothing of the theory which underlies the Vatican decrees.   They thought that they were conferring an extraordinary privilege on the Roman see, by giving to it a certain measure of jurisdiction outside its own suburbicarian domain, and that they were thus honouring the memory of S. Peter, whose successor Julius was reputed to be.   So they thought, and they were quite right.   The new privilege which they then conferred was extraordinary.[1]   Their in-

---

[1] Archbishop De Marca of Paris (*De Concord. Sac. et Imp.* vii. iii. viii.) rightly says, "The words of the canon prove that the institution

tention was to add to the primacy of honour which the see of Rome already possessed, a primacy of jurisdiction—of *limited* jurisdiction, no doubt, but still a primacy of jurisdiction, and one which should affect the whole Church. They failed in carrying out their full design, because these canons were never received in the East in such sense as to be applicable (without modification) to the East;[1] and they were

of this right was *new*. 'If it please you,' says Hosius of Cordova, the president of the council, 'let us honour the memory of S. Peter the apostle.' He says not that the ancient tradition was to be confirmed, as was wont to be done in matters which only require the renewal or explanation of an ancient right."

[1] The Sardican canons were included in the collection of· John Scholasticus, the schismatic patriarch of Constantinople, who was intruded by Justinian into the place of S. Eutychius; and they received a certain recognition at the Trullan Council, along with other documents, more or less inconsistent with them, as, for example, the canons and letters of the Councils of Carthage in the time of S. Aurelius, which expressly rejected the Sardican system of appeals. Pope Nicholas I. (Coleti, ix. 1297), in his first letter to Photius, alleged the 10th (al. 13th) canon of Sardica, in proof of the uncanonical character of Photius' elevation to the patriarchal throne of Constantinople; but Photius, who was the most learned man who ever sat on that throne, absolutely denied, in his reply, that those canons were received in the Constantinopolitan Church (Migne's *Patrol. Græc.*, cii. 600, 601). The later Greek canonists, finding them in some way sanctioned by the Trullan Council, interpret the canons which deal with the appeal to Rome as applying, in the letter, only to the Churches of the West. They hold that, so far as they are applicable to the East, the appeal is to the see of Constantinople, which is new Rome (cf. Beveridge's *Synodicon*, i. 486, 489). But, when we pass from the theories of canonists to the actual practice of the Church, we find that the Sardican discipline about appeals was never carried out in the East. The Councils of Antioch, Constantinople, and Chalcedon, had worked out a totally different scheme of appeals, in which the pope does not appear at all. And the real fact is that it is very difficult to discover much trace of the actual carrying out of the Sardican system, even in

only received in certain parts of the West. But in whatever Western provinces they were received, they had the effect of aggregating those provinces for certain purposes to what may now be called the Roman patriarchate. The ultimate effect of these canons was to revolutionize the whole theory and practice of ecclesiastical government, at any rate within the Latin portion of the Church. For here we have the first beginning of that which, in the course of ages, was enlarged by accretion and successful usurpation into that plenitude of power which, wherever it is acknowledged, makes the Church to be the bond-servant of the pope.

Having thus considered the two great Councils of Nicæa (A.D. 325) and Sardica (A.D. 343 or 344) in their bearing on our general subject, we are in a position to revert to the pontificate of Damasus, who occupied the Roman chair from A.D. 366 to A.D. 384. I have already implied several times that this pontificate constitutes a fresh starting-point in the history of the growth of the papal claims. It was during the episcopate of Damasus that a worldly spirit became very marked among many of the members of the clergy of the Roman Church. It was also during his time that, by legislative action on the part of the emperors, a certain measure of coactive jurisdiction was conferred by the state upon the popes. My limits will not allow me to treat this branch of the

the West, before the ninth century. Compare De Marca's *De Concord. Sac. et. Imp.*, lib. vii. capp. iv. et seqq.

subject in much detail, but I propose to illustrate my statement by reference to a certain decree of the Emperor Gratian, which was promulgated in response to the petition of a synod held at Rome under the presidency of Damasus. The synod was held in the year 378,[1] and it petitioned Gratian to give orders that if any bishop, after being condemned, should wish wrongly to keep possession of his bishopric, or if, when summoned to be tried by his brethren, he should contumaciously refuse to come, he should be brought to Rome either by the prefect of the prætorium of Italy, or by the vicarius of the city of Rome; or, if the trouble arose in the more distant parts, that the duty of trying the case should be committed to the local metropolitan; or, if the metropolitan was himself the guilty party, that he should be ordered to go without delay to Rome, or to such judges as the Bishop of Rome might appoint. They further asked that, if the accused bishop should for any reason doubt the fairness of his metropolitan, or of any other of his episcopal judges, he should have the right to appeal to the Bishop of Rome, or to a synod of at least fifteen of the neighbouring bishops.[2]

[1] The synodical letter is addressed to Gratian and Valentinian II., no mention being made of either Valens or Theodosius; and the imperial reply runs also in the name of the same two emperors. Tillemont (viii. 775, 776) and Coleti (ii. 1190) conclude that both letter and reply must be assigned to the latter portion of the year 378, between the death of Valens in August, 378, and the accession of Theodosius in January, 379. Mansi agrees; and so does F. Ryder (*Catholic Controversy*, p. 68, 2nd edit.).

[2] Cf. Coleti, *Concilia*, ii. 1189. It is clear from the letter of the

Such was the request which the Synod of Rome, in the year 378, sent to the young Emperor Gratian, who was only nineteen years old. The bishops who sat in this council came from various parts of Italy.[1] Presumably, they were the pope's suburbicarian suffragans. The emperor granted to them all that they asked; and when one comes to look into his rescript, one discovers that, by the addition of about five words, he gave to them a great deal more than they asked. They had asked that contumacious bishops should be compelled by the prefect of the prætorium of Italy, or else by the vicarius of the city of Rome, to come to Rome to be tried. This mention of the officials who were to coerce the refractory prelates limits the scope of the application of the enactment, for which the synod petitioned, to Italy and Illyricum.[2] The emperor in his rescript

synod, and also from the emperors' reply, that earlier in the reign of Gratian, apparently when he was the colleague of his father Valentinian I., there had been some imperial decree enacting that the Bishop of Rome should have the right to try the other bishops of the Churches. That earlier decree, probably made in 367, would seem to have covered the whole ground of the synod's petition. The synod asks for no new law, but for the better execution of the earlier law. It says, "Idcirco statuti imperialis non novitatem sed firmitudinem postulamus" (Coleti, ii. 1188). The earlier decree was evidently called forth by the schism of the anti-pope Ursinus; but it was probably restricted in its scope to the provinces comprised within the civil jurisdiction of the prefect of the prætorium of Italy. If it had referred to the Western empire generally, the Roman Synod of 378 would assuredly have laid stress on the fact, and that synod's petition would have asked for the renewal of such a far-reaching jurisdiction (see p. 157).

[1] "Ex diffusis Italiæ partibus . . . congregati."

[2] The prefecture of Illyricum was at that time administered by the

brings in the prefect of the prætorium of Gaul and the proconsuls of Africa and Spain, and thus extends the system of appeals, which he is establishing, to the whole of the Western empire, to Gaul, Britain, Spain, and Africa, as well as to Italy and Illyricum.[1] It sometimes seems to me that ecclesiastical historians have hardly done justice to the immense importance of this act of imperial legislation. By one stroke of his pen the Emperor Gratian created, so far as the civil power could create, a patriarchal jurisdiction over the whole Western empire, and vested it in the Bishop of Rome. The powers granted by the rescript go far beyond anything which was attempted by the Council of Sardica. At Sardica there was no question of any one being tried at Rome. But, according to the

Prefect of Italy. The very learned Jesuit, Daniel Farlati (*Illyricum Sacrum*, tom. i. p. 84, ed. 1751), says, " Illyricum integrum, nullâque sui parte dimiuutum Valentinianus in suâ potestate retinuit, *ejusque plenam administrationem Præfecto Prætoriano Italiæ reliquit, vel mandavit*, ad quem paucis ante annis Jovianus, vel Julianus eamdem revocaverat. Hæc forma et descriptio Imperii atque Illyrici retenta est sub Gratiano et Valentiniano juniore." So Sextus Petronius Probus was Prefect of Italy and also of Illyricum from 368 to 375 (see Tillemont, *Histoire des Empereurs*, v. 685, 686, ed. 1701); and Mamertinus from 362 to 365 (Tillemont, *Op. cit.*, v. 21); and it seems probable that Hesperius, the son of the poet Ausonius, administered the prefectures of Italy and Illyricum in 378 (see Tillemont, *Op. cit.*, tom. v. p. 712 et seq.; and Jac. Gothofred., *Cod. Theodos.*, tom. vi. p. 366, ed. Lugd., 1665). On the two prefectures being held during the reigns of Valentinian and Gratian by one prefect, compare Le Quien, *Oriens Christianus*, ii. 3, 4.

[1] The Roman synod in its petition had used the words : " seu ab illustribus viris præfectis prætorio Italiæ vestræ, sive a vicario." Gratian in his rescript says, " aut ab illustribus viris præfectis prætorio *Galliæ atque* Italiæ, sive *a proconsulibus*, vel vicariis " (Coleti, *Concilia*, ii. 1191).

rescript, all the metropolitans of the Western empire are liable to be dragged to Rome, whether they will or no, by the secular arm, in order that at Rome they may be judged by the pope.   Moreover, bishops who are dissatisfied with the judgment of their metropolitan and his synod may appeal to Rome, and the appeal may apparently be heard by the pope in person; whereas, according to the canon of Sardica, all that the pope could do was to order a rehearing of the case by bishops of the provinces bordering on the province of the accused.   We have no reason to suppose that the bishops of Gaul or Spain or Africa had ever wished that this new system should be made applicable to them, or that they assented to it.   Even Damasus himself and his Italian synod had not proposed such an enormous extension of the Roman patriarchate.   The emperor seems to have thrown in Gaul, Britain,[1] Spain, and Africa, as if he thought that he might as well do the thing thoroughly while he was about it.   But we must observe carefully that there is not a word in the rescript about the Eastern empire.   Let no one suppose that it was a recognition by the state of the inherent primacy of jurisdiction over the whole Church which Ultramontanes suppose to have been granted by our Lord to S. Peter, and to his successors, the popes.   The new system applies only to the West.   It is limited, local.   It is therefore patriarchal, not papal.   Moreover, its extension

---

[1] Britain was, in the time of Gratian, under the civil jurisdiction of the prefect of the prætorium of Gaul.

to Gaul, Britain, Spain, and Africa had no synodical action for its basis. The patriarchal jurisdiction over those countries was the creation of the state, not the creation of the Church. Ecclesiastically, the new legislation, so far as it applied to those more remote countries, was null and void. Still it was law, and the powers given to the pope were capable of being enforced by the whole might of the Roman empire. Was I not right in saying that the pontificate of Damasus forms a new point of departure in regard to all matters connected with the growth of the papal jurisdiction? I sometimes think that the Roman pontiffs, having acquired this vast extension of jurisdiction by the act of the civil power without any concurrence of the Church, were driven to devise some presentable theory which should constitute a religious basis for the new authority which they had acquired. Their vague claim to be successors of S. Peter would be an obvious basis to put forward. That claim being really unhistorical and baseless, there could be no definition of the privileges conferred by it, either in scripture or tradition. This absence of authoritative definition would leave them free to plead their succession from S. Peter as a religious basis for jurisdiction derived from the emperor. / Whether Damasus did so plead it I cannot say, but I find in the decretals of Siricius, the successor of Damasus, a new way of speaking about the privileges supposed to be inherited by the Roman see from S. Peter. I must, however, finish what I have to say about Damasus before passing on to Siricius.

A few months after the Emperor Gratian had issued the rescript which so greatly enlarged the power of the pope, he joined Theodosius to himself as a partner in the government of the empire, and he assigned to Theodosius the East, while he reserved the West as his own immediate share. The empire had been divided in this way on previous occasions, but Gratian's partition did not proceed exactly on the old lines. Hitherto as a rule the whole of Illyricum had belonged to the West. *Now* Gratian divided Illyricum into two parts, and united Eastern Illyricum to that part of the empire which he committed to Theodosius.[1] Damasus saw very clearly that there was great danger that Eastern Illyricum would pass away from his sphere of influence, or rather (to use what would now be the more accurate expression) from his jurisdiction, unless something was done to safeguard his rights. We may be certain that the canons of Sardica, though they were not at that time known in Africa, were well known in Eastern Illyricum. Sardica is itself situated in Eastern Illyricum, and three of the Sardican canons[2] dealt with local matters connected with the Church of Thessalonica, the most powerful see in Eastern Illyricum. If the canons of Sardica were in

---

[1] Tillemont (*Histoire des Empereurs*, ed. 1701, tom. v. pp. 716–718) shows that Gratian gave Eastern Illyricum to Theodosius, *when he made him Emperor*, i.e. in 379. Compare Duchesne (*Origines*, p. 41).

[2] Namely, the sixteenth, eighteenth, and nineteenth, according to Hefele's numbering.

force there, then undoubtedly Damasus had a certain jurisdiction of a limited kind in the Eastern Illyrian provinces.[1] But besides the jurisdiction conferred by the canons of Sardica, there was the new and much fuller jurisdiction quite lately conferred by Gratian. The rescript of Gratian had, I believe, been issued before the partition of Illyricum, and if so, it doubtless had force of law there.[2] Damasus would be very loth to lose those fair provinces from his patriarchate.[3] At the same time, it would not be very easy for him to interfere otherwise than exceptionally in the affairs of provinces which belonged to the Eastern emperor. He therefore gave a commission to Ascholius, Bishop of Thessalonica,[4] creating him his vicar in Eastern

---

[1] It is worth mentioning that one of the Sardican canons on appeals to Rome, namely, the fourth, was proposed by a bishop of Eastern Illyricum, Gaudentius of Naissus, in Dacia.

[2] It is fair to add that some great authorities assign the rescript of Gratian to 380 or 381; that is to say, to a date later than 379, when Illyricum was divided. I may mention Hefele (*Councils*, ii. 292, E.T.) and Duchesne (*Liber Pontificalis*, p. 214). If their view be correct, the Canons of Sardica might seem to be the sole basis of the pope's claim to jurisdiction over Eastern Illyricum, since Gratian's rescript, which was limited in its scope to the Western division of the empire, would have given him no authority there. But it must be remembered that there had been an earlier decree of Gratian (see note on pp. 155, 156), which conferred certain large powers on the Roman bishop. I think that it is almost certain that in that earlier decree mention had been made of the Praetorian Prefect of Italy, whose sphere of administration extended at that time over the whole of the undivided Illyricum. If that be so, the pope had in any case acquired through the action of the state patriarchal powers throughout Illyricum, before the division of that prefecture in 379, and my argument will remain unaffected, even though Gratian's second rescript be assigned to 380 or 381.

[3] Cf. Duchesne, *Origines*, p. 41.

[4] The fact that this commission was granted to the Bishop of

Illyricum, and authorizing him to exercise the powers which belonged to himself as Patriarch of the West.[1] This was the first instance of the popes attempting anything of this kind. Until the Council of Sardica there would have been no ground for such action, because up to that time the popes had no jurisdiction of any sort or kind outside the suburbicarian provinces. But Gratian's rescript had made Damasus a very great potentate, a sort of spiritual prefect of the prætorium throughout the West; and as the prefects had their vicars, so the popes would think that it was natural for them to have vicars also. Accordingly Ascholius of Thessalonica was empowered by Damasus to exercise whatever jurisdiction he, the pope, possessed in the provinces of Eastern Illyricum.[2]

Thessalonica shows that the vicariate was created by the pope after Illyricum had been divided. Sirmium, not Thessalonica, had been the capital of the undivided Illyricum.

[1] If Damasus had thought that there was any possibility of making good a claim to universal jurisdiction over the whole East, there would have been as much necessity for him to create vicars in Egypt and Syria and Asia Minor as in Eastern Illyricum.

[2] The proof of this statement may be seen in the letters of Pope Innocent I. to Anysius and Rufus, two successive bishops of Thessalonica, in which he confirms to Anysius and imparts to Rufus vicarial powers over Eastern Illyricum, and in which he refers to the similar action taken by his predecessors, Damasus and Siricius, in favour of Ascholius, the predecessor of Anysius, and of Anysius himself (cf. Coleti, *Concilia*, v. 845, 846). The letters of Damasus to Ascholius are lost; for the two which were read at the Roman Council under Boniface II., in A.D. 531, have nothing to do with this particular subject, and appear to me to be spurious. The original letter from Siricius to Anysius is also lost, but a second letter referring to some of the contents of the first is extant (cf. Coleti, *ubi supr.*). Duchesne, in an article entitled *L'Illyricum ecclésiastique* (*Byzantinische Zeitschrift*, erster Band, p. 543, 1892), seems to pass over the action of Damasus in

While the see of Rome was thus enlarging the bounds of its jurisdiction in the West by the help of the imperial power, its relations with the East remained unchanged, so far as jurisdiction was concerned. No doubt the East was conscious that a great ecclesiastical power was rising in the West, but it was a power to which it owed no allegiance, but only the debt of Christian brotherhood and charity, and the respect due to the see which had the primacy of honour. The attitude of the East towards Rome comes out very clearly in connection with the schism of Paulinus at Antioch. The origin of that schism goes as far back as the year 330, when S. Eustathius, the orthodox Bishop of Antioch, was deposed on false charges of Sabellianism and immorality, by Eusebius of Nicomedia, Eusebius of Cæsarea, and other bishops, who sympathized with Arianism. The Emperor Constantine banished S. Eustathius from Antioch; but before the saint departed he enjoined on his people the duty of patiently continuing in the Church of Antioch, even though Arianizing bishops might be set over them. They were to remain and strengthen the faith of the poor and uninstructed, and to do what they could to resist the wolves who would otherwise ravage the flock.[1] S. Chrysostom, who tells us this, adds that events showed the wisdom of the

this matter, and to suppose that the vicariate of Thessalonica was created by Siricius. I do not understand how the clear statement of Pope Innocent can be got rid of; but, whichever view is finally adopted, my argument remains unaffected.

[1] Cf. S. Chrys. *Hom. in S. Eustathium*, § 4, *Opp.* ed. Ben., ii. 609.

saint's counsel, for the great mass of the Catholics refused to set up any separate conventicles, but attended the principal churches of the city, even when the bishops thrust in by the Arianizing emperors were heretical; and so the flock remained Catholic, though it had a succession of heretical chief pastors.[1]   At last, by the good Providence of God, a saintly and orthodox bishop, Meletius, who had formerly occupied the see of Sebaste in the Lesser Armenia, was appointed Bishop of Antioch.   Catholics and Arians united in electing him, the Arians supposing him to be Arian, and the Catholics having reason to believe that he was Catholic.   In his first sermon he plainly declared his sentiments, and openly professed the Catholic faith in its fulness in the presence of the Arian Emperor Constantius.   Now, it happened that there was a small body of ardent Catholics in Antioch who had, ever since the banishment of S. Eustathius, held aloof from the main body of the Antiochene Church, and had worshipped separately, having as their leader a worthy priest named Paulinus.   There was, no doubt, much to be said in justification of the course which they took, although it was in opposition to the council of S. Eustathius, whom they specially professed to follow, and after

[1] Tillemont (x. 524) says that these Arianizing bishops of Antioch "were not visibly separated from the communion of the universal Church, and most of them concealed their heresy somewhat;" but this can hardly be said of Stephen, who was excommunicated by name at the Council of Sardica. It is, however, most probable that the proceedings of that council remained unknown for several years to the Church people of Antioch.

whose name they were commonly called Eustathians.
But now that at length the bishop, accepted by the
great majority of the Church people in the city, was
thoroughly Catholic, there was a splendid opportunity
for healing the schism. However, Paulinus and his
party still held aloof. A few months after Meletius
had been enthroned in the episcopal chair, the very
celebrated and very influential Council of Alexandria
was held under the presidency of S. Athanasius. This
Council carefully considered the position of affairs
at Antioch, and it recommended that the whole
body of Catholics in that city should unite together.[1] It accordingly appointed a commission,
headed by S. Eusebius of Vercellæ, which was
to proceed to Antioch and bring about the much-
desired reunion. Unfortunately a hot-headed bishop
from Sardinia, named Lucifer, who immediately
afterwards broke away from the Church with his
followers, reached Antioch before the commission
sent by S. Athanasius and by the other Fathers of
the Council of Alexandria. Instead of reuniting the
two parties of Catholics, and inducing them all
to acknowledge S. Meletius as bishop, which was
obviously the right thing to do,[2] Lucifer consecrated

---

[1] Dom Montfaucon, the Benedictine editor of S. Chrysostom, in the
Monitum to S. Chrysostom's homily *De Anathemate* (*Opp.* S. Chrys.
ed. Ben., Venet., 1734, tom. i. p. 690), describes the action of S. Athanasius thus : "Athanasius in Synodo Alexandrinâ anno 362, totis
viribus nitebatur, ut Eustathiani Meletianis adjungerentur, omnesque
Catholici unum Meletium Episcopum agnoscerent."

[2] See Cardinal Newman's *Arians of the Fourth Century*, 3rd edit.,
1871, pp. 374, 375.

Paulinus the priest of the Eustathians. Thus the schism was made tenfold more difficult to heal. Bishop was now pitted against bishop. But the blame of the schism must be laid on Lucifer who consecrated, and on Paulinus who allowed himself to be consecrated. This grievous scandal took place in the year 362. S. Gregory of Nyssa describes it as an attempt to corrupt the chastity of the Church of Antioch, which Church, however, remained faithful to her pastor, S. Meletius, who was espoused to her.[1] The great majority of the orthodox Christians of Antioch were in the communion of S. Meletius, while a small minority followed Paulinus. Apparently for some years the Roman Church was undecided as to which side should receive her support; but in the year 375 Pope Damasus openly declared himself in favour of Paulinus, and wrote letters to him treating him as the one Catholic Bishop of Antioch, and ignoring altogether the claims of S. Meletius. Two years later, in 377, Pope Damasus went further, and in the presence of Dorotheus, a priest whom S. Basil had sent to Rome, spoke of S. Meletius and of the glorious S. Eusebius of Samosata as if they were Arian heretics. One cannot help seeing a certain analogy between the state of things in Antioch at that time and the state of things in England now. The Church of Antioch under S. Meletius numbered in its fold the great majority of those who held the Catholic faith, as the Church of England does at the present day

---

[1] S. Greg. Nyss. *Orat. Funebr. in S. Melet., Opp.* ed. Migne, iii. 857.

The minority of separatists under Paulinus had the support of Damasus and the Roman Church, and thus occupied a position in some way parallel to the Romanist communion in this country, though there can be no question that Paulinus would have rejected with horror the Vatican decrees, if they had been proposed to him for his acceptance. All the great saints of the Eastern Church, and above all S. Basil, supported S. Meletius. They were on the spot, they knew the facts, and they treated S. Meletius with the greatest veneration as a saint, and as the occupant of the apostolic throne of Antioch.[1] They communicated with him, although Rome ignored him ; they rejected the communion of Paulinus, although Rome supported him.

Towards the end of the year 376 a fresh complication added to the confusion. The heresiarch Apollinaris openly separated himself from the Church, and consecrated Vitalis, or Vitalius, to be the Apollinarian Bishop of Antioch. This made a third bishop in that unfortunate city. Three years before there had arrived in Antioch a young man, twenty-seven years old, who was destined to play an important part in the history of the Church. His name was Jerome. He was a Latin, born in Dalmatia, but

---

[1] In the year 379 a great council of Eastern bishops was held at Antioch. One hundred and forty-six prelates attended, amongst whom were S. Eusebius of Samosata, S. Pelagius of Laodicea, S. Eulogius of Edessa, and S. Gregory of Nyssa. As Tillemont (viii. 367) says, it was one of the most illustrious councils ever held in the Church. S. Meletius presided. The whole East accepted him as the rightful bishop, though he was rejected by the Church of Rome.

catechized and baptized at about the age of twenty in Rome. He was a member of the local Roman Church, and had formed his conceptions of the position of the Roman Church in Rome itself, where, as I have said, he received his instruction in Christianity. He came to Syria to practise the ascetic life, and he established himself among the monks of the desert of Chalcis. After he had stayed among these monks for about four years he began to find his position uncomfortable, on account of the disputes at Antioch. As a member of the Roman Church, he would naturally sympathize with Paulinus, who was in communion with Pope Damasus. But the monks for the most part would be in communion with S. Meletius, who was the bishop generally recognized in Antioch and the East. S. Jerome therefore wrote a curious letter to the pope, asking for directions as to what he was to do. Any one who is acquainted with S. Jerome's writings, knows that he is a writer who never minces his words. He is apt to exaggerate. He throws himself violently into one side of a disputed question, and perhaps a few years afterwards he throws himself with equal violence into the opposite side of that same question. God forbid that I should even seem to depreciate the many noble qualities and noble gifts which he possessed; but no one is faultless, and S. Jerome would have been the last person to claim faultlessness for himself.[1]

[1] Ultramontane writers make no scruple about pointing out S. Jerome's faults, when it suits them to do so. The Jesuit, Father

Certainly, if ever there was a case when a man might be excused for exaggerating the authority of the Roman see, such an excuse might be pleaded on behalf of S. Jerome. A Latin, living in the East, and suffering continual personal annoyance arising out of the religious divisions of the East, he might well turn to Rome, the Church of his baptism, which was living in comparative quiet, and was basking in the sunshine of the world's favour, and was supporting faithfully the traditional teaching of the Church, and might seek for direction from the great pontiff who ruled in the capital of the empire, and who, in S. Jerome's view, sat in S. Peter's own chair. Practically at the time when S. Jerome wrote, the whole West was Catholic, and Rome was the centre of the West; while the East was suffering persecution from an Arian emperor, and was split and divided and weakened. Twenty years before, when Pope Liberius had given way, and had surrendered the Nicene formula,[1] and when, shortly afterwards, the Western bishops were deluded into signing an Arian creed at the Council of Ariminum, no one would have looked to the pope or to the West for trustworthy guidance.

Bottalla, in his treatise on the *Infallibility of the Pope* (ed. 1870, p. 185), speaking of S. Jerome, says, "This holy Doctor's tendency to give too ready credence to unauthorized rumours is well known. Thus, as is pointed out by Zaccaria, he represents S. Chrysostom as an Origenist, and *he adopts the falsehoods spread abroad by the adherents of Paulinus to the prejudice of S. Meletius of Antioch.*"

[1] Hefele admits that Liberius "renounced the formula $\delta\mu oo\acute{u}\sigma\iota os$," and that he "renounced the letter of the Nicene faith".(*History of the Church Councils,* vol. ii. pp. 235, 246, Eng. trans.).

Then S. Athanasius stood alone against the world. But things were altered now, and S. Jerome wrote in his perplexity to Pope Damasus as follows: "Since the East tears into pieces the Lord's coat, . . . therefore by me is the chair of S. Peter to be consulted, and that faith which is praised by the apostle's mouth, thence now seeking food for my soul, whence of old I received the robe of Christ. . . . I speak with the successor of the fisherman, and the disciple of the Cross. I, who follow none as my chief but Christ, am associated in communion with thy Blessedness, that is, with the see of Peter. On that rock the Church is built, I know. Whoso shall eat the Lamb outside that house is profane. If any one shall not be in the ark of Noah, he will perish when the flood prevails. . . . I know not Vitalis [the Apollinarian]; I reject Meletius; I am ignorant of Paulinus. Whoso gathereth not with thee scattereth; that is, he who is not of Christ is of Antichrist."[1] As far as I know, in all the writings of the Fathers during the first four centuries this passage stands alone. Of course, no Catholic would dream of departing from the general teaching of the Fathers in order to adhere to the exaggerated statements of one young man, who was in sore perplexity.[2] We can make excuses

[1] *Ep.* xx., *Opp.* ed. Vallars., i. 37, 38. Tillemont (xii. 44) gives 376 as the date of this letter.

[2] That he was a young man appears clearly from his own statement. Three years before he wrote the above-quoted letter to Damasus, he had written a letter (*Ep.* xiv.) to his friend Heliodorus. Later on he describes this letter to Heliodorus as having been written "dum essem adolescens, immo pene puer" (cf. *Ep.* lii. ad Nepotian..

for him, we can try and see how he ever came to use such words, but we unhesitatingly set them aside as exaggerated and unworthy. If they are taken literally and accepted, we must say that all the glorious Eastern saints of that age were living in deadly sin. They were supporting those who were "profane;" they were communicating with those who were "not in the ark," and who were off "the rock." Take S. Basil as an example. He was the great leader of the Catholic army of the East; fighting a tremendous battle with heresy; undoubtedly the most heroic man of his time. Not a comparative novice like S. Jerome, who had only been baptized ten years before; but a man in the maturity of his power, forty-seven years old, the metropolitan of the great see of Cæsarea in Cappadocia. He also had before him the same question to decide. Should he communicate with Meletius, whom Rome rejected, or with Paulinus, whom Rome supported? He decided the question by communicating with Meletius and by rejecting Paulinus. It is doubtful whether the ideas expressed in S. Jerome's fine phrases had ever presented themselves to his mind. If they had, he had seen through their shallowness. Moreover, he had had some experience of what Pope Damasus was like, and whether he really was a rock from which a man might derive solid support. Over and over again he had written to Damasus to ask him, living,

Opp., i. 252). If he was "pene puer" in 373, he was certainly a young man in 376.

as he was, in comparative peace and quiet, to help
the Eastern Churches which were suffering persecution; but nothing was done, although much might
have been done. It was proposed in the year 376
that fresh letters should be written to the West, to
be sent by a zealous priest named Dorotheus. S.
Basil, writing to S. Eusebius of Samosata, says, "For
myself, then, I do not see what one should send by
him, or how agree with those who send. . . . It occurs
to me to use Diomed's language [to Agamemnon in
the *Iliad* about Achilles]: 'Would that thou hadst
never sued for aid,'[1] since, saith he, the man 'is
arrogant.' For indeed disdainful tempers, treated
with attention, are wont to become more contemp-
tuous than usual." S. Basil is, of course, speaking
of Damasus. He goes on, "And if the Lord should
be gracious unto us, what other support do we need?
But if the wrath of God remain upon us, what help
can we get from Western superciliousness? They
who neither know nor endure to learn the truth,
but, preoccupied with false suspicions, are doing now
just what they did before in the case of Marcellus,

---

[1] *Iliad*, ix. 694, 695. We may suppose that the whole passage was
running in S. Basil's mind; I therefore subjoin the late Lord Derby's
translation (Homer's *Iliad*, ix. 805-811):—

> "Would that thou ne'er hadst stooped with costly gifts
>   To sue for aid from Peleus' matchless son;
>   For he before was over-proud, and now
>   Thine offers will have tenfold swollen his pride.
>   But leave we him according to his will,
>   To go or stay: he then will join the fight,
>   When his own spirit shall prompt, or Heaven inspire."

when they quarrelled with those who reported to them the truth, and by their own action supported heresy. For I myself, without concert with any, was minded to write *to their leader* [Damasus]: nothing indeed about ecclesiastical matters, except so much as to hint that they neither know the truth of what is going on among us, nor accept the way by which they might learn it; but generally about the duty of not attacking those who are humbled by trials, and of not taking disdainfulness for dignity, a sin which of itself is sufficient to set a man at enmity with God." [1]   It is worth while to quote, by the way, Bossuet's comment on this passage. He says, " It is clear that the confirming of heresy was roundly and flatly, without any excuse, without any attempt to modify, imputed by Basil to two decrees of Roman pontiffs *de fide.*" [2]   What I gather from the whole passage is that S. Basil had no conception of the Bishop of Rome being the divinely appointed monarch of the Church. [3]   He thought of him as a

[1] *Ep.* 239, *Opp.* ed. Ben., 1730, iii. 368.

[2] *Gallia Orthodoxa*, cap. lxv., *Œuvres*, ed. Versailles, 1817, tom. xxxi. p. 138.

[3] One may illustrate S. Basil's conception of the papal office, as described in the text, by the salutation prefixed to the letter which S. Meletius, S. Basil, and thirty other Eastern bishops sent to Pope Damasus and other Western bishops by the hands of the Milanese deacon, S. Sabinus, in the year 372. The salutation runs as follows: " To the most religious and holy brethren and fellow-ministers, the like-minded bishops of Italy and Gaul, Meletius, Eusebius, Basil, etc, send greeting in the Lord " (S. Basil, *Ep.* 92, *Opp.* ed. Ben., iii. 183). Tillemont (ix. 668, 669) shows that the term " Italy " in this salutation includes Rome and the suburbicarian Churches. S. Basil in his 243rd *Epistle* (*Opp.* iii. 372) addresses Damasus and the

very powerful bishop, as, of course, he was, but still as one who was essentially his equal, to whom he owed no allegiance, with whose help he could dispense, and whose actions or inaction he was entitled freely to criticize. If S. Jerome in his younger days thought otherwise, his opinion must be quoted for what it is worth, either as his own personal view, or at most as the theory which he had imbibed at Rome. It was not the general view of the saints or of the Church. It does not represent the tradition received from the apostles.

And practically what did S. Jerome gain by following the lead of Damasus? Why, this! that he joined himself to the separatist body of which Paulinus was bishop, and rejected the communion of S. Meletius, the true occupant of the apostolic see of Antioch. Five years after his letter to Damasus, he must have had his Romanizing views somewhat rudely shaken. By that time the Eastern Church had got out of its difficulties. The persecuting Emperor Valens was dead. The orthodox Theodosius was on the throne. The second Ecumenical Council was assembled at Constantinople, and S. Jerome himself was residing in that city. The Ultramontane historian, Cardinal Orsi, tells us that "perhaps there has not been a council in which has been found a greater number of

Western bishops in similar terms. Mansi (iii. 468), speaking of the sending of the first of these letters, says that the Eastern bishops "synodicam Sabino tradunt *Damaso* deferendam." Imagine the Anglo-Roman bishops of the present day writing in this fashion to Pope Leo XIII. and to the bishops of Italy and France.

confessors and saints." [1]   *There* were gathered S. Gregory of Nazianzus, S. Gregory of Nyssa, S. Peter of Sebaste, S. Amphilochius of Iconium, S. Pelagius of Laodicea, S. Eulogius of Edessa, S. Cyril of Jerusalem, and many more.   And who was the prelate who was recognized by all as worthy of presiding over this wonderful assemblage?   Cardinal Orsi shall tell us.   "But above all," he says, "S. Meletius was pre-eminent, both for the dignity of his see, and for the excellency of his virtue." [2]   We must remember that S. Meletius was still out of communion with Rome.   Damasus still supported the separatist body under Paulinus, and still refused letters of communion to Meletius.   However, that blessed saint, though rejected by Rome, was accepted with veneration by the Church ; and by the agreement of all he took his seat in the presidential chair of the second Ecumenical Council. [3]   According to S. Jerome's youthful view, he was off " the rock," he was " outside the ark," he was among " the profane."   One may fairly suppose that this object-lesson on a large scale must have driven

[1] Orsi, *Ist. Ecc.*, xviii. 63 (tom. viii. p. 135, ed. Rom. 1751): " Dimodochè non v'è forse concilio, nel quale si sia trovato un maggior numero di confessori, e di santi."

[2] " Sopra tutti però risplendeva sì per la dignità della sede, sì per l'eccellenza della virtù s. Melezio."

[3] Orsi (xviii. 64, tom. viii. p. 137) says, " Il capo, il condottiere, il padre, e la guida di questa sacra adunanza finchè egli visse, fu s. Melezio, e dopo la sua morte s. Gregorio, e finalmente dopo la sua dimissione Nettario."   Orsi here enumerates the three prelates, who in succession presided over the Council, viz. S. Meletius, S. Gregory of Nazianzus, and finally Nectarius.   Hefele (*Councils*, Eng. trans., ii. 344) says, " Meletius of Antioch at first presided, and after his death Gregory of Nazianzus."

those fancies out of S. Jerome's mind. I do not think that he ever again recurs to them.[1] While the Council was still going on, S. Meletius died, still out of communion with Rome.[2] One may say that he was canonized there and then. The saints vied with each other in preaching his panegyric. We still possess S. Gregory Nyssen's discourse on the occasion. The people flocked to get strips of linen which had touched his body. That body was embalmed and transported with all honour to Antioch; and five years afterwards, S. Chrysostom, preaching on his festival, tells us of the devotion which the faithful of Antioch felt towards their glorious saint.[3] Even Rome had ultimately to alter her views; and though the pope repudiated and insulted him as an Arian during his life, the Roman Church invokes him as a saint now that he is dead. His name is entered in the Roman Martyrology on the 12th of February. I think that I was justified in saying that, however much Pope Damasus might have succeeded, with the help of the imperial power, in enlarging his jurisdiction in the West, the East continued firm in her traditional belief and practice, and acknowledged no jurisdiction, but only a primacy of honour, in the occupant of the papal chair.

[1] See Note E. in the Appendix, pp. 392–395.

[2] Tillemont (xvi. 662) says, "Si tous ceux qui meurent hors de la communion de Rome, ne peuvent meriter le titre de Saints et de Confesseurs, c'estoit à lui [Baronius] à faire effacer du Martyrologe S. *Melece* et S. Flavien d'Antioche, S. Elie de Jerusalem, et S. Daniel Stylite." I have discussed more fully the question whether S. Meletius died out of communion with Rome on pp. 238–253.

[3] *Hom. in S. Melet., Opp.* ed. Ben., 1734, ii. 518–523.

LECTURE V.

THE GROWTH OF THE PAPAL POWER DURING THE SIXTY YEARS WHICH FOLLOWED THE DEATH OF DAMASUS.

IN my last lecture I tried to show you how the popes began, in the middle of the fourth century, to acquire jurisdiction outside the suburbicarian Churches. We saw that the Council of Sardica gave to them a strictly limited power of receiving appeals in the case of deposed bishops. But as the canons of Sardica were for a long while neither received nor known in the East, and were only received in certain parts of the West, the jurisdiction derived from the Sardican canons did not go very far. But then we saw how, during the pontificate of Damasus, the Emperor Gratian conferred on the pope a very large measure of jurisdiction over the bishops of the whole Western empire. This jurisdiction received from the emperor had no canonical basis, but it was felt to be a power with which the Western Churches had to reckon; because the pope, when acting in accordance with the provisions of Gratian's rescript, was able to enforce

N

his authority upon contumacious bishops by the help
of the secular mag'strates. The result of this was
to give a certain legally authoritative character to all
the official acts of the popes, and amongst those acts
to the letters[1] which they from time to time sent out
in response to the requests for advice which came to
them from the provinces. From very early times it
had been customary in the West to consult the see of
Rome as being the only Western apostolic see. There
was a similar custom in the East of consulting the
various Eastern apostolic sees. Whether in the East
or in the West, the apostolic sees were consulted,
because they were presumed to have retained in
special purity the original deposit of tradition, which
they had received from the apostles. The answers
which arrived from Rome or from other apostolic
sees were received with great respect, although it
was not supposed that they had the force of law.
Sometimes it would happen that some specially valuable letter written by an occupant of one of the
great sees, or even occasionally by some bishop of an
inferior see who might be in high repute for sanctity
and learning, would be received by some Council as
stating accurately the law or custom of the Church,
and such a letter would, by the action of the Council,

---

[1] Gratian's rescript made the pope the court of final appeal for the
bishops of the West, and the normal court of first instance for the
metropolitans of the West, but it did not define the law which he was
to administer. This omission left it free to the popes to make their
own law, and they were able to give to their decretal letters a force
equivalent to that of the canons.

become a canonically authoritative document. This
happened not infrequently in the East. For example,
the Church in the East accepted as of binding
authority what were called the canonical epistles of
S. Denys the Great of Alexandria, of S. Gregory the
wonder-worker of Neocæsarea, of S. Peter and of
S. Athanasius, both of Alexandria, of S. Basil of
Cæsarea, of S. Gregory of Nyssa, of S. Gregory of
Nazianzus, of S. Amphilochius of Iconium, of Timothy,
of Theophilus, and of S. Cyril, all of Alexandria,
and of S. Gennadius of Constantinople.[1] In the West,
although the popes must often have written letters of
advice in reply to inquiries, we do not find that any
of their letters were accepted as having legal force,
until we come to the letters of Siricius (who followed
Damasus) and his successors. No doubt Pope Stephen
had tried, in the time of S. Cyprian, to legislate for
the whole Church, by means of letters, on the subject
of the baptism of heretics ; but he failed. However, in
the time of Siricius the pope had become, by the action
of the state, a great potentate in the West, and some
of the Western provincial Churches were prepared to
accept his replies to their inquiries as having force
of law. Under these altered circumstances the popes
not unnaturally assumed a more authoritative tone.
They no longer gave mere advice, but they laid down
the law, and in some cases threatened bishops, who
should disobey, with the penalty of being cut off

---

[1] See the second canon of the Council in Trullo (Coleti, *Concilia*,
vii. 1345).

from the communion of the Roman Church. They
still professed, however, not to be making new law,[1]
but to be authoritatively declaring what was the
already existing law. But often, under cover of declaring the old law, they really made new law. For
example, old laws might belong to different categories.
Some laws would be general laws binding the whole
Church, or at any rate binding the whole West, others
would be local laws or customs received only at Rome
and in the suburbicarian region. The popes, writing
to distant provinces in Spain, Gaul, or elsewhere
might refer to local Italian customs as old laws, and
set them forth as binding on distant Churches,[2] and
thus, by the authority of their decretal epistle, make
them to become law in places where hitherto they
had had no canonical force.

But it must be observed that this legislative or
quasi-legislative action of the popes through decretal

---

[1] Compare the letter of Pope Innocent I. (A.D. 402–417) to Victricius
of Rouen (Coleti, iii. 8): " Non quo nova præcepta aliqua imperentur,
sed ea quæ per desidiam aliquorum neglecta sunt, ab omnibus obser-
vari cupiamus." Pope Innocent has copied this sentence, almost
word for word, from the letter of his predecessor Siricius to the bishops
of Africa (Coleti, ii. 1225).

[2] Compare the letter of Pope Innocent I. to Decentius of Eugubium
in which he says that the Churches throughout Italy, Gaul, Spain,
Africa, Sicily, and the adjacent islands ought to follow the customs of
the Roman Church. He proceeds to give a number of liturgical and
ritual directions, *e.g.* as to the point in the altar service, when the kiss
of peace is to be given, and the like. He gives the Roman rule, and
asserts that the Western Churches ought to conform themselves to it
(cf. Coleti, iii. 4). That was doubtless the papal view, but it was not
carried out. The traditions of Gaul, Spain, and even of North Italy,
were entirely opposed to such liturgical conformity. See Duchesne,
Origines du Culte Chrétien, chap. iii. pp. 81–99, *et passim.*

epistles was confined to the West. It was a very rare thing for any Eastern prelate to write to Rome such letters of inquiry on matters of discipline as often came from Western Churches. I do remember one such case. Alexander, Bishop of Antioch, wrote a letter of inquiry to Pope Innocent I. (*circa* 415); and Innocent sent an answer, but it never became part of the Eastern canon law. On the contrary, one very important portion of Innocent's letter, in which he laid down that the Bishop of Antioch ought to have patriarchal jurisdiction over the Bishops of Cyprus, was practically annulled, if it ever had any force, by the Ecumenical Council of Ephesus held sixteen years afterwards, which declared that, if the statement of facts contained in the petition of the bishops of Cyprus was correct, they were to remain free, and (to use the technical expression) autocephalous.[1] As may be supposed, the decision of the Council prevailed over that of the pope; although that is hardly an accurate way of stating the case, for the pope's decretal could have had no legal or canonical force in the East.

It follows, from what I have said, that the quasi-legislative authority of Rome which was exercised after the time of Damasus through the papal decretals, being an authority which was only received in the West, was part of the pope's *patriarchal* power. It was not a power belonging to his primatial position with reference to the whole Church.

---

[1] The Church of Cyprus remains autocephalous to this day.

The fact is, that as primate of the whole Church he had no jurisdiction, but only honour and influence : as state-made Patriarch of the West he had a jurisdiction derived from the emperor: in those Western provinces, where the canons of Sardica were received, he had, over and above his state-given authority, a very limited jurisdiction derived from the synodical action of the Church : and, finally, in the suburbicarian Churches he had a very full and commanding metropolitical jurisdiction derived from ancient custom—that is to say, if we go to the bottom of the matter, derived from the delegation or concession of the bishops of Central and Southern Italy, and regulated and confirmed, as time went on, by the canons of councils.

As we have seen, it was in the time of Damasus that the state made the pope Patriarch of the West, and it was in the time of Damasus' successor Siricius that the first decretal epistle having force of law anywhere outside the suburbicarian region was issued. It was addressed to Himerius, Bishop of Tarragona in Spain. That letter to Himerius was the beginning of the long line of the genuine papal decretals. In later ages, when it was believed that the popes had always from the beginning been monarchs of the Church, men must have thought it strange that the decretals should begin with Siricius. And so in the ninth century the pseudo-Isidore forged decretals, which he attributed to the earlier popes, from S. Clement of Rome, who, according to the old mistake, was supposed to be S,

Peter's immediate successor, onwards.   But I must
not be tempted into discoursing now about the forged
decretals.   If we fix our attention on the genuine
decretals, we find that Pope Siricius and his successors
were ashamed to base their asserted legislative
authority on the rescript of the Emperor Gratian;
they therefore, as I intimated in my last lecture, fell
back on their vague claim to be successors of S. Peter
in his chair; and in their decretals they began to
speak in a semi-mystical way of S. Peter living on
in them, and acting and judging and defining through
them.   Let me give a few examples.   Pope Siricius
in his first decretal to Himerius says, " We bear
the burdens of all who are heavily laden; *or rather
the blessed Apostle Peter bears them in us;* for he,
as we trust, in all things protects and defends us who
are the heirs of his government."[1]   Similarly
Xystus III., who became pope about thirty-four years
after the death of Siricius (viz. in A.D. 432), says in
one of his letters that " the blessed Peter *in his
successors* has delivered that which he received."[2]
Thus the popes of that age taught that S. Peter was in
some sense in them, his successors, bearing the burdens
of the heavily laden, and delivering in them and
through them the deposit of the faith which he had
originally received.   And this doctrine about S. Peter
living and acting in the popes, which was being put
forth by the popes, was naturally repeated by papal
legates and by other persons closely connected with

---

[1] Coleti, *Concilia,* ii. 1213.   [2] Coleti, iii. 1697.

the Roman see. Thus we find Philip, one of the papal legates at the Council of Ephesus, saying that "the most blessed Peter, the prince and head of the apostles, . . . up to the present time and always lives and judges in his successors."[1] We must certainly say that all this is new doctrine; new and therefore false; an attempt to give a religious sanction to the great position which the Roman pontiffs had acquired mainly through the legislative action of the state. It would be easy to quote further illustrations of the increasing tendency to make large and baseless claims on behalf of the Roman see, which may be found in the letters of Pope Innocent (402–417), Pope Zosimus (417–418), Pope Boniface (418–422), and their successors; but what I have said under this head is, I think, sufficient. One more point, however, ought to be noticed. Practically these popes of the early part of the fifth century did not attempt to legislate for the East, or to exercise in any specially papal way jurisdiction over it. They probably knew that their claims would be ignored or repudiated. They pressed their new theories on the West especially on those parts of the West which lay outside the suburbicarian provinces, and which had only recently been brought within their jurisdiction by the action of the State. They asserted their new claims on Gaul, and on Illyricum, and on Spain, and on Africa. Having no valid ground for this new jurisdiction of a religious

---

[1] Coleti, iii. 1153.

or ecclesiastical character, all that they could do was to refer perpetually to S. Peter, and to the rights which they inherited from him. But of course, any divinely instituted rights coming to the popes from S. Peter as primate, if they existed at all, would be universal in their range. The popes were thus forced to lay down principles which applied to both East and West, though for the present they did not urge them on the East. They were building up a Western patriarchate, but the arguments which they used, if they were sound, really pointed to a universal patriarchate—in other words, to an ecumenical papacy. As time went on, they must have felt this; and when the opportunity presented itself in the time of S. Leo, and still more in the time of S. Leo's successors,[1] the claim to ecumenical jurisdiction came openly to the front.

But how did the Western provinces accept the new patriarchal yoke which was being pressed upon them? Naturally, the way in which it was received varied according to circumstances. Apparently the patriarchal authority of Rome was received with least opposition in Eastern Illyricum, the most eastern division of the West.[2] On the other hand, it

---

[1] *E.g.* Felix III., Gelasius, Symmachus, and Hormisdas.

[2] Ecclesiastically, Eastern Illyricum belonged to the West. Even there the bishops protested, when the popes first began to receive appeals from the decisions of the local synods. In the time of Pope Innocent I. (*circa* 414) the Macedonian bishops objected to the pope rehearing the cases of Bubalius and Taurianus, who had been condemned in Macedonia: see the eighteenth epistle of Innocent in Dom Constant's collection of the Letters of the Roman pontiffs (i. 841,

met with the sturdiest rejection in Africa. The great Church of North Africa was at the height of its glory, and, one may add, of its sanctity. It had splendid traditions reaching back to the time of S. Cyprian and to the still earlier times of the second century. In the beginning of the fifth century, it was illuminated by the combined holiness and genius of S. Augustine. And S. Augustine was but one, although the greatest, among a number of saints; as, for example, to name two of them, S. Aurelius of Carthage and S. Alypius of Tagaste. The African Church had from early times been accustomed to act as one body under the leadership of the Bishop of Carthage. But the Bishop of Carthage, though leader, had no exaggerated authority. His relation to the African bishops was very different from the relation of the Bishop of Alexandria to the Egyptian bishops, and from the relation of the Bishop of Rome to the suburbicarian bishops. Everything in Africa seemed to bear on it the stamp of primitive freedom. Consequently the African bishops were not at all disposed to accept meekly the new claims which were being put forth by the popes. I might illustrate this statement by referring to the various episodes which occurred during the course of the Pelagian controversy, but for my present purpose I prefer to speak of the case of Apiarius.

842). Dom Coustant, commenting on the words of Innocent, says, "Hence we may conclude that Bubalius and Taurianus, having been judged by the Macedonians, had appealed to the apostolic see, and that the Macedonians were indignant that their judgment should be reviewed."

Apiarius was a priest of the Church of Sicca, a place situated in what was called the proconsular province, the province of which Carthage was the metropolis. He fell into certain sins—we are not told the details in regard to them—and he was deposed and excommunicated, though perhaps with some informality, in the year 418 by Urban, Bishop of Sicca, who had been a pupil of S. Augustine. Apiarius appealed from his bishop to Pope Zosimus. Probably he knew that if he appealed to the Provincial Synod, the witnesses of his crimes would be forthcoming, and his condemnation would undoubtedly be ratified. He therefore appealed[1] to distant Rome. Cardinal Baronius tells us[2] that Zosimus received the appeal, and admitted Apiarius to communion, and restored him to the exercise of his priestly functions. Apparently Apiarius, when he was in Rome, made various counter accusations against his bishop Urban, poisoning thereby the mind of Pope Zosimus. Whereupon Zosimus sent three legates, namely, Faustinus, Bishop of Potentia, a city in the March of Ancona, and two Roman priests, Philip and Asellus. These three Zosimus sent as legates to Africa. After their arrival a Council was held in the autumn at Carthage, at which the Roman legates were present. They said that they had been charged by the pope to treat with the African bishops about four points.

---

[1] The appeal must have been made before the great Council of May, 418; compare p. 195.

[2] *Annal. Eccl.*, s.a. 419, tom. v. pp. 463, 464, ed. 1658.

They asked (1) that the African bishops should be allowed to appeal to the Roman See; (2) that bishops should not go so often to the imperial court; (3) that priests and deacons, if rashly excommunicated by their bishop, should be allowed to appeal to the neighbouring bishops; (4) that Bishop Urban of Sicca should be excommunicated or even sent to Rome, if he did not amend his ways. They quoted, in support of the first point, the fifth canon of Sardica, which, as I showed in a previous lecture, granted a very limited right of appeal to Rome. But the legates did not quote it as a canon of Sardica, but as a canon of the Ecumenical Council of Nicæa. The canons of Sardica were not accepted in Africa as authoritative; and, in fact, although Gratus, Bishop of Carthage, had been there, all recollection of the true Council of Sardica seems to have completely passed away from the mind of the African Church.[1] But the Council of Nicæa was venerated in Africa as elsewhere, and its canons were received as authoritative. When the legates quoted the Sardican canon as if it were Nicene, the African bishops at Carthage

[1] At the Council of Carthage, held in the year 348, Bishop Gratus referred to the Council of Sardica by name, and recalled the provisions of the 15th (*al.* 19th) Sardican canon (Coleti, ii. 749). But the only Council of Sardica known to S. Augustine in 397, when he wrote to Eleusius (*Ep.* xliv., *Opp.* ii. 103), and in 406, when he wrote against Cresconius (*Contra Crescon.,* iii. 34, et iv. 44, *Opp.* ix. 454, 509), was the Arian Conciliabulum of Philippopolis. The reference to the Council of Sardica, in the report of the speech of Bishop Novatus, at the Council of Carthage, in May, 419 (Coleti, iii. 446), has evidently crept into the text from the margin.

must have been thoroughly puzzled. They thought
that they knew the Nicene canons well, and this
canon quoted by the legates, which allowed appeals
to Rome, was completely new to them. It was not
in the copy of the Nicene canons which Bishop Cæci-
lian of Carthage, who had been present at the Council
of Nicæa, had brought back with him to Africa ; nor
in any of the other copies, whether in Greek or Latin,
which were preserved in the archives of the Church of
Carthage.[1] However, the bishops behaved in the most
conciliatory way, and wrote to Pope Zosimus, telling
him that the canon quoted by his legates was not in
their copies of the Nicene canons, but that they would
provisionally consent to observe it until further
investigation had cleared the matter up. It is not
certain whether Pope Zosimus ever received this
letter, as he died in the latter part of December in
that year, and was succeeded by Pope Boniface. On
May 25, of the following year, 419, a general Council,
at which all the African provinces were represented,
was held at Carthage under the presidency of S.
Aurelius, the bishop of that see. Next to S. Aurelius
sat Valentinus, the Primate of Numidia. After him
Faustinus, the papal chief legate. Then followed in
due order all the African bishops who were present,
217 in number, including S. Augustine and S. Alypius.

---

[1] At the Council held in May, 419, S. Alypius, speaking of the
canons alleged by Faustinus, said, evidently with a twinkle in his
eye, "When we inspected the Greek copies of this Niceno Synod,
somehow or other, I know not why, we utterly failed to find them
there" (Coleti, iii. 445).

Last of all sat the two Roman priests, Philip and
Asellus, the junior legates of the pope. The Council
determined, in spite of the protest of the legate
Faustinus, that they would write to the bishops of
Constantinople, Alexandria, and Antioch, and ask
them to send to Carthage authenticated copies of the
Nicene canons, as preserved in the archives of their
several Churches, so that the question might be once
for all settled whether the canon alleged by Pope
Zosimus and his legates was really a genuine canon
of Nicæa or not. They also determined to write to
the new Pope Boniface, inviting him to make similar
inquiries. Moreover, they ratified the action of the
Council held the year before, when Faustinus first
arrived in Africa; and determined that provisionally
they would act upon the canons alleged by the pope;
that, if on inquiry it should clearly appear that those
canons were really Nicene, they would accept them
absolutely, and act upon them in the future; but
that, if it should appear that the pope had made some
mistake, a Council should be convoked which should
decide what was to be done. As for Apiarius, he
besought the Council to grant forgiveness to him, and
then the legate Faustinus interceded for him, and
so it was determined that he should be restored to
communion and to the exercise of his priestly
ministry, but that he should be required to remove
out of the diocese of Sicca, where he had given much
scandal. The Council could not help observing that,
even if the canons alleged by the legates were really

Nicene and consequently binding in Africa, they gave
no authority to the pope to summon bishops to Rome,
nor to restore priests to communion in Rome when
they had been excommunicated in their own diocese
or province. Zosimus, while quoting the canons of
Sardica to the Africans, had in no way observed
them himself. The Council therefore, in its letter to
Pope Boniface, writes as follows: "To the most
blessed lord and honourable brother Boniface; . . ."
then, after a summary of what had taken place, they
continue, " We took care also to intimate last year by
our letter to the same Zosimus, bishop of venerable
memory, that we would for a short time permit these
rules to be observed without any injury to him, until
we had investigated the statutes of the Nicene
Council. And now we request of your Holiness to
cause us to keep whatever was really ordained by
the Fathers at Nicæa, and also to take care that
those rules, which are written in the instructions
brought by the legates, be really carried out by you
in Italy;" and then they quote the words of the
Sardican canons alleged by the legates. They go on
to say, "These rules we have at all events inserted
in the acts of our Council until the arrival of the
genuine copies of the Nicene Synod. And should
they be there contained, . . . and should they also
be observed strictly by you in Italy, we request that
we should by no means be compelled to endure such
treatment as we are unwilling to mention, or should
suffer what is unbearable." In other words, the

Council means to say, "If your alleged canons are really Nicene we will keep them, but we must beg that they be kept strictly by you also. There must be no pretence of undoing our African sentences in Rome, as Zosimus professed to restore Apiarius; and there must be no claim to summon our bishops to Rome, as was threatened by Zosimus in regard to our brother Urban, Bishop of Sicca.[1] Such modes of action are unmentionable and unbearable." Then remembering that Zosimus was now dead, and that Boniface was pope, they continue, "But we trust, by the mercy of our Lord God, that while *your Holiness* presides over the Roman Church, we shall not have to endure such arrogance as that (non sumus jam istum typhum passuri); and that a course of proceeding shall be maintained towards us such as ought to be observed, even without our having to speak about it."[2] Such was the style in which this great Council of more than two hundred bishops, under the guidance of such glorious saints as S. Augustine, S. Aurelius, and S. Alypius, thought that it was right and proper for them to address the pope. I leave you to consider whether any Roman Catholic synod would think of writing such a letter now. On the principles of the Vatican Council, they could not do it. On our Anglican principles, or rather on our Catholic prin-

---

[1] The African fathers had quoted in their letter at full length the Sardican canons, which require that, in the case of an appeal to Rome, the rehearing shall take place, not at Rome, but in the country where the cause began.

[2] The whole letter is given by Coleti (iii. 528–530).

ciples, it would be the most natural thing in the world. How does this come about? It comes about, because S. Augustine and the African saints thought of the pope substantially as we should have thought of him, if, with our present views, we had lived in the fifth century.[1] But the modern Roman Catholics, who accept the Vatican Council, think of him in a totally different way. We are quite content to find ourselves, in such a matter, on S. Augustine's side.

Before we go on with the story, we ought to notice that the pope did not apparently venture to base his claims to receive appeals on any inherent right of his see derived from S. Peter. It was very well to do that when writing to simple-minded bishops in Illyria or Spain, but when writing to Africa, he knew that he was dealing with bishops, some of whom were the most learned and able theologians then alive. To use Petrine arguments of the Roman sort when in controversy with them, would be to run the risk of having the whole fallacy of those arguments exposed with all the force and persuasiveness of such a pen as S. Augustine's. Pope Zosimus no doubt felt that discretion was the better part of valour, and therefore humbly based his claim on the grant of the Church, as expressed in the canons which he alleged, and which he wrongly called Nicene. This highly discreet method of proceeding ought to be remem-

---

[1] Of course the extravagant papalism of later times, and especially the decrees of the Vatican Council, have forced us into a position into which S. Augustine was not forced.

bered. It is very characteristic. However, though in one sense the pope may have acted discreetly, his whole proceeding was so utterly un-Catholic, that it called forth from the African Church a well-deserved rebuke. The pope's action, in their view, was "intolerable," "unmentionable," and the outcome of "arrogance;" and they do not hesitate to use these very plain expressions when reviewing the whole matter in a letter to Zosimus' successor. There is, of course, in all this no cause for surprise. It is what one would expect from such great saints.

But to return to our story. Towards the end of the year 419, replies from S. Atticus, Bishop of Constantinople, and from S. Cyril, Bishop of Alexandria, arrived in Carthage. These two prelates sent correct copies of the Nicene canons, which were found to tally with the copies already at Carthage. Naturally the Sardican canons alleged by Rome were not among them. A Council might have been convened at once to put an end to the provisional acceptance of the Sardican system of appeals. But apparently the African Church preferred to wait until a convenient opportunity for reopening the matter occurred. Nothing is more remarkable throughout this history than the wisdom and moderation of the great men who at that time guided the African Church. The fitting opportunity did not in their judgment present itself until five, or, as some say, seven years had passed. During that interval or parenthesis appeals to Rome from Africa were allowed in the case of bishops, in accordance with the agreement. The matter was reopened in consequence of fresh scandals arising in connection with Apiarius. Since his restoration to communion he had been living at Tabraca, in the proconsular province. Here he acted in such a way that the inhabitants were obliged to accuse him of enormous crimes, and he was cut off from communion. Instead of attempting to justify himself, he went off to Rome, pretending that he had appealed to the pope, although he certainly never did appeal in any formal way. Of course the African bishops would never have allowed a mere priest to appeal to Rome, for such an appeal was not allowed even by the canons of Sardica. Appeals to Rome by priests were unknown in Africa until Apiarius, in his previous trouble, had first led the way. The African Church had promptly taken measures to prevent the repetition of such an irregular proceeding[1] by passing a canon in the great Council of May, 418, which concluded as follows: "Whoever appeals to a court on the other side of the sea [*i.c.* to Rome], may not again be received into communion by any one in Africa."[2] It is there-

---

[1] Compare Hefele, ii. 463, Eng. trans.

[2] Hefele's *Councils*, Eng. trans., ii. 461; see also p. 463. It is worth while quoting the extraordinary explanation of this canon, given by Father Bottalla, S.J., a professor in S. Beuno's College, North Wales. He says (*Supreme Authority of the Pope*, p. 151), "The African Synod, in the above-mentioned canon, forbade nothing but the formal and judicial appeal of the inferior clergy to the see of Rome; it did not, and it could not, forbid their private recourse to the supreme pastor of the Church; and if, under any exceptional

fore evident that on this second occasion Apiarius
did not appeal in any formal way. Such a formal
act would not have been allowed. He simply slunk
off to Rome, and besought the pope to admit him to
communion. By this time Boniface was dead, and
Celestine had succeeded him. Celestine, without any
communication with Africa, restored him to communion. It seems most extraordinary that pope after
pope should have acted in this scandalous manner.
Apparently, in order to assert the papal jurisdiction
over Africa, the popes were willing to break the most
fundamental canons of the Church, and to run the
risk of presenting the Roman Church to the eyes of
the world as an accomplice in foul and enormous
crimes. Pope Celestine went on to add insult to
injury.—He wrote to the African Church expressing
his joy at finding Apiarius innocent, although he had
never had any opportunity of hearing what the accusers of that wicked priest had to say; and then,
to make things worse, he sent him back to Africa
to be readmitted to communion, and with him he
sent, as legate, that same Bishop Faustinus who had
given such just cause of umbrage to the African
Church on the previous occasion. When Faustinus

circumstances, the pope saw fit, he might suspend the effect of the
general canon, and enable the condemned priest or deacon to lay a
formal and judicial appeal before his court." Assuredly, if the Fathers
of the African Church had accepted all this, they would never have
ventured to meddle with a matter so completely beyond their control.
In their letter to Celestine they expressly call on the pope to reject
these private appeals to his see, which they describe as "improba
refugia," a very proper title for such scandalous transactions.

arrived, a general Council of all Africa was convoked;[1] and the bishops, under the presidency of S. Aurelius of Carthage, wrote an admirable letter to Celestine. It was addressed "to the most beloved lord and honourable brother Celestine." They begin by expressing the wish that, as Celestine had written to them about Apiarius with joy, so they could make their reply concerning him with similar joy. Then the gladness on both sides would be better founded, and the pope's satisfaction in regard to Apiarius would appear less hasty and precipitate. Then they proceed as follows, and I will give their exact words. They say, "When our holy brother and fellow-bishop Faustinus arrived, we assembled a Council; and we believed that he had been sent with that man, in order that as by his help Apiarius had formerly been restored to the priesthood, so now by his exertions the same Apiarius might be cleared of the very great crimes charged against him by the people of Tabraca. But the course of examination in our Council brought to light such great and monstrous crimes, as to overbear Faustinus, who acted rather as an advocate than as a judge, and who manifested rather the zeal of a lawyer engaged for the defence than the impartiality of an umpire. For first he vehemently opposed the whole assembly, inflicting on us many affronts under pretence of asserting the privileges of the Church of Rome, requiring that we should

---

[1] According to Hefele in A.D. 424; according to Tillemont in A.D. 426.

receive Apiarius back into communion, because your Holiness, believing him to have appealed, though he was unable to prove that he had appealed, had restored him to communion. But to act in such a way was quite unlawful, as you will also better see by reading the acts of our synod. After a most laborious inquiry carried on for three days, during which, in the greatest affliction, we investigated the various charges against him, God the righteous Judge, strong and patient, put a complete stop to the obstacles raised by our brother-bishop Faustinus and to the evasions of Apiarius himself, by which he was trying to conceal his execrably shameful acts. For his foul and disgusting obstinacy was overcome, by which he endeavoured to cover up, through an impudent denial, all this dirty mire; for our God put pressure upon his conscience, and published even to the eyes of men the secret things which He was already condemning in that man's heart, a very sty of wickedness; so that, notwithstanding his crafty denial, Apiarius suddenly burst forth into a confession of all the crimes with which he was charged, and of his own accord convicted himself of every kind of incredible infamy; and thus he changed to groans even the hope we had entertained, believing and desiring that he might be cleared from such shameful blots; except indeed that he mitigated by one consolation this our sorrow, in that he released us from the labour of a longer inquiry, and by confession had applied some sort of remedy to his own wounds, though, sir and brother (domine frater), it was done unwillingly and with a struggling conscience. Premising, therefore, our due regards to you,[1] we earnestly beg of you, that for the future you do not easily admit to a hearing persons coming to Rome from Africa, nor choose to receive to your communion those who have been excommunicated by us; because your reverence will readily perceive that this has also been decreed by the Nicene Council. For, although this seems to be there forbidden in respect of the inferior clergy or the laity, *how much more did the Council will this to be observed in the case of bishops*, lest those who have been suspended from communion in their own province might seem to be restored to communion hastily or precipitately or in some undue way by your Holiness.[2] Let your holiness reject, as is worthy of you, that bad taking shelter with you of priests and of the clergy of lower degree, *both because by no ordinance of the fathers has this right been with-drawn from the African Church, and the Nicene decrees have most plainly committed the inferior clergy and the bishops themselves to their metro-politans.*[3] For they have ordained with great pru-

---

[1] "Præfato itaque debitæ salutationis officio."

[2] "Vel festinato vel præpropere vel indebite." The pope had no right to receive to his communion African Christians who had been excommunicated by the African Church, until they had been restored by their own Church. If he did so, he would be acting hastily and precipitately and in an undue way. The great principle on which the Council insists, is "that all matters shall be terminated in the places where they arise." Mr. Rivington (*Dependence*, pp. 226, 227) has failed to realize this.

[3] It will hardly be believed that Father Bottalla, speaking of this

dence and justice that *all matters shall be terminated in the places where they arise;* and they did not think that the grace of the Holy Spirit would be wanting to any province, by which grace the bishops of Christ would discern with prudence and maintain with constancy whatever was equitable; especially since any party, who thinks himself wronged by a judgment, may appeal to the synod of his province, or even to a general Council [of all Africa]; *unless it be imagined by any one that our God can inspire a single individual with justice, and refuse it to an innumerable multitude of bishops assembled in council.*" I must break off here to point out how faithfully the great African Church had guarded the tradition which she possessed nearly two hundred years before, in the time of S. Cyprian, who, you will remember, implied that no Christian would

letter (*Supreme Authority of the Pope*, p. 142), says that the African fathers "made no objection to appeals of bishops to the Roman pontiff, but only to those of the inferior clergy." He goes on to say (p. 143), "The African Church never denied the right of the pope to receive appeals in the case of bishops and even of priests. Such a denial was impossible, since that Church had always looked upon the Roman bishop, as not only its patriarch, but also the supreme pastor of the universal Church." Father Bottalla's argument may be retorted upon himself. As the African Church clearly did deny the right of the pope to receive appeals in the case of bishops and also of priests, it follows, on Father Bottalla's principles, that that Church did not look on the pope either as its patriarch or as "the supreme pastor of the universal Church." It is fair to add that all Roman Catholic divines are not like Father Bottalla. Tillemont (xiii. 862-866, and 1031-1039) and others, candidly admit what ought never to have been denied. The Council of Carthage, under S. Aurelius, was carrying on the old principle laid down by S. Cyprian (see p. 57).

be likely to think that the authority of the bishops in Africa was inferior to the authority of the pope except some few "desperate and abandoned men." I now continue my quotation from the letter of the Council of Carthage to Pope Celestine. They go on to say, "How shall we be able to trust a sentence passed beyond the sea, since it will not be possible to send thither the necessary witnesses, whether on account of the weakness of sex, or of advanced age, or through any other impediment?[1] For that any legates *a latere* should be sent by your holiness, we can find ordained by no synod of the fathers." Then they go on to say that the Sardican canon, quoted by Faustinus, is not a genuine Nicene canon, as was made apparent by the authentic copies of the canons of Nicæa, which they had received from Alexandria and Constantinople. Finally, they conclude their letter thus. They say, "Moreover, refrain from sending any of your clergy to execute your orders, refrain from granting this, *lest it should seem that we are intro-*

---

[1] The whole of this reasoning is just as valid for the case of bishops as for the case of the inferior clergy. It goes to prove that "*all matters*" should "be terminated in the places where they arise." There is a passage in S. Augustine's forty-third (*al.* 162nd) letter, addressed to Glorius and others (*Opp.* ed. Ben., ii. 91), which is sometimes quoted as if it implied that African bishops could appeal to Rome from the sentences of the regular ecclesiastical tribunals in Africa, but that priests and deacons could not so appeal. Such a view proceeds from a complete misunderstanding of the passage and of the circumstances connected with the origin of the Donatist schism, to which S. Augustine is referring. It would take too long to deal with the matter in a note. The reader may be referred to Archbishop De Marca, *de Concord. Sac. et. Imp.*, lib. vii. cap. xvi. §§ vi.-ix., coll. 1053-1056, ed. Böhmer, 1708; and to Tillemont, vi. 15, 16.

*ducing the smoky arrogance of the world into the
Church of Christ,* which sets before those who desire
to see God the light of simplicity and the splendour
of humility. For now that the miserable Apiarius
has been removed out of the Church of Christ for
his horrible crimes, we feel confident respecting our
brother Faustinus, that, through the uprightness and
moderation of your Holiness, the charity of the
brethren will by no means have to endure him any
longer in Africa. Sir and brother, may our Lord
long preserve your Holiness to pray for us."[1]

Such was the celebrated letter[2] of the Church of
North Africa to Pope Celestine. I cannot imagine a
more complete repudiation of the papal idea. That
idea involves the principle that *jure divino* every
member of the Church, whether clerical or lay, has
an inherent right to have "recourse to the pope's
judgment in all causes which appertain to the
jurisdiction of the Church." The African fathers
absolutely deny that right. Because if they had
believed in it, they must have safeguarded it. No

---

[1] Coleti, iii. 532–534.

[2] Bossuet (*Def. decl. cler. Gall.* xi. 14, *Œuvres,* xxxiii. 334, ed.
1818) calls this letter "nobilem illam epistolam." The Ultramontane
Lupus naturally calls it " infelicissimam, et scatentem erroribus," and
the synod which wrote it he describes as "erraticam, deviam ac
prævaricatoriam." The unfortunate Lupus, with his Ultramontane
ideas, continually finds himself completely out of sympathy with the
great saints of the fourth and fifth centuries. They and he lived in
two different worlds of thought. They in all the splendour and freedom
of the Catholic faith, he in the prison-house of Ultramontanism.
Bossuet well describes his pettifogging criticisms on the African
Fathers who wrote this letter, as "inepta, ne dicam impia " (p. 337).

Christian man would pass over and ignore a matter of divine revelation. No assembly of Christian subjects could venture to dictate to their divinely appointed sovereign, that he should refrain from using one of his divinely given prerogatives. Ultramontane writers ask of us impossibilities when they ask us to believe that. Let them say, if they like, that the African Church was wrong, heretical in fact, in regard to that matter which, in the opinion of De Maistre, is the "necessary, only, and exclusive foundation of Christianity;" but, as honourable men, let them refrain from pretending that the Church of North Africa, in the time of S. Augustine, believed in the principles laid down by the Vatican Council. Such a pretence is an impertinence and an act of folly, which must alienate every person of good sense and Christian simplicity who is cognisant of it. Let the Church of S. Augustine, S. Aurelius, and S. Alypius be branded as heretical, if the Ultramontanes choose to have it so; we for our part are quite willing to stand side by side with those great saints, and to share their condemnation. There is the possibility, some may think the probability, that at the awful tribunal of our Lord hereafter the note of heresy may be otherwise assigned.

It is hardly worth while to refer to the absurd cavil which the Romanists[1] make, when they set forth, as if it overthrew the whole argument which arises out of the synodical letter which has been so

---

[1] *E.g.* Father Bottalla, *loc. cit.*

largely quoted, the fact that Anthony, Bishop of
Fussala, appealed in A.D. 421 (or 422) to Pope Boniface from the decision of a Council in Numidia, which
had passed sentence on him; and that at a later stage
S. Augustine wrote to Pope Celestine (Boniface
having died on the 4th of September, 422), imploring
him not to reinstate Anthony in the see of Fussala,
thereby acknowledging his right to do so.[1] Will it be
believed that the whole of this transaction happened
during that interval of five or seven years when the
African Church, in pursuance of its temporary compact,

---

[1] Cf. S. Aug. *Ep.* ccix., *Opp.* ed. Ben., ii. 777–780. It appears from
this letter that Anthony argued that he ought either to have been
deprived of the episcopate altogether, or to have been left in possession
of his see of Fussala. His contention was that a bishop could not be
punished with a minor penalty. In his reply to this argument,
S. Augustine, writing to the pope, naturally looks about for precedents
of minor penalties being inflicted on bishops in sentences, which had
been sanctioned by the see of Rome. He says, " There exist examples,
in cases in which the apostolic see either pronounced judgment or
ratified the judgment of others, in which bishops for certain faults
have neither been deprived of the honour of the episcopate, nor been
left altogether unpunished. I will not search out cases very remote
from our times, but I will mention recent cases." Then he mentions
three cases of bishops, who had been punished recently with minor
penalties. All the cases had arisen in the African province of Mau-
ritania Cæsariensis. As Tillemont (xiii. 1036) suggests, they may
all have belonged to the period between 418 and 424 (or 426), during
which the African Church allowed appeals to Rome. In some of these
cases Rome may have ratified the African sentence ; in others Rome
may have softened a more stringent sentence, and may have appointed
a minor penalty. As for the " cases very remote from our times,"
which S. Augustine declines to search out, they may have been cases
which arose in the suburbicarian region, in which the pope was
metropolitan, or in Eastern Illyricum, where appeals to Rome were
allowed. The explicit statements of the Council of Carthage cannot be overthrown by doubtful hypotheses concerning precedents of
which we know nothing.

allowed bishops to appeal to Rome ? The argument deducible from S. Augustine's action in this matter falls entirely to the ground, and ought never to have been put forward. But there is one point connected with this case of Anthony of Fussala which it may be well to notice. When Pope Boniface sent messengers into Africa with letters ordering that Anthony should be reinstated in his see, if he had made a true statement of his case to the pope, the people of Fussala were threatened with coercion by the secular arm, and they were told that soldiers would be sent to Fussala to force them to obey the sentence of the apostolic see. Here we see the effects of Gratian's rescript. The decisions of the pope in such a case, though they had no canonical force in Africa except under the temporary compact, had complete legal validity, and they could be enforced by the whole power of the Roman empire. No wonder that in places where the bishops did not rise to the height of heroic sanctity which characterized S. Augustine and some of his African brethren, the local Churches gave way to the papal pretensions, and accepted law and justice from the pope's mouth. There is nothing more absolutely certain in the history of the Church than that the papal *jurisdiction*[1] outside the suburbicarian pro-

---

[1] It may be well to call attention to the fact that I am dealing in the text with papal *jurisdiction*. The primacy of honour and influence enjoyed by the Roman Church, as an apostolic Church planted in the metropolis of the civilized world, can be traced back to sub-apostolic times.

vinces mainly arose out of the legislation of the state. One may truly say that Erastianism begat it, and forgery developed it. I except, of course, the very restricted jurisdiction given at Sardica by canons which were at first only received in a small part of the Western Church, and which were never received in the East as applicable to the East.

Let us now pass from Africa to Gaul, and inquire how the new papal claims were treated there. I might draw your attention to the case of Proculus, Bishop of Marseilles, a man of saintly life, who was treated in a very unbecoming manner by Pope Zosimus. That pope ventured to summon Proculus to Rome, but to this summons Proculus paid no attention; and Zosimus took steps to deprive him of his see, no doubt trusting to the aid of the civil power to secure that these uncanonical acts, which constituted an invasion of the jurisdiction of the provinces of Gaul, should practically take effect. But the death of Zosimus put an end to the whole affair.

I prefer, however, to dwell on the case of S. Hilary of Arles, because his righteous resistance to the arbitrary interference of Pope S. Leo, though it con-stitutes an additional reason for honouring his holy memory, was nevertheless the occasion of the issuing of another imperial rescript, which enlarged the papal power, and did much to rivet its chains on the Churches of the Western empire. S. Hilary was Metropolitan of Arles, a see which appears to have enjoyed, in the fifth century, a certain pre-eminence among the metropolitan sees of Gaul. He was a great friend of S. German of Auxerre, a saint to whom our own island is so greatly indebted, in that he was God's instrument for putting down Pelagianism in the British Church. In the year 444 S. Hilary was visiting S. German at Auxerre. While he was there, various illustrious persons and others came to him and to S. German, bringing complaints against Chelidonius, Bishop of Besançon. I am bound to say that the complaints would not strike us, in the nineteenth century, as anything very serious. But S. Hilary and S. German would, of course, look at them according to the ideas of the fifth century, and according to the actual discipline of the Church at that time. It appears that Chelidonius had, as a layman, married a widow; and the canons ordered that such a person should never be consecrated to the episcopate, even after his wife's death. A rule of that kind had been formulated at the Council of Valence, in the year 374,[1] and it appears also in the decretal epistle of Pope Siricius to Himerius of Tarragona.[2] Moreover, it was thoroughly accepted by S. Leo, and by the whole Western Church of that age. It was a sort of extension of S. Paul's rule, that a man who had been the husband of more than one wife was not a proper person to be ordained.[3] Chelidonius had also, before his ordination, held some judicial office, in the fulfilment of which he had been obliged to condemn various people to death;

---

[1] Coleti, ii. 1067.   [2] Ib., ii. 1217.   [3] 1 Tim. iii. 2, 12.

and according to the ecclesiastical law this fact disqualified him for the episcopate. There was no question that if the allegations were well-founded, then, according to the canons of the Church in that age, Chelidonius ought to be deposed. Accordingly a Council was summoned to meet at Besançon, at which both S. Hilary and S. German were present, and S. Hilary presided. The Council determined that the facts were proved, and that Chelidonius ought to resign his office. This he apparently refused to do, and consequently the Council proceeded to depose and excommunicate him, as a rebel against the authority of the Church.[1] Thereupon Chelidonius went to Rome, and complained that he had been unjustly condemned. Tillemont says that Pope S. Leo, apparently without any investigation, admitted Chelidonius at once to communion. Herein, as Tillemont points out, S. Leo seems to have followed the example of his predecessors, Zosimus and Celestine, who, without proper inquiry, admitted the miserable Apiarius to communion when he took refuge with them. The Roman Church seems to have been so possessed with the desire of domination, that it thought nothing of overthrowing the fundamental rules on which the discipline and unity of the Church rest.[2] When S. Hilary heard what had

---

[1] After Chelidonius' deposition Importunus was consecrated to fill the vacant see (see Tillemont, xv. 85).

[2] I think that the words used in the text are a not unfair description of the general spirit of the Roman Church, from the time of Damasus onwards; but I am not prepared to say that, in his admis-

happened at Rome, he started off on foot in the middle of winter, and, crossing the Alps, he arrived, still on foot, in the eternal city. He visited first the tombs of the two great apostles and the relics of the martyrs, and then he went to pay his respects to the pope. He begged him, very deferentially, to see that the Church's rule was not broken by the admission of persons to communion in Rome who had been formally excommunicated in Gaul. S. Hilary in no way proposed to accept S. Leo as judge in this matter. The pope had no ground for claiming such a position. All that S. Hilary wished to do was to state clearly the facts of the case, and to beg the pope to maintain in Rome the discipline of the Church.[1] S. Hilary had a great deal to put up with

sion of Chelidonius to communion, when that excommunicated bishop arrived in Rome, S. Leo was actuated by any wrong motive. In all probability he was firmly persuaded that he had a right to receive an appeal from the decision of a Gallican synod, and to rehear the case in Rome; and he may also have supposed that the effect of the sentence of the court below was suspended until the appeal had been heard. Holding these ideas, he would seem to himself to be acting rightly when he admitted Chelidonius to communion, although, according to the earlier discipline of the Church, which had never been canonically altered, his action cannot be justified. The primitive discipline is admirably illustrated by an interesting episode in the history of the Roman Church. When the heretic Marcion, who had been excommunicated by his father, the Bishop of Sinope in Pontus, arrived in Rome about the year 140, and begged to be admitted to communion, the rulers of the Roman Church declared that they were unable to act in the matter contrary to the decision of Marcion's venerated father (Cf. S. Epiph., *Panar.*, hær. xlii.).

[1] It seems evident that the canons of Sardica were not received as binding in Gaul in the time of S. Hilary. If the limited appeal to Rome, allowed by the Council of Sardica, had been accepted by the

during his sojourn in the city. His biographer, S. Honoratus of Marseilles, tells us that he in no way feared those who threatened him; that he overcame those who disputed with him; that he did not yield to the powerful; that, even though he was in danger of his life, he would in no way admit to his communion a man whom he, in conjunction with such great men as S. German of Auxerre and the other Gallican bishops, had condemned.[1] While he was in Rome he attended a synod of bishops, at which Chelidonius also was present, and, apparently, he shocked the delicate Roman ears by the plainness of speech which he used in asserting the independence of the Church in Gaul.[2] He would not plead his cause before S. Leo, who, as S. Hilary rightly felt, had no jurisdiction in the matter. To the Roman mind this was insolence, and accordingly S. Hilary was actually put under arrest. As usual, the Church of Rome, in order to gain its point, fell

---

Gallican Church, S. Hilary could never have told S. Leo "se ad officia non ad causam venisse" (*Vit. Hilar. Arel.*, cap. xvii.). He would have had to allow that Chelidonius had a right to appeal, though he might have insisted that the appeal should be heard in Gaul, and not in Rome.

[1] See S. Honoratus' *Vita S. Hilarii Arelatensis,* in Quesnel's edition of S. Leo's works, ed. 1700, i. 369.

[2] S. Leo (*Ep.* x. cap. iii., *Opp.* ed. Baller.), speaking of S. Hilary's conduct at this synod, says that he uttered things "which no layman would have dared to say, and to which none of the bishops would listen" (quæ nullus laicorum dicere, nullus sacerdotum posset audiro). In the preceding chapter of his letter, S. Leo had said that S. Hilary "would not suffer himself to be subject to the blessed Apostle Peter" (ut se beato Apostolo Petro non patiatur esse subjectum).

back on the help of the civil power.   However, when things had come to that pass, S. Hilary felt that it was time for him to return to Gaul.   He therefore slipped away from his guards, and got back to Arles in the middle of February.   S. Leo then acquitted Chelidonius, and issued an order that he should be re-established in his bishopric, on the ground that there was no proof that he had ever married a widow.   Chelidonius was apparently re-established in his bishopric by the strong arm of the state. But S. Leo went further in the matter.   He seems to have listened to all the tittle-tattle brought to his ears by those who felt aggrieved in any way by S. Hilary's saintly severity and apostolic spirit of discipline, and who were encouraged by what had happened to send their complaints to Rome.   Tillemont and Fleury assert that S. Leo actually separated S. Hilary from his communion.[1]   Whether this be so

---

[1] See Tillemont xv. 80, 89; and Fleury, *Hist. Eccl.*, l. xxvii. § 5 (tom. vi. p. 269, ed. 1722).   It is quite certain that S. Hilary did not communicate with S. Leo during the whole time that he was in Rome, for S. Leo (*Ep.* x. cap. vii.) says of him that "he thought it right to withdraw himself by a shameful flight (turpi fuga), *having no share in the apostolic communion, of which he did not deserve to partake;* God, as we believe, bringing this about, Who, in a way unexpected by us, both drew him to our judgment seat, and also brought to pass his secret departure in the midst of the investigation, *to prevent his sharing in our communion.*"   It seems to me that S. Leo implies that during the process of the investigation S. Hilary could not communicate with the Roman Church, but that he probably would have done so if he had remained to the end.   It is to me uncertain whether S. Hilary's inability to communicate with S. Leo during the course of the investigation was the result of S. Leo's action, or of S. Hilary's own unwillingness.   If the first view is correct, then S.

or not, the pope certainly professed to deprive him
of his metropolitical authority, and he made various
other arrangements in regard to the Churches of
Gaul which could not be justified by the canons, and
which, as Tillemont observes, were not carried out.[1]

It seems to have been because S. Leo feared that
the bishops of Gaul would not pay much attention to
his revolutionary decrees, that he applied again to the
civil power; that so, however much his orders might

Hilary must have been authoritatively suspended from communion,
and so far Tillemont and Fleury would be justified. If the second
view is correct, we have the spectacle of a great saint going to Rome
and staying there for some time, but refusing to communicate with
the pope. S. Hilary would hardly have acted in that way if he had
held the Vatican doctrine of the papacy. Whichever way the question
is decided, my argument remains unaffected. S. Hilary's disciple
and biographer, S. Honoratus, tells us that while in Rome S. Hilary
was threatened, was in peril of his life, and was put under arrest
(*Vita S. Hilar. Arelat.*, cap. xvii.). The knowledge of these facts
may mitigate our view of the "*shamefulness*" of his flight. Even
Ultramontane historians have been compelled to acknowledge that
S. Leo's conduct towards S. Hilary was, to say the least, unfortunate.
Thus Cardinal Baronius, speaking of an angry letter written by S.
Leo's successor, Pope Hilary, against another great light of the
Church of Gaul, S. Mamertus of Vienne, says, "There is no cause
for wonder that the Roman pontiff, Hilary, should have so vehemently attacked Mamertus, a man, as events proved, illustrious
by his sanctity; for in these litigious cases it is very easy for any
one to be deceived. Something very similar happened to S. Leo,
who inveighed most bitterly against S. Hilary for very much the
same reason. Who does not know that it often happens that the
ears of pontiffs are filled with false accusations, by which they are
deceived? and, when they imagine that they are acting in accordance
with justice, they are really harassing the innocent" (Baron., *Annal.
Eccl.* s.a. 464).

¹ Tillemont, xv. 80, 81, 85, 86; compare the remarks of Stephan.
Baluzius in De Marca's *De Concord. Sac. et Imp.*, v. xxxiii., coll. 631-
636, ed Böhmer, 1708.

be lacking in canonical validity, they might, at any
rate, be clothed with all the majesty of the imperial
authority. The Emperor Valentinian III. was then
ruling in the West. He was a feeble and con-
temptible prince, stained with every vice, who
murdered with his own hands Aetius, the only great
man in his service. It was to this Valentinian that
S. Leo applied for help in his contest with S. Hilary.
The emperor did all that S. Leo wished, and addressed
a rescript, in the year 445, to that same Patrician
Aetius whom he afterwards killed. In this rescript
the emperor says, among other things, that "the
peace of the Churches will then only be preserved,
when the whole body of them acknowledge their
ruler. Hitherto this has been inviolably observed;
but now Hilary of Arles, as we have learnt from the
faithful report of the venerable man, Leo, the Roman
pope, has, with contumacious daring, attempted certain unlawful things, and thus an abominable confusion has invaded the Churches north of the Alps."
Towards the end of the rescript the emperor adds,
"We decree, by a perpetual edict, that nothing shall
be attempted contrary to ancient custom, either by
the Gallican bishops or by the bishops of other
provinces, without the authority of the venerable
man, the pope of the eternal city; but whatever the
authority of the apostolic see has sanctioned or shall
sanction, let that be held by them and by all for a
law; so that if any of the bishops shall neglect, when
summoned, to come to the tribunal of the Roman

prelate, let him be forced to come by the civil governor of the province."[1] Thus did the decrepit autocracy of the dying empire plant in the home of freedom, the Church of God, the hateful likeness of itself. This rescript of Valentinian goes far beyond the rescript of Gratian. It makes the pope's word law, and it makes the bishops his humble servants.[2] It is grievous to think that so noble a man as S. Leo really was, should have stained his history by his share in this degrading act of legislation. The Roman Catholic Tillemont justly observes, that those who have any love for the liberty of the Church, and any knowledge of her discipline, will agree that this rescript will redound through all ages as little to the honour of Leo, whom it praises, as it does to the hurt of Hilary, whom it condemns.[3] Succeeding popes knew well how to use such a law in their own interest.

In the meanwhile, the blessed Hilary[4] spent the

---

[1] *Constitutio* Valentiniani III. Augusti, *inter Leoninas Ep.* xi., *Opp.* S. Leon., ed. Baller.

[2] The subsequent history shows what an effect it had in Gaul. The Gallican bishops were much more compliant with the papal claims, after the promulgation of Valentinian's constitution, than they had been previously.

[3] Tillemont, xv. 83, 84.

[4] When S. Hilary got home to Arles, he showed the Christian meekness of his spirit by sending first the Priest Ravennius, and afterwards the Bishops Nectarius and Constantius, to pacify S. Leo's wrath. However, he would not yield on the main point; and his friend Auxiliaris, the Prefect of Rome, who had acted as host to the Bishops Nectarius and Constantius, urged him to use "a certain soft-ness" (*quâdam teneritudine*) in his messages, which would conciliate "the ears of the Romans" (*aures Romanorum*). Tillemont (xv. 85), after quoting this letter of Auxiliaris, observes that we are not told

four remaining years of his saintly life working
out his own salvation · and promoting that of his
people. He gave himself to prayer and preaching,
and the practice of good works; he redoubled his
austerities; he helped the poor of his diocese with
gifts, and consoled them by his sympathy.[1] At
length he died, and, if Tillemont is right, he was at
his death still out of communion with Rome. His
body was carried to S. Stephen's Church, the people
crying out with one accord, "This day has for ever
brought to an end the reproaches of an unjust
accusation."[2]　S. Honoratus, who was present, tells
us that the saint's remains were nearly torn to pieces
by the crowds who pressed around to touch them.

Thus was gathered into the joys of Paradise
one more of the long line of saints who have
withstood the usurpations of the Roman pontiffs,
and who, in many cases, have died outside their
communion. One is thankful to know that after
S. Hilary's death, S. Leo spoke of him[3] as a man
"of holy memory;"[4] and his commemoration occurs

---

that S. Hilary followed the prefect's advice, or that he made any
further effort to appease S. Leo.

　[1] Tillemont, xv. 89.

　[2] "Hæc dies querelas injustæ imputationis perpetuo resecavit"
(*Vit. S. Hilar. Arel., ap. Opp. S. Leon.,* ed. Quesnel, 1700, i. 371).

　[3] *Ep.* xl. *ad Episcopos per Arelatensem Galliæ provinciam constitutos
Opp. S. Leon.,* ed. Baller.

　[4] These words of S. Leo would not of themselves prove that S.
Hilary died in the Roman communion. In a letter to Bishop Pascha-
sinus (*Ep.* lxxxviii. cap. iv., ed. Baller.), and also in a letter to the
Emperor Marcian (*Ep.* cxxi. cap. ii.), S. Leo calls Theophilus of
Alexandria a man "of holy memory." Now, Theophilus had been

on the 5th of May in the Roman martyrology. It is well for the Church in all ages to meditate on the example of such saints, and to celebrate their names with honour from generation to generation.

It will not be possible for me in these lectures to trace the further development of the papal power, as it shows itself in the authentic records of the history of the Church. The rescript of the Emperor Valentinian III. formed a new starting-point, and all manner of causes combined together to help forward the evil growth. The barbarian invasions of the West, the Mohammedan conquest of the East and of Africa, the long succession of successful forgeries which formed a chain of which the forged decretals of the pseudo-Isidore constituted only one link, the final breach between the East and the West, the temporal sovereignty which the popes acquired, the Crusades, the close alliance between the State and the Church, the dependence of the later monastic orders and of the friars on the Roman see, the systematizing labours of the schoolmen and the canonists, working as they did so largely on spurious authorities,—all these causes, and many more, helped to develop the papal power from what we see that it was in the time of S. Leo, into what it became in the time of Bellarmine and into what it is now, as set forth in the Vatican decrees. The thing itself

excommunicated by the Roman Church for what he had done against S. Chrysostom, and he died outside the Roman communion (see Tillemont, xi. 495).

is not of God. It is of the earth earthy. It is impossible to exaggerate its weakening effect on those portions of the Church which have accepted it. For a long while its worst excesses were rejected by the noblest provinces of the Roman communion, as, for example, by the illustrious Church of France. Now it seems as if its deadening influence had been bound upon the whole of that communion by the Vatican decrees of 1870. We ought to thank God every day that in His great mercy He has delivered the Church of England from that bondage. We must indeed mingle with our thanksgivings the deepest penitence and humiliation, when we think how unfaithful we have been in our use of our freedom ; when we think of our lack of discipline, of our miserable Erastianism, of our worldliness, of our Laodicean self-satisfaction, of our very imperfect grasp of certain aspects of primitive truth. We may, however, in all humility hope that in some degree we are improving. Thank God! it is no part of *our* creed that the Church which we love is without spot or wrinkle.[1] *We* are free to see our faults, and to confess them, and to do what we can to amend them. The more we strive to amend what we see to be wrong, the more will our vision be purged, so that we shall become conscious of evil which we had not before suspected. Let us pray that we may be more and more weaned from

---

[1] Cf. S. August., *de Perfect. justit. hom.*, cap. **xv.** § 35 (*Opp.* ed. Ben., 1690, x. 183); see also S. Aug., *Retractt.*, lib. i. cap. vii. § 5 (*Opp.* ed. Ben., 1689, i. 10).

trust in all mere earthly supports. It is not enough that we reject the earthliness of the *papacy;* we must seek to be freed from all *reliance* on the earthly accidents of our ecclesiastical position, on our connection with the State, on our ancient endowments, on our social position. I do not say that we are necessarily to agitate for a revolution in these matters. The time may arrive when such an agitation may become necessary. But what we are bound to do is to wean our hearts from all *reliance* on these things, and to struggle continually against all that is corrupt and wrong, which may have crept into the Church in consequence of them. Our only real strength is in our true Head, Jesus Christ our Lord. If the Church had kept the eyes of her heart fixed on our Lord in the fourth century, as they had been fixed during the three previous centuries, that inroad of worldliness could never have taken place. It was the inroad of worldliness which in the West resulted in the papacy. We have got rid of the papacy, but we have not got rid of the worldliness. We need to live in much closer fellowship with our ascended King, not only in our individual life, though that, of course, must form the foundation, but also in our ecclesiastical life. We have to bring home to ourselves the living union which exists between Christ and the Church. No matter what clouds of danger and difficulty are lowering on the horizon, threatening the ship of the Church with an overwhelming storm, we have Christ with us in the ship, and He has pledged His word that He will bring us safely through. People often fly over to Rome, because they are so conscious of the terrible difficulties which threaten the Church on all sides, and they think somehow that a compact organization under an earthly head would give the Church the strength she needs. Alas! the earthly head, being no part of the institution of Christ, does not reveal the heavenly Head, but hides Him. It is the power of the heavenly Head which we are to trust. It is His organic connection with the Church that we are to realize. It is His guidance which is pledged to us. It is His Headship which will reveal itself most marvellously in the hour of greatest need, to those who are looking to Him. If we do not look to Him, we shall certainly be swept away, either into heresy, or into unbelief, or into the false unity of the papal communion. All those things are doomed to an awful ending. But through all the terrors of the last times Christ will purge and protect His own Church, and guard the faith of His people, who are trusting in Him and looking for the day of His glorious appearing.

PART II.

LECTURE VI.

THE UNITY OF THE CHURCH.—I.

In the preceding lectures I have spoken of the position of the Roman see during the first four and a half centuries of our era; of its primacy of honour and influence, and of the causes which brought about that primacy; of its metropolitical jurisdiction over the suburbicarian Churches from the earliest times; and of the patriarchal jurisdiction over the Churches of the Western empire which it gradually acquired during the fourth and fifth centuries, partly through the legislation of the Council of Sardica, but mainly through the action of the civil power. We have noticed the upgrowth in Rome of the notion of the popes being in some sense successors of S. Peter in S. Peter's own chair, and attention has been called to the great use which was made of this notion to give an appearance of apostolic and even of divine sanction to claims whose real origin was partly synodical, but mainly secular; and we have observed how the use of these Petrine arguments during the process of building up the Western patriarchate prepared the way for the claim of an ecumenical jurisdiction over the whole Church, which was unmistakably put forth in the time of S. Leo. We have had occasion to notice over and over again how the great saints of the Church, especially in the East and in Africa and in Gaul, repudiated the papal jurisdiction, when from time to time an attempt was made to put it in force outside the suburbicarian limits; and we have seen how entirely the supporters of the definitions of the Vatican Council concerning the papal primacy fail, when they attempt to prove those definitions by an appeal to Holy Scripture.

I propose in these supplementary lectures to drop the discussion of the origin and growth of the papal jurisdiction, and to deal with the cognate subject of the claim of the Roman see to be the necessary centre of communion for the whole Church. The discussion of this claim will, I hope, throw light on the true nature of the Church's unity, a very important point which is often much misunderstood.

In order that we may know precisely what the Roman claim is, I will quote a remarkable passage from a remarkable article by the late Cardinal Wiseman.[1] He says, "According to the doctrine of the ancient Fathers, it is easy at once to ascertain who are the Church Catholic, and who are in a state

---

[1] The article appeared in the *Dublin Review* for August, 1839. It is the famous article in which occurred a sentence quoted from S. Augustine, which produced the strange effect on Newman so graphically described in the *Apologia* (pp. 211-213, ed. 1864).

of schism, by simply discovering who are in communion with the see of Rome, and who are not."[1] Thus, according to the teaching of this distinguished Roman Catholic prelate and divine, who was in every sense a representative man, communion with the Roman see is a test of fellowship with the Catholic Church; those who are out of communion with the Roman see are in schism; and this statement is put forth, not as the description of the *de facto* state of things in this or that age of the Church's history, but as " the doctrine of the ancient Fathers," which is presumably in accordance with the revealed will of God, and therefore obligatory for all time.

It is obvious that the theory of the Church's unity which underlies Dr. Wiseman's statement is the notion that that unity is always *visible;* that the different provinces and patriarchates into which the Church militant is divided are at all times in visible communion with the see of Rome, their divinely appointed centre, and, as a consequence, in communion with each other. If at any time any patriarchate or province ceases to be in communion with the pope, it necessarily on this theory ceases for the time to be in fellowship with the Catholic Church; it has lapsed into schism. Such is the view which

---

[1] *Dublin Review*, vol. vii. p. 163. The Jesuit Perrone (*Prælectt. Theoll., Tractat. de Locc. Theoll.*, part. i. sect. ii. cap. ii. prop. iii. n. 576, ed. 1841, vol. ii. pars i. p. 408) inculcates the same teaching. Speaking of the Fathers, he says, "Opponebant hæreticis et schismaticis auctoritatem ecclesiæ romanæ *quâcum si quivis haud communicaret, frustra speraret sese ad ecclesiam pertinere.*"

is held, I suppose, universally by modern Roman Catholics, which is implied in the second paragraph of the third chapter of the Vatican dogmatic decree, "*de Ecclesiâ Christi,*" but which to us seems so strange, and, in the face of the acts and writings of the saints, so absolutely untenable.

Not that we make light of the importance of visible unity. The fundamental law of the Church is the law of love; and to whatever degree the main body of the Church is dominated by that law, there will be a proportionate yearning for visible unity, and a readiness to give up a great deal in order to attain to it. The different members of the Church, or a majority of them in the various provinces, being inwardly united by love, the provincial or national Churches will manifest the love which dwells in the hearts of the faithful,[1] by external fellowship and intercommunion. Moreover, intercommunion is not merely an outcome and expression of love; it is in itself a sacred duty which cannot be set aside except in obedience to some higher law. But this visible unity, at which the Church is bound to aim, and which expresses the supernatural love which dwells in her, is no mechanical unity resulting from an iron necessity; it is produced by the action of the Holy Ghost, who dwells in the Church and in the hearts of the Church's members, and by the free co-operation

---

[1] Obstacles resulting from past unfaithfulness may hinder at times this manifestation of love, but the spirit of unity and the tendency to unity are inseparable accompaniments of true love.

of their sanctified wills. On the Roman theory, the external unity of the Church is a mechanical unity; it is a unity which *cannot* be broken. Those who are in fellowship with the pope are in the Church, those who are not in fellowship are outside. On this theory, the visible unity of the Church is not the outcome of the free co-operation of the members of the Church with the unifying influences of the Spirit of God; it is the rigidly necessary result of the way in which the Church is defined. It would be hardly conceivable that any one should on this theory pray that the Church may be visibly one;[1] the Church *must* be visibly one at all times, for the Church consists of the pope and those who are in visible communion with him. No amount of sin and unbelief can suspend or mar this Roman unity. The area of its fold may be diminished, but the external unity itself cannot be touched or affected. Very different is the primitive idea of visible unity, which is also our own. According to the primitive idea, visible unity is no mere logical deduction from a definition; it is the outcome of the unifying operation of the

---

[1] It is true that in the baptismal service we pray that the child may be regenerated, although we are quite certain that it will be regenerated. But there is no analogy between such a prayer and a prayer for the visible unity of the Church offered by one who holds the Ultramontane theory of visible unity. Our certainty concerning the regeneration of the child depends upon our trust in God, and in His faithfulness to His promises; but on the Ultramontane theory the visible unity of the Church is the *necessary* consequence of the definition of the Church. It does not depend on the action of God, or on the promise of God. We can no more pray for it than we can pray that two and two may make four.

Holy Spirit, which may be thwarted, and which often
has been thwarted. The faithful, and more especially the rulers of the Church, have to pray and
labour continually that this unity may be maintained
when it exists, and may be recovered when at any
time it is lost. It is the good gift of our ascended
Lord, for which we are dependent on Him.

No doubt there is an underlying invisible unity
which never ceases. All true parts of the Church are
united by their profession of one faith in essentials,
by their possession of the same spiritual powers
transmitted from Christ and His apostles through the
unbroken succession of the episcopate, by their ad-
herence to the fundamental laws of the Church's
polity and discipline, and above all by their organic
union with their invisible Head and Centre, Christ
our Lord. In this sense the Church is always one.[1]
But that essential unity is perceived by faith, and not
by sight. The Church must never be content with
the invisible unity which never fails. It is her duty
to do all she can to manifest to the world, by the
visible intercommunion of her various parts, that
she is indeed indwelt by the spirit of unity and
love.

From what has been said, it will have been gathered
that according to the Roman idea the Church is
always visibly one; but according to the primitive
teaching, the visible unity of the Church, though a

---

[1] On account of this abiding invisible unity, we are always able to
confess our faith in "the *one* holy catholic and apostolic Church."

great blessing which is always to be aimed at, is nevertheless not strictly necessary.[1] The essential unity of the Church remains, even though the outward unity may from time to time be broken.

It will be well, before investigating the teaching of the Fathers, to whom Cardinal Wiseman rightly appeals, to consider whether Holy Scripture throws any light on the matter. I shall not attempt to exhaust the scriptural argument, but shall set before you two principal points, one connected with the Old Testament, and the other with a passage in our Lord's great prayer, which He offered just before His entrance on His Passion.

It seems to me that some considerable light comes to us, in regard to the matter which we are considering, from the history of God's ancient people, Israel. If we have any true perception of the relation between the old covenant and the new, we shall expect to find some close analogies between the organization and history of Israel and the organization and history of the Church; and so in fact we do. The Israelite nation was organized in twelve tribes

---

[1] It must always be remembered that there is a great difference between the visibility of the Church and the visibility of the unity of the Church. The Church militant is always a visible body; it is not always a visibly united body. The distinction is sometimes overlooked. It may be worth noticing that the distinction between the two ideas was clearly perceived by the divines and canonists who were appointed to prepare materials for the Vatican Council. In the "*Schema Constitutionis dogmaticæ de Ecclesiâ Christi Patrum examini propositum,*" the fourth chapter has for its title, "Ecclesiam esse societatem visibilem," and the fifth chapter has the title, "De visibili Ecclesiæ unitate" (see the *Collectio Lacensis,* tom. vii. coll. 568, 569).

under twelve tribal princes.[1] These princes were co-ordinate one with the other. No one of them had jurisdiction over the rest. It may perhaps be allowed that Judah at the first start had a slight pre-eminence in honour. During the journey through the wilderness, they of the camp of Judah " set forth first." [2] But there was no central monarchy. The Lord God was the King of Israel and the only King ; and when He saw fit He raised up heroes sometimes from one tribe and sometimes from another,[3] to act as His people's leaders in war, and as their supreme judges in peace. The organization seems to have been devised in such a way as to leave the people dependant on God for the preservation of their national unity. There was no permanent supreme controlling power here on earth. The people were not headless, but the Head was invisible. The constitution, to be workable, pre-supposed a lively faith. In later times the people's faith grew weak. They came to Samuel and said, " Make us a king to judge us like all the nations; "[4] and so they "rejected" the Lord, that He " should not be King over them." [5] As Samuel said to them some time afterwards, " Ye said unto me, Nay ; but a king shall reign over us : when the Lord your God was your King." [6] So the Lord " gave them a king in His anger; " [7] and first Saul, and

---

[1] Numb. i. 4–16.   [2] Numb. ii. 9.
[3] *E.g.* Joshua from Ephraim, Gideon from Manasseh, Jephthah from Gad, Samson from Dan.
[4] 1 Sam. viii. 5.   [5] 1 Sam. viii. 7.
[6] 1 Sam. xii. 12.   [7] Hos. xiii. 11.

then David, and then Solomon, reigned over them.   It
is most interesting to notice how, so long as the people
were content with their twelve co-ordinate princes, and
looked only to their invisible King to keep them one,
their unity was preserved.   But very soon after they
had established an earthly monarchy, the germs of a
schism began to manifest themselves.   When, after the
overthrow of Absalom, King David crossed back over
the Jordan, "the men of Israel came to the king, and
said unto the king, Why have our brethen the men of
Judah stolen thee away?"[1]   And they said to the men
of Judah, "We have ten parts in the king, and we have
also more right in David than ye. . . . And the words
of the men of Judah were fiercer than the words of
the men of Israel."[2]   The whole passage shows clearly
that the quarrel between the north and the south had
begun.[3]   And at last the separation took place; and
Rehoboam reigned in the south, and Jeroboam in the
north.   The visible unity of the people of God was
suspended.   But the people remained one.   God's
people were not limited to the two tribes who
followed the house of David.   When the prophet,
who was Elisha's messenger, poured the oil on Jehu's
head, he said unto him, "Thus saith the Lord, the
God of Israel, I have anointed thee king *over the
people of the Lord, even over Israel.*"[4]   Israel had its
great saints and prophets as well as Judah.   One

---

[1] 2 Sam. xix. 41.   [2] 2 Sam. xix. 43.

[3] Compare Blunt's *Undesigned Coincidences*, pp. 162–175 (8th
edit.).

[4] 2 Kings ix. 6.

may almost say that in Elijah and Elisha Israel had greater saints than Judah; and the prophet expressly tells us that Samaria " did not commit half of Jerusalem's sins." [1] Notwithstanding the suspension of visible unity the essential unity of the nation continued. S. Paul speaks of " the promise made of God unto our fathers; unto which promise *our twelve tribes*, earnestly serving God night and day, hope to attain." [2]

I cannot doubt that this history of Israel was a prophecy of the Church of the new covenant. The Church, which is the new Israel, was organized by our Lord under twelve co-ordinate apostles. The apostles and their successors the bishops were the earthly guardians of the Church's unity; but in some sense the earthly organization was incomplete. There was no one central authority, no one permanent controlling power here on earth. The Church's Head was to be on high, within the veil. The constitution of the new Israel, as of the old, pre-supposed a living faith animating the militant Church and keeping it dependant on its Head. If the Church militant were a merely human creation, it would need, like other human societies, " a head in the same order of life as the rest of the body." [3] But the Church is a divine creation; and though it has a human Head, that Head is the Incarnate Son of God enthroned in glory, organically

[1] Ezek. xvi. 5.   [2] Acts xxvi. 6, 7; cf. S. James i. 1.
[3] See the Rev. L. Rivington's *Authority*, p. 5.

united to the Church on earth, the permanent Source of her essential unity, and perfectly able to secure her visible unity, whenever He sees that her faith and love and humility and unworldliness make it safe and desirable to grant to her that boon. In the early ages of the Church the Lord Jesus did grant to His Church the gift of visible unity. The Church was persecuted and unworldly and full of faith and love, and the Lord took care that her essential unity should be manifested visibly. Afterwards the Church made terms with the world, and the world was admitted within the sacred enclosure, and some leading portions of the Church began to cry out like Israel of old, "Nay; but a king shall reign over us." Some were prepared to subject the Church to the emperor, "the divine head,"[1] as he was called by the imperial commissioners at the Council of Chalcedon. Others were willing to subordinate the whole Church to the usurped jurisdiction of the Roman pontiffs. But the mere fact that the notion of an earthly head[2] should be seriously entertained was a token of how grievously the Church had fallen from her primitive fulness of realization of the things unseen. As the West came more and more under

---

[1] τῇ θείᾳ κορυφῇ (Coleti, iv. 1461).

[2] The Bishop of Rome may be called "head" in two senses. He may be called "head," as possessing from very ancient times a primacy of honour among bishops, just as the Duke of Norfolk may be called the head of the English nobility. He may also be called "head," as possessing a supposed primacy of jurisdiction over the whole Church. It is in this latter sense that the word is used in the text.

the dominion of the papal head at Rome, it became increasingly evident that the Church would lose, at any rate for a time, her visible unity. Our Lord would not allow His Church to remain visibly united under any head but Himself; and so in process of time the East and the West became separated, and later on Rome withdrew her communion from England. The analogy between Israel and the Church as regards this matter has been singularly complete.[1]

And now to pass to a very important New Testament passage, which is often quoted as if it favoured the Roman theory that the Church is at all times a visibly united body. Our blessed Lord prayed on

[1] It may be objected that, though there was no king at first in Israel, there was a high priest. But the high priest had, by the original constitution, no controlling power over the nation. The twelve tribal princes were not dependant on him. The Lord God was the only King. When the nation asked for a king, they did not reject the high priest; they rejected God. The high priest went on as before, at the head of the ministers of worship. The appointment of a king was not the substitution of one visible governor for another; it was the substitution of a visible for an invisible head. Among the Israelites the government of the people was not entrusted to the priesthood; but in the Church the bishops are not only priests but princes, and it is as princes that they act as guardians of the Church's unity. If the Roman theory were true, the pope would be not only the high priest but also the monarch of the Church; and it would be as monarch that he would claim to be the centre of unity and the possessor of supreme jurisdiction. If the history of Israel before the Babylonish captivity is to help us in the present discussion, we must fix our attention on its kings and princes, rather than on its priests and Levites. It need hardly be added that, when I speak of the bishops as princes, I am alluding not to any co-active jurisdiction which may in this or that country be granted to them by the civil power, but to the inherent spiritual jurisdiction which they inherit from the apostles.

the night of His Passion, not only for His apostles, but, as He said, "for them also that believe on Me through their word; that they may all be one; even as Thou, Father, art in Me, and I in Thee, that they also may be [one] in us: that the world may believe that Thou didst send Me" (S. John xvii. 20, 21).[1] This was undoubtedly a prayer which was intended to result in the unity of Christian believers, and the unity of which our Lord spoke was a *visible* unity. It was to be a unity which the world could perceive, and which would, when perceived, draw the world to faith in the divine mission of Christ. So far we shall all agree. But then the Roman argument goes on to assert, that what our Lord prayed for must· necessarily be granted in all ages of the Church as a permanent gift. It is supposed that Christ's prayer for visible unity is equivalent to a divine promise that visible unity shall never fail. Surely that is a very doubtful hypothesis. The final object of the prayer was that the world should believe in the divine mission of Christ; but the world as a whole has never yet believed in our Lord's divine mission,

---

[1] The passage discussed in the text is admitted by Roman Catholics to be a passage of primary importance in connection with the teaching of Holy Scripture about the unity of the Church. Mr. Allies, in the third section of his treatise on the *See of S. Peter* (ed. 1866, p. 113 *f.*), in which he deals with the unity of the Church as being "the end and office of the primacy" of the pope, starts with a discussion of S. John xvii. And Father Bottalla, in the first section of his book on "The supreme authority of the pope" (ed. 1868, pp. 8-10), begins his discussion of unity by a consideration of our Lord's words recorded in S. John xvii. 20-23.

Doubtless the time will come when it will do so. The time will come when "the earth shall be full of the knowledge of the Lord, as the waters cover the sea;"[1] when "the kingdom of the world" shall "become the kingdom of our Lord and of his Christ."[2] I quite believe that that future conversion of the world will be brought about by a very wonderful restoration of visible unity to the Church, connected, it may be, with the future conversion of Israel;[3] for, as S. Paul says, "What shall the receiving of" Israel "be, but life from the dead?"[4] But the point to be noticed is that, though our Lord prayed with the intention that, as the result of His prayer, the world should believe in Him, that result has not yet been produced.[5] Our Lord's prayer, so far

[1] Isa. xi. 9.

[2] Rev. xi. 15.

[3] The Jesuit, Father Knabenbauer, quotes and adopts a very apposite passage from Cornelius a Lapide, bearing on this matter. He says, "Bene notat *Lap.:* 'tunc enim Antichristi regno everso Ecclesia ubique terrarum regnabit et fiet tam ex Judæis quam ex Gentilibus unum ovile et unus pastor'" (Knabenb., *Comment. in Daniel.,* vii. 27, p. 202, ed. 1891).

[4] Rom. xi. 15.

[5] When our Lord says (S. John xvii. 20, 21), "Neither for these only do I pray, but for them also that believe on Me through their word; that (ἵνα) they may all be one; even as Thou, Father, art in Me, and I in Thee, that (ἵνα) they also may be [one] in us: that (ἵνα) the world may believe that Thou didst send Me;" we are not to understand that our Lord is praying directly either for the visible unity of believers or for the conversion of the world. He prays for believers in general, as He had prayed for the apostles (vers. 11–15 and 17–19), that the Father would "*keep them*" and "*sanctify them.*" That was the immediate intention of his prayer. But our Lord looks forward beyond the immediate intention. He wishes the faithful to be "kept" and "sanctified," *in order that* (ἵνα) they may be one in

as it deals with the conversion of the world, is not
equivalent to a promise applicable to all ages. And
if the plain facts which history records, and which
we see around us, compel us to this conclusion in
regard to one object of the prayer, who shall venture
to say that the same principle is not applicable to
the other object? especially as the two objects of
the prayer are so closely connected. Why may not
the visible unity of all believers be reserved for
the future, as the conversion of the world is evidently reserved for the future ?[1] Moreover, it seems
clear that the visible unity, which is to result in

the Father and in the Son, and *in order that* (ἵνα) that unity visibly
manifesting itself may result in the conversion of the world. The
Church's visible unity and the world's conversion are the ultimate
objects of His prayer. Compare the parallel prayer for the apostles in
verse 11, in which the immediate intention and the ultimate object
are also distinguished.

[1] Mr. Richardson (*What are the Catholic Claims?* p. 30) enumerates
twelve claims, which he makes on behalf of the Roman communion. He
formulates the fourth of these claims thus: "That not only did Christ
pray to His Eternal Father for this visible unity, but that He also
proclaimed the immediate answer to His prayer by the words, 'And
the glory which Thou hast given Me I have given to them, that they
may be one as We also are One,' etc. (John xvii. 22)." On p. 49 he
appears to identify this gift of "glory" with "the outward expression
of unity." All this is very strange and novel exegesis. The Fathers
interpret the passage quite differently, and so does the great Jesuit
commentator Maldonatus. S. Gregory Nyssen (*in illud, Tunc Ipse
Filius subjicietur, Opp.* ed. Migne, i. 1320, 1321) understands the
"glory" to be the gift of the Spirit. S. Augustine and S. Bede
understand it of the future glory in the world to come. S. Chrysostom and his followers understand it of the gift of miracles. Maldonatus understands it of the love which our Lord felt for His followers.
In any case the "glory," which our Lord had given, cannot be "the
outward expression of unity." Our Lord implies that that is to be
the ultimate result of the gift; it is not the gift itself.

the conversion of the world, will be an unmistakable fact which the whole world will recognize. Its recognition will not depend on the world's accepting the private theory of one particular body of Christians. Roman Catholics may choose to imagine that they are the only people who really believe in Christ through the word of the apostles, and that, as they are visibly united, the first of the two objects, mentioned by our Lord in S. John xvii. 20, 21, has been attained in them. But it is evident that such a very partial realization of unity is no adequate fulfilment of our Lord's intention. What the world sees at present is a disunited Christendom ; what our Lord desired was a completely united Christendom ; and until that is attained, the promise implied in His great prayer remains unfulfilled. It is impossible to deduce from these words of Christ a pledge that the visible unity of the Church shall *never* fail. The true deduction from what we are told about our Lord's prayer is just the opposite. If those for whom our Lord prayed constitute a body which *of necessity* is always visibly one, we should be obliged to say with all reverence that on that most sacred night our Lord had offered a needless prayer. We may gather, from the fact that He prayed, that the unity for which He prayed was a difficult thing, which could only be accomplished through the mighty power of the grace of God. Our Lord had in view a unity which would be brought about by the shedding forth of the Spirit of love, and by the Church's complete surrender of herself to the influences of that Spirit of love. He was not praying for a unity, which should be the logically necessary outcome of a definition. Such a unity as our Lord prayed for is set before us in the history of the primitive Church, and such will be the visible unity of the finally reunited Church. For the present the Church and the world have made terms with each other; love has grown cold, and disunion is the necessary result. It is for us to labour and pray, and thus prepare the way for those " times of refreshing,"[1] which we know, on the sure testimony of Holy Scripture, are to come at last.

But on this question of the nature of the Church's visible unity, and on the cognate question as to whether communion with the see of Rome is a necessary condition of membership in the Catholic Church, Cardinal Wiseman appeals to "the doctrine of the ancient Fathers." To the Fathers, therefore, let us go. We shall have to reconsider, from a different point of view, some incidents of Church history which have already been discussed in the lectures dealing with the jurisdiction of the papal see, but I hope that I shall be able to avoid monotonous repetition.

It will be remembered that Pope Victor (A.D. 188–198) "proscribed the Asiatic Christians by letters," and proclaimed that they " were all *utterly* separated from communion,"[2] because they kept Easter on the

---

[1] Acts iii. 19.   [2] Euseb., *H. E.*, v. 24.

day of the Paschal full moon, on whatever day of the
week that event might happen to fall.   This, as far
as I remember, was the first occasion when, on any
large scale, the Church had an opportunity of showing by her action whether she really held the
principle enunciated by Cardinal Wiseman, that
communion with the see of Rome is the test which
enables Catholics to be distinguished from schismatics.
The Asiatic brethren were " entirely " (ἄρδην) cut off
from the communion of the pope.   The question
arose, Were they entirely cut off from the unity of
the Church ?   Eusebius tells us that " Victor *endeavoured* to cut off the Churches of all Asia, together with the neighbouring Churches, as heterodox,
from the common unity ?" [1]   The pope *endeavoured,*
but did not succeed.   Separation from the communion
of the pope did not decide the question of separation
from the unity of the Catholic Church, even though
the crime for which the Asiatics had been condemned
was the most serious one of "heterodoxy."   The pope
decreed that they were heterodox, but the great
majority of the bishops held them to be orthodox,
and they maintained their communion with Polycrates
of Ephesus and his colleagues, and severely rebuked

---

[1] Dom Coustant (*Romanorum Pontificum Epistt.*, tom. i. col. 100, ed.
1721) says, " Neque propterea secum pugnare credendus est Eusebius
cum Victorem dicit conatum esse Asianos abscindere.   Et abscidit
enim re verâ Asianos, cum eos a communione suâ removit; et conatus
est ab Ecclesiæ corpore segregare, cum ceteris Episcopis ad idem
præstandum et literis et exemplo auctor fuit.   At plerique eum
potius commonendum censuerunt, ut in proposito non permaneret."

the pope for his obstinacy,[1] until at last he gave way,
and the peace of the Church was restored. Assuredly
Cardinal Wiseman's theory is not borne out by the
episode of the Paschal controversy.

In a previous lecture I have gone so fully into the
history of the baptismal controversy in the time of
S. Cyprian, that there is no need to traverse the
ground again. I will only recall the fact that Pope
Stephen cut off from his communion S. Cyprian and
the whole North African Church,[2] and also S. Firmilian and the Churches of Cappadocia and of the
neighbouring provinces; but those great saints maintained their ground, knowing well that they retained
their membership in the Catholic Church, although
deprived of the communion of the Roman see; and
the whole Church, from their day to ours, has justified
their view on this point, even though, in regard to
some other aspects of the general controversy, the
Africans and Asiatics would find few supporters at
the present time. I hardly suppose that any one
will be ready to come forward in defence of the
notion that S. Cyprian and S. Firmilian and the
Churches of the East and of the South were all in
schism after Stephen had cut them off from his communion; but undoubtedly they must be pronounced
to be schismatics, if Cardinal Wiseman's principle is
a trustworthy test.

[1] Pope Nicholas I. confessed that "Videamus Victorem papam . . .
pæne a totius Ecclesiæ præsulibus pertinaciæ redargutum " (Coleti,
ix. 1360).

[2] See Note A. in the Appendix, pp. 325-333.

I pass on to the consideration of the case of S. Meletius of Antioch, and of the Eastern saints who communicated with him. I have given the outlines of S. Meletius' history before.[1] During twenty years, namely, from 361 to 381, he presided as bishop over the great Church of Antioch; and during the whole of that time he was excluded from the communion of the Roman see; and during the last six years of his episcopate his rival, Paulinus, the Bishop of the Eustathians, was recognized by the pope as the legitimate Catholic Bishop of Antioch. It will, I think, throw light on the way in which Cardinal Wiseman's principle would have been viewed by great saints of the early Church, if I quote from a letter which S. Basil the Great wrote to the Count Terentius on the occasion of the arrival in Antioch of the letters recognizing Paulinus, which were written by Pope Damasus in the year 375. S. Basil says that he hears that the brethren of Paulinus' party are " carrying about letters from the Westerns which commit the bishopric of the Church of Antioch to them, and which defraud (of his due) the most admirable bishop of *the true Church of God*, Meletius.[2] . . . However, since we accuse no one, but, on the contrary, wish to be in charity with all men, especially with those of the household of faith, we congratulate those who have received letters from Rome; and if, moreover, he [Paulinus] should have some

---

[1] See pp. 163-176.

[2] Παραλογιζόμενα δὲ τὸν θαυμασιώτατον ἐπίσκοπον τῆς ἀληθινῆς τοῦ Θεοῦ ἐκκλησίας Μελέτιον.

honourable and grand testimony (concerning himself), we pray that it may prove true, and be confirmed by his actions. *But not because of this shall
we be able to persuade ourselves either to ignore
Meletius, or to lose thought of the Church under him,
or to consider the questions, about which from the
beginning the separation arose, as small matters, or
to think of them as having little profit towards the
aim of godliness. As for me, if any one, having
received a letter from men, should pride himself upon
it, not only shall I never suffer myself because of this
to shrink back;* but, even if such a letter should have
come from heaven itself, but should not agree with
the sound word of the faith, I am not able to consider
such a one as being in communion [with myself] *in
sacris*"[1] (κοινωνὸν τῶν ἁγίων). It should be noticed
how in this passage S. Basil speaks of the Church
under S. Meletius as "*the true Church of God,*" with
which he holds communion, although on Cardinal
Wiseman's principle it was no true Church, but a
schismatic body. Moreover, S. Basil declares that the
"letters of *men*"—that is, the letters from the pope—
will not make him shrink back. He says that the
matters in dispute have a close bearing on orthodoxy,[2]

---

[1] *Ep.* 214, *Opp.* ed Ben., 1730, iii. 321.

[2] S. Basil is no doubt referring, at any rate primarily, to the dispute
in regard to the use of the word "hypostasis." S. Basil and the
other Cappadocian Fathers, and the East generally, spoke ordinarily of
three "hypostaseis" in the one God. Paulinus, following what might
then be called the Western usage, spoke of *one* "hypostasis." S.
Meletius' and S. Basil's phraseology has ultimately prevailed throughout the Church, both in the East and in the West. In reality the two

and that he would not communicate with an unsound man, even if he received letters from heaven itself.[1] Thus he clearly lays down that the papal decision is not decisive on the question of orthodoxy. He does not excuse S. Meletius on the ground of invincible ignorance, or on the ground that circumstances over which he had no control prevented his being in the Roman communion. Such a line would have been impossible, for there was nothing to prevent S. Meletius from being in the communion of Rome. He had only to submit to Paulinus, and he would be in that communion at once. The pope had declared, with all the authority of the Roman see, that Paulinus was the true Bishop of Antioch; but S. Meletius differed from the pope on that point, and S. Basil agreed with S. Meletius. Consequently S. Basil held not only that S. Meletius was a Catholic, but that his followers constituted the true Church of God in Antioch, and S. Basil would not hold communion *in sacris* with Paulinus.[2]

But S. Meletius was upheld against Paulinus and his powerful supporter, not only by S. Basil, but by all the Catholic bishops of Syria and Asia Minor. In

parties were substantially at one in their doctrinal teaching, though they differed as to the precise meaning which should be attached to the word *hypostasis*, when used in theological statements; and in consequence expressed the faith, which they held in common, by formulas which were apparently irreconcilable.

[1] S. Basil is, of course, referring to S. Paul's words in Gal. i. 8.

[2] Dom Maran, in his preface to the third volume of the Benedictine edition of S. Basil (p. xi), says, speaking of S. Basil, " Non immerito ergo communionem cum Paulino ineundam negabat; quippe cum iniri non posset, quin Meletius rejiceretur, qui solus Antiochiæ legitimus erat episcopus."

the year 379 S. Meletius presided over a great Council
held at Antioch, at which 146 prelates attended
among whom were some illustrious saints.[1] It was at
this Council that the Eastern bishops under S. Meletius received and signed a dogmatic letter, drawn up
two years before by a Council held at Rome under
the presidency of Pope Damasus.[2] This letter is called
" the tome of the Westerns " in the 5th canon of the
second Ecumenical Council. A copy of this letter
with the signatures of the Antiochene Fathers attached, was sent to Rome, and was preserved there
in the archives of the Church. The signature of
S. Meletius, as president of the Council, stands first.[3]
Father Ryder, of the Birmingham Oratory, considers
that the fact that this document was laid up in the
Roman archives is a proof that S. Meletius " had been
admitted " " to immediate communion with Rome,
although his right to the see of Antioch was not admitted to the prejudice of Paulinus."[4] Mr. Rivington

---

[1] See the note on p. 167. The *codex Vaticanus* gives 163 as the
number of bishops present at the council.

[2] Hefele (ii. 291, 361, 362, Eng. trans.) supposes that the Roman
letter or tome was drawn up at a Council held in 369. Merenda, in his
Gesta S. Damasi (Migne's *Patrol. Lat.*, xiii. 190, 191), thinks that the
"tome of the Westerns" really consisted of three dogmatic letters
which were put forth by Roman Councils in 369, 374, and 377. The
first of those letters is extant, and fragments of the others remain.
The subscriptions of the Antiochene Fathers immediately follow the
fragments of the synodical letter of 377; and I believe that it was
that letter, and no other, which was signed at Antioch. Mansi (iii.
463–468) agrees, but in some details his discussion of the matter
needs to be corrected by Merenda.

[3] Coleti, ii. 1047, 1081; Mansi, iii. 461, 462, and 511.

[4] Ryder's *Catholic Controversy*, 2nd edit., p. 60.

S

says, with even less appearance of reason, that S. Meletius' "subscription" "proves ... to demonstration " that he was " living in communion with Rome "[1] two years afterwards, when he presided over the second Ecumenical Council. It is difficult to see how S. Meletius' subscription could "prove to demonstration" anything of the kind. The preservation of a document of that sort in the Roman archives might, under some circumstances, be accepted as fairly good proof that the signatories were in communion with the Roman Church. But such an inference cannot safely be drawn in the present case, for S. Meletius signs distinctly as Bishop of Antioch. His subscription is thus worded : " I Meletius, *Bishop of Antioch,* consent to all the things written above, so believing and holding; and if any one holds otherwise, let him be anathema." If the acceptance and preservation of a document so signed is to be considered as a proof that S. Meletius was " in immediate communion with Rome," we must go further, and say that it was also a proof that he was recognized at Rome as the Bishop of Antioch. But such a view is quite irreconcilable with facts to be presently mentioned. In the meanwhile, it is easy to explain how the document may have got into the Roman archives. It is most probable that among the 146 signatories there were some, perhaps many, who had always been in good relations with the Roman see. Damasus himself had hardly got to the point of considering all those who

---

[1] Rivington's *Authority,* 2nd edit., p. 93.

were outside his communion as being therefore outside of the communion of the Catholic Church, and as imparting the taint of schism to those Churches which maintained friendly relations with them. We cannot suppose that Damasus considered the whole East to be in schism, because the Eastern bishops communicated with S. Meletius and rejected Paulinus. He never refused his communion to S. Basil. Rome herself, in the fourth century, would hardly have accepted Cardinal Wiseman's theory, that those who are not in communion with the see of Rome are necessarily in a state of schism.[1] It follows, therefore, that there were probably some, and perhaps many, of the Fathers of the Council of Antioch who were in friendly relations with Damasus. One or more of these bishops would send to Rome the copy of the "tome of the Westerns," to which were appended the 146 signatures of the Easterns. The pope, having received the document from a friendly source, and

---

[1] Some Ultramontane writers, when confronted with the case of S Meletius, attempt to get out of their difficulty by replying that Meletius was at any rate in "*mediate* communion" with the see of Rome, because of his communion with S. Basil, who himself communicated with Pope Damasus. This argument seems to make the see of Cæsarea the centre of communion for the whole Church. It would be interesting to know whether, in the nineteenth century, it is held to be allowable for a bishop who is out of communion with Rome, to exercise authority in a city, in which there is another bishop recognized by the pope; and whether it would be said, concerning such a rebellious bishop, that he was in "*mediate* communion" with Rome, because the Archbishop of Goa might choose to ignore the papal decision, and to grant his communion to the rebel. The whole notion of "*mediate* communion" seems to me to be irreconcilable with the modern papal theory.

perceiving its great importance as establishing the
fact that the schism at Antioch rested on no fundamental difference of belief, would naturally lay it up
in his archives; but it is unreasonable to contend
that such an action proves that S. Meletius was admitted to immediate communion with the Roman see.
As I have hinted above, subsequent events show
clearly that S. Meletius never was in communion
with the Western Church.   But let us trace the
course of the history.

It appears to be admitted that the Antiochene
Council of 379 failed to heal the breach which
divided the Catholics under S. Meletius from the·
Eustathians under Paulinus.   Father Ryder, after
mentioning the Council, says that S. Meletius "*soon
after* entered into terms of communion with his
rival."[1]   Tillemont (viii. 368) shows that the Protestant Blondel was wrong in supposing that a compact
between the two parties was made *at the Council.*[2]
But undoubtedly a compact was made later on, probably in the spring of the year 381.   On the 10th
of January in that year, the Emperor Theodosius
published at Constantinople his constitution "*Nullus
hæreticis,*" in which he ordered that all Churches
which were in the hands of heretics should be given
over to the Catholics.   On the 28th of February of
the previous year, he had published at Thessalonica
another constitution, the "*Cunctos populos,*" in
which he had declared that he wished all his subjects

---

[1] *Loc. cit.*   [2] Compare also Hefele (ii. 291, Eng. trans.).

to accept the faith as held by Damasus of Rome
and Peter of Alexandria, who were, of course, the
two prelates of highest dignity in the Catholic
Church. The emperor entrusted to a high official
named Sapor the duty of seeing to the execution
of the law of January, 381.[1] When Sapor came to
Antioch, he found great difficulty in deciding which
party ought to be put in possession of the Churches.
The Catholics under S. Meletius, the Eustathians
under Paulinus, and the Apollinarians under Vitalis,
all claimed to hold the same doctrine concerning the
blessed Trinity that was held at Rome by Damasus
and at Alexandria by Peter. Finally Sapor decided
in favour of S. Meletius. It is clear that at the time
of Sapor's visit the breach was still unhealed. Very
soon after this decision of Sapor, S. Meletius left
Antioch for Constantinople, to attend the second
Ecumenical Council, at which he presided, and in
the course of which he died. It must have been
during the very short interval which came in between Sapor's visit and S. Meletius' final departure
from Antioch,[2] that a compact was at last made

---

[1] Tillemont, in his *Histoire des Empereurs* (note vii. on Theodosius
I., tom. v. pp. 728, 729, ed. 1701), shows by very convincing reasons
that it was to carry out *the law of January*, 381, that Sapor came to
Antioch.

[2] The second Ecumenical Council commenced its sessions in May,
381; and the emperor's decree, which Sapor had to administer, was
dated January 10, 381. When allowance has been made for Sapor's
journey from Constantinople to Antioch, and for S. Meletius' journey
from Antioch to Constantinople, it will be seen that the interval
between Sapor's visit and S. Meletius' departure could not be more
than three months at the outside. It was, in fact, probably less.

between the saint and his rival. S. Meletius had been for a long time most desirous of entering into some arrangement which should put an end to the scandal of the division, or at any rate prevent its perpetuation; but hitherto his efforts had been without fruit. However, at length Paulinus relented, and the two parties came to an agreement, according to the terms of which, whenever either of the two bishops died, the survivor was to be recognized as the one legitimate bishop of the whole body of orthodox Christians in Antioch. So far as I know, there is no proof that the agreement settled anything beyond the question of the succession to the see. We are not told that S. Meletius and Paulinus communicated together, or that intercommunion was established between the two bodies of Christians.[1] Of course, no personal agreement between S. Meletius and Paulinus could bring the latter into communion with the episcopate of the Eastern Church, or the former into communion with Rome and the West. There is no sort of reason to suppose that the other bishops, either of the East or of the West, were in

Merenda (*De Sancti Damasi Gestis*, cap. xii.; Migne's *Patrol Lat.*, xiii. 181) holds that Sapor did not arrive at Antioch until March, 381.

[1] Socrates (*H. E.*, v. 5) says that "the people had peace, and so no longer quarrelled with one another." Two Catholic bishops in the same city, each with his own flock, was such an unusual spectacle in the early Church, that, if it had been part of the compact that the two bodies should actually communicate together, one would have expected the particulars to be recorded. However, if any one thinks that inter-communion was established between the two parties, I have no wish to gainsay him.

any way parties to the compact. It seems probable
that the whole thing was done in a hurry, and that
S. Meletius had to leave for Constantinople before
any consultation with the Church elsewhere could
be had.[1]

Information concerning the compact was, however,
sent to the West. An important synod, representing
Northern Italy, Pannonia, Gaul, and Africa, met at
Aquileia in September, 381, under the presidency of
S. Valerian of Aquileia, and under the leadership of
S. Ambrose of Milan; and a letter of that synod,
addressed to the three emperors, Gratian, Valentinian II., and Theodosius, makes two references to
the compact (*pactum*) which had been concluded
between the two orthodox parties at Antioch. In
that letter the substance of the compact is accurately
stated, and the emperors are requested to take care
that, when one of the two bishops dies, the Churches
shall remain under the government of the survivor,
and that no attempt shall be made to consecrate a
bishop to succeed in the place of the one who should
have passed away.[2] Further on in the letter the
synod refers again to the compact, and expresses its
wish that it should remain in force.[3] When this

---

[1] Sozomen (vii. 3), after describing the termination of the contest,
says, " When these things had thus come to pass, Meletius proceeded
to Constantinople."

[2] " Oblatas pietati vestræ opinamur preces nostras, quibus *juxta
partium pactum* poposcimus, ut altero decedente penes superstitem
ecclesiæ permanerent, nec aliqua superordinatio attentaretur" (Coleti,
ii. 1186).

[3] " Pacto, quod stare volumus."

letter was written, the Aquileian Fathers did not
know that the compact had practically come to an
end two or three months before. S. Meletius had
died in. May or June, during the session of the
Ecumenical Council of Constantinople, and that
Council had decided to ignore the compact, and to
authorize the election and consecration of a new
Bishop of Antioch in succession to S. Meletius, no
account being taken of the claims of Paulinus. The
fact was that S. Meletius died before the compact
had been accepted and ratified by the bishops.[1] The
episcopal college could not be bound by the private
agreement made between S. Meletius and Paulinus,
in regard to matters which affected not only the
diocese of Antioch, but also the whole of the Antiochene province and patriarchate, and in some degree
the whole Eastern Church. It is, I think, allowable
to express regret that the bishops at Constantinople

---

[1] Socrates (v. 5) and his imitator Sozomen (vii. 3) tell us that six
leaders among the clergy of Antioch, belonging to either party, took
an oath at the time when the compact was made, by which they
bound themselves to take no part in any election to the bishopric, and
to refuse to be themselves elected, so long as either S. Meletius or
Paulinus was alive. These historians also tell us that S. Flavian,
who actually succeeded S. Meletius, was one of those who took the
oath. If so, S. Flavian's episcopate originated in a violation of his
sworn promise. It would require very much stronger evidence to
make me believe that so illustrious a saint could be guilty of such a
crime; or that so many great saints, as were then found among the
bishops of the East, could have become accomplices in that crime.
Tillemont (viii. 371, and x. 527) evidently disbelieves the story.
However, even if the story were true, the oaths of the Antiochene
clergy would only bind themselves. They could not swear away
the rights of the bishops.

did not voluntarily ratify the compact in the interests of peace. What they actually did was canonically legitimate, but it may be doubted whether it was either wise or charitable; and S. Gregory Nazianzen resigned the bishopric of Constantinople and withdrew from the Council in testimony of his disapprobation of what was being done.

But to return to the Council of Aquileia. We have seen that, when they wrote their letter to the emperors in September, 381, they supposed that S. Meletius was still alive.[1] But in various parts of the letter they imply that S. Meletius had not yet been admitted to their communion, nor were they willing to admit him to their communion at the Council which they were then holding. They say, "Paulinus, who has always maintained his communion with us inviolate, is reported to be troubled by the dissensions of others, whose faith in former times vacil-

---

[1] Three or four months later a Council of the bishops of North Italy was held at Milan under the presidency of S. Ambrose. This Council also addressed a letter to the Emperor Theodosius (Coleti, ii. 1193). In the course of this letter the Council refers to the fact that in the letter from their previous Council at Aquileia they had written that "the city of Antioch had two bishops, Paulinus and Meletius," and they called to mind the arrangement about the succession, which they had urged the emperors to maintain in force; but they go on in their letter from Milan to say that "*now*, Meletius having died, and Paulinus remaining as the survivor, . . . it is reported that, contrary to justice and ecclesiastical order, a fresh bishop has been, not exactly substituted in the place of Meletius, but rather superposed." This passage from the Milanese letter proves to demonstration that the Council of Aquileia had not heard of S. Meletius' death. The news of that event reached North Italy during the interval between the Council of Aquileia and the Council of Milan.

lated. And these last we should wish to admit to our fellowship, *if it can be done, and if a full belief recommends them (si fieri potest, et si fides plena commendat)*; but in such a way that the privilege of our long-established fellowship be still maintained with the other side. And our care for these persons [S. Meletius and his flock] is not unnecessary. First of all, because, when a common fellowship has been established, no cause of complaint should be allowed to remain ; and, secondly, because some time ago we received letters from both parties, and specially from those who were causing the dissension in the Church of Antioch [that is, the party of S. Meletius]; and unless we had been hindered by an incursion of the hostile [Goths], we had arranged to send certain of our number, who would have acted as mediators and arbitrators to restore peace, if it were possible. But because at that time, owing to public disturbances, our desires could not take effect, we think that our petition should be offered to your piety, by which we pray that, according to the compact made between the parties, if one dies the Churches may remain subject to the survivor,[1] and that no intrusive conse-cration (*superordinatio*) should be attempted. And so we beseech you, most clement and Christian emperors, to convoke the whole body of Catholic bishops to a Council to be held at Alexandria, *who may fully discuss and settle the question as to who are to be admitted to communion, and who are to*

---

[1] " Ut altero decedente penes superstitem ecclesiæ permanerent."

have their communion with us maintained." [1] It
seems perfectly clear from this letter that S. Meletius,
up to the time of his death, was still cut off from the
communion of the Western Church, which was so
fully represented at Aquileia. [2] It is true that the
Roman Church was not represented there. The
Roman Church was at that time harassed by a
domestic trouble. The anti-Pope Ursinus was once
more disputing possession of the Roman see with
Damasus. [3] But, if the pope had granted his communion to S. Meletius, it is in the highest degree
improbable that S. Ambrose and the rest of the
West should have been ignorant of the fact, and
that they should be petitioning the emperors to
summon an Ecumenical Council at Alexandria to
decide whether or no communion should be granted
to S. Meletius and to his flock. There is not any

---

[1] Coleti, ii. 1186.

[2] S. Gregory Nazianzen, in his *Carmen de Vitâ suâ* (1611–1616,
Opp. ed. Ben., 1840, ii. 758), describes the dispute in the Ecumenical
Council as to the succession to the see of Antioch after S. Meletius'
death. He gives in verse the substance of the speech which he
made, counselling that Paulinus should be left undisturbed. In this
speech the following passage occurs: " As long as the divine bishop
[Meletius] was in the midst, and it was not clear how ever they of the
West would receive the man, for hitherto they had been wrath, it was
in a way pardonable to grieve somewhat these self-styled defenders of
the canons [viz. Damasus and the Western bishops]. For a meek
man [like Meletius] is an antidote to anger." S. Gregory seems
clearly to imply that the dissension with the West continued during
S. Meletius' life, but peace followed, when, on his death, Paulinus
was left sole bishop ($\mu o\nu \acute{o}\theta\rho o\nu o s$, cf. 1586); and S. Gregory is anxious
that that peace should not be disturbed by the election of a successor
to the saint.

[3] Hefele (ii. 375, E.T.).

shadow of a proof that the pope had, without inform-
ing the rest of the West, admitted S. Meletius to his
communion, and to assert that he must have done
so seems to me to be entirely unreasonable. I submit that it has now been conclusively shown that
S. Meletius presided over an Ecumenical Council,
when for years he had been occupying the great
see of Antioch in defiance of the pope, who recognized his rival, and when, in consequence, he had
been excluded from the communion of Rome and of
the West.[1]   I submit, further, that it has been shown
that he died in this condition; and that, if Cardinal
Wiseman's theory is true, he was a schismatic in life
and a schismatic in death; and that consequently
the second Ecumenical Council [2] and all that wonderful galaxy of saints, which rendered it so specially
illustrious, were all implicated in the deadly sin of
schism.   It must further be noticed that, having, on
the Roman hypothesis, died in schism, he was nevertheless canonized, first by the Council, and afterwards
by the Western Churches, and specially by the Church

[1] It must be remembered that the Vatican Council, in the constitution *De Eccl. Christi* (cap. iii.), declared that it was part of the
Catholic teaching, from which no one can deviate and be saved, that
"all pastors of whatever dignity" and "all the faithful" "are bound
to the jurisdiction of the Roman pontiff by the duty of true obedience"
"in things which pertain to the discipline and government of the
Church diffused throughout the whole world," "so that, unity of communion being preserved with the Roman pontiff, the Church of
Christ may be one flock under one supreme pastor."   S. Meletius
seems hardly to have realized the truth of this teaching.

[2] It was this Council which enlarged the Nicene Creed and brought
it substantially into its present form, excepting always the "Filioque"
clause, which was long afterwards added in the West.

of Rome, in whose Martyrology his name occurs. All
these incredible propositions must be maintained, unless people are willing to admit that Cardinal Wiseman's theory is untenable, or at any rate that it does
not agree with the teaching of the Fathers of the
fourth century. But if so, Cardinal Wiseman was
imprudent when he appealed to the Fathers. After
all, is it not safer, from the Roman point of view, to
brand the appeal to the Fathers as treason ?

Let us now consider the case of S. Flavian, the
successor of S. Meletius, and that of S. Chrysostom,
who was the spiritual son of both those great saints.
As we have seen, it was the second Ecumenical
Council which determined, whether wisely or un-
wisely, that Paulinus' claims to the see of Antioch
should be ignored, and that a bishop should be chosen
and consecrated to take the place of S. Meletius.
S. Flavian, who was probably more than seventy
years old, and who had been for forty years, first as
a layman and afterwards as a priest, a prominent
leader of the Catholics at Antioch, was consecrated to
fill the patriarchal throne of that city.[1] S. Chrysostom
describes how the sorrow of the faithful at the death
of Meletius was changed into joy by the consecration
of Flavian. It seemed to them that Meletius had
risen from the tomb, and in the person of Flavian

---

[1] The title "patriarch" had hardly come into use; but the sixth
Nicene Canon shows that Antioch had for a long time possessed
special privileges, such as were afterwards called "patriarchal." Cf.
S. Hieron., *Lib. contra. Joann. Jerosol.*, § 37 (*Opp.* ed. Vallars, ii.
447). See also Duchesne's *Origines du culte*, pp. 19–21.

was seated once more in the pontifical chair.[1]   Flavian
was acknowledged as the true bishop by all the
suffragans of the Antiochene province and patriarchate, and also by the episcopate of the three
exarchates of Asia, Pontus, and Thrace.   But Egypt
and the West recognized Paulinus.   In the summer
of the year 382, the majority of the bishops who had
attended the second Ecumenical Council met again
in synod at Constantinople, and addressed a synodical
letter to the Western bishops, who were holding a
Council at Rome.   The Blessed Theodoret gives the
letter at full length, in proof, as he says, of the
manly spirit and wisdom of the bishops.[2]   In
the course of their letter they inform their Western
brethren [3] that the episcopate of the province of
Antioch and of the patriarchate of the East [4] "have
canonically ordained the most reverend and most religious Flavian to be bishop of the very ancient and
truly apostolical Church of Antioch."[5]   But the
Western bishops in their Council at Rome took a
different view of the matter.   They had always supported Paulinus, and they continued to support him

[1] S. Chrys., *Serm. cum Presb. fuit ordin.*, *Opp.* ed. Ben., i. 442.

[2] Theodoret, *H. E.*, v. 8.

[3] The letter is addressed "to the very honoured lords and most
reverend brethren and fellow-ministers, Damasus, Ambrose, Britton,
Valerian," etc.

[4] τῆς ἀνατολικῆς διοικήσεως.   The Constantinopolitan Fathers add
that the whole of the local Church of Antioch was consenting to
Flavian's ordination, and as it were with one voice gave him honour.
They also state that they themselves had synodically received this
"legitimate ordination."

[5] Theodoret, *H. E.*, v. 9.

now. Sozomen tells us that "the bishop of the
Romans and all the priests (*i.e.* bishops) of the West
were not a little indignant; and they wrote the
customary synodical epistles to Paulinus, as Bishop
of Antioch, but they entered into no communication
with Flavian; and they treated Diodorus of Tarsus
and Acacius of Berœa, and those who acted with
them, the consecrators of Flavian,[1] as guilty persons,
and they held them to be excommunicate."[2]

Thus the old state of things went on. The orthodox
of Antioch continued to be divided into two camps,
as they had been divided ever since the banishment
of S. Eustathius in 330. The great majority acknowledged S. Flavian as the true bishop, and he enjoyed
the communion of the Church throughout the Eastern
empire, with the exception of the bishops of Egypt,
Cyprus, and Arabia. The small body of the Eustathians still clung to Paulinus, who was recognized by
Rome and the West. Of course, if the theories of
the Vatican Council and of Cardinal Wiseman are
true, S. Flavian and Diodorus and Acacius were
excommunicated schismatics, and the whole Eastern
episcopate, who supported them and communicated
with them, were *fautores schismaticorum.* However,
the blessing of God seemed to rest upon them. It
was at Antioch, in the midst of this nest of so-called
schismatics, that S. Chrysostom was growing day by
day in sanctity, and was becoming famous for the

---

[1] τοὺς ἀμφὶ Διόδωρον . . . καὶ Ἀκάκιον.
[2] Sozom., *II. E.,* vii. 11.

eloquence and unction and fruitfulness of his preaching. As may be supposed, when the fact that he was a great Eastern saint and doctor is remembered, he took no heed of the papal pronouncement against S. Flavian. Antioch was an Eastern see, and the Eastern bishops had sanctioned Flavian's consecration, and had determined that it was canonical, as in fact it was. In such a matter it was for the Eastern bishops to judge; and S. Chrysostom, being well versed in the Church's laws, threw himself heart and soul into S. Flavian's cause. His whole life had hitherto been spent out of communion with Rome. In A.D. 369, when he was about twenty-two years old, he had been baptized by the great S. Meletius, and in the following year had been admitted by him into the minor order of readers. In 381, S. Meletius, just before leaving Antioch for the last time, had raised S. Chrysostom to the diaconate, and five years afterwards, early in the year 386, the saint was ordained priest by S. Flavian. It was not until twelve years later that S. Chrysostom, after his elevation to the episcopal throne of Constantinople, entered into communion with the see of Rome. He was then fifty-one years old, and the main bulk of his homilies and commentaries had been by that time written. When we are reading any of S. Chrysostom's works, or when they are being quoted controversially either on the one side or the other, it is desirable that we should remember that in the majority of cases what is being read or quoted was

written by the saint at a time when, according to
Cardinal Wiseman's theory, he was living in schism.
The mere statement of such an absurd consequence
appears to me to constitute of itself a disproof of the
theory which logically leads to it.

I said that S. Chrysostom threw himself heart and
soul into S. Flavian's cause.   In many of his sermons
he gives expression to the feelings of veneration and
affection which he entertained for his saintly bishop
and leader.   On one occasion, after quoting the great
promise to S. Peter, "Thou art Peter, and upon this
rock I will build My Church," he says that the
apostle inherited the name of Peter, "not because he
did miracles, but because he said, 'Thou art the
Christ, the Son of the living God.'"   "Thou seest,"
he continues, "that his very being called Peter took
its beginning, not from working miracles, but from
ardent zeal.   But, since I have mentioned Peter,
another Peter occurs to me, our common father and
teacher, who, being his successor in virtue, has also
inherited his see.   For this too is one of the privileges of our city, that it received at the beginning for
its teacher the first of the apostles."[1]   Thus did S.

[1] S. Chrys., *Hom. in Inscript. Actt.*, ii., *Opp.* ed. Ben., iii. 70.   S.
Chrysostom goes on to mention that, while Antioch had yielded up
S. Peter's body to the imperial city of Rome, she had nevertheless
kept S. Peter himself, because she kept S. Peter's faith.   I think that
it is quite possible that S. Chrysostom, in the ardour of his love and
veneration for the apostolic founder of the Church of Antioch, may
have been betrayed sometimes into an exaggerated tone, when speaking of S. Peter (but see Note F. in the Appendix, pp. 396–400).   It is,
however, to be noted that he never connects the Petrine primacy with
any supposed primacy of jurisdiction in the see of Rome.   As has been

Chrysostom regard S. Flavian, though excommunicated by Rome, as "another Peter," the successor of the apostle in virtue, as he was also, according to the belief of that age, Peter's successor in the episcopal throne of Antioch. In another homily he speaks of S. Flavian as his "tenderly loving father."[1] In another preached, when the bishop was not present, he speaks of his "fervent, fiery, warm charity, which could not be restrained."[2] But such passages are too numerous to quote, and would become wearisome.

But as S. Chrysostom was full of affection and admiration for S. Flavian, so also he is very earnest in warning his flock against the dreadful sin of leaving the true Church of Antioch in order to "go over" to the Eustathian schismatics who enjoyed the communion of Rome. In his eleventh Homily on the Ephesians, he says, "If we desire to partake of that Spirit which is from the Head, let us cleave one to another. . . . Nothing will so avail to divide the Church as love of authority. Nothing so provokes God's anger as the division of the Church. . . . When the Church is warred upon by her own children, it disgraces her

mentioned already, he was, during the greater part of his life, out of communion with the see of Rome, and consequently he would not be likely to magnify the Roman claims. But he had a great devotion to S. Peter, and it is conceivable that in his homilies, when he is giving expression to that devotion, his fervid rhetoric may have carried him beyond the strict limits of accurate statement.

[1] τῷ πατρὶ φιλοστόργῳ. *Hom. in illud In Fac. Petr. Rest., Opp.* ii. 362.

[2] *Hom. i. de Incomprehensib., Opp., i. 445.*

even in the face of her enemies. For it seems to
them a great mark of hypocrisy that those who have
been born in her, and nurtured in her bosom, and
have learned perfectly her secrets, that these should
of a sudden change, and treat her as an enemy. Let
these remarks be taken as addressed to those who
give themselves indiscriminately to those who divide
the Church. For if, on the one hand, those persons
have doctrines also contrary to ours,[1] then on that
account further it is not right to mix with them; if,
on the other hand, they hold the same opinions, the
reason for not mixing with them is greater still.
And why so ? Because then the disease is from lust
of authority. . . . Shall it be said, ' Their faith is the
same; they are orthodox as well as we ' ? If so, why
then are they not with us ? There is ' one Lord, one
faith, one baptism.' If their cause is right, then is
ours wrong; if ours is right, then is theirs wrong.
. . . Dost thou think this is enough, tell me, to say
that they are orthodox ? Are then things connected
with the appointment of the clergy past and done
away ?[2] And what is the advantage of all things

---

[1] S. Chrysostom is doubtless referring to the disputes about the use
of the word *hypostasis*, in connection with the doctrine of the Holy
Trinity (see the note on pp. 239, 240).

[2] τὰ τῆς χειροτονίας. The reference is to the uncanonical consecration of Paulinus by the firebrand Lucifer, when the see of Antioch
was already occupied by S. Meletius (see p. 165); or, if this homily
was preached after the death of Paulinus, there would be a reference
not only to Paulinus' own illegal consecration, but also to the entirely
uncanonical act by which before his death he consecrated, without
any assisting bishops, Evagrius to be his successor, as bishop of the
Eustathians. I shall give reasons further on for setting aside as most

else, if this be not strictly observed? For as we must needs contend for the faith, so must we for this also. . . . . If any amongst us are convicted of deeds the most disgraceful, and are about to undergo some penance, great is the alarm, great is the fear on all sides, lest he should start away, people say, and join the other side. Yea, let such an one start away ten thousand times, and let him join them. And I speak not only of those who have sinned, but if there be any one free from imputation, and he has a mind to depart, let him depart. I am grieved indeed at it, and bewail and lament it, and am cut to the very heart, as though I were being deprived of one of my limbs; and yet I am not so grieved as to be compelled to do anything wrong through such fear as this. . . . . I assert and protest that to make a schism in the Church is no less an evil than to fall into heresy. . . . . Of what hell shall he not be worthy who slays Christ and plucks Him limb from limb? . . . Speak, ye women that are present—for this generally is a failing of women—relate to the women who are absent what I have mentioned, startle them. . . . . Those who, forsooth, seem to be in earnest, these are the very persons who work this mischief. Yet surely, if it is for these things ye are in earnest, it were better that ye also were in the ranks of the indifferent; or rather it were better still that neither they should be indifferent, nor ye such as ye are. I speak not of

improbable the notion that the death of Paulinus preceded the delivery of this homily (see note on pp. 262, 263).

you that are present, but of those who are going
over.   The act is adultery. . . . One of the two [sets
of clergy] must have been appointed contrary to law.
If, therefore, you suspect [the rightfulness of our
position], we are ready to yield up the government
to any one you like.   Only let the Church be one.
But if we have been lawfully appointed, persuade
those who have illegally mounted the [episcopal]
throne to resign. . . . Be earnest, I entreat you, in
establishing yourselves firmly henceforward, and in
bringing back those who have seceded, that we may
with one accord lift up thanksgiving to God."[1]

If there are any English Churchmen who are
tempted to "go over" to the Anglo-Roman body, it
might be well for them to read carefully the whole of
the preceding extract.   The forcible reasoning which
S. Chrysostom employed against the Romanizers of
his day, is entirely applicable to their representatives
in the present generation.   There is no doubt one
great difference in the situation.   In those days, the
days of Pope Siricius, the papal idea was only the
germ of a germ.   It was not completed as a germ
until the time of S. Leo and his immediate successors.
Now the Leonine germ has reached an enormous

---

[1] S. Chrys., *Hom.* xi. in *Epist. ad Ephes., Opp.* ed. Ben., xi. 86–89.
In the Benedictine preface to the Homilies on the Ephesians, Dom
Montfaucon shows clearly that they were preached at Antioch, and
he draws his primary argument from this very passage; concerning
which he says, "Omnino loqui videtur de schismate Eustathiano, tunc
Antiochiæ perseverante."   The preface to the Oxford translation
gives a summary of Montfaucon's other arguments.   Compare also
Tillemont, xi. 628, 629.

development, and will no doubt develop much more as time goes on. The Eustathians themselves would have been amazed if they could have foreseen the future.

The Eustathian Bishop Paulinus seems to have died in A.D. 389 or 390.[1] Before his death he conse-

---

[1] Paulinus' death is sometimes assigned to the year 388, but that date appears to be too early. Socrates (*H. E.*, v. 15) and Sozomen (*H. E.*, vii. 15) imply that he died about the time when Theodosius celebrated his victory over Maximus by a triumph at Rome. That triumph took place in June, 389. But as Socrates and Sozomen also tell us that Evagrius did not long survive his consecration, and as he was certainly alive when the Council of Capua was held—that is, during the winter of 391–392, and as the two historians are not very accurate in their chronological indications, it is perhaps more probable that Paulinus did not die till 390, or even till the beginning of 391. During the short episcopate of Evagrius, Theophilus of Alexandria and the Egyptian bishops, who had communicated with the Eustathians as long as Paulinus lived, withheld their communion from them, in consequence, I suppose, of their uncertainty about the canonicity of Evagrius' consecration. It is a moot point whether Evagrius enjoyed the communion of Rome and the West. Theodoret (*H. E.*, v. 23) asserts that he did ; but I should be inclined to gather from S. Ambrose's 56th Epistle, which is addressed to Theophilus, that not only Egypt, but also Rome and the West, withheld their communion from Evagrius as well as from his rival, S. Flavian. If so, it is just possible that, when S. Chrysostom preached his eleventh Homily on the Ephesians, quoted on pp. 258–261, the Eustathians were not in communion with Rome. I hardly think it likely that that homily was preached after the death of Paulinus, because it is difficult to imagine what could move "earnest" people, who held no peculiar or heretical doctrine, to leave the great Catholic community, which acknowledged S. Flavian, and which enjoyed the communion of the whole episcopate of the East, in order to join Evagrius, who was at the head of a small sect, and who was *ex hypothesi* neither in communion with the East nor with the West, but stood absolutely alone as an isolated bishop. Certainly S. Chrysostom makes not the faintest allusion either to the supposed isolation of the Eustathians or to the withdrawal of Roman support from them, as reasons for regarding them as schismatics. Obviously he could not use the latter

crated Evagrius to be his successor. This act, as I have already pointed out, involved a most serious breach of the canons. The consecration took place without the consent of the bishops of the province and patriarchate. It was performed with no assisting bishops; and, moreover, it was the case of a bishop consecrating his own successor, a proceeding which the Church has always forbidden. The fact was that no single bishop in the patriarchate of the East supported Paulinus, or communicated with him. The Western Council of Capua, held during the winter of 391–392, granted the communion of the West to all orthodox bishops of the East, with the exception of the rival bishops at Antioch, S. Flavian and Evagrius. The Council committed to Theophilus of Alexandria and to the other Egyptian bishops the duty of arbitrating

argument, for he had never been in communion with Rome himself. There was nothing in S. Chrysostom's principles to prevent his preaching the homily during the lifetime of Paulinus, and it seems to me that we have every reason for supposing that it was so preached. With regard to Paulinus, I notice that Mr. Richardson (*What are the Catholic Claims?* p. 117) entitles him "*Saint* Paulinus." I very much doubt whether he could produce any proof of the Church having ever commemorated him as a saint. The two Catholic bishops of Antioch, S. Meletius and S. Flavian, were canonized; but the Eustathian leaders, Paulinus and Evagrius, never attained to that honour. It is true that S. Flavian, with great wisdom and magnanimity, inserted their names in the diptychs, but that is a very different thing from canonizing them. S. Atticus, in a letter to S. Cyril of Alexandria, mentions that "Paulinus and Evagrius, who were leaders of the schism in the Church of Antioch, were inscribed after their death in the sacred diptychs with a view to the peace and concord of the people" (*Opp.*, S. Cyril. Alex., ed. Aubert, vi. 203). The name of Paulinus of Antioch does not appear in the Roman Martyrology.

between those two.   S. Flavian, however, very naturally declined to commit his cause, which had been canonically decided in his favour by his proper judges, the bishops of the East, to the arbitrament of the Egyptians, who had for years been communicating with the schismatic Eustathians, and had thus been fomenting division in his city and diocese.   As it happened, the situation was soon afterwards simplified by the death of Evagrius.   The great influence of S. Flavian prevented any bishop being appointed to carry on the Eustathian succession, and so at last a real prospect of peace dawned upon the Christian people of Antioch.   However, the Eustathians still kept up their separate assemblies for worship under the leadership of their presbyters.   It was not until 398, after S. Chrysostom's consecration to the bishopric of Constantinople, that the long breach between Rome and Antioch was brought to an end.   This happy result was effected by the mediation of S. Chrysostom.

The Emperor Arcadius, the son and successor of Theodosius, had summoned Theophilus of Alexandria to Constantinople, to take part in S. Chrysostom's consecration, and Theophilus was in fact his principal consecrator.   In this way it came to pass that S. Chrysostom, for the first time in his life, was admitted to the communion of the see of Alexandria. It was also at this time of his consecration that he negotiated the reunion of Theophilus with S. Flavian.[1]

---

[1] Tillemont, x, 809,

Thus the three great sees of Constantinople,[1] Alexandria, and Antioch entered into a league of peace
with each other. It only remained to bring Rome
and the West into the confederation, and then the
visibility of the Church's unity, which had been so
long in abeyance, would be once more restored.
Accordingly Acacius, Bishop of Berœa, one of S.
Flavian's consecrators, was sent to Rome by S. Chrysostom, and S. Isidore, a priest of Alexandria, was
sent with him by Theophilus. Acacius carried with
him the decree of S. Chrysostom's election to the
episcopal throne of Constantinople, and the two
legates, who travelled together, took to the pope
documentary proof of the fact that S. Flavian was
in full communion with Theophilus.[2] Pope Siricius
seems to have made no difficulty about receiving
S. Flavian and S. Chrysostom to his communion.
There is not the smallest reason to suppose that
they expressed any sorrow for their previous line of
action, or any acknowledgment of any divinely appointed primacy in the see of Rome. There is no
trace of any such notion in S. Chrysostom's voluminous writings. S. Flavian and S. Chrysostom appear
to have maintained the ground which they had
always taken, and they were received on their own
terms; and so the Church was, after many years of
division, restored to a state of peace. Acacius and

---

[1] Constantinople had been given precedence over Alexandria by the
second Ecumenical Council.

[2] Tillemont, *loc. cit.*

S. Isidore returned from Rome to Egypt together; and Acacius was able to carry on to Antioch "letters of communion for S. Flavian and his flock from the bishops of Egypt and of the West."[1] A certain number of the Eustathians still kept up a separation, although, after the reunion of the Church, a great many were received by S. Flavian into the Catholic fold. The schism finally came to an end about the year 415, during the pontificate of Alexander, Bishop of Antioch. S. Flavian himself had previously died, about the year 404, at the great age of ninety-five. For sixty-seven years, that is to say, from the time when he was twenty-two to the time when he was eighty-nine, he had lived outside the Roman communion. As we have seen, there is no reason to suppose that, when peace was restored, he made any act of reparation for what Cardinal Wiseman would consider to be a life spent in schism. Nevertheless the learned Ultramontane, Pietro Ballerini, describes him as "a most celebrated bishop, who was the master of S. John Chrysostom, and whose name was enrolled in the register of the saints."[2]

---

[1] Sozomen, *H. E.*, viii. 3; compare Socrat., *H. E.*, vi. 9. Notice how Sozomen mentions the bishops of Egypt before those of the West, although the latter included the pope. How could he have expressed himself in that way if he had accepted the papal theory?

[2] "Episcopus celeberrimus, qui S. Joannis Chrysostomi magister extitit, et in Sanctorum album relatus fuit" (Petr. Ballerin. *de vi ac rat. primat. Rom. Pont.*, ed. 1845, p. 135).

LECTURE VII.

THE UNITY OF THE CHURCH.—II.

The Acacian Troubles.

IN this lecture I intend to continue, and if possible to conclude, what I have to say on the true nature of the unity of the Church, giving further illustrations, from the sayings and actions of the saints, of the great principle, that separation from the communion of the see of Rome does not necessarily carry with it exclusion from the fellowship of the Catholic Church.

During the greater part of the last lecture we were considering the troubles caused by the Eustathian schism. I propose now to pass over nearly a hundred years, and to deal with the dissension which arose in the Church in consequence of the excommunication and deposition of Acacius, the Patriarch of Constantinople, by Felix III.[1] of Rome, in the year

[1] He is commonly called Felix III., but he was really the second and not the third pope of that name. The so-called Felix II. was an anti-pope intruded into the Roman see by the Arian Emperor Constantius, at the time when Liberius was living in exile at Berœa (see p. 139).

484. By that time the Roman see had very much enlarged and consolidated its power. As we have seen, S. Leo had, in A.D. 445, obtained from the murderer Valentinian III. an imperial constitution, which, so far as the law of the state could do so, subjected the bishops to the will of the pope.[1] Moreover, at the Council of Chalcedon, in A.D. 451, although much was done which S. Leo disliked extremely, yet for the first time in the history of the Church the legates of the pope presided at an Ecumenical Council,[2] and the sanction which the Council gave to S. Leo's great dogmatic letter to S. Flavian of Constantinople, given, as it was, after careful examination and comparison of its statements with the writings of earlier Fathers, helped largely to consolidate the reputation of the Roman see for

---

[1] See pp. 212, 213.

[2] At the Council of Ephesus, although S. Cyril held Pope Celestine's proxy, empowering him to "join the authority" of the Roman see to that of his own Alexandrian see for the particular purpose of deposing and excommunicating Nestorius, if he should continue in the heresy which he openly avowed, yet, as Bossuet (*Def. Cler. Gall.*, vii. xiii. 7) rightly observes, "Cyril had not been expressly delegated to the Council, of which Celestine had as yet no thought when he commissioned Cyril to represent him." The pope sent other legates, namely, two bishops and a priest, to represent him at the Council; and they in the pope's name promulgated his assent and the assent of all the West to what had been there done. Nevertheless Cyril, as being the highest dignitary present, presided, taking precedence of the legates who represented Celestine in the Council. This was quite in accordance with the Church's ancient custom. So Hosius, though he was not the pope's legate, took precedence at Nicæa of the two priests who represented Sylvester; and at Carthage S. Aurelius took precedence of Faustinus, the legate first of Boniface and afterwards of Celestine.

orthodoxy.   Again, S. Leo presented the unusual
spectacle of a pope who was also a theologian; and
in the terse Latin of his sermons he had worked out
what may be called the first systematic exposition
of the papal interpretation of the great Petrine
texts. S. Leo showed the way, and his successors
boldly followed. One may mention specially Felix
III. (483-492); Gelasius I. (492-496); Symmachus
(498-514); and Hormisdas (514-523).[1]

The quarrel with Acacius began in the year 482,
during the pontificate of Simplicius. There can be
no question that Acacius was very much to blame,
and it seems to me that he richly deserved to be
deposed and excommunicated. He had been made
Patriarch of Constantinople in A.D. 471, and for
eleven years in all his public actions had appeared
to be a champion of the Catholic faith, as it had been
defined at Chalcedon. But in the year 482, the see
of Alexandria having become vacant, John Talaia,
an orthodox priest, was canonically elected to the
throne of S. Mark. Unfortunately, the letter which,
according to custom, he wrote to the Patriarch of
Constantinople, to announce his election and consecration, miscarried. Acacius took offence at the
seeming want of courtesy, and he watched for oppor-
tunities, when he was conversing with the Emperor

---

[1] Hilary (461-467) and Simplicius (467-483) intervened between
S. Leo and Felix III., and Anastasius II. (496-498) intervened between Gelasius and Symmachus. Anastasius was less grasping and
in every way more attractive than his immediate predecessors and
successors.

Zeno, to disparage the new Patriarch of Alexandria.
He proposed to the emperor that Peter Mongus, the
Monophysite anti-patriarch, should be recognized as
the true patriarch, on the condition that he should
accept and promote the so-called *Henoticon*, a document inspired, if not drawn up, by himself, which
was intended as a compromise on the basis of which
Catholics and Monophysites might unite. It recognized the dogmatic decisions of the first three Ecumenical Councils, but, though it anathematized
Eutyches, he was silent on the subject of the binding authority of the Chalcedonian definition.[1] The
emperor fell in with Acacius' proposal, and Peter
Mongus on his side accepted the *Henoticon*. Accordingly, he was enthroned at Alexandria as the patriarch
recognized by the emperor, and in his letters to Pope
Simplicius and to Acacius he professed to accept the
Council of Chalcedon. At heart he remained a
Monophysite; and very soon, when he found that
by his compliance with Catholic orthodoxy he was
losing his old Monophysite adherents, he anathematized Chalcedon and the tome of S. Leo. Then again,
when Acacius called him to account, he once more
accepted "the holy Council of Chalcedon."[2] Altogether he was a most unfit person to sit as a suc-

---

[1] It is important to remember that the Henoticon was not in itself
heretical, but it needed to be supplemented by other tests, if Monophysites were to be excluded from communion (see Natalis Alexand.,
Hist. Eccl., ix. 615, ed. 1786, Dingii ad Rhenum).

[2] The letter of Mongus to Acacius may be read in the *Church
History* of Evagrius (iii. 17).

cessor of S. Mark and S. Athanasius. Acacius had undoubtedly sullied his own orthodoxy by promoting Mongus' intrusion into the see of Alexandria, and by remaining in communion with him, when it became evident that the purity of his faith was more than doubtful.[1]

Meanwhile the true patriarch, John Talaia, had fled to Rome, where he was honourably received by Simplicius. That Pope, however, died a few weeks after Talaia's arrival, and was succeeded by Felix III.; and to him Talaia addressed a formal petition and complaint, in which various charges were brought against Acacius. The pope sent two suburbicarian bishops, Vitalis of Truentum and Misenus of Cumæ, as legates to Constantinople; they carried with them letters to Acacius and to the emperor, and also a formal citation commanding Acacius to present himself without loss of time at Rome, there to answer before a synod (*in conventu*) of his brother-bishops the charges brought against him.[2] When the legates arrived in Constantinople, they were first imprisoned and then bribed, and ultimately they gave in to the

---

[1] But it is difficult for us to judge with any certainty as to the *degree* of Acacius' faultiness. We do not know whether he had convincing proofs of Mongus' heresy. Heretics are often very slippery; and it should be remembered that in the fourth century the see of Rome was for a long while deceived as to Marcellus of Ancyra. The popes held him to be orthodox long after the Catholic bishops of the East had detected his unsoundness. S. Basil's complaints about the way in which the popes had "supported heresy" in the case of Marcellus have been quoted on pp. 172, 173.

[2] Colcti, v. 217, 218.

wishes of the emperor and the patriarch. They
publicly communicated with Acacius and with the
representatives of Peter Mongus, and during the
course of the service the name of Mongus was recited
in the reading of the diptychs. On the return
journey they took back with them a letter from
Acacius to Felix, in which Mongus was praised, and
in which Acacius avowed that he held communion
with him. The pope lost no time in summoning a
Council of the suburbicarian bishops which met at
Rome in July, 484. In that Council the legates were
deposed from the episcopate and excommunicated;
and either at the Council or shortly after its conclusion, the pope passed sentence on Acacius, in which
he professed to deprive him of the episcopate and of
Catholic communion, and to cut him off from being
numbered among the faithful.[1]

As I have already said, I think that Acacius
thoroughly deserved to be deposed and excommunicated. But it is quite another question whether the
pope had authority to do what he did in the matter.
He certainly had the right to separate Acacius from
the communion of the Roman Church, and if his
sentence was sanctioned by the Roman synod, it
would avail to cut Acacius off from the communion
of the suburbicarian Churches generally. But separation from the communion of the Roman Church, or
even of the suburbicarian Churches, would not effect
the separation of Acacius from the fellowship of the

<hr>

[1] Coleti, v. 167-169.

Catholic Church, unless the Roman sentence were confirmed by the episcopate at large, expressing their judgment either in an Ecumenical Council or in separate local Councils. The proper tribunal before which Acacius ought to have been brought, and which would have had authority to depose him and to cut him off from the unity of the Church, would have been the synod of the whole patriarchate of Constantinople, which included the three exarchates of Asia, Pontus, and Thrace.[1] The synod of the patriarchate, or the

---

[1] Strictly speaking, the tribunal of first instance would have been the synod of the province, with an appeal to the synod of the patriarchate, whose decision was final, unless an Ecumenical Council were assembled to consider the case (see the sixth canon of the second Ecumenical Council). S. Chrysostom, in a letter to Pope Innocent I., describes how, when the Emperor Arcadius wished him to try Theophilus, Patriarch of Alexandria, he begged to be excused, " knowing the laws of our fathers, and out of respect and honour to the man, having moreover letters from him, which pointed out that causes should not be drawn beyond the countries to which they belonged, *but that the affairs of each province should be transacted therein*" (S. Chrys., *Ep.* i. *Innocentio Episc. Rom., Opp.* ed. Ben., iii. 516). From this letter it appears clear that both S. Chrysostom and Theophilus agreed that a patriarch should be tried first of all by the bishops of his province. Moreover, as S. Chrysostom was writing to the pope, and refers to the principle as if it was established, we may conclude that he anticipated that the pope would agree on this point with himself and his enemy Theophilus. It is possible, however, that at Constantinople the exceptional institution, known as the σύνοδος ἐνδημοῦσα, would have taken the place of the Provincial Synod. But, whatever might have been the strict law in regard to the tribunal of first instance, in practice, when the case of a patriarch was to be investigated, the larger synod of the patriarchate or even of the whole East would have been assembled. One may instance the synods at Antioch, which tried Paul of Samosata ; and compare Tillemont, xi. 195. It is worth while noticing, as a proof of the growth of the papal and Italian claims, that in A.D. 381 or 382 the Council of Milan, under S. Ambrose, writing to the Emperor Theodosius on

synod of the whole East, or the supreme tribunal of an Ecumenical Council, would have been fully competent to exercise jurisdiction over Acacius. The synod of the suburbicarian bishops was wholly incompetent to do anything more than separate Acacius from the particular communion of their Churches. His episcopal office and his membership in the Catholic Church was not subject to their jurisdiction. Perhaps it will be replied that, owing to the confusions in the East and the complicity of the emperor with the misdoings of Acacius, it was impossible to expect a synod to be assembled, which should have the courage to do justice in the case, and that there was need for the pope to intervene, and if necessary

the subject of the disputed succession at Antioch and also about a similar difficulty at Constantinople in connection with Maximus the Cynic and Nectarius, pleads that the East alone ought not to settle such matters, but that an Ecumenical Council was needed. S. Ambrose and his council expressly say, "*We do not assume to ourselves the prerogative of examining such things, but we ought to have a share in their examination*" (S. Ambros., *Ep.* xiii., *Opp.* ed. Ben., iii. 856). The emperor wrote back to the Italians that their request was unreasonable and offensive to the Eastern bishops, and that their argument in favour of the necessity for an Ecumenical Council was insufficient; that the affairs of Nectarius and Flavian were in the East, and all the parties were there present, and consequently that these cases ought to be settled in the East and by the East, and that there ought to be no innovation in the bounds which the Fathers had set (see Tillemont, x. 150). There can be no question that the emperor was stating the immemorial practice of the Church, not only in the East, but in Africa and elsewhere. The Italians had to give way. However, the point to be noticed is that in 381 the Italians only claimed in a humble sort of way *a share* in the decision; whereas in 484 the local Roman Council professed to depose Acacius, who was an Eastern prelate, without the East having anything to say in the matter. The claim was simply revolutionary.

to stretch his prerogative, so that somehow the Church's orthodoxy might be vindicated. An argument of that kind seems to be based on notions which imply forgetfulness of the relations of the Church to our Lord, and of His promises to her. Our Lord, who is the one and only Head of the Church, is quite able to take care of her, and in His own time and way to lead her out of her difficulties and confusions into complete unity in regard to all necessary articles of faith. He can, when He sees fit, secure for her the opportunity of exercising such acts of discipline as will purge her from seeming complicity with heresy. There was no need for the pope or for any one else to transgress the bounds of his jurisdiction. In the times of the Arian troubles the Church had been in much greater difficulty and confusion than she was in the time of Acacius and Peter Mongus, and yet our Lord guided her in the midst of the storm, and brought her at last into unity through the truth. I grant that extreme cases might arise, when large sections of the Church might appear to have lapsed into undisguised heresy, and when, on the principle that *necessity has no law*, it would be competent for any bishop to intervene in dioceses beyond his jurisdiction, and to do what he could to provide faithful pastors for the flock of Christ. If the pope had acted in this case on that principle, a good defence might perhaps be made on his behalf. But Pope Felix never attempted to defend his conduct on the plea of necessity. He acted throughout

as if he was the possessor of a universal jurisdiction
inherited from S. Peter.   He must have sanctioned the
synodical letter of the council of forty-two Italian
bishops which met in the basilica of S. Peter at Rome
in October, 485.   They wrote as follows: "As often
as the priests of the Lord [*i.e.* the bishops] are
assembled within the limits of Italy to treat of
ecclesiastical causes, especially those which concern
the faith, the custom is observed that the successor of
the bishops of the apostolic see, as representing the
entire episcopate of all Italy, should himself make all
decrees, that he may exercise that care of all the
Churches which belongs to him as the head of all.
For the Lord said to the blessed Apostle Peter, ' Thou
art Peter, and on this rock I will build My Church,
and the gates of hell shall not prevail against it.'   In
obedience to which words, the 318 holy Fathers
assembled at Nicæa granted the right of confirming
and initiating [ecclesiastical] proceedings to the holy
Roman Church,[1] both of which rights the succession
[of pontiffs] by the grace of Christ preserves, even to
this our age."   Then they proceed to apply what has
been said to the case of Acacius, on whom, " following
the decree of the apostolic see," they pronounce
anathema.[2]   This, then, was the authorized Roman
account of the conduct of Pope Felix.   He claimed
the right to depose Acacius from his bishopric and to

---

[1] Confirmationem rerum atque auctoritatem sanctæ Romanæ ecclesiæ
detulerunt.

[2] Coleti, v. 248–250.

cut him off from the number of the faithful, on the ground that he, as Roman pontiff, was the head of all the Churches, having the care of all. And these rights are traced up ultimately to our Lord's words to S. Peter, and proximately to a decree of the Nicene Council. To what Nicene decree does the Roman Synod refer? No such decree appears among the genuine canons of that Council. As usual, the Roman claims are based upon a spurious interpolation. Certainly, if for one moment one could conceive these claims to be legitimate, one would have to say that the popes have been the most unfortunate set of people that have ever existed. On this hypothesis, it would follow that a true claim, which, if it is true, may be rightly described as the chief point in the whole of the Christian system, has been perpetually commended to the acceptance of the world on grounds which will not bear examination. To use Père Gratry's words, "The question has been gangrened with fraud." There can be no doubt that in this instance the Roman Council is referring to the spurious clause interpolated at the beginning of the sixth Nicene Canon, "The Roman Church always had the primacy." That clause occurred in the copy of the Nicene Canons which was used by the Roman legates at the Council of Chalcedon; and in this Acacian controversy Gelasius, the successor of Pope Felix, refers to it in a certain *tractatus*,[1] of which

---

[1] Coleti, v. 341; and compare the note by the Ballerini in Migne's reprint of their edition of S. Leo's works (tom. iii. col. 393).

fragments remain. The clause is spurious,[1] but even if it were genuine, it is difficult to see how the Roman Council of 485 could extract out of its somewhat vague wording any proof that the Fathers of Nicæa granted the right of confirming and initiating proceedings to the Roman Church.[2] And yet, if the Council did not refer to this spurious clause, there is absolutely nothing else in the genuine canons of Nicæa which bears in the remotest way on the claims to primatial jurisdiction put forth by the popes. The authority asserted by Felix, when he passed sentence of deposition and excommunication on Acacius, was undoubtedly a usurped authority, which the Eastern Churches could not recognize without danger to their own liberties and to the liberties of the whole Church.[3] Acacius deserved punishment, but the

---

[1] The spuriousness of the clause about the primacy is evidently acknowledged by Perrone, for, speaking (*Prælectt. Theoll.*, tom. ii. pars i. p. 418, ed. 1841) of the sixth canon of Nicæa and the twenty-eighth of Chalcedon, he says, "Cum igitur de ecclesiæ Romanæ primatu nullo modo agatur in allatis canonibus." Compare Hefele, i. 397, Eng. trans.

[2] Nor was any such right granted to the see of Rome by the Sardican canons, which the popes of the fifth century used to quote as if they were Nicene.

[3] It must be remembered that Acacius was not accused of being personally a heretic. His principal fault (and it was a very great one) was that he was too easy in accepting the assurances of Peter Mongus that he venerated "the holy Council of Chalcedon;" while all the time the crafty heretic was repudiating that council among his Monophysite friends in Alexandria. Acacius must, one would think, have been aware of this, and if he had been really zealous for the revealed doctrine of our Lord's Incarnation, he would have taken measures to expose the double dealing of Mongus, and would then have withdrawn from his communion.

punishment inflicted on him by Felix was *ultra vires,* and therefore invalid. It was, as a matter of course, ignored by Acacius himself and by the whole Eastern Church; and the result was that there ensued a complete breach of communion between the East and West for thirty-five years—that is to say, from A.D. 484 to A.D. 519.

It is important to notice that the breach of communion was *complete.* A hundred years earlier Pope Damasus could refuse his communion to S. Meletius, and yet could remain in communion with S. Basil, who energetically supported S. Meletius.[1] The popes did not then put forth the view that all those whom they separated from the communion of the Roman Church were in consequence separated from the communion of the Catholic Church. But the Roman claims had very much developed between the time of Damasus and the time of Felix and Gelasius. It was not merely Acacius who was excommunicated, but by the Roman party it was held that all who in any way communicated with Acacius, whether during his lifetime or after his death, were tainted with the taint of communion with Peter Mongus; and so the anathema which had been pronounced on Acacius was extended to them, and they became, in the view of the pope, altogether external to the Church. The completeness of the breach is shown very clearly by what took place at a Council of Rome under Gelasius in the year 495. At that council, Misenus, the former

---

[1] Compare the remarks of Tillemont, xvi. 642.

Bishop of Cumæ, who had been sent by Pope Felix
as one of his legates to Constantinople, and who had
there been induced to communicate with Acacius and
with the representatives of Peter Mongus, and who
had in consequence been deposed from the episcopate
and excommunicated, was restored to communion
with the Church and was re-established in his former
see. The documents containing his humble petition
for mercy and his recantation are preserved in the acts
of the Council. Misenus professes before the Council
that he rejects all heresies, " especially the Eutychian
heresy with its originator Eutyches and his follower
Dioscorus, and those who succeeded the latter, and
those who held communion with him, namely,
Timothy the Cat,[1] Peter [Mongus] of Alexandria,
Acacius of Constantinople, Peter [the Fuller] of
Antioch, and all their accomplices and *all those who
communicate with them ;* ' all these he repudiates,
condemns, and for ever anathematizes, and all these
and all like them he curses with dreadful impre-
cations,[2] and promises that he will never have any
sort of fellowship with such, and that for the future
he will be utterly separate from all of them." After
this, Pope Gelasius made a long speech to the Council,
which concludes as follows: " In consideration of the
fact that Misenus has, according to the rule, professed
that he detests all heresies, and especially the

---

[1] For an account of the origin of this singular nickname, see Dr.
Bright's article in Smith and Wace, iv. 1031.

[2] " Horribiliter execrari."

Eutychian heresy, together with Eutyches, Dioscorus, Timothy the Cat, Peter of Alexandria, Acacius of Constantinople, and Peter of Antioch, and all their successors, and *all those who follow and communicate with them,* and that he strikes them with an everlasting anathema, let him again partake of the grace of apostolic communion and of the episcopal dignity which he originally received by a Catholic consecration." Then all the bishops[1] and priests rose up in the synod and exclaimed fifteen times, "O Christ, hear us! long life to Gelasius!" and twelve times they said, "Lord Peter, preserve him!" and seven times they said, "May he hold the see of Peter during the years of Peter!"[2] and six times they said, "We see thee, who art the vicar of Christ!" and again they said, "May he hold the see of Peter during the years of Peter!" and this they repeated thirty-seven times.[3] Such was the spirit which the popes of the latter part of the fifth century had managed to infuse into the bishops whom they consecrated, and who were under their immediate rule.

We must now turn to the East, and see how the Eastern Church was faring during these thirty-five years, when it was absolutely cut off from fellowship with the Roman Church, and when, according to the

---

[1] There were forty-six bishops, probably all of them suburbicarian.

[2] Alluding to the utterly unhistorical tradition that S. Peter was Bishop of Rome for twenty-five years.

[3] See the whole of the acts in Coleti, v. 397–402.

Roman view, it was in consequence cut off from the Catholic Church, and was abiding in a state of execrable schism.

Acacius had died during the lifetime of Felix in 489. He was succeeded in the patriarchal throne of Constantinople by Fravitas, who, however, died three or four months after his consecration. He had written to Pope Felix announcing his succession to the see, and asking for his communion. The pope's reply arrived in Constantinople after the death of Fravitas, and was received by his successor Euphemius. The consecration of Euphemius seemed to be providentially ordered, with the view of giving to the Church an opportunity of getting the schism healed. He was a courageous and holy man, full of zeal for the Catholic faith, and ready to suffer in its defence. Before his enthronement a synodical letter arrived from Peter Mongus, addressed to Fravitas ; but, when Euphemius perceived that Mongus in this letter anathematized the Council of Chalcedon, he cut him off from his communion and expunged his name from the diptychs of the Church of Constantinople. Mongus died shortly afterwards, and was succeeded in the see of Alexandria by one who bore the honoured name of Athanasius. Unfortunately, this successor was also a Monophysite in doctrine, and Euphemius refused to hold communion with him. For the same reason Euphemius refrained from communicating with Palladius of Antioch ; while, on the other hand, he admitted to his communion

Sallustius, the Patriarch of Jerusalem, who accepted the decrees of Chalcedon. Euphemius, on his accession, wrote a synodical letter to Pope Felix, having first reinserted his name on the diptychs of his Church.[1] The pope accepted the letter, and, having read it, felt assured of Euphemius' doctrinal orthodoxy, and was well inclined towards him; but he would not grant to him episcopal communion, because Euphemius had not expunged the names of Acacius and Fravitas from the diptychs.[2] Thus the schism between the Churches of Rome and Constantinople continued. Assuredly the responsibility lay now entirely on the pope. There could be no pretence of supposing that Euphemius was inclined to tamper with the faith. But he was not prepared to acknowledge the validity of Acacius' deposition,[3] which had been the act of an Italian Council without any participation of the Eastern Church. Whether Acacius was worthy of censure or not, he had remained free from any valid censure during his lifetime, and now Euphemius was entitled to argue that he had passed away from the judgment of men.[4] The real point which divided the

---

[1] It had been removed by Acacius, after his so-called deposition by Felix.

[2] Niceph. Callist. *H. E.*, xvi. 19, in Migne's *Patrol. Græc.*, cxlvii. 153.

[3] Euphemius seems to have laid stress on the fact that the pretended deposition had been the act of only *one* man, viz. the pope (see Gelas., *Commonitor. ad Faustum*, Colcti, v. 295).

[4] Nicole and other Roman Catholic writers, who uphold the righteousness of the cause of Euphemius, allege, as a further justification of his proceedings, that *dictum* of S. Augustine in which he deprecates the excommunication of those who are likely to draw after them a

Churches was no longer the duty of safe-guarding the true faith of the Incarnation, and the authority of the Council of Chalcedon, but the claim of the pope to depose an Eastern patriarch, who was not personally heretical, and to cut him off from the number of the faithful. If Euphemius had given way on that point, he would have betrayed the Catholic system of Church government, and he would have been worthy of all censure. The pope was fighting for his own baseless claim to autocracy, and it was the duty of every well-instructed Catholic to resist him.

Our information in regard to this breach of communion between the East and the West is mainly derived from the letters of the popes and from the acts of Roman Councils, who of course regard it from the Roman point of view. It may therefore be well to quote an account of the matter from an Eastern

multitude of persons ("*qui habent sociam multitudinem*"). I will quote one paragraph of Nicole's argument: "Quoiqu' on ne puisse douter qu' Acace ne fut coupable, il n'est pas certain néanmoins que tout coupable puisse être déposé et excommunié par toutes sortes de juges. Les Orientaux prétendoient qu'un Patriarche de Constantinople ne pouvoit être jugé ni déposé que par un concile auquel l'Église d'Orient eût part. D'ailleurs la règle de Saint Augustin: Qu'il ne faut point excommunier ceux qui entraînent avec eux une multitude de personnes, '*qui habent sociam multitudinem*,' étoit trés considerable à l'égard d'un Patriarche qui attiroit avec lui tout l'Orient. Ainsi les Evêques attachez [sic] à la cour s'étant unis à Acace, les plus saints Evêques d'Orient ne crurent pas se devoir séparer de sa communion, de peur d'augmenter le mal au lieu de la guérir" (Nicole, *de l'Unité de l'Église*, liv. ii. chap. x. pp. 308 *f.*, ed. 1708). This treatise of Nicole is styled by Mgr. Bouvier, Bishop of Le Mans, who died in 1854, an "*exquisitum opus.*"

writer; and one could not go to a better authority than to Cyril of Scythopolis, the friend and biographer of several of the saints who lived during the period of the schism. Cardinal Baronius says of him that he was the most accurate and trustworthy writer of saints' lives that he knew, always excepting S. Athanasius and S. Jerome.[1] He also says of him that he was "illustrious on account of his sanctity."[2] Alban Butler refers to him as "one of the best writers of antiquity."[3] This Cyril of Scythopolis, speaking in his life of S. Sabas about S. Elias of Jerusalem, says, "When the Patriarch Elias had obtained the see of Jerusalem in the third year of the reign of the Emperor Anastasius[4] [A.D. 494], the Church of God was thrown into confusion, being divided into three parts; for the bishops of Rome dissented from those of Byzantium because the name of Acacius, a former bishop of Constantinople, had been inserted in the sacred diptychs; and Acacius had not followed the preciseness ($\tau \grave{\eta} \nu \ \dot{\alpha} \kappa \rho \acute{\iota} \beta \epsilon \iota \alpha \nu$[5]) of the

[1] *Annal.*, s.a. 491, tom. vi. p. 468, ed. Antverp., 1658.

[2] See Baronius' annotated edition of the Roman Martyrology, in his notice of S. Sabas, who is commemorated on December 5 (p. 533, ed. Antverp., 1589).

[3] In the *Life of S. Euthymius* (January 20).

[4] The reign of Anastasius lasted from 491 to 518.

[5] There is, I think, a slight touch of irony in the application of the word $\dot{\alpha} \kappa \rho \acute{\iota} \beta \epsilon \iota \alpha$ to the Romans. So, more than 120 years earlier, S. Basil, in a letter to S. Eusebius of Samosata, with very marked irony describes Pope Damasus and the Roman clergy as $\dot{\alpha} \kappa \rho \iota \beta \acute{\epsilon} \sigma \tau \epsilon \rho o \iota$ (*Ep.* cxxxviii., *Opp.* ed. Ben., iii. 230). And S. Gregory Nazianzen describes the pope and the Westerns as "the self-styled defenders of the canons" (see p. 251). There was a something about Roman ways which made the great saints of the East shrug their shoulders.

Romans.   Moreover, the Byzantine bishops dissented from the Alexandrians, who were anathematizing the Council of Chalcedon, and were communicating with the memory of Dioscorus, who had been deposed by that synod.   The result was that Elias was only able to communicate with Euphemius, the Bishop of Byzantium; for, as has been said, *the Westerns had separated themselves,*[1] and Palladius of Antioch, in order to curry favour with the emperor, was anathematizing the decrees of Chalcedon, and was embracing the communion of the Alexandrians."[2]   It apparently did not occur to S. Elias that it would be his duty at all hazards to get into communion with Rome.   From the Eastern point of view, " the Westerns had separated themselves."   And this was strictly true.   The separation was the act of the pope, and the responsibility for the schism lay on him.   S. Elias was not a courtier bishop.   If he had been he would have communicated with the Monophysite bishops of Alexandria and Antioch, who were favoured by the emperor.   He was an orthodox Eastern Catholic, and he therefore naturally embraced the communion of Euphemius.   Nineteen years afterwards, in A.D. 513, he was driven from his see by the heretical emperor, and was banished to the shores of the Red Sea, because he refused to communicate with the Monophysite Severus, who had been intruded by the emperor into the see of Antioch.   There he died in

---

[1] Τῶν δυτικῶν ὡς εἴρηται ἀποσχοινισάντων.
[2] Cf. Cyril. Scythop., *Vit. S. Sab.*, cap. 1.

the year 518, ten days after the death of his persecutor. He died, as he had lived, out of communion
with the Roman Church ; but he is venerated by that
Church as a saint, and is commemorated in the
Roman Martyrology on July 4.

Euphemius had been previously driven from his see
by Anastasius in the year 495. He lived for twenty
years in exile, dying at Ancyra in 515. His name
ought to be had in honour throughout all generations
as a confessor for the Catholic doctrine of the Incarnation, and as a firm defender of Catholic liberty
against papal usurpation. He also died, as he had
lived, out of communion with the Roman see.

His successor at Constantinople was S. Macedonius.
During the whole of his episcopate this saint was
being persecuted by the emperor, because he maintained the true faith in regard to the Incarnation,
and upheld the authority of the Council of Chalcedon.
In the year 511 the emperor banished him, as he had
banished his predecessor; and he died at Gangra in
515, and was buried in the church of the holy martyr
Callinicus. S. Theophanes tells us that after his
death many miracles of healing were wrought at his
tomb.[1] He died, as he had lived, out of communion
with Rome ; and in the year 519, when the breach
was healed between the Churches of Rome and
Constantinople, Pope Hormisdas, regardless of S.
Macedonius' sufferings for the faith and his sanctity,
insisted on his name being expunged from the Con-

---

[1] S. Theoph., *Chronograph.*, A.C. 508.

stantinopolitan diptychs.   This was done by the
then Patriarch John, a poor-spirited man.   But the
exclusion did not last long.   The Church of Constantinople soon replaced the name of her saintly patriarch
on the sacred tablets, and he was reckoned among
the saints.   His feast is kept by the Eastern Church
on the 25th of April.

But there would be no end, if I were to go into full
details in regard to all the saintly names which make
glorious the annals of the Eastern Church during
that period, when she was separated from the communion of Rome.   I will, however, make a list of
some of them, arranging them according to the patriarchates into which the greater part of the Eastern
Church was divided.   To each name I will prefix
the day on which he is commemorated either in the
Eastern service-books or in the Roman Martyrology,
and in connection with most of the names I will add
a few historical notes.

In the patriarchate of Constantinople.
>   April 25.—S. Macedonius the Patriarch (died in
>   A.D. 515).
>   June 27.—S. Sampson the Receiver of Strangers
>   (died during the schism according to
>   Baronius).
>   October 1.—S. Romanus the Melodist (flourished
>   *circa* A.D. 500).
>   December 11.—S. Daniel the Stylite (died *circa*
>   A.D. 494).

In the patriarchate of Antioch.

> July 4.—S. Flavian II. of Antioch (died in A.D. 518).
>
> July 31.—The 350 Martyrs of Syria Secunda (died in A.D. 517).
>
> October 28.—S. James of Sarug (died in A.D. 521).

In the patriarchate of Jerusalem.

> January 11.—S. Theodosius the Cœnobiarch (died in A.D. 529, at the age of 106).
>
> January 26.—S. Gabriel the Archimandrite (died in A.D. 490).
>
> July 4.—S. Elias the Patriarch (died in A.D. 518).
>
> September 29.—S. Cyriacus the Anchorite (died in A.D. 556, at the age of 108).
>
> October 28.—S. John the Chuzibite (flourished during the schism).
>
> November 30.—S. Zosimas the Wonder-worker (flourished during the schism).
>
> December 5.—S. Sabas the Great (died in A.D. 532, at the age of 93).
>
> December 8 (but in Rom. Mart. May 13).— S. John the Silentiary (died in A.D. 558, at the age of 104).

In the patriarchate of Alexandria.

> July 27.—The 3911 Martyrs at Negrân (died in A.D. 522 or 523).
>
> October 24.—S. Aretas and his 340 companions (martyred in A.D. 522 or 523).

October 27.—S. Elesbaan the King (was flourishing in A.D. 525).
October 27.—S. Pantaleon and his eight companions (were flourishing *circa* A.D. 500).

Some of these saints died before the healing of the
schism, and therefore out of communion with Rome.[1]
Others did not die until after the schism was healed,
but they had become illustrious by their sanctity,
and in some cases by their miracles, while they were
out of communion with Rome. I do not remember
that in any case there is the smallest particle of
evidence to show that they viewed their restoration
to communion with Rome as an event of any personal
importance to themselves. They doubtless rejoiced
that the unity of the Church was once more rendered
visible, and that the breach of communion between
the Eastern and Western bishops had come to an

---

[1] Mr. Richardson (*What are the Catholic claims?* p. 118) has a
curious passage, in which he speaks of S. Meletius' separation from the
communion of the Roman see as being a "unique example in
antiquity." What can Mr. Richardson mean? Does he really think
that S. Meletius was the only saint recognized by the Church, who
lived outside the Roman communion? If that is his opinion, he is
under a complete delusion, and either he has forgotten what he
learnt when he was sitting on the "hard bench," of which he speaks
in the note, or the instruction given to him must have been very mis-
leading. Various passages in his somewhat flimsy book tempt one to
speculate as to which of these two alternative suggestions gives the
truer account of the mistakes into which he falls. For example,
on p. 61 he speaks of the "*eternal Syncatabasis of the Son.*" If I
had used such an expression when I sat on "hard benches" at
Cambridge and at Cuddesdon, I should have been in some way made
to understand that I was either grievously heretical or grossly
ignorant.

end; but there is not the least reason for supposing
that they regarded themselves as having been outside
the Church before the pacification, and as having
been brought within the true fold by means of that
event. I doubt if such an idea ever crossed the mind
of any Eastern Catholic during the whole course of
the controversy.[1] The notion of the pope being the

---

[1] Among the Easterns I do not include the bishops of the provinces
of Eastern Illyricum, who had always been reckoned as ecclesiastically
belonging to the West (see pp. 160–162). In the Acacian controversy
many of them adhered to the East, but in doing so they broke away
from their natural connection. S. Cyril of Alexandria, in a letter to
the Patriarch John of Antioch, speaking of the pope and the Western
bishops, says, "They have also written copies to Rufus, the most
reverend Bishop of Thessalonica, and to some others of the reverend
bishops of Macedonia, *who always agree with their decisions*" (S. Cyril.
Alex., *Ep. ad Joann. Antiochen., Opp.* ed. Aubert, vi. 43). It should
in fairness be mentioned that certain communities of monks belonging
to the order of the Acœmetæ, or *Sleepless ones,* who were very zealous
for the Council of Chalcedon, and who considered that that Council was
disparaged by the Henoticon, on account of its silence, refrained from
communicating with the Patriarchs Euphemius and S. Macedonius,
and on the other hand did communicate with the West. Fifteen years
after the breach between the East and the West, the two monasteries of
S. Dius and S. Bassian in Constantinople, and the mother-house of the
Acœmetæ, called the Irenæum, on the opposite shore of the Bosphorus,
besides a community of nuns, were still maintaining their separation from
S. Macedonius. However, they had returned to Catholic communion
before the pacification of Constantinople and Rome in 519. For in
the previous year I find that the Archimandrites of the three above-
mentioned monasteries joined with the Archimandrites of the other
Constantinopolitan monasteries in petitioning the Eastern bishops
assembled in the σύνοδος ἐνδημοῦσα at Constantinople to reinsert the
names of Euphemius and S. Macedonius in the diptychs. Those
names were an abomination to Rome, as they were also an abomination
to the Monophysites, but they were rightly dear to Eastern Catholics.
In their petition they speak of the Constantinopolitan patriarch as
"our most holy archbishop, *the Ecumenical Patriarch,* John" (cf.
Coleti, v. 1141, 1144).

necessary centre of communion, which had been gradually developed in Rome, was a novelty even there, and was completely ignored in the East, where the original teaching about the Church's unity, as it had come down from the apostles, was faithfully retained and handed on.

I proceed to set down a few historical particulars concerning most of these holy persons.

S. Sampson the Receiver of Strangers established a hospital at Constantinople, which was afterwards named after its saintly founder. His feast was celebrated at Constantinople with considerable solemnity. The law courts were closed on that day until divine service was finished. His name also occurs in the Roman Martyrology. Baronius thinks that he died during the reign of Anastasius; and, if so, he must have passed from earth to Paradise during the schism.[1] It is fair to say that Alemannus holds that there is no absurdity in supposing that he lived on into the reign of Justin,[2] or even to the beginning of that of Justinian.[3] Father Verhoven, S.J., thinks that his death may not have occurred until 530 or 531.[4] In any case, his career of sanctity must have commenced during the schism, and there is high authority for the view that he did not live to witness the pacifi-

---

[1] See Baronius' notes to the Martyrology, under June 27.

[2] The Emperor Justin reigned from 518 to 527, and was succeeded by his nephew Justinian.

[3] Cf. Du Cange, *Constantinop. Christian.*, iv. B. 114 (*Hist. Byzant.* ed. Venet., 1729).

[4] Cf. *Acta. SS.*, tom. v., Jun., p. 264.

cation, which, so far as Constantinople and the exarchate of Thrace was concerned, took place in 519.[1]

S. Romanus the Melodist seems to have been the earliest writer of the class of liturgical hymns called κοντάκια. He was at first a deacon of the Church of Berytus, and afterwards belonged to the staff of clergy attached to the Church of Blachernæ at Constantinople. Dr. Neale gives as his date, "about A.D. 500."[2]

S. Daniel the Stylite was one of the best known of the pillar-saints. He had visited S. Symeon in his youth, and had received his cowl as a legacy. He lived for thirty-three years on a pillar, four miles from Constantinople, and died during the schism, about the year 494. He was attended during his last moments and was buried by the holy patriarch Euphemius, who was out of communion with Rome. Before his death he wrote his dying wishes for his disciples in the form of a will. In this document he says, "Separate never from the Church your mother." Under all the circumstances of the case, we may be sure that he communicated with the Church under Euphemius. He is commemorated in the Roman Martyrology, as well as in the Eastern service-books.[3]

---

[1] But the bishops of the exarchates of Asia and Pontus and of the patriarchates of Antioch and Jerusalem did not come into communion with the West until 521 or 522. See the letter of Epiphanius of Constantinople to Pope Hormisdas (Coleti, v. 669), and the reply of Hormisdas (Coleti, v. 1120-1125).

[2] Cf. Cardinal. Pitr., *Analect. Sacr. Spic. Solesm.*, i. xxv.; and see Neale's *General Introduction*, p. 843.

[3] Compare Tillemont, xvi. 439-452.

S. Flavian II. of Antioch was patriarch in that city from A.D. 498 to A.D. 512. He was then banished by the persecuting emperor, Anastasius, to Petra in Arabia, and he died in exile in July, 518. One must suppose that his sanctity was the sanctity of penitence, and that it was developed during the years of his banishment. His conduct during his episcopate was extremely weak and halting. The most interesting point about his history is that, having lived for thirty-four years out of communion with Rome, and having died in the same condition, he is nevertheless venerated as a saint by the Roman Church, and his name finds a place in the Roman Martyrology.

The 350 martyrs of Syria Secunda were orthodox monks who were going on pilgrimage to the sanctuary of S. Symeon Stylites, when they were attacked and murdered by a band of assassins, hired by Severus, the Monophysite Patriarch of Antioch, and Peter, the Monophysite Metropolitan of Apamea.[1] This took place apparently in the year 517. These martyrs are commemorated in the Roman Martyrology, and Baronius asserts that they were in the Roman communion when they died.[2] I hope to show, in the Appendix, that that is a mistake.[3]

S. James of Sarug, who "enjoyed an extraordinary reputation for learning and holiness,"[4] was born in

---

[1] Apamea was the metropolis of Syria Secunda.
[2] *Annal. Eccl.*, s.a. 517, tom. iv. p. 694, ed. 1658.
[3] See Note G. in the Appendix, pp. 401–407.
[4] Smith and Wace, iii. 327.

the year 452, and died in November, 521.   From the age of thirty-two to the age of sixty-nine he lived out of communion with Rome; and it is quite probable that he died in the same condition, though it is just possible that he may have come into communion with Rome a month or two before his death.[1]   In any case, his learning and holiness were established long before. Assemani and Mgr. Abbeloos [2] have shown that he was thoroughly orthodox.   The Maronites, who are in communion with Rome, commemorate him at the mass along with S. Ephrem Syrus, in these words, "Let us commemorate S. James and S. Ephrem, the most eloquent mouths and the pillars of our holy Church."[3]   The Bollandist, Père Matagne, calls S. James, " sanctissimus episcopus." [4]

S. Theodosius the Cœnobiarch was the superior of all the cœnobites, who lived under the jurisdiction of the Patriarch of Jerusalem.   He was a most ardent champion of the true doctrine of the Incarnation and of the authority of the Council of Chalcedon, and on that account he was banished by Anastasius.   Two

---

[1] On March 26, 521, Pope Hormisdas sent a letter from himself at Rome to Epiphanius, Patriarch of Constantinople, commissioning him to act as his representative in the work of bringing the bishops of Pontus, Asia, Palestine, and of the patriarchate of Antioch into communion with Rome and the West (cf. Coleti, v. 1120–1125). Considering the slowness of communication in those times, and the magnitude of the work to be done, it must remain doubtful whether, in the distant diocese of Sarug, which was beyond the Euphrates reunion was accomplished before S. James' death in November.

[2] Cf. J. B. Abbeloos, *de Vitâ et Scriptis Sancti Jacobi Batnarum Sarugi dissertatio historico-theologica* (Lovan. 1867).

[3] *Acta SS.*, tom. xii., Octobr., p. 830.   [4] *Ibid.*, p. 824.

lives of him have come down to us, one by Cyril of Scythopolis, the other by Theodore, Bishop of Petra, who had been his disciple. He is credited with miraculous and prophetic gifts. Baronius calls him, "the celebrated Theodosius, great in name and illustrious in deeds;"[1] he also describes him as "most holy."[2] He was out of communion with Rome from the age of sixty-one to the age of ninety-eight. He lived to the age of one hundred and six, so that he survived the reunion of the patriarchate of Jerusalem with the West eight years.

S. Gabriel the Archimandrite was one of the disciples of S. Euthymius the Great. He became abbot of S. Stephen's monastery at Jerusalem, and died there, out of communion with Rome, in the year 490. His feast is celebrated on January 26.

S. Cyriacus the Anchorite was ordained deacon at the age of thirty-six, in the year 484, the very year when the breach of communion between the East and the West took place. He had already been nineteen years living the monastic life. He was ordained priest at the age of fifty-two, in the year 500, in the middle period of the schism. Baronius applies to him the epithet of "*sanctissimus.*"[3] He was out of communion with Rome from the age of thirty-six to the age of seventy-three. He died at the age of one hundred and eight, in the year 556.

---

[1] *Annal. Eccl.*, s.a. 511, tom. vi. pp. 617, 618, ed. 1658.
[2] *Ibid.*, s.a. 491, tom. vi. p. 468.
[3] *Ibid.*

He is commemorated in the Roman Martyrology on September 29.

S. John the Chuzibite was one of the wonder-working saints. He was a disciple of S. Sabas, and was illustrious for his sanctity and miracles in the laura of Chuziba. John Moschus, in the *Pratum Spirituale* (cap. 25), tells how, when S. John was abbot of that laura, he was accustomed to see some visible token of the descent of the Holy Ghost at the consecration of the Holy Eucharist. There is also an account of one of his miracles in Evagrius' History.[1] Before the pacification of the Church he had ceased to be abbot of his laura, and had become Bishop of Cæsarea, and in that capacity took part in the synod at Jerusalem, which was held in the year 518.[2] All the members of that synod were out of communion with Rome. He wrote a defence of the faith of Chalcedon.

S. Zosimas the Wonder-worker was a friend of S. John the Chuzibite, and like him was endowed with the gifts of prophecy and miracles. Evagrius recounts several instances of the saint's exercise of these gifts.[3] In one of these S. John the Chuzibite took part; and from the fact of S. Zosimas speaking of him as "the Chuzibite," one would suppose that it took place before S. John's elevation to the episcopate. On the other hand, S. John was at Cæsarea when this miracle was worked, and that fact may

---

[1] *H. E.*, iv. 7. [2] *Acta SS.*, Octobr., tom. xii. p. 587 *ff*.
[3] *H. E.*, iv. 7.

indicate that he had already become Bishop of Cæsarea.[1]   If the miracle was worked before S. John's consecration, S. Zosimas' thaumaturgic powers must have been developed when he was out of communion with Rome.   If it took place afterwards, the point must remain doubtful.   S. Zosimas is commemorated in the Roman Martyrology on November 30.

S. Sabas the Great was, as Alban Butler truly says, "one of the most renowned patriarchs of the monks of Palestine."   He was the superior general of the anchorites who lived under the jurisdiction of the Patriarch of Jerusalem, just as S. Theodosius the Cœnobiarch was the superior of the cœnobites in the same region.   The details of his wonderful and most edifying life have been preserved for us by Cyril of Scythopolis, his biographer; and the English reader may study them in the pages of Alban Butler.   S. Sabas was out of communion with Rome from the time that he was forty-five to the time that he was eighty-two, and it was during those years that the most striking events of his life happened, and that his most heroic deeds were accomplished.   The Roman Martyrology says of him, "He shone out as a wonderful example of sanctity

---

[1] S. Zosimas himself was abbot of a monastery at a place sixty miles away from Cæsarea, yet he used to visit that city; so there is no reason why S. John, when he was Abbot of Chuziba, may not have done the same.   The fact that he was elected to the see of Cæsarea might tend to show that he was known to the clergy and to the faithful of the place, and that he had therefore visited it, when he was an abbot.

in Palestine, and he laboured strenuously for the Catholic faith against those who impugned the holy Council of Chalcedon." Those strenuous labours belong to the period when, according to the teaching of Cardinal Wiseman, he was living in schism. He died in the year 532, at the age of ninety-three. A church and monastery were built at Rome in his honour; and the monastery, which he himself founded in the wildest part of the rocky desert to the west of the Dead Sea, is visited to this day by most travellers in Palestine.

S. John the Silentiary was born in the year 454. He became Bishop of Colonia, in the province of Armenia Prima, in 481. He resigned his see in 491, and lived as an anchorite in Palestine until his death in 558. He was out of communion with Rome from the age of thirty to the age of sixty-seven. He lived to be one hundred and four. Some of the most remarkable events of his life, and some of his most wonderful miracles, took place while he was out of communion with Rome. Cyril of Scythopolis, who knew him, wrote his life in the year before he died. The Eastern Church keeps his feast on the 8th of December, but his name occurs in the Roman Martyrology on the 13th of May.

I have reserved for the last the saints of the patriarchate of Alexandria, because of the peculiar circumstances of that patriarchate during the time of the schism. Between the years 482 and 538 the patriarchs of Alexandria were all of them Monophy-

sites.　Nevertheless, both the orthodox Church of
the East and also the Latin Church celebrate the
memories of S. Aretas and the martyrs of Negrân
in Southern Arabia, and also of S. Elesbaan, the
King of Ethiopia.　It is most unlikely that these
persons would have been venerated as saints if they
had been Monophysites, and yet it is difficult to clear
them of having lived in communion with Timothy II.,
the Patriarch of Alexandria from 520 to 537, who
certainly was a Monophysite.　All that can be said
is, that at any rate in the earlier years of his episcopate Timothy may have concealed his Monophysite
belief.[1]　That he was in fact a Monophysite has been
proved by the discovery of a treatise written by him
against the Council of Chalcedon, among the Syriac
MSS. of the British Museum.[2]

S. Aretas and the martyrs of Negrân were put to
death by orders of the Jewish king of the Homeritæ,
Dhu'n Navvâs, in the year 522 (or 523), in a manner
so cruel that the memory of it is preserved in the
Koran,[3] written a hundred years later.　The number
of martyrs was altogether 4252, as is mentioned in
the very accurate acts of their martyrdom.　Out of
this great number, S. Aretas, the governor of the
city, and 340 of the chief men are commemorated
in the Roman Martyrology on October 24.　The

---

[1] The earlier years of Timothy's episcopate coincided with the
reign of the Emperor Justin, who was very much opposed to
Monophysitism.

[2] Cf. *Acta SS.*, tom. x., Octobr., pp. 710, 711.

[3] In the Sûrah of the Zodiacal signs, the 85th.

memory of the others is celebrated on July 27. The news of this massacre was communicated to the rest of Christendom by Simeon,[1] Bishop of Beth Arsam, who had been sent, in A.D. 524, by the Emperor Justin as an ambassador to one of the Arabian kings. Simeon gives the details in a letter to the Abbot of Gabula, in which he expresses a hope that the news of the martyrdom may be spread throughout the Church, and that the martyrs may receive the honour of commemoration.[2] The Bollandist Father Carpentier thinks that it is probable that the public veneration of these martyrs began at Constantinople within five years of their glorious death, and that a commemoration of them was inserted into the typicum of S. Sabas during the lifetime of that saint.[3] There seems to be no doubt that these Arabian Christians acknowledged the Bishop of Alexandria as their patriarch;[4] nevertheless the Bollandist stoutly maintains that they were not themselves tainted with heresy.[5] I incline to believe that he is right, though the question is surrounded with difficulties. There can, however, be no difficulty in deciding that they were out of communion with Rome. Timothy of Alexandria may have concealed his Monophysitism from fear of the emperor,[6] but

---

[1] Assemani decides that Simeon was Catholic, and not Monophysite.

[2] See the article on *S. Elesbaan* by the Dean of Christ Church, in Smith and Wace, ii. 73.

[3] *Acta SS.*, tom. x., Octobr., p. 715.   [4] *Ibid.*, p. 713.

[5] *Ibid.*, pp. 695, 701, 713.

[6] *Ibid.*, p. 711 ; et tom. xii. pp. 317, 319.

he did not share in the general pacification of the Church, which took place in the years 519–521. When Pope John I. came to Constantinople in the year 525, he said Mass in Latin on Easter-day, and communicated with all the bishops of the East *except Timothy of Alexandria.*[1] The Acts of S. Aretas tell us that during the Eastertide of that. very year "the most blessed Bishop Timothy, having assembled in the church of the holy Apostle Mark all the orthodox and a multitude of monks from Nitria and Scete, decreed that there should be a day of intercession,[2] and celebrated a vigil, and on the morrow, when he had concluded the Eucharistic service, he placed the Divine Oblation in a silver vessel, and sent It by a presbyter to the King of the Ethiopians,"[3] that is to S. Elesbaan, and exhorted him to go and lead his army against the wicked tyrant Dhu'n Navvâs.

I must not dwell any longer on these Alexandrian saints, but must refer the reader to Father Carpentier's disquisitions on S. Elesbaan and also on S. Pantaleon and his eight companions in the twelfth volume of the Bollandist October. I lay less stress on the Alexandrian saints than on those of the other patriarchates, because they lived in a barbarous

---

[1] Cf. Pagi, *Critica,* ii. 525, ed. 1727.

[2] ἐκήρυξε λιτανείαν: the word λιτανεία may mean a litany, or a procession, or a supplication. This public service of intercession for S. Elesbaan took place at Alexandria, in April 525. Easter-day fell that year on March 30 (cf. *Acta SS.,* tom. xii., Octobr., p. 319).

[3] *Acta SS.,* tom. x., Octobr., p. 743.

country, and there is a shade of uncertainty about their orthodoxy.[1] S. Macedonius and S. Elias and S. Flavian II sat on the great patriarchal thrones of Christendom, and knew perfectly well that they were out of communion with Rome, and that they, as patriarchs, were responsible for the separation of the whole East from Rome; and S. Sabas and S. Theodosius and S. John the Silentiary are among the shining lights who rendered illustrious the lauras and monasteries of Palestine. The united testimony of these and of others like them, of whom I have spoken, proves conclusively that the saints of the Eastern Church, in the time of the Acacian troubles, knew nothing of Cardinal Wiseman's doctrine that "it is easy at once to ascertain who are the Church Catholic and who are in a state of schism, by simply discovering who are in communion with the see of Rome and who are not." Pope Gelasius probably did hold something of this sort; for, as we have seen, he compelled the ex-legate Misenus to "strike with an everlasting anathema" Acacius and his successors and "all those who follow and communicate with them;" and it was only on condition of Misenus doing this that the pope restored him to communion and to his episcopal see.[2] But we for our

---

[1] But it must be remembered that Romanists cannot object to their evidence being brought forward, because the Roman Church commemorates them as saints. I refer to S. Aretas and other martyrs of Negrân, and to S. Elesbaan.

[2] Seo pp. 280, 281. Tillemont (xvi. 658), when he describes Misenus' curses against those who communicated with Acacius, says very truly

part wholly decline to accept the witness of the popes
in their own favour.   We have in this case the popes
on one side, and a large body of saints on the other,
and we feel that it is safer to follow the saints; and
the more so because the saints were handing on the
traditional teaching of the Church.   The mantles of
S. Cyprian and of S. Basil and of S. Chrysostom had
fallen upon them.

The reader will naturally want to know how this
Acacian trouble came to an end.   It would take too
long to go into the matter fully, but I will give a
brief account of how it came about.

The persecuting Emperor Anastasius died in July,
518.   He was succeeded by Justin, who had risen
from the ranks.   Justin was a rough soldier, who
could neither read nor write, but he had one great
advantage over his predecessor, in that he was
fervently attached to the Catholic faith.   At that
time John the Cappadocian was Patriarch of Constantinople.   He had succeeded the Monophysite
Timothy,[1] who had been intruded into the see by
Anastasius when S. Macedonius was banished.[2]
During the whole of Timothy's episcopate the faithful people of Constantinople, who had been well

"That is to say, he cursed more than half the Church, and among
others S. Sabas, S. Theodosius, S. Daniel the Stylite, S. Elias of
Jerusalem, etc.   That is terrible!"   It is indeed terrible, but it is the
natural outcome of Gelasian principles.

[1] Timothy removed from the diptychs the names of Euphemius and
of S. Macedonius, and also the entries referring to the Council of
Chalcedon and to S. Leo, the author of the *Tome.*

[2] See p. 287.

trained in orthodoxy by their holy patriarchs
Euphemius and S. Macedonius, refused to communicate with the heretical intruder.   Their joy was
great when Justin came to the throne; and on the
Sunday following they flocked to the church, and
when the Patriarch John and the rest of the clergy
entered, a strange proceeding took place.   The congregation burst into acclamations, which lasted for
hours.   "Long live the emperor!" they said: "Long
live the empress!" "Long live the patriarch!"
"Thou art orthodox, of whom art thou afraid?"
"Why do we remain without communion?" "Why
have we not communicated for so many years?"
"We wish to communicate from thy hands!" "Let
the holy synod [of Chalcedon] be put on the diptychs!" "An orthodox emperor reigns, whom dost
thou fear?" "The faith of the orthodox people is
conquering!" "Long live the new Constantine!"
"Long live the new Helena!" "Bring back the
relics of Macedonius at once!" "Restore the relics
of Macedonius to the church!" "Let the names of
Euphemius and Macedonius be given a place at
once!" "Put the four [ecumenical] synods on the
diptychs!" "Put Leo the Bishop of Rome on the
diptychs!" "Long live the orthodox emperor!"
"Bring the diptychs at once!"[1]   There is a curious
record of all these acclamations, which was solemnly
read out before the important Council of Constantinople, at which S. Mennas presided in the year

[1] I have given merely a selection from the long list of acclamations.

536. The record goes on to say, "Then the most holy and most blessed Archbishop and Ecumenical Patriarch John, receiving the diptychs, ordered the four holy synods to be entered, . . . and also the names of Euphemius and Macedonius of holy memory, the defunct Archbishops of this Royal City, and also the name of Leo, who was Archbishop of Rome. Then with a great voice all the people, as with one mouth, exclaimed, 'Blessed be the Lord God of Israel, for He hath visited and redeemed His people;' "[1] and so at last the patriarch was able to accomplish the holy service of the altar.

Thus, after a period of unsatisfactory vacillation in regard to the faith, brought about by the intrusion of the heretic Timothy, the Church of Constantinople was happily restored to orthodoxy;[2] but it was still out of communion with Rome. However, the new emperor was quite determined that the whole Church throughout his empire should be bound together in a fellowship which should be visibly one. He therefore wrote to Pope Hormisdas, and the Patriarch John also wrote. Hormisdas replied cordially, but made it quite clear that, if the East wished to be in communion with the West, the name of Acacius must be expunged, and a certain formulary (*libellus*), which had been sent from Rome to Constantinople in

---

[1] Coleti, v. 1148–1156.

[2] It will be remembered that the great body of the Church had remained orthodox all along, but a heretical emperor had intruded a heretical bishop into the see.

the time of the Emperor Anastasius, must be signed.
In the following year (A.D. 519) legates arrived from
Rome, bringing this formulary with them. It contained a very high-flying statement of Hormisdas'
claims on behalf of his see, such a statement as no
Eastern bishop or saint had ever signed before. It is
only fair that the most important clauses of this
formulary should be set forth in full. The words
are, of course, the pope's words; but he requires the
Eastern bishops to sign them, if they wish to be
admitted to his communion. The formulary runs
as follows: "The first point of salvation is, that we
should keep the rule of right faith, and in no way
deviate from the tradition of the Fathers: because it
is not possible to pass over the determination of our
Lord Jesus Christ, who said, 'Thou art Peter, and on
this rock I will build My Church.' These words are
proved by their effects, for in the apostolic see the
Catholic religion is always kept inviolable.[1] Wishing,

---

[1] This was a dangerous argument to use. It may be doubted
whether Hormisdas would have inserted this clause if he could have
foreseen that one of his successors, S. Leo II., would in the year 683
write to the Emperor Constantine Pogonatus concerning Pope Honorius
as follows, "We anathematize Honorius, who, instead of labouring to
keep this apostolic Church pure by the teaching of apostolic tradition,
suffered it, the immaculate, to be polluted through his profane betrayal," or, as the last words run in the Latin form of the epistle,
"attempted to subvert the immaculate faith by a profane betrayal"
(Coleti, vii. 1156). The same Pope S. Leo II., having included his
predecessor Honorius in a list of heretics, says, "*All these*, preaching one
will and one operation in the Godhead and Manhood of our Lord Jesus
Christ, *impudently attempted to defend heretical doctrine*" (*Ep.*, Leonis
Papæ II., *ad Ervigium regem Hispaniæ*, ap. Coleti, vii. 1462). It is
important to remember that, according to the teaching of the popes,

therefore, not to fall from this faith, and following in all things the ordinances of the Fathers, we anathematize all heresies, but especially the heretic Nestorius, . . . and together with him we anathematize Eutyches and Dioscorus, . . . who were condemned in the holy Council of Chalcedon, which we venerate and follow and embrace ; . . . joining him to these, we anathematize Timothy the parricide, surnamed the Cat and his disciple Peter [Mongus] of Alexandria. . . . We similarly anathematize their accomplice, who became their follower, Acacius, formerly Bishop of Constantinople ; and those, moreover, who persevere in their communion and fellowship : for if any one embraces the communion of these persons, he falls under a similar judgment of condemnation with them. . . . We approve and embrace all the epistles of blessed Leo, Pope of the city of Rome, which he wrote concerning the right faith.   Wherefore, as we have said before, following in all things the apostolic see, we preach all things,

they themselves are liable " to defend heretical doctrine in an impudent manner."   This teaching was faithfully handed down in the Roman see ; and so we find that Pope Adrian VI. in his *Quæstiones de Sacramentis in quartum Sententiarum librum* (fol. xxvi. coll. iii., iv.), when treating of the minister of Confirmation, discusses the question, " Utrum papa possit errare in his quæ tangunt fidem " ?   He replies, " Dico primo quod si per ecclesiam Romanam intelligat caput ejus, puta pontifex, certum est quod possit errare, etiam in iis quæ tangunt fidem, hæresim per suam determinationem aut decretalem asserendo. Plures enim fuerunt pontifices Romani hæretici."   I quote from the edition published by Pope Adrian in 1522 during his pontificate, under his own eye at Rome.   It must be remembered that Acacius had never explicitly " defended heretical doctrine," as Honorius did, nor asserted heresy in a decretal, as other popes did.

which have been by her decreed; and consequently
I hope that I shall be in one communion with you,
the communion which the apostolic see preaches, in
which is the whole and perfect entirety (*soliditas*) of
the Christian religion. We promise for the future
that at the celebration of the holy mysteries there
shall be no mention made of the names of those who
have been separated from the communion of the
Catholic Church—that is, of those who do not agree
in all things with the apostolic see. . . ."[1] The
Patriarch John knew well that the emperor was
determined that the Church of Constantinople should
come into communion with the Church of Rome.
His own record was not one that could bear investigation, nor had he any large share in the courage and
firmness of the saints. He had been syncellus or
confidential chaplain to his heretical predecessor;
and he had been appointed to his present exalted
position by the heretical Emperor Anastasius, who
had compelled him to anathematize the Council of
Chalcedon, as the price to be paid for his elevation
to the patriarchate. In the present conjuncture he
knew that, if he was to retain his see, he must
sign the Roman formulary; but, poor-spirited as
he was, he was not prepared to sign it as it stood.
He insisted on prefacing it by a preamble. After
the usual compliments to his "brother and fellow-
minister" Hormisdas, he says, "When I received
your letter, I rejoiced at the spiritual charity of your

---

[1] Coleti, v. 622.

Holiness, because you are seeking to unite the most holy Churches of God according to the ancient tradition of the Fathers, and you are hastening to drive away those who have torn the rational flock of Christ. Know therefore, most holy one, that, according to what I have written, I too, loving peace, renounce all the heretics repudiated by thee: *for I hold the most holy Churches of your elder and of our new Rome to be one Church; I define that see of the Apostle Peter and this of the imperial city to be one see.*" [1] Then he expresses his complete assent to everything that was done at the four Ecumenical Councils, concerning the confirmation of the faith and the state of the Church, and denounces all disturbers of the same, and then proceeds to adopt and make his own the words of the papal formulary. It will be noticed that by means of this preamble the Patriarch John managed to blunt very considerably the edge of the formulary; for, by identifying in some curious fashion his own see of new Rome with the papal see of old Rome, he managed to claim for the Constantinopolitan see a share in all the special privileges which in the formulary were assigned to the Western apostolic chair. However, the document, as modified by the patriarch, was accepted by the legates, and intercommunion was once more established between Rome and Constantinople. Rome could congratulate herself on having won a very substantial victory, in so far as the name of Acacius

---

[1] Coleti, v. 621, 622.

was struck out of the Constantinopolitan diptychs. Rome also won for a time another victory, which was less to her credit. By command of the pope,[1] the legates insisted on the names of Euphemius and S. Macedonius being also removed from the diptychs. Those names had been triumphantly replaced a few months before, namely, on the day of the great acclamations. However, as part of the price to be paid for the reunion of the Church, they were now once more removed. But, as has been already stated,[2] no long time elapsed before they were again re-placed; and since then S. Macedonius has been reckoned by the Constantinopolitan Church as one of the saints, and venerated accordingly.[3]

The formulary which the legates had brought was signed not only by the Patriarch John, but also by the other bishops who happened to be in Con-stantinople at that time. It was probably signed by all, or almost all, the bishops of Thrace, and by some of those in Pontus and Asia. But Justinian, the Emperor Justin's nephew, wrote to the pope in the year 520, that "a considerable part of the Eastern bishops[4] could not be compelled, even by the use of fire and sword, to condemn the names of the bishops who died after Acacius." Incidentally we learn from this passage what sort of pressure was put upon the bishops to compel them to accept the Roman demands.

---

[1] Cf. Coleti, v. 613.   [2] See p. 288.
[3] Cf. *Acta SS.*, tom. iii., April, p. 373.
[4] "Pars orientalium non exilis" (Coleti, v. 667).

The Patriarch Epiphanius, who had succeeded John the Cappadocian, wrote at the same time to Hormisdas, and told him that "very many of the holy bishops of Pontus and Asia, and above all of the patriarchate of Antioch, found it to be difficult and even impossible to expunge the names of their former bishops." Consequently, Epiphanius recommends the pope to follow "the pathway of humility" in his effort to reunite the Church.[1] The Emperor Justin also wrote to much the same effect, and speaks of "the threats and persuasions" used to induce the clergy and laity of these dioceses to agree to the removal of the names; but "they," he says, "esteem life harder than death, if they should condemn those, when dead, whose life, when they were alive, was their people's glory." Then he urges the pope to abate his demands, "in order to unite everywhere the venerable Churches, *and especially the Church of Jerusalem, on which Church all bestow their good will, as being the mother of the Christian name, so that no one dares to separate himself from that Church.*"[2] The pope, in his answer to the emperor, urges him to use force to compel uniformity.[3] He at the same time wrote to the Patriarch Epiphanius, empowering him to represent himself, so that whoever was admitted to communion with the Church of Constantinople was to be reckoned as being in communion with the Church of Rome. He also begs Epiphanius to send him a list of those whom he

<hr>

[1] Coleti, v. 669.   [2] *Ibid.,* v. 672, 673.   [3] *Ibid.,* v. 681.

shall thus admit, and to state the contents of the declaration of faith which each should make on his reception;[1] and he inserts a concise statement of doctrine, the substance of which is to be enforced on all who are received. This statement of doctrine has reference to our Lord's Incarnation, and there is nothing in it bearing on the prerogatives of the see of Rome.[2] So it came to pass that in the end the pope receded from the extreme claims which he had made at first, and left the whole matter practically in the hands of Epiphanius. The larger part of the Eastern Church was admitted back into communion with the West on its own terms, and not on the pope's terms.[3] The Eastern bishops had all along been ready to give pledges of the orthodoxy of their faith;[4] but they had rightly refused to give way by subjection to the usurping claims of the Roman see. Throughout the patriarchates of Antioch and Jerusalem, and in the greater part of the exarchates of Pontus and Asia, the names of Euphemius and of S. Macedonius were never expunged from the diptychs, and the bishops refused to append their signatures to the obnoxious formulary of Hormisdas.[5] We are

---

[1] Coleti, v. 1121, 1122.   [2] *Ibid.*, v. 1123, 1124.

[3] Except that the name of Acacius was probably removed from the diptychs.

[4] I except, of course, the patriarchate of Alexandria, which had been cut off from the communion of the Church of Constantinople by Euphemius in the year 490, and which was still given over to Monophysite misbelief. The see of Alexandria was not admitted back into fellowship with the rest of the Church until the consecration of the Patriarch Paul by S. Mennas of Constantinople in A.D. 538.

[5] The very learned historian Pagi, of the order of the Conventual

indeed told by Father Bottalla (*Supreme Authority of the Pope*, p. 115) that " all the bishops of the Eastern Church, with their patriarchs and their emperor, signed the formula of union, amidst shouts and tears of universal joy ; " and by " the formula of union " Father Bottalla means the original formulary of Hormisdas. He goes on to say that " this precious document of the faith of the East, signed by all the patriarchs, and accepted, of course, by the whole Western Church, has a weight of authority not less than that of a definition of faith pronounced by an Ecumenical Council." This passage is thoroughly characteristic of the way in which history is written by some Ultramontane controversialists. As we have seen, instead of the formula having been signed by " all the bishops of the Eastern Church," it was signed by about half the bishops of one out of the four Eastern patriarchates ; the patriarch himself

Minorites, arrives at the same result. He says, " We come to this conclusion, namely, that Hormisdas, who at first wished to compel the Eastern bishops to subscribe the formulary put forth by himself, and offered to them by his legates, at last yielded to their opposition. For, if he had insisted on their subscribing that formulary, there would have been no need for Epiphanius to report to him what the *libelli*, or professions of faith, set forth by the aforesaid bishops contained, and with what form of words they subscribed. . . . It appears, therefore, that the Eastern bishops were at length admitted to the communion of the apostolic see, although they had not condemned Euphemius and Macedonius, and had not allowed their names to be expunged from the diptychs. That the name of Macedonius remained on the diptychs, in which it had been inscribed, and was restored to those from which it had been removed, is clearly proved by the sacred *cultus* which the Greeks pay to him, as appears from their menæa." (Pagi, *Critica*, ii. 515, ed. 1727).

refusing to sign it, until he had prefixed a preamble which took away almost all its point. And, again, instead of the formulary being "a precious document of the faith of the East," it was drawn up by the pope, and was pressed upon the East by the emperor with threats of fire and sword; and yet, notwithstanding those threats, it was rejected by the majority of the Eastern bishops. Even if it had been signed by them all, it would be ludicrous to compare the authority of such a document so signed with the authority of "a definition of faith pronounced by an Ecumenical Council." The formulary had not been synodically accepted in a free Council, and therefore did not bind future generations. Each bishop, who freely signed, was personally bound by his own signature, but he could not bind his successors. The Church's laws, whether dogmatic or disciplinary, are not made in such a fashion as that. To crown his other enormities, Father Bottalla informs us in the note that "Rusticus—who wrote under Justinian, the successor of Justin—says that the formulary of Hormisdas was signed by 2500 priests (*sacerdotes* bishops) of the Eastern Church." Rusticus says nothing of the kind. What he does say is that the Council of Chalcedon was "an Ecumenical Synod, which has often been confirmed by the harmonious judgment of all the Churches, not only by the encyclical letters [1] [of various patriarchal and pro-

---

[1] These are, I imagine, the synodical letters printed by Coleti (iv. 1834–1934); they are, for the most part, addressed to the Emperor Leo.

vincial Councils] in the reign of [the Emperor] Leo, but also by the *libelli* (professions of faith) of perhaps 2500 bishops in the reign of the Emperor Justin, after the schism of Peter [Mongus] of Alexandria and of Acacius of Constantinople."[1] Rusticus is no doubt right when he says that all these 2500 *libelli* contained an explicit acceptance of the Council of Chalcedon; but he nowhere identifies these *libelli* with the original formulary of Hormisdas, nor does he suggest that they were all worded in accordance with one pattern. If he had committed himself to either of these statements, he would have come into collision with our contemporary sources of information; as it is, his testimony harmonizes completely with the whole body of facts which has reached us through other channels.

Here I must bring to a conclusion what I propose to say at the present time on the subject of the Acacian troubles. To my mind the history of those troubles shows clearly that the great Eastern saints of the fifth and sixth centuries had no conception of the papacy as the divinely appointed and necessary centre of communion. If they really thought that to be out of communion with the pope was equivalent to being out of communion with the Catholic Church, one would be bound to say that their actions would prove that they were very wicked men. On that *hypothesis*, they were content to remain outside the

<hr>

[1] Rustic., *contra Acephalos disputat.* (Migne, *Patrol. Lat.*, lxvii. 1251).

Church for thirty-five or thirty-seven years. Nay, more; some of them were content to die in that appalling condition. No one, who knows anything of primitive theology, could suppose that S. Macedonius and S. Elias and S. Sabas and their brethren held the common Protestant notion that it does not matter whether you are in the Church or out of it. Assuredly they believed, as every one believed, that *"extra ecclesiam nulla salus."* If, therefore, they supposed that the Church was restricted to that body of persons who were for the time being in communion with the pope, they manifested a most culpable carelessness about their salvation, seeing that they took no pains to get back into the Catholic unity.   Let those who choose to do so, throw mud at those holy men. I, for my part, entirely disbelieve in the theory of their wickedness; but that is equivalent to saying that I entirely disbelieve in the notion that they accepted the modern Roman teaching about the relation of the papacy to the unity of the Church.

I should much like to pursue the history of the Church Catholic and of the Roman see through the century which followed the pontificate of Hormisdas. One would have to tell of how the great and illustrious Church of North Africa, meeting in council under the presidency of Reparatus of Carthage, " synodically separated Vigilius, the Roman bishop, the condemner of the three chapters, from Catholic communion, reserving, however to him a place of repentance;"[1] and of how in February, 552, S. Mennas, Patriarch of Constantinople, anathematized the same Pope Vigilius, and was himself anathematized by the pope.[2] The two prelates were reconciled in the following June; and two months afterwards S. Mennas died in the odour of sanctity; he is venerated by the Roman Church as a saint on August 25. One would have to narrate the very remarkable proceedings of S. Eutychius of Constantinople and the fifth Ecumenical Council; of how it anathematized the person as well as the writings of Theodore of Mopsuestia, and also certain writings of Ibas and of the Blessed Theodoret; although it must have known well that it was acting in defiance of the wishes of Pope Vigilius, who was in Constantinople at the time, and who refused to come to the Council. One would have to tell how for six months the Pope refused his assent to what had been done by the Council, but how at last in a letter to S. Eutychius he confessed that it was the devil who had deceived him, and had led him to despise brotherly charity, so that he was carried away into discord, but that now he wishes to retract his former opposition, and to condemn Theodore of Mopsuestia, and such

---

[1] This was in A.D. 550 (cf. Coleti, v. 1395, 1396). Surely the mere fact that a Western Church like the African could act in this way, is proof positive that the papal theory was unknown in that age to the Church at large. On that theory such action would have been suicidal.

[2] Dom Coustant, in his *Dissertatio de Vigilii Papæ Gestis*, § 88, ap. Cardin. Pitr., *Analect. Novissim. Spic. Solesm.*, p. 427, says, "Nobis autem non displicet quod Theophanes de mutuo Vigilii in Monam, et Menæ in Vigilium anathemate scribit."

writings of the same Theodore and of Ibas and of
Theodoret as had been condemned by the Council.[1]
One would have to narrate the history of the
dissensions which arose in the West in consequence
of Vigilius having assented to the decrees of the
Fifth Council; of how the bishops of Tuscany,
Liguria, Venetia, and Istria withdrew from communion with the Roman see; and of how the
province of Aquileia remained out of communion
with the pope for nearly one hundred and fifty years.[2]
One would have to point out that many who lived
and died at that time outside the Roman communion,
have since been reckoned among the saints. To give
one instance, ten bishops of Como,[3] who were never
in communion with the pope, are venerated as saints
by the Church of Como to this day, and this veneration has been sanctioned by the Congregation of
Rites. One might go on to quote the celebrated letter
written by the glorious missionary S. Columbanus to
Pope Boniface IV., in which he justifies the refusal
of many of the bishops of North Italy to communicate
with the papal chair. It is true that S. Columbanus
makes some mistakes in his historical statements,
but the principles which he lays down show that he
had no notion of accepting the papal theory.[4] But,

---

[1] Coleti, vi. 239–246.   [2] From A.D. 557 to A.D. 698.

[3] These ten bishops' names are these: S. Flavian I. (Feb. 26); S.
Adalbert (June 3); S. Agrippinus (June 17); S. Martinianus (Sept.
3); S. John II. (Oct. 3); S. John III. (Oct. 20); S. Octarianus (Oct.
23); S. Benedictus (Oct. 30); S. Flavian II. (Nov. 26); S. Rubianus
(Dec. 16); cf. *Acta SS.*, tom. x., Octobr., pp. 106–108.

[4] He says to the pope in one passage of his letter, "Rightly do

interesting as these subjects are, I must resist the temptation to discuss them. Enough has been said, I think, to show that Cardinal Wiseman committed a rash act when he appealed to " the doctrine of the ancient Fathers " in favour of his theory, that "it is easy at once to ascertain who are the Church Catholic, and who are in a state of schism, by simply discovering who are in commmunion with the see of Rome, and who are not." [1]

No! the ancient Fathers taught a doctrine concerning the distinction between Catholics and schismatics, and concerning the true nature of the unity of the Church, which differs very widely from the teaching of the Vatican Council and of Cardinal Wiseman. In ancient times, if the question arose, Is such and such a bishop a prelate of the Catholic Church? various points would have to be investigated before an answer could be given. It would have to be considered whether the bishop had been validly ordained in the line of the apostolical succession; whether the faith which he publicly professed was in agreement with the doctrinal tradition of the Church; whether he was the canonical occupant of his see; whether the see itself had been canonically erected. These would seem to be the principal questions which would need to be satisfactorily answered in such a case. It is quite certain that the mere fact of being in com-

your juniors resist you, and rightly do they refuse to communicate with you" (*Ep.* v. *ad Bonifacium Papam* iv., § ix., Migne, *Patrol. Lat.,* lxxx. 279.

[1] See pp. 220, 221.

munion with the pope or out of communion with the
pope would in no way be a certain test of a bishop's
status. S. Meletius was out of communion with
Damasus, yet his people constituted "*the true Church
of God*" at Antioch.[1] Paulinus was in communion
with Rome, yet his position was illegitimate ; he had
"*illegally mounted the throne;*" his partisans were
guilty of "*dividing the Church.*"[2]

According to the teaching of the Fathers, the
true canonical bishops of the Catholic Church constituted a college, of which Christ our Lord was
the one and only Head. If they, as a whole, were
looking to Him, and depending on Him, He was
able and willing to safeguard the visible unity of
the episcopal body. If their faith in their invisible Head failed, if they began to put their trust
in secular princes or in an ecclesiastical monarch of
their own creating, they ran the risk of experiencing
the withdrawal of the Lord's hand, and of losing, at
any rate for a time, the precious gift of visible unity.
Even so, each separate section of the canonical
episcopate remained united to our Lord, and through
Him, and through the common faith and the fundamental institutions of the Church, retained an organic
union with the other sections. The invisible unity
remained, though the visible unity was in abeyance.
Even in our present divided condition the Lord still
governs His Church, and through her begets new

---

[1] S. Basil. *Ep.*, ccxiv., *Opp.* ed. Ben., iii. 321.

[2] S. Chrys., *Hom.* xi. *in Epist. ad Ephes.*, *Opp.* ed. Ben., xi. 86, 89.

children, and feeds and guides those whom He has begotten ; but how miserably weakened is the divided Church's witness in the face of the unbelieving world, and how feeble is her use of her supernatural weapons in her warfare with Satan and his spiritual hosts of wickedness ! Assuredly, if we long for the restoration of the Church to her ancient spiritual glory, we must yearn for the restoration of her visible unity. For this we must pray, for this we must work. But that unity can only be restored in accordance with the institution of Christ. If we could have a perfect unity by some human device of our own, by building up a papacy into a great tower of Babel, to prevent our being "scattered abroad upon the face of the whole earth,"[1] it would but result in an increase of confusion. The Church can be united under Christ's Headship, and under His only. He has not chosen to appoint one great ecclesiastical potentate as His vicar, to represent His Headship over the Church. Each bishop is Christ's vicar for the diocese over which he presides; but for the whole Church the Invisible Head appoints an Invisible Vicar,[2] even the Holy Ghost, whose principal instrument in the external government of the Church is the collective episcopate. Therefore the only way which will really lead

---

[1] Gen. xi. 4.

[2] Tertullian (*de Præscript. Hæret.*, cap. xxviii.) and S. Jerome (*Hom.* xxii. *in Luc., Opp.* ed. Vallars., vii. 314) both call the Holy Ghost the Vicar of Christ. S. Jerome says, " When the Lord Jesus came, and sent the Holy Ghost, His Vicar (Vicarium Suum), every valley was exalted." Compare S. John xiv. 16.

towards a restoration of visible unity, is a more complete subjection of the bishops to the Holy Ghost. We ought to pray for a great outpouring of the Holy Ghost upon the whole of the Catholic episcopate, that so in all parts of the Church the rust of party-spirit and prejudice and ignorance and worldliness and ambition may be purged away, and by the mysterious unifying power of the Spirit, those who have long been severed may be drawn together, and obstacles to unity may be removed, and the attraction of love may bind and unite, and the whole body of the Church's rulers may look up to Christ in faith and trust, and from Him receive their impulse and direction. May our Lord hasten this in His own time.

We know not whether it is our Lord's purpose to accomplish this unifying work before His return. It may be that, in punishment for His people's sins, the visible unity of the Church will remain suspended until the Church herself has been purged through the fires of the last great persecution, which shall be in the days of Antichrist. It may be that the outpouring of the Spirit will not be granted until Israel "shall turn to the Lord," when "the veil is taken away."[1] It may be that the prophecies of the conversion of the world shall find their fulfilment in that new order of things, which shall issue out of Christ's "appearing and kingdom,"[2] when the nations shall be ruled with a rod of iron by the saints who have

---

[1] 2 Cor. iii. 16.　　　　　　[2] 2 Tim. iv. 1.

overcome,[1] and who have been caught up to be with
our Lord.[2] We must not venture to be over-con-
fident in regard to the sequence of future events.
But we know that all God's promises shall be
wonderfully fulfilled in due season. Heaven and
earth shall pass away, but His words shall not pass
away. Ultimately "the Lord shall be King over all
the earth: in that day shall the Lord be one, and
His Name one."[3] Ultimately "all flesh shall come
to worship before Me, saith the Lord."[4] Ultimately
the world shall believe that the Father sent the Son,
because the followers of Christ, who believe in Him
through the apostolic word, shall be "perfected into
one."[5]

[1] Rev. ii. 26, 27.

[2] 1 Thess. iv. 17.

[3] Zech. xiv. 9.

[4] Isa. lxvi. 23.

[5] Cf. S. John xvii. 20-23.

APPENDIX.

NOTE A.

The Excommunication of S. Cyprian (see pp. 82, 83).

SOME Roman Catholic writers have done their best to make out that Pope Stephen, in his dealings with S. Cyprian, never proceeded beyond *threats* of excommunication, and that no actual rupture took place. It is difficult to understand how such a view could ever have been seriously taken by candid persons; but it is easy to see that Ultramontanes would shrink from admitting that so illustrious a saint as Cyprian persisted in upholding the opinion concerning baptism which he had inherited from his predecessors, although the retaining of that opinion had resulted in his being separated from the communion of the Roman Church. If S. Cyprian and S. Firmilian were really excommunicated, and if they nevertheless refused to alter either the teaching or the practice condemned by Rome, then it is clear that neither of these saints nor their colleagues in Africa and Asia Minor could have considered that communion with the pope was an essential matter. It would follow from this conclusion that their witness would have to be reckoned as adverse to the truth of the Ultramontane theory concerning the papacy. Having thus pointed out the importance of the question, I proceed to discuss it.

I have quoted in my second lecture the clear statements of S. Firmilian on the subject of the excommunication, but it will be worth while to repeat them in this place. That great saint, writing to S. Cyprian, after mentioning the fact that there had been in various matters a diversity of practice in the different provinces of the Church, says, "And yet there has not been on that account at any time any departure from the peace and unity of the Catholic Church. This Stephen has now dared to make, breaking the peace with you [Cyprian], which his predecessors ever maintained with you in mutual affection and respect."[1] And further on in the same letter S. Firmilian apostrophizes Stephen, and says, "How great a sin hast thou heaped up against thyself, when thou didst cut thyself off from so many flocks! For thou didst cut thyself off. Deceive not thyself. For he is truly the schismatic who has made himself an apostate from the communion of the unity of the Church. For while thou thinkest that all may be excommunicated by thee, thou hast excommunicated thyself alone from all."[2] Then he goes into particulars about the way in which Stephen had treated the bishops sent to Rome as envoys or legates by the synod of the North African Church; how Stephen "would not admit them even to the common intercourse of a conference," and how "he commanded the whole brotherhood that no one should receive them into his house; so that not only peace and communion, but shelter and hospitality, were denied them on their arrival."[3] Yet in the face of all this Mr. Rivington says, "There is *no* evidence that S. Cyprian was *ever* under excommunication."[4] It seems incredible that such a statement should be made.

---

[1] *Ep. S. Firmil., inter Cyprianicas* lxxv., *Opp.* ed. Ben., p. 144

[2] *Ep. cit.*, p. 150.   [3] *Ep. cit.*, pp. 150, 151.

[4] *Authority*, p. 103, 2nd edit.

Evidence there clearly is, and more of the same kind might have been quoted. Later on Mr. Rivington reveals to us the theory by which he gets rid of the plain evidence of S. Firmilian. He says that, as the sentence, in which the statement concerning S. Cyprian's excommunication occurs, "contains a most exaggerated account of the situation, we may feel ourselves at liberty to regard this statement also as exaggerated."[1] But how does he know that the account of the situation is exaggerated? Our only knowledge of the embassy of the legates from Carthage to Rome is derived from this letter of S. Firmilian. I am not aware that that embassy is mentioned by any other writer. There is, therefore, no counter-evidence which might lead us to suppose that S. Firmilian had given an exaggerated description of the treatment accorded to the legates. S. Firmilian had just received despatches[2] from S. Cyprian containing, no doubt, an account of the whole transaction ; and it would be inconceivable that, in writing back to S. Cyprian, he should falsify the account received from him ; and still more inconceivable that, if *per impossibile* he had done so, S. Cyprian should have translated his letter into Latin and published it to the world. How can any nineteenth-century writer pretend to know better than these great saints of the third century the details of what happened in Rome on the occasion of the visit of the legates? If one may set aside evidence in such a way as that, history becomes an impossibility, and universal scepticism is the inevitable result. What Mr. Rivington's theory really means is that he thinks that S. Firmilian lied, and that S. Cyprian translated and published his lies. I am aware that other Roman Catholic writers have taken

---

[1] *Authority,* p. 105.

[2] The despatches were carried from Carthage to Cappadocia by the deacon Rogatianus.

the same line as Mr. Rivington.   The fact is that they are
driven into a corner, and that the simplest way of escape is
to deny the truth of the evidence, however well attested it
may be.   But, in justice to our brethren of the Roman
communion, it must not be supposed that their best writers
follow such a hopeless course.   Such a course would be
impossible to a historian like Tillemont ; but I prefer to
quote an authority from the south side of the Alps.   I
know of no greater name among Ultramontane historians
of the last century than that of Archbishop Mansi of
Lucca, best known by his great edition of the Councils.[1]
Mansi, in his animadversion on Natalis Alexander's dis-
sertation concerning the subject which we are discussing,
says, " So openly does Firmilian write to S. Cyprian that
Pope Stephen broke the peace, and that he accordingly
deprived them of his communion, that it seems that it
cannot be doubted that he went beyond threats and at
length pronounced sentence of excommunication against
them."   Mansi proceeds to quote S. Firmilian's words, and
to show that they are decisive in favour of his position.
Then he adds, " But the answer of Natalis appears to be
altogether futile.   He says that Firmilian has described a
mere threat of excommunication in the same terms as if it
had really been fulminated, because he took up his pen
when he was somewhat angry with Stephen.   I say again
that such an answer appears to me to be altogether futile,
because it would necessarily follow that Firmilian had
forgotten all the rules of Christian behaviour and of honesty,
if, in order that he might excite odium against Stephen, he
had lied in so serious a matter. . . .[2] And who, I ask, could

---

[1] The Jesuit professor of theology in the university of Innsbruck,
Father Hurter, in his useful *Nomenclator Literarius* (iii. 101), speaking
of Mansi, says, " De illo jam agemus, qui totâ hâc epochâ omnium
fuit celeberrimus deque Ecclesiâ atque re literariâ optime meritus."

[2] " In re tam gravi mentitus esset."

conceive that, if Stephen had done no more than threaten, Firmilian would have compared him to the traitor Judas, and would have charged him with insolence, wickedness, and folly ? Assuredly these are the words of one who is impatiently bearing a wound which he has received, and who is kindled with wrath against the man who has inflicted on him a deadly wound. . . . It is clear that Stephen broke the peace and refused communion, because he did not refrain from excommunicating Firmilian, Cyprian, and the others."[1] Mansi goes on to quote the letter of S. Denys of Alexandria to Pope S. Xystus II., a fragment of which has been preserved by Eusebius. In that letter S. Denys, speaking of Stephen, says, "He therefore had written previously concerning Helenus (of Tarsus) and concerning Firmilian, and concerning all those in Cilicia and Cappadocia and Galatia and the neighbouring nations, *saying that he would not communicate with them* (ὡς οὐδὲ ἐκείνοις κοινωνήσων) for this same cause, namely, that they rebaptize heretics."[2] S. Denys in his letter, so far as it has been preserved to us, dealt entirely with Stephen's

---

[1] *Animadvers. in Dissert.* xii. Art. i., ap. *Natal. Alexandr. Hist. Eccl.,* ed. 1786, Bingii ad Rhenum, tom. vi. pp. 222, 223.

[2] Euseb., *H. E.,* vii. 5. I have appended the original Greek of S. Denys' summary of the operative part of Stephen's letter, the English translation of which is italicized in the text. Mansi rightly translates these words as follows: "quod neque cum illis communicare vellet;" and Baronius renders the passage in the same way. I mention this, because Valesius has seriously altered the sense by translating S. Denys' words thus: "sese ab illorum communione discessurum." There is a difference between announcing that in the future you will not communicate with certain people, and announcing that in the future you will separate from their communion. The first formula implies that separation has already been effected, or is being effected by the document in which the formula occurs. The second formula threatens a separation in the future. S. Denys represents Stephen as having effected the separation, and not as having merely threatened it.

relations with the Eastern bishops, and says nothing of his relations with the Church of North Africa ; but Mansi points out that if the pope excommunicated the Easterns he must have also excommunicated the Africans, since the latter entirely agreed with the former in their teaching and practice.[1] Thus the witness of S. Denys corroborates the witness of S. Firmilian and of S. Cyprian. Here we have a threefold cord, which will not easily be broken by any amount of *a priori* Ultramontane reasoning.

When it is once admitted that three contemporary writers of such high character, and of such esteem in the Church, as the three saints mentioned above, agree in their witness that an excommunication was not merely threatened but also pronounced and promulgated,[2] and when it is also admitted that there is no shred of contemporary evidence on the other side, the discussion might fairly be brought to an end ; but Natalis Alexander and others lay stress on the fact that S. Augustine, writing a century and a half later, seems to have thought that the estrangement between Rome and Carthage never amounted to a breach of com-

---

[1] On this point Natalis Alexander would have agreed with Mansi. His words are express : "Una erat causa Firmiliani et Cypriani ; . . . non est igitur verisimile quod Firmilianum communione privaverit Stephanus cum Orientalibus suis, et Cyprianum cum Africanis pace et communione frui permiserit" (*Hist. Eccl.*, ed. 1786, tom. vi. p. 218).

[2] The objection might be raised that, if Eusebius had supposed that Stephen had actually excommunicated the Easterns, he would have given an exact account of how the breach was healed. If Eusebius had lived some centuries later, when a papal excommunication was the direst thing that could happen to any Christian community, he would no doubt have done so ; but Eusebius would not think of the matter quite in that light. In *H. E.*, v. 24, he gives an account of the excommunication of the Asiatics by Pope Victor, and he describes S. Irenæus' mediation, as here he describes S. Denys' peace-making efforts, but neither there does he make mention of the close of the dispute.

munion.[1] It is true that Tillemont does not so understand
S. Augustine. He thinks that S. Augustine admits that
the pope withdrew his communion from S. Cyprian, but he
supposes that S. Augustine holds that, as S. Cyprian did
not retort on the pope by a counter-excommunication, but
remained united to him by the bond of charity, the breach
was not complete.[2] Out of respect for the great name of
S. Augustine, I will consider whether his view of the
matter can really avail to counterbalance the evidence of
the three contemporary saints, whose witness has been
discussed above ; and for the sake of conciseness I will take
no account of Tillemont's explanation of S. Augustine's
meaning, and I will assume that the saint really supposed
that Stephen never withdrew his communion from S. Cyprian
and from the other African bishops.

On that view of the case, I have no hesitation in saying
that S. Augustine's representation of the matter cannot
possibly avail to counterbalance the direct testimony of
S. Firmilian and S. Cyprian, confirmed as it is by the
corroborative evidence of S. Denys ; for there is every
reason to believe that S. Augustine had not got the full
evidence before him. The contemporary evidence of the
excommunication of S. Cyprian, which has come down to
us, is primarily contained in S. Firmilian's letter, as
translated and published by S. Cyprian. But that letter
was not in the collection of the Cyprianic correspondence
on the subject of the rebaptizing of heretics, which was in
the hands of S. Augustine. The collecting of S. Cyprian's
letters was a work of time. We now possess seven letters,
either written by or to S. Cyprian on the question of rebaptism ; but S. Augustine had only five of these in his

---

[1] Cf. S. Aug., *De Baptismo contra Donat.*, v. 25, *Opp.* ed. Ben.,
1688, ix. 158, et *De unic. Bapt. contra Petil.*, cap. xiv., *Opp.*, ix. 538.

[2] Tillemont, iv. 150, 151.

collection. In his controversy with the Donatists he was obliged to go most minutely into the arguments about baptism contained in the Cyprianic documents. He discusses them clause by clause.[1] He actually takes the trouble to reply separately to each of the eighty-six speeches made by the eighty-five bishops who sat in the great Council of Carthage,[2] over which Cyprian presided, and which was the last of the Cyprianic Councils on rebaptism.[3] So it comes to pass that we know exactly what documents S. Augustine possessed, and what were missing; and we find that he never refers either to the synodical letter [4] written to Stephen by S. Cyprian in the name of the second of the three Councils on rebaptism, or to the letter [5] addressed to S. Cyprian by S. Firmilian.[6] S. Augustine was quite aware that documents existed bearing on the controversy about baptism in the time of S. Cyprian, which had not

---

[1] S. Aug., *De Baptismo contra Donatistas*, libb. ii., iii., iv., v.

[2] S. Cyprian, as president, made two speeches, the first and the last.

[3] *Op. cit.*, libb. vi., vii.

[4] S. Cypr., *Ep.* lxxii.   [5] *Ep.* lxxv.

[6] S. Augustine's words, in his refutation of the speech of Crescens of Cirta (*De Bapt. contra. Donat.*, vi. 15, *Opp.* ed. Ben., 1688, ix. 171), show clearly that S. Cyprian's synodical letter to Stephen, which had been known to Crescens, was not known to him. Compare Mr. C. H. Turner's *Note* appended to Dr. Sanday's *Essay on the Cheltenham List* (*Studia Biblica et Ecclesiastica*, iii. 324, 325). In his third book against Cresconius (*Opp.* ed. Ben., 1688, ix. 435), S. Augustine implies that Cresconius had referred to "the letter of certain Orientals," as witnessing to their approval of S. Cyprian's doctrine about rebaptism. He quotes in the second chapter some words from Cresconius, which seem to me to imply that this letter was a synodical epistle expressing the formal assent of some Eastern synod to the conclusions of the third Carthaginian Council on rebaptism. I doubt if S. Augustine had seen the letter; and the fact that it was written, not by one man, but by several, seems to me to be a proof positive that it was not the letter of S. Firmilian, with which we are acquainted. Tillemont (iv. 158) gives further reasons for concluding that S. Augustine had never seen S. Firmilian's letter to S. Cyprian.

come into his hands. He says in one place, "Not all the things which were transacted among the bishops at that time were committed to memory and to writing, and *not all the things which were so committed have come to my knowledge.*"[1] It is clear from all this that the whole evidence, as we now possess it, was not before S. Augustine; and in point of fact the last of the Cyprianic documents of which he had knowledge was the summarized report of the proceedings at the final Council on rebaptism. *But that Council preceded the excommunication;*[2] and it is therefore no matter for wonder that S. Augustine was unaware of the fact that a complete rupture finally took place. To put the whole matter briefly. The principal evidence for the excommunication is to be found in S. Firmilian's letter. That letter was not known to S. Augustine. It is perfectly clear from that letter that both S. Cyprian and S. Firmilian were excommunicated. We thus know of their excommunication from themselves. It seems unreasonable to set aside the best possible contemporary evidence in deference to certain *dicta* of S. Augustine, who lived a century and a half later, and who had never seen the document which constitutes the principal proof. It is plain that the objections raised by Natalis Alexander have no real solidity. I submit that the excommunication of S. Cyprian and S. Firmilian and their colleagues by Pope Stephen must be accepted as historically true.

[1] *De Bapt. contr. Donat.*, ii. 4, *Opp.*, ix. 98.

[2] Tillemont, iv. 155; and compare the *Acta SS.*, tom. iv. Septembr., pp. 305, 306, where Father Suyskens, S.J., the author of the Bollandist *Life of S. Cyprian*, replies to Dom Maran's arguments, and shows that the African legates who were rejected by Stephen were sent by the third Council on rebaptism, and not by the second.

NOTE B.

Concerning passages from S. Cyprian's works, which are quoted by Ultramontanes in support of their contention that S. Cyprian held the papal theory (see p. 89).

S. CYPRIAN's witness in favour of the Catholic system of Church government and against the papal theory is consistently maintained throughout his acts and writings. But the Ultramontane divines naturally do what they can to discover passages which may seem to qualify the crushing force of his testimony against the later claims of Rome. Without attempting to exhaust the subject, I will take the passages from the Cyprianic documents which are quoted by Father Bottalla as supporting his views (*Supreme Authority of the Pope*, pp. 10–13), and will point out how consistent they are with S. Cyprian's general teaching in regard to the organization of the Church.

Father Bottalla says, "The Fathers and all Christian antiquity acknowledge the closest connection between the unity of the Church as represented by Christ, and the headship of one universal pastor." In proof of this statement Father Bottalla quotes S. Cyprian's letter to Magnus (*Ep.* lxxvi., ed. Ben., p. 153). S. Cyprian there says, " Wherefore the Lord, intimating to us a unity that cometh of divine authority, declareth and saith, 'I and the Father are one.' To which unity reducing His Church, He further saith, 'And there shall be one flock and one shepherd.'"[1] S. Cyprian is quoting two passages from the tenth chapter of S. John's Gospel. The words of the second passage, as they were spoken by our Lord, referred to the one flock of the Catholic Church, consisting of Jews and Gentiles, under Himself the one Shepherd. S. Cyprian, however, in his application of the passage, somewhat varies from the original meaning. He is showing that each local Church forms an organized unity under one head, the bishop. This is a very favourite subject with S. Cyprian. Magnus had asked him whether Novatians, on their conversion to the Church, ought to be rebaptized. S. Cyprian says, Yes, "for the Church is one, and, being one, cannot be both within and without. For if it was with Novatian, it was not with Cornelius. But if it was with Cornelius, who by a legitimate ordination succeeded the Bishop Fabian, ... Novatian is not in the Church ; nor can he be accounted a bishop, who, despising the evangelic and apostolic tradition, succeeding to nobody, has sprung from himself." The Novatian schism arose out of a dispute in the local Church of Rome. Two bishops, Cornelius and Novatian, claimed each of them to be the legitimate Bishop of Rome. It was not a question of the rights of the pope as against the rights of some other bishop or bishops. The question was, Which of two claimants was the rightful Bishop of Rome? S. Cyprian held that S. Cornelius was undoubtedly the true bishop. He had been consecrated first, and his election and consecration had been carried out in a thoroughly canonical and orderly way. He was the true successor to the previous Bishop, Fabian.

I give my own translation in the text. The Latin runs as follows : "Idcirco Dominus insinuans nobis unitatem de divinâ auctoritate venientem ponit et dicit : *Ego et Pater unum sumus.* Ad quam unitatem redigens ecclesiam suam denuo dicit: *Et erit unus grex et unus pastor.*"

Afterwards Novatian was consecrated in an entirely uncanonical manner, when the see was no longer vacant. Novatian succeeded to nobody. It will now be evident that when S. Cyprian quotes our Lord's words, "There shall be one flock and one shepherd," he is referring to the local Church at Rome, and he is showing that the Roman flock had already its one shepherd, Cornelius, and that consequently Novatian was a schismatical intruder, and that those who communicated with him shared in his guilt, and according to S. Cyprian's notion ought to be rebaptized. There is not a single word in the whole epistle which deals with "the headship of one universal pastor" over the whole Catholic Church of Christ. So far from that being the case, the letter was written by S. Cyprian in the course of the controversy about rebaptism, which culminated in his excommunication by Stephen; and the whole letter is intended to prove to Magnus that the theories about the validity of schismatic baptism, which were favoured at Rome, were altogether wrong. Father Botalla was unfortunate in his first Cyprianic quotation. Let us pass on to his second proof.

He says, "The same doctrine was inculcated by those confessors of Christ who returned from the Novatian schism to the unity of the Church." These confessors were members of the local Roman Church, who had been imprisoned for the faith after the martyrdom of Pope S. Fabian in January, 250. For a whole year they witnessed a good confession for Jesus Christ. However, in the year 251 some of them were beguiled into giving their support to the party of Novatian, who was commencing his schism at Rome. S. Denys of Alexandria and S. Cyprian wrote letters of remonstrance to them, and finally they were led to see their mistake, and to sue for readmission into the Church. On their readmission, they confessed their error and made a profession of allegiance to S. Cornelius, as being their legitimate bishop. The whole dispute turned on the question, Who was the rightful Bishop of Rome? Both Cornelius and Novatian claimed to be the Bishop of the Catholic Church at Rome, and each one accused his rival of being the head of a schismatic body. The confessors' profession on their readmission was as follows: "We acknowledge that Cornelius is Bishop of the most holy Catholic Church [in this city], chosen by God Almighty and Christ our Lord. We confess our error; we have suffered from imposture. We were circumvented by crafty and perfidious speeches. For although we seemed, as it were, to have held a kind of communion with a schismatic and heretic, yet our mind was ever sincere in the Church. For we are not ignorant that there is one God, one Christ the Lord, Whom we confessed, one Holy Ghost, and that there ought to be one bishop in a Catholic Church."[1] I have added in brackets the words "in this city," which express the true meaning. I see that Tillemont does the same. He says (iii. 460), "S. Cornelius reports word for word the act by which the confessors recognized him as the sole bishop of the Catholic Church [in Rome]." The confessors call the body adhering to Cornelius "the most holy Catholic Church," in contrast with the schismatic body adhering to Novatian. Father Bottalla tells us that "the name of Catholic Church is applied" in this passage "to the Church of Rome exclusively—that is, to S. Peter's chair—on account of its being the centre, the root, the source, and the matrix of Catholic unity." But such an interpretation is obviously very far-fetched. The relation of the so-called chair of S. Peter to Catholic unity was not in dispute. The question was, Who was the true occupant

---

[1] *Ep.* Cornelii *ad Cypr., inter Cyprianicas* xlvi., *Opp.* ed. Ben., pp. 60, 61.

of that chair ?   Which was the legitimate Catholic flock in Rome ?

Father Bottalla proceeds, "In the same sense Pope Cornelius, in his epistle to Fabius, Bishop of Antioch, used the following expression, pointing out the crime of Novatus :[1] 'This assertor of the gospel did not know that there can be but one bishop in the Catholic Church.'"[2]   Unfortunately, Father Bottalla makes a slip in his translation of this passage.   It should be, "that there can be but one bishop in *a* Catholic Church," not "in *the* Catholic Church."   S. Cornelius, who wrote to his brother of Antioch in Greek,[3] used the expression, ἐν καθολικῇ ἐκκλησίᾳ, not ἐν τῇ καθολικῇ ἐκκλησίᾳ.   When this correction has been made, it will be at once perceived that the passage is useless for Father Bottalla's purpose.   On the contrary, it helps to show that I have rightly interpreted the profession of allegiance made by the penitent confessors, for that profession was doubtless either drawn up or sanctioned by S. Cornelius ; and the plain meaning of his letter to Fabius may be safely used to clear up phrases, if there are any, which may be thought ambiguous in the profession.

But let us now go back to Father Bottalla's statement that the Church of Rome is "the centre, the root, the source, and the matrix of Catholic unity."   Truly, if that could be solidly proved, I should not care to write this book ; and for the first time in my life I should begin to fear that the faith which God in His great mercy has ever given me in the Catholicity of my mother the Church of England, has been the result of some illusion.   Father Bottalla

---

[1] Father Bottalla, following Eusebius, calls the anti-pope *Novatus;* but Eusebius is mistaken. The man's real name was Novatian. Novatus was a different person.

[2] Cf. Euseb., *H. E.*, vi. 43.

[3] Valesius, the editor of Eusebius, conclusively shows in a note that the letter was written in Greek, as we have it in Eusebius.

refers in a note to S. Cyprian's forty-fifth letter, addressed to S. Cornelius ; and he quotes S. Cyprian's words, "the root and womb of the Catholic Church,"[1] by which words he supposes that S. Cyprian means to describe the Roman Church, as being the centre and source of Catholic unity. We English Churchmen have been taught that the Catholic Church diffused throughout all the world, in her essential unity, is the root and womb and mother and head of individual Catholics and of particular local Churches, wherever they may be, whether at Rome, or at Canterbury, or at Oxford, or elsewhere. The whole Church is organically connected by the joints and bands of the apostolic faith and of the apostolical succession with the apostolic Church, which was set up on earth by our Lord ; and the whole Church is also organically connected, through her episcopate and through the Sacraments and through the operation and indwelling of the Holy Ghost, with her ascended Head, our Lord Jesus Christ, who holds the angels of the Churches in His right hand.[2] All local Churches derive their being, as Churches, from her. As Tertullian well expressed the matter, "These Churches, so many and so great, are but that one primitive Church from the apostles, whence they all spring. Thus all are the primitive, and all apostolical, while all are one."[3] Therefore the whole Church in her unity is the mother and womb and root of the particular local Churches ; and each local Church, if she is abiding in Catholic unity, is the local representative of the whole, and shares in the attributes of the whole ; so that each local Catholic Church becomes, in consequence of her relation to the whole, the mother and womb and root of the individual Catholics who belong to her. This is true of the particular local Church

---

[1] "Ecclesiæ Catholicæ radicem et matricem" (*Opp.* S. Cypr., ed. Ben., p. 59).   [2] Cf. Rev. i. 20.   [3] *De Præscr. Hær.*, xx.

of Rome, but it is true equally of all other local Churches. So we English Catholics have been taught, and so S. Cyprian in his day believed. I will refer to a few passages which occur in his letters, so as to illustrate his view. In April, 251, the Council of Carthage, hearing of the dispute at Rome as to the succession to the bishopric of the Church in that city, sent two African bishops, Caldonius and Fortunatus, to Rome with instructions that they were to endeavour to pacify the quarrel between the followers of Cornelius and the followers of Novatian, and also that they were to ascertain the truth as to whether the election and consecration of Cornelius had been canonical, and whether the charges brought against him by Novatian were supported by any solid evidence. Later on, when the African Church had been fully satisfied that Cornelius was the legitimate Roman bishop, S. Cyprian wrote to him concerning the recent mission of Caldonius and Fortunatus as follows: "We lately sent, dearest brother, our colleagues Caldonius and Fortunatus; that not only by the persuasion of our epistles, but by their presence and the advice of you all, they might endeavour, as far as they could, and labour effectually to bring the members of the divided body to the unity of the Catholic Church and to join them [to it] by the bond of Christian love. But since the self-willed and inflexible obstinacy of the adverse party *has not only refused the bosom and embrace of her who is their root and mother,*[1] but has also, with discord increasing and widening worse and worse, appointed a bishop for itself, and, contrary to the· mystery of the divine appointment and of Catholic unity once delivered, has set up an adulterous and opposed head without the Church ; . . . we have directed our letters to you."[2] Here

---

[1] "Radicis et matris sinum atque complexum recusavit."
[2] *Ep.* xlii. *ad Cornelium, Opp.* ed. Ben., p. 56.

it is evident that what S. Cyprian calls "*the root and mother*" is the unity of the Catholic Church, represented no doubt at Rome by the legitimate Bishop Cornelius and his flock of adherents. Cornelius and his party are not "*the root and mother*" because the pope is the centre of unity to the whole Church, but because they were recognized as legitimate by the whole Church, and because they joined in communion with her, and therefore represented her in Rome. In another letter, written about the same time, S. Cyprian urges the confessors who had got entangled in Novatian's party to "return to the Church your mother and to our brotherhood."[1] They were to return to the Church their mother by recognizing Cornelius as their true bishop, who was himself recognized by the Catholic episcopate. The question whether Cornelius as pope had a primacy of jurisdiction over the whole Church, did not arise. It was to the motherhood of the Church at large, not to any supposed ecumenical motherhood of the Roman see as such, that they were pressed to return.[2] I

---

[1] "Ad ecclesiam matrem et ad nostram fraternitatem revertamini" (*Ep.* xliv. *ad Confessores Romanos, Opp.* ed. Ben., p. 58).

[2] I do not for a moment deny that the local Roman Church was in a certain sense the mother-Church of large parts of the West, and more especially of the suburbicarian Churches; but there is no allusion to Rome's position as the original spring of evangelization in the West, and as the ecclesiastical metropolis of Central and Southern Italy, in these expressions of Cyprian. He is dealing with a much more vital fact, namely, the motherhood which appertains to the Catholic Church—"our brotherhood," as he calls it, a society extending all over the known world. So in his seventy-third *Epistle to Jubaianus (Opp.* ed. Ben., p. 137), in a passage where there is not the remotest allusion to Rome or to the local Church of Rome, he says that, when heretics understand that all baptism outside the Church is invalid, "they hasten to us more eagerly and more promptly, and implore the privileges and gifts of *Mother Church*" (munera ac dona *ecclesiæ matris* implorant). And still more appositely, in his forty-third epistle which he sent to Cornelius, enclosing it as a covering letter along with his letter to the confessors, he says, referring to his letter to the confessors,

pass on to the letter quoted by Father Bottalla, giving first
a short explanation of the circumstances under which it
was written.   While the two African bishops, Caldonius
and Fortunatus, were making their investigations in Rome,
their colleagues in Africa determined that Cornelius should
not be publicly recognized in Africa as the Roman bishop.
The canonicity of his election had been disputed, and it
was necessary that all doubts should be removed before
the African Church committed herself as championing his
side.   It was therefore determined that, until a final
decision should be given, official letters to the Roman
Church should be addressed to the priests and deacons
of that Church, and not to Cornelius.   This rule had been
broken at Adrumetum through a mistake, and letters from
that colony had been directed to Cornelius himself ; but
after a visit which S. Cyprian paid to Adrumetum, the
mistake was rectified, and all subsequent letters to the
Roman Church were for a time directed to the priests and
deacons of that Church, and not to the bishop.[1] Cornelius
noticed the change, and noticed also that the change had
come about in consequence of S. Cyprian's visit to Adrumetum, and he not unnaturally supposed that S. Cyprian
was inclined to favour the claims of the anti-pope Novatian.
Accordingly he wrote to S. Cyprian to expostulate. S.
Cyprian in his reply gave a full explanation of the whole
matter, and animadverts on the way in which the simplest
incidents get misreported and misrepresented. Then he goes

"In my letter I would prevail with them, from mutual affection, to
return *to their mother, that is the Catholic Church*" (ad matrem suam,
id est ecclesiam catholicam). But the passages in which the whole
Church is called our mother are practically innumerable.

[1] These letters would, in the great majority of cases, be letters of
commendation, introducing this or that African Catholic, who might
be travelling to Rome, to the authorities of the Church in the
imperial city, and certifying to the fact that the bearer was in full
communion with the Catholic Church.

on to say, "We, who furnish all who sail hence with instructions, lest in their voyage they any way offend, know well that we have exhorted them to hold *the root and womb of the Catholic Church.*"[1] Evidently S. Cyprian meant by these words to warn his people against attending schismatic worship when away from Africa, and to urge them to find out, in every place where they might sojourn, the legitimate bishop who was recognized by the whole body of Catholic bishops. The Church in communion with the legitimate bishop would be the true representative of the Catholic Church at large, and would in a subordinate way share with that Church the prerogative of being "the root and womb" of the children of God. Persons sailing from Africa would more often be on their way to Rome than to any other place, because Rome was the capital of the empire, the metropolis of the civilized world. S. Cyprian therefore would certainly intend that his advice should be of help to his people, if they should chance to be in Rome ; and in fact the reference to that advice in this letter to Cornelius shows that in S. Cyprian's mind the advice had a special bearing on the existing circumstances of the Roman Church. This fact will enable us to reject at once Father Bottalla's view that the Roman Church was itself "the root and womb," as being the centre of unity to the

---

[1] "Nos enim singulis navigantibus, ne cum scandalo ullo navigarent, rationem reddentes, scimus nos hortatos eos esse ut *ecclesiæ catholicæ radicem et matricem* agnoscerent ac tenerent" (*Ep.* xlv. *ad Cornelium, Opp.* ed. Ben., p. 59). The word "matrix" sometimes means "stem," which would agree well with "*radix*" (*root*), and would suit the sense as well as the more usual meaning "*womb.*" But the fact that in *Ep.* xlii. S. Cyprian had joined *radix* with *mater*, seems to me to make the meaning "*womb*" the more probable. Bossuet, in his *Instruction Pastorale sur les Promesses de l'Église* (*Œuvres,* ed. 1816, xxii. 411, 412), favours the meaning "stem." He understands the "*radix et matrix,*" as I do, of the Church's unity :—"cette tige, cette racine de l'unité" (p. 412).

whole Catholic Church. For, on account of the schism
raging in the local Church of Rome, the difficulty was to
decide which was the true Church of Rome. If the
Roman Church was itself "the root and womb," then,
whether they joined Cornelius or Novatian, they would
suppose that they had adhered to "the root and womb."
But S. Cyprian's advice was evidently meant to help them
to *discriminate*. He in effect tells them, "You must
adhere to that party which shall prove itself to have a
right to the communion of the Catholic Church. When
you are on the spot, and know the circumstances, you will
soon be able to find out which of the two parties has the
better right. If you cannot decide, you must wait and see
how the matter will be decided by the bishops in Africa
and elsewhere. Whatever you do, take care to adhere to
that party only which either is already or immediately
will be, in fellowship with the Church at large. You must
avoid separatist cliques, and abide in Catholic unity. So
my advice is, Hold to the root and womb of true Christians—I mean, your mother the Catholic Church."[1] I do
not doubt that S. Cyprian felt sure in his own mind that
S. Cornelius was the legitimate bishop; but he was
precluded for the present from openly telling his people
to communicate with the party of Cornelius, because, as I
have said, the matter was supposed to be in suspense
until the return of the two African legates.[2]

I will quote one more passage which throws light on

---

[1] From what I have said, it will, I hope, be clear to those of my
readers who know Latin, that in the expression, *"ecclesiæ catholicæ
radicem et matricem,"* the words *" ecclesiæ catholicæ "* are in the genitive
of *apposition*, so that the whole expression signifies, "the root and
womb, which is the Catholic Church."

[2] Baronius says that the African bishops had "suspended communion " (communicationem suspenderant) both with Cornelius and
with Novatian, until the legates' return (*Annall.,* s.a. 254).

S. Cyprian's use of the word "root" (radix). In his epistle to Jubaianus S. Cyprian undertakes to prove that the followers of Novatian ought to be rebaptized on their reconciliation with the Church. In the course of his argument he says, "We, who hold the head and root of the one Church, know assuredly and are confident that to him [Novatian], being outside the Church, nothing is awful ; and that baptism, which is one, is with us, where he also himself was formerly baptized."[1] Here it is clear that the Church herself is "the head and root" of individual Catholics. S. Cyprian cannot possibly mean that the pope or the Church of Rome is "the head and root," for he is contrasting himself with Novatian, who claimed to be the true Bishop of Rome. In such an argument S. Cyprian could not say, "I hold to the Church of Rome and to the pope, and therefore I know that Novatian can do nothing lawful ; " because Novatian would naturally answer, "I am the pope ; I am the head and root of the one Church." In the controversy with Novatian it was impossible to rest the Catholic cause on any supposed prerogative of the Roman Church, because both sides claimed to have the Roman Church with them. S. Cyprian rests the proof on the general consent of the episcopate spread throughout the world. He could plead that consent with crushing force against Novatian. It is the universal Church gathered up into its main organ of government, the college of bishops, which is "the head and root" of true Catholics.[2] Moreover, in this

---

[1] "Nos autem, qui ecclesiæ unius caput et radicem tenemus, pro certo scimus et fidimus nihil illi extra ecclesiam licere, et baptisma, quod est unum, apud nos esse, ubi et ipse baptizatus prius fuerat" (*Ep.* lxxiii. *ad Jubaianum, Opp.* ed Ben., p. 130).

[2] So in his treatise on *The Unity of the Church* (*Opp.* ed. Ben., p. 195), in a celebrated passage in which he contrasts the oneness of the whole Church with the multiplicity of the progeny of the Church, S. Cyprian says, "Yet is there one head, one source, one mother, abundant in the results of her fruitfulness" (unum tamen caput est, et origo

particular controversy about rebaptism S. Cyprian was opposing Pope Stephen. Almost immediately after the letter to Jubaianus was written he must have received an epistle from the pope, threatening him with excommunication, and in the autumn of that same year he actually was excommunicated. It would have been absurd to base his argument in favour of baptizing Novatians on his fellowship with Stephen, who was treating him as a heretic because he baptized Novatians.

These various passages, as it seems to me, throw light on each other. If we compare them together, they are seen to teach the same doctrine. In S. Cyprian's view, the Church Catholic is our mother,[1] and she who is our mother

una, et una mater fæcunditatis successibus copiosa). The argument requires us to interpret these expressions of the Church Catholic in her entirety; but care must be taken to read the treatise in an uninterpolated edition, such as Hartel's. Father Bottalla (*Supreme Authority of the Pope*, p. 12) has the courage to assert that "unquestionably" these expressions and others like them, occurring in the passage of the *De Unitate*, to which I am referring, denote "the primacy and the authority of S. Peter." In the whole treatise there is not a word about any peculiar authority either in S. Peter or in the Roman see. Peter, as the first-chosen apostle, is historically the first bishop, and so the commencement of the episcopate, and consequently he is a fitting *symbol* of the unity of the Church. But in the passage with which we are dealing S. Cyprian has passed on from the symbol to that which is symbolized. and from the historically first bishop to "the one and undivided episcopate" which governs "the Church" which "is spread abroad;" and it is a perversion of his whole argument to interpret "the sun" and "the root" and "the fountain" of Peter and of Peter's authority. These expressions set forth the relation of the whole Church in her unity to her separate members, that is to her manifold "progeny," to use S. Cyprian's expression. For proof, I can only refer the reader to the treatise itself, where the meaning is so plain that no comments can make it plainer. It is evident that Father Bottalla has been deceived by the interpolations. The words which he quotes in the note are taken from one of them. On these interpolations, see pp. 350, 353, 354.

[1] See pp. 340, 341.

is also our root,[1] and she who is the root, out of which we grow, is also the womb,[2] in which we were conceived by grace, and the head by which we are governed. There is in them no trace of Father Bottalla's idea,[3] that S. Cyprian held that the Church of Rome is " the centre, the root, the source, and the matrix of Catholic unity."

I have treated at length concerning this Cyprianic phrase, " the root and matrix of the Church." I must try and deal in a more summary way with S. Cyprian's statements about S. Peter. As we might expect, S. Cyprian holds the scriptural and Catholic teaching about S. Peter's leadership among the apostles, which resulted from the

---

[1] See pp. 343-345.　　　　[2] See pp. 343, 344.

[3] It must surely have been through forgetfulness of the state of affairs at Rome during the first few months of the Novatian schism, that Father Bottalla has quoted two passages from S. Cyprian's epistles, as if they proved that S. Cyprian held that " to be in communion with the Bishop of Rome is equivalent to being in communion with the whole Catholic Church." The first passage occurs in S. Cyprian's forty-fifth epistle (*Opp.* ed. Ben., p. 59), which was addressed to Pope Cornelius. Owing to the schism in Rome, the African Church had, as we have seen, suspended communion with both Cornelius and Novatian. When at length the question was cleared up, and it was made evident that Cornelius was the legitimate Catholic bishop, it was agreed that all the African bishops should send letters to Cornelius, " that so," as S. Cyprian says, " all our colleagues might approve of and uphold thee and thy communion—that is, the unity and charity of the Catholic Church." The second passage occurs in the fifty-second letter, which is addressed to Antonianus (*Opp.* ed. Ben., p. 66), and is practically to the same effect as the other. To uphold Cornelius and his flock and to reject Novatian and his followers, when once it had been proved that Cornelius was the legitimate bishop, was in fact to support the unity of the Catholic Church as against schism, and the charity of the Catholic Church as against factiousness. The words could have been written concerning the legitimate bishop of any see. They have nothing to do with any special Roman privilege. Such arguments as these of Father Bottalla's seriously damage the cause on behalf of which they are used.

fact that to him first the apostolic office was promised (or given),[1] and which showed itself by the initiative which he so largely took in the first founding of the Church. I have dealt with this subject in my third lecture, to which I must refer my readers.[2] The point which is characteristic of S. Cyprian is the stress which he lays on the *symbolical* character which he assigns to S. Peter. That apostle, as *primus inter pares*, is the symbol of the Church Militant;[3] just as, according to the teaching of S. Augustine, S. John, the beloved disciple, who leaned back on the Lord's breast at the supper, is the symbol of the Church Triumphant.[4] This teaching of S. Cyprian about the symbolical character of S. Peter was thoroughly assimilated and reproduced by S. Augustine. Take one passage as a sample. In his 295th sermon, preached on the Feast of S. Peter and S. Paul, S. Augustine says, " Among these [the apostles] almost everywhere it was granted to Peter alone to represent the Church (gestare personam Ecclesiæ). On account of this character, which he alone bore of representing the whole Church, was it granted him to hear the words, ' To thee will I give the keys of the kingdom of heaven.' *For these keys not one man, but the unity of the Church received.* Hereby then is the excellence of Peter set forth, that he was an emblem of the whole body and of the unity of the

---

[1] See the note on pp. 351, 352.   [2] See pp. 111–115.

[3] Mr. Rivington says (*Authority*, pp. 96, 97), " How could Peter be a symbol of unity, unless he bore a special relationship to the other apostles?" He did bear a special relationship to them. He was the first-called apostle, and so he naturally became the leader of the band; but he was not their ruler or king, and his leadership ended with himself. It was a leadership in founding, and it involved no jurisdiction over the other apostles for himself, nor any jurisdiction over the universal episcopate for his supposed successors at Rome. S. Peter's precedence in designation was no doubt the reward of his personal faith and loyalty and courage.

[4] Compare p. 100.

Church, when it was said to him, 'I give to thee,' what in fact was given to all."[1] It was not that S. Peter possessed the power of the keys in some supereminent sense. The other apostles possessed that power equally with him. But he, as the first-called apostle, was fitted to symbolize the Church in her unity, so that it should be understood that the power of the keys was given to the unity of the Church—that is, to the united body or society of the Church. This was exactly S. Cyprian's view. I will quote in illustration the opening passage of the argument of S. Cyprian's treatise on the Unity of the Church. S. Cyprian says, " The Lord saith unto Peter, ' I say unto thee,' (saith He,) ' that thou art Peter, and upon this rock I will build My Church, and the gates of hell shall not prevail against it. And I will give unto thee the keys of the kingdom of heaven, and whatsoever thou shalt bind on earth, shall be bound also in heaven, and whatsoever thou shalt loose on earth, shall be loosed in heaven.' Upon one he builds His Church ; and although to all His apostles after His resurrection He gives an equal power,[2] and says, ' As My Father sent Me, even so send I you ; receive ye the Holy Ghost : whosesoever sins ye remit, they shall be remitted to him, and whosesoever sins ye retain, they shall be retained ;' yet in order to manifest unity, He by His authoritative utterance [to S. Peter] arranged for that same unity an origin beginning from one. Certainly the other apostles also were what Peter was, endued with an equal fellowship both of honour and power ; but the commence-

---

[1] S. August., *Opp.* ed. Ben., 1683, v. 1194. It should be noted that S. Augustine, when he has occasion in another place (*De Bapt.*, lib. iii. cap. xviii., *Opp.* ed. Ben., ix. 117) to treat of the commission to remit and retain sins, given to the ten apostles on Easter day, says that they all " *represented the Church* " (gerebant personam Ecclesiæ).

[2] " Super unum ædificat ecclesiam, et quamvis apostolis omnibus post resurrectionem suam parem potestatem tribuat," etc.

ment starts from unity, that the Church may be set before us as one.[1]   Which one Church in the song of songs, the Holy Spirit, speaking in the Person of our Lord, designates, and says, ' My dove, My undefiled is but one ; she is the only one of her mother, she is the choice one of her that bare her.'   He who holds not this unity of the Church, does he think that he holds the faith ?   He who strives against and resists the Church is he assured that he is in the Church ? "[2]   Now, I put it to any candid Roman

[1] "Tamen ut unitatem manifestaret, unitatis ejusdem originem ab uno incipientem suâ auctoritate disposuit.   Hoc erant utique et ceteri apostoli quod fuit Petrus, pari consortio præditi et honoris et potestatis, sed exordium ab unitate proficiscitur, ut ecclesia Christi una monstretur."   It seems to me that the word "auctoritas" in this passage should, according to a well-known use of the word, be taken in a concrete rather than in au abstract sense ; but, if any one should think otherwise, my argument will not be affected, as it in no way depends on my suggestion being adopted.   The passage quoted in this note is a good illustration of the meaning of another passage, which occurs in the synodal epistle of S. Cyprian's first Council on rebaptism.   This epistle was no doubt written by S. Cyprian, and is numbered as the seventieth.   The Council says, " Et baptisma unum sit et Spiritus Sanctus unus et una ecclesia a Christo Domino nostro super Petrum origine unitatis et ratione fundata ; " of which passage the sense may be thus expressed, " There is both one baptism, and one Holy Ghost, and one Church founded by Christ the Lord upon Peter, for an origin and showing forth of unity " (*Opp.* ed. Ben., p. 125). The ablatives seem to be without construction, and to have a general reference to the sentence.

[2] " Qui ecclesiæ renititur et resistit in ecclesiâ se esse confidit ? " (*Opp.* ed. Ben., pp. 194, 195).   In the text I have translated this passage from the latest critical edition of S. Cyprian's works, by Hartel, published in 1871 at Vienna.   Cardinal de Fleury, the Prime Minister of France under Louis XV., forced the Benedictines to insert the interpolated passages, which had been expunged from every critical edition, and which had been erased by Baluzius, who prepared the edition, which after his death was brought out and fathered by them (see Chiniac de la Bastide Duclaux' *Histoire des Capitulaires des Rois François*, pp. 226-228, ed. 1779).   The evidence against the interpolations is overwhelming.

Catholic, Is this the way that he would write on the great subject of the Church's unity ? Perhaps such a one rejoiced, when he perceived that S. Cyprian starts his argument with the Petrine text about "*the Rock*." But the very fact that he begins by quoting that text, makes his subsequent comment on it the more significant. Why, when he is dealing at length with such an important subject as the Church's unity, does he say nothing about that institution which Roman Catholics consider to be the divinely ordained source and guarantee of unity ? Why is there nothing about Peter's jurisdiction over the Church ? Why is there nothing about the infallible popes, the successors of S. Peter, who are supposed to be the principle and centre of unity ? You may read the whole treatise on unity from beginning to end, and you will not find one single word about Rome, or about the pope, or about any papal jurisdiction derived from S. Peter. S. Cyprian sees in S. Peter, not the *guarantee* of unity, but, as being the first-designated apostle, the *symbol* of unity. The apostolate was promised, or, as S. Cyprian would perhaps have said, *given*[1] to S. Peter

---

[1] It is curious that the majority of the Fathers seem not to have noticed that our Lord's words to S. Peter, recorded in S. Matt. xvi. 18, 19, convey a *promise*, not a gift. S. Chrysostom (*Hom.* liv. *in Matt., Opp.* ed. Ben., 1741, vii. 548) does indeed speak of the words as containing "two *promises*" (ὑποσχέσεων δύο); but the Fathers in general speak as if the apostolical authority were then and there given. And yet the Lord's words are quite unmistakable: "I *will* give (δώσω) unto thee the keys of the kingdom of heaven," etc. Later on, the promissive nature of the words was generally acknowledged. Theophylact (tom. vii. p. 647, *in Matt. Hom.*, lxv. 4, quoted by Mr. Gore, *Rom. Cath. Claims*, 4th edit., p. 87) acknowledges it very explicitly. In a treatise addressed to Ladislas, King of Poland and Hungary, in 1441, the University of Cracow speaks of our Lord's " verba *promissiva*, Tu es Petrus, et tibi dabo," etc. (cf. Launoi., lib. i. *ep.* x., *ad Christoph. Fauvæum, Opp.* ed. 1731, tom. v. pars i. p. 105). Baluzius, the writer of the notes to the Benedictine S. Cyprian, says (*Opp.* S. Cypr. ed. Ben., p. 414), speaking of the words *Tibi*

first, in order that, a beginning being made from one, unity
might be *manifested*, and the Church *be set before us* as
one.   To a Romanist all this must seem very poor and thin.
To an English Catholic it is meat and drink ; for it sets
forth, both in what is said and in what is not said, the very
central truth about the polity of the Church which he has
received to hold.   Notice how twice over in this short
passage S. Cyprian insists that S. Peter received no peculiar
power, that "the other apostles were what Peter was,
endued with an equal fellowship both of honour and power."
Can anything be more frigid, I had almost said senseless,
than the Ultramontane reply that S. Cyprian is speaking
of the power of order and not of the power of jurisdiction ?
that the apostles were all equally with S. Peter bishops,
but that S. Peter, though no more than a bishop in order,

dabo claves, "Quamvis istic claves non dentur Petro, sed *promittantur,*"
etc.   And even Father Bottalla (*Supreme Authority of the Pope,* p.
33), says, "Although Peter by a prophetic name, and by an explicit
promise of an eminent office, had been designated by Christ to be the
head and the ruler of His Church, yet Christ, as long as He remained
on earth, did not invest him with the high dignity of œcumenical
pastor."   The Gospel record makes it clear that the apostolate was
promised to S. Peter first (S. Matt. xvi. 18, 19); afterwards it was
promised to all the twelve (S. Matt. xviii. 18); finally it was conferred
on the whole body simultaneously on the evening of the day of our
Lord's resurrection (S. John xx. 21–23).   This was the actual
order of events; but I am inclined to think that S. Cyprian
thought that, while all the twelve received precisely the same commission, and were invested with precisely the same ecumenical
jurisdiction, S. Peter was actually made an apostle some little time
before the others.   This, S. Cyprian thinks, was done for symbolical
reasons, to show forth the unity of the Church, that the commencement of the Church might start from unity. The symbolism is equally
preserved if the truer view be accepted.   Unity may be conceived to
be set forth by the promise of the apostolical office being made to one
first, and later on to the others ; while the equality of the apostles is
well brought out by the simultaneous conferring of the apostolate on
Easter day.

was a bishop of bishops—yea, was the monarch of the Church in jurisdiction? Why does not S. Cyprian say that? The subject of the Church's unity required some treatment of the central jurisdiction. So S. Cyprian felt; but he knew of no more central jurisdiction than the jurisdiction of the apostolic college; and when he passes on to later times, he knows of no more central jurisdiction than "the one and undivided episcopate" (episcopatum unum atque indivisum).

When in after ages the papal idea began to grow up in the Roman Church, it was felt how unsatisfactory from the papal point of view S. Cyprian's teaching was, and a remedy for the supposed mischief was sought. It is generally supposed that Pope Gelasius proscribed his writings, as well he might, for night and day are not in more direct contrast than Gelasius and Cyprian. In a decree ascribed to that pope lists of books recommended and books proscribed are given, and the works of Thascius Cyprianus occur as an item in the prohibitory index. Afterwards some person or persons unknown forged certain sentences about the grievous consequences of deserting the see of Peter, and inserted them into S. Cyprian's treatise.[1] This just supplied the lacking papal element; and a few lines were enough to give a different turn to the whole argument. Some have supposed that it was after these interpolations had been forged that another clause, irreconcilable with the above-mentioned item, crept into the copies of the Gelasian decree. According to this other clause, S. Cyprian's writings, instead

---

[1] Ultramontane writers suggest that the interpolations were marginal notes, which crept into the text by the carelessness of copyists. With every wish to be charitable, I feel no doubt myself that the forgery was deliberate. Anyhow, whether forged or not, they very conveniently got into the text, and entirely changed the impression produced by the whole argument.

of being rejected, were placed first on the list of works commended to the faithful for study.[1]

But let us pass to another Cyprianic passage about S. Peter. In his twenty-seventh epistle, which is addressed to the lapsed, S. Cyprian writes as follows : "Our Lord, whose precepts and warnings we ought to observe, *determining the honour of a bishop* and the ordering (rationem) of His Church, speaks in the Gospel, and says to Peter, 'I say unto thee, that thou art Peter, and on this rock will I build My Church ; and the gates of hell shall not prevail against it. And I will give unto thee the keys of the kingdom of heaven ; and whatsoever thou shalt bind on earth, shall be bound in heaven ; and whatsoever thou shalt loose on earth, shall be loosed in heaven.' Thence the ordination of bishops and the ordering (ratio) of the Church runs down through the changes of times and successions, *so that the Church is settled upon the bishops*, and every act of the Church is controlled by these same rulers."[2] Notice, again, how the great Petrine passage suggests to S. Cyprian, as it suggests to us, not the government of the Church by popes, but the government of the Church by bishops. S. Peter was not the pope over the apostles, but one among them ; the first called,[3] and therefore the natural leader and spokesman and representative, but with no larger jurisdiction

[1] The decree with its two irreconcilable clauses is given in Colcti (v. 387, 390).

[2] *Opp.* ed. Ben., pp. 37, 38.

[3] The author of the article "*Pope*," in the *Catholic Dictionary* by Messrs. Addis and Arnold (p. 671), says very strangely, "Peter, of course, was not chosen first in order of time." One can only suppose that the writer has confused the calling of S. Peter to be a *disciple*, as recorded in S. John i. 41, 42, with his calling to be an *apostle*, as recorded in S. Matt. x. 1, 2. As we have already seen, S. Cyprian held that S. Peter was not only called first, but that he was also consecrated first. This notion is doubtless based on a mistake, but it ought to be kept in mind, if we would understand S. Cyprian aright (see the note on pp. 351, 352).

than the others. What he was, they all were, namely, founders and foundations and rulers of the Church of God. Their successors in their ruling office, and therefore his successors, were the bishops. S. Peter might or might not have special diocesan successors in particular sees, such as Antioch or Rome. S. Cyprian says nothing here about such local successions. Even if there were such local successions they would be, from S. Cyprian's point of view, accidental, not essential or vital. The vital point was and is that the bishops everywhere inherit the whole ordinary jurisdiction of the apostolic college. They are all the successors of the apostles, and as of the others, so specially of the representative apostle, Peter. " The Church is settled upon the bishops." This is good Catholic teaching, which it has been the glory of the English Church to treasure up, and hand down, and consolidate, as the basis of her whole system of polity. We are grateful to the Latin communion for some precious things, which she has guarded more faithfully than we have guarded them ; but in regard to other matters, and specially in regard to the divinely ordered constitution of the Church, it is for her to learn from us.

I think that the teaching of S. Cyprian about the relation of S. Peter to the Church's unity and to the episcopate, which I have gathered from these two passages, will suggest the true interpretation of several other passages in the holy martyr's writings, and will make it unnecessary for me to treat them at length. I append them to this note in an *Addendum*,[1] so that the reader may be in possession of all the Cyprianic passages which have been quoted in favour of the papal theory.

I have now fulfilled my promise[2] to deal with the various

---

[1] See pp. 357–363.

[2] I have dealt with the passage in which S. Cyprian calls the

passages from the Cyprianic documents which are quoted
by Father Bottalla in support of his notion that S. Cyprian
acknowledges " the closest connection between the unity of
the Church, as represented by Christ, and the headship
of one universal pastor." I confidently assert that the
meaning of each one of the quoted passages has been
misrepresented by Father Bottalla. I of course exonerate
him from any intentional deceit ; but the fact remains that
the meaning of the passages has been misrepresented. I
do not believe that the idea of a " headship of one universal
pastor " over the whole Church ever entered S. Cyprian's
mind, either as a thing to be accepted or rejected.[1] His
whole notion of the Church presupposed a college of
essentially co-equal bishops owning no divinely appointed
personal superior, excepting only our Lord Jesus Christ.
In one sense this note does injustice to S. Cyprian. The
necessity of disproving Father Bottalla's statements has
compelled me to dwell on those few sentences in the
Cyprianic documents, which might conceivably be twisted

Church at Rome the *cathedra Petri et ecclesia principalis*, in my
second lecture. See pp. 53–56.

[1] Compare Archbishop Benson's words quoted in the note on p. 80.
If any one supposes that S. Cyprian was conscious of a claim made on
the part of Pope Stephen to be the " universal pastor " of the Church,
then it will follow that the saint deliberately rejected the papal idea
(see the passage quoted on pp. 77, 78). Either way his witness is
diametrically opposed to the Ultramontane theory set forth in the
Vatican decrees. It should be remembered that those decrees assert
that the supremacy of S. Peter and of his supposed successors, the
popes, over the whole Church is not a new development, but is due to
the immediate institution of Christ, and has been known to all the
ages of the Church's history. In this connection it is worth while
recalling a statement made by the late Cardinal Pitra, a learned
Ultramontane, who occupied the post of " Librarian of the Holy
Roman Church." He says that there is no place in the history of
Christian Rome " pour *la conception rationaliste* d'un lent progrès du
saint Siège " (*Analecta Novissima*, 1885, tom. i. p. 15).

into a papal meaning. I hope that I have successfully untwisted them. But S. Cyprian's whole view must be gathered, not from those few passages, but from his writings at large, and still more from his actions. S. Cyprian was the most glorious saint and the most illustrious Church-ruler of his age. The whole Church has venerated him with special honour ever since his martyrdom : we know more about him than about any other post-apostolic saint of the first three centuries : the circumstances of his life led him to deal specially with matters connected with the government of the Church : and both his writings and the story of his life remain as a perpetual witness against the papal and in favour of the episcopal constitution of the Church of God.

Addendum to Note B.

In this *Addendum* I propose to collect such passages from S. Cyprian's writings as have been or might be quoted in favour of the papal theory, and which have not been discussed either in the second lecture or in Note B. It will not be necessary for me to comment on them at any length, because I trust that what I have written on pp. 347–355 will enable the reader to perceive at once S. Cyprian's meaning.

1. In his Epistle to Quintus, S. Cyprian says, "For neither did Peter, whom the Lord chose first, and on whom He built His Church, when Paul afterwards disputed with him about circumcision, claim anything to himself inso-lently, nor arrogantly assume anything ; so as to say that he held the primacy, and that he ought rather to be obeyed by novices and those lately come ; nor did he despise Paul because he had previously been a persecutor of the Church, but he admitted the counsel of truth, and readily yielded to the legitimate argument which Paul pressed ; furnishing

thereby a lesson to us both of concord and patience, that we should not obstinately love our own opinions, but should rather adopt as our own those which at any time are usefully and wholesomely suggested by our brethren and colleagues, if they be true and lawful."[1]   According to S. Cyprian's view, which has been discussed in the note on pp. 351, 352, the apostolate was given to S. Peter before it was given to the other apostles, and to him it was given, when the Lord said to him, "On this rock I will build My Church."   S. Peter had no greater powers than the other apostles, but his seniority by consecration made him the symbol of the Church's unity.   S. Cyprian holds that for a short time he was the only foundation, the other apostles not having received their powers until some time had elapsed ; and so, on this view, the Church may be said to have been built on S. Peter in a certain pre-eminent way.   This is the meaning of the "*super quem ædificavit ecclesiam suam.*"   When S. Peter and S. Paul are compared as regards their apostolic office, there is no question that the former had a priority both in time and order. But S. Cyprian points out that, if in consequence of this priority S. Peter had expected S. Paul to obey him, he would have been guilty of insolence and arrogance.   In other words, S. Peter had no primacy of jurisdiction.   S. Paul was his "brother and colleague."

2. In his epistle to Jubaianus, S. Cyprian says, "To Peter, in the first place, upon whom He built the Church, and whence He appointed and shewed forth the origin of unity, the Lord gave that power, namely, that whatsoever

---

[1] "Nam nec Petrus, quem primum Dominus elegit, et super quem ædificavit ecclesiam suam, . . . vindicavit sibi aliquid insolenter aut arroganter assumpsit, ut diceret se primatum tenere et obtemperari a novellis et posteris sibi potius oportere . . . quæ aliquando a fratribus et collegis nostris utiliter et salubriter suggeruntur . . ." (*Ep.* lxxi. *ad Quintum, Opp.* ed. Ben., p. 127).

he should loose on earth should be loosed in heaven."[1] The comment on the previous passage applies also to the first clause of this one. The appointment and manifestation of the origin of unity through S. Peter's priority of consecration is illustrated by the passage from the *De Unitate*, quoted and discussed on pp. 349–353.[2]

3. In one of his epistles to S. Cornelius, S. Cyprian says,[3] "Peter, however, on whom the Church has been built by the same Lord, one speaking for all, and answering in the voice of the Church, says, 'Lord to whom shall we go?'" After what has been said previously, there is no need to make any comment here.

4. In an earlier part of the same letter, S. Cyprian had said, "For this has been the very source whence heresies and schisms have taken their rise, that obedience is not paid to God's bishop (sacerdoti), nor do they reflect that there is for the time one bishop (sacerdos) in a Church [*i.e.* in each Church], and one judge for the time

---

[1] "Nam Petro primum Dominus, supra quem ædificavit ecclesiam, et unde unitatis originem instituit et ostendit, potestatem illam dedit ut id solveretur in cælis quod ille solvisset in terris" (*Ep.* lxxiii. *ad Jubaianum, Opp.* ed. Ben., p. 131). The conclusion, which S. Cyprian draws from this premiss, is not that the pope is the monarch of the Church or its necessary centre of unity, but that "they only, who are set over the Church, and are appointed by the law of the gospel and the ordinance of the Lord, may lawfully baptize and give remission of sins, . . . and that no one can usurp to himself, against bishops and priests, what is not in his own right and power." As usual, S. Cyprian sees in the promise of our Lord to S. Peter the institution of the episcopate.

[2] I have already pointed out (see pp. 345, 346) the very strained relations which existed between S. Cyprian and Pope Stephen when this letter was written. S. Cyprian was on the verge of being excommunicated by Rome, and would certainly not insert passages at such a time in support of the necessity of union with Rome.

[3] "Petrus tamen super quem ædificata ab eodem Domino fuerat ecclesia unus pro omnibus loquens et ecclesiæ voce respondens ait : ' Domine ad quem ibimus ' " (*Ep.* lv. *ad Cornelium, Opp.* ed. Ben., p. 83).

in Christ's stead; whom if the whole brotherhood would
obey, according to the divine injunctions, no one would
stir in anything against the college of bishops (sacerdotum)."[1] It need hardly be said that in S. Cyprian's
writings, as in the writings of many of the other Fathers,
the word "*sacerdos*" almost always means *bishop*, and
hardly ever *presbyter*. I should not have loaded my pages
with this passage if I had not noticed that it is quoted by
some Ultramontane writers as if it proved that the pope
is the "one judge," who judges the whole Church "in
Christ's stead." The wording of the passage and the
whole argument of the epistle show that S. Cyprian is
speaking of the functions of each bishop in his own
Church, and not of any supposed ecumenical functions
of the pope in regard to the Church universal.

5. In his epistle to Florentius Puppianus, S. Cyprian
says, "There (S. John vi. 67–69) speaks Peter, upon
whom the Church was to be built; teaching and showing
in the name of the Church that, although a contumacious
and proud multitude of such as will not obey may withdraw, yet the Church does not depart from Christ, and
they are the Church who are a people united to the bishop
(sacerdoti), and a flock adhering to their own pastor."[2]

---

[1] "Neque enim aliunde hæreses obortæ sunt aut nata sunt schismata
quam inde quod sacerdoti Dei non obtemperatur, nec unus in ecclesiâ
ad tempus sacerdos et ad tempus judex vice Christi cogitatur . . . ."
(*Opp.* ed. Ben., p. 82). I will insert here a few references to passages,
in which bishops are styled "Vicars of Christ," or "Vicars of the
Lord." Ambrosiaster says that a bishop "vicarius Domini est" (*in*
1 *Cor. xi.* 10; ap. S. Ambros. *Opp.*, vii. 173, ed. Ben., 1781, Venet.).
Pope Hormisdas, in a letter to the bishops of Spain, describes bishops
as "Vicars of Christ" (Coleti, v. 604). The same expression is used
of bishops by the Synod of Compiègne in the year 833, by that of
Thionville in 844, and by that of Meaux in 845 (Coleti, ix. 801, 942,
961).

[2] "Loquitur illic Petrus, super quem ædificanda fuerat ecclesia
. . . . et illi sunt ecclesia, plebs sacerdoti adunata et pastori suo grex

The words about S. Peter will be understood from previous
explanations. The definition of the Church at the end of
the passage contains no allusion to the pope. It speaks
of the flock in each diocese adhering to their own bishop.

6. In the treatise *De Bono Patientiæ*, S. Cyprian says,[1]
" Peter likewise, on whom the Church was founded by
the good pleasure of the Lord, lays it down in his Epistle."
Comment is needless.

7. In an epistle addressed to his Carthaginian flock,
S. Cyprian says,[2] "There is one God, and one Christ, and
one Church, and one chair founded by the word of the
Lord on Peter (super Petrum).[3] Another altar cannot be
set up, nor a new priesthood made, besides the one altar
and one priesthood." S. Cyprian is warning his people
against the schism of Felicissimus, who had set up a
separate altar at Carthage and had got five Carthaginian
priests to join him. S. Cyprian explains that in each
local Church there is but one episcopal chair ; one priesthood—that is, the one true bishop and the clergy adhering
to him ; and one altar. The "one chair"—that is, the
episcopate of the one canonical bishop—is founded on Peter,
for according to S. Cyprian and the Fathers generally all
legitimate bishops are the successors of Peter.[4] In the

adhærens ";(*Ep.* lxix. *ad Florentium Puppianum, Opp.* ed. Ben., p.
123).

[1] " Item Petrus, super quem ecclesia Domini dignatione fundata
est, in epistola sua ponit " (*De Bon. Pat., Opp.* ed. Ben., p. 250).

[2] Deus unus est, et Christus unus, et una ecclesia, et cathedra una
super Petrum (*al.* petram) Domini voce fundata. Aliud altare con-
stitui aut sacerdotium novum fieri præter unum altare et unum
sacerdotium non potest" (*Ep.* xl. *ad plebem, Opp.* ed. Ben., p. 53).

[3] Some manuscripts read ".super petram," "on the rock." The
sense would be the same. I follow Hartel in the text. The Benedictines read " petram."

[4] See the passages from S. Cyprian, to which I have referred or
which I have quoted and discussed on pp. 346, 354, 355. Compare
also a passage from S. Chrysostom quoted on p. 383, and see S. Greg.

words " the one chair " there is not the most remote allusion
to the episcopal chair of the bishops of Rome. The see
of Rome was at that time vacant, and there had been as
yet no Roman condemnation of the Carthaginian schismatics.
It was against Cyprian that they were rebelling, and it is
his own chair of which he is speaking.[1] Any Carthaginian
Christian who separates himself from the one Bishop of
Carthage "remains without the Church."   It is to me
most astounding that Mr. Rivington should have quoted
the passage about " the chair," as if it referred to "the
Church of the Romans."[2]

I have now gone through the whole of my collection
of Cyprianic passages, which have been quoted by Ultramontanes in proof of their idea that S. Cyprian held the
papal theory. I have not intentionally withheld any passage,
though of course it may easily happen that I may have
failed to notice one or more. I feel morally sure that I
have quoted all those on which stress is usually laid. I
submit very confidently my case to the candid reader.
I do not believe that in any one of these passages there is
the smallest ground for supposing that S. Cyprian intended
to teach papalism. If this is all that Ultramontanes can
discover in his writings, which may seem to favour their
cause, they had much better say nothing about him. His
real view of the authority of the bishops of Rome is set

Nyss., *De Castigat., Opp.* ed. Migne, iii. 311, and Bossuet, *Def. Cler.
Gall.*, lib. viii. capp. 12, 13, *Opp.* ed. 1817, xxxii. 602–611.   According to the Fathers, the bishops are all successors of the apostles, and
therefore of S. Peter, the representative apostle.

[1] Sometimes the Fathers describe "the one episcopate" as the
apostolic chair; so S. Basil in his 197th epistle (*Opp.* ed. Ben., iii.
288) congratulates S. Ambrose, Bishop of Milan, on his elevation to
the episcopate, and he says, "The Lord Himself translated you from
among the judges of the earth to the chair of the apostles " (ἐπὶ τὴν
καθέδραν τῶν ἀποστόλων).

[2] *Authority*, p. 99.

forth in numerous passages of his letters and treatises, and above all by his acts. Fully to discuss those passages and those acts would require a volume. I have given a short account of some of them in my second lecture [1] and in note A. [2] The defenders of the English Church may safely stake their case, so far as it relates to the papal claims, on the witness borne by S. Cyprian. May the prayers of that blessed martyr draw down upon the Church of England and upon us her children a full measure of the divine blessing and protection !

[1] See pp. 51–90.   [2] See pp. 325–333.

NOTE C.

S. Peter's primacy, as held by representative Anglican divines (see p. 113).

I HAVE been surprised to notice that Mr. Rivington, in his book entitled *Dependence* (p. 33), says that, "as an Anglican," he "for a long while held, as a more logical view, that S. Peter excelled the others in natural qualities only;" and in an earlier book entitled *Authority*,[1] he commits himself to the extraordinary statement that "the idea that all the apostles were equal, except in natural qualities," is "a fundamental point of Anglican teaching."[2] I cannot imagine what can have led him into such a complete misapprehension. The English divines, handing on the tradition of the Fathers, no doubt teach that the apostles were equal, not only in regard to order, but also in regard to jurisdiction. They deny altogether that any one apostle had jurisdiction over the others; or that the jurisdiction of any one apostle over the Church was of a different kind from the jurisdiction of each of the other apostles over the Church. But while doing full justice to the doctrine of the Fathers about the equality of the apostles, they also do justice to the scriptural and patristic teaching about S. Peter's priority of place, to his leadership or foremanship in the apostolic college. I do not know that any of them identify that leadership with S. Peter's superiority in

[1] *Authority*, p. 59.

[2] Compare also *Authority*, pp. 69, 70.

natural qualities, or suppose that it simply arose out of those natural qualities without any reference to acts and words of our blessed Lord. Even if English divines of repute could be found, who held such a view (which I doubt), yet assuredly the general tradition of the English Church has been the other way ; and it would be absurd to say that the view held by Mr. Rivington, when he was an Anglican, is "a fundamental point of Anglican teaching."

No doubt, S. Peter's leadership among the twelve does not occupy the same important position in Anglican teaching that it occupies in Romanist teaching. From the nature of the case, a priority of place is a much less important matter than a supremacy of jurisdiction ; and the difference of view in the estimate of importance is greatly intensified when the priority of place is supposed to belong to S. Peter personally, whereas the supremacy of jurisdiction is supposed to belong to him officially, and to have been transmitted by him to a long line of successors. From the English point of view, it is a matter of no doctrinal importance whether or no S. Peter's priority of place was retained by him to the end of his life ; or, again, whether it had reference to the whole body of the apostles, or to the apostles of the circumcision only. Such questions may afford interesting points for scriptural or patristic investigation, but whichever way they might be decided, they would not affect the substance of our faith ; nor would that faith be affected, if we came to the conclusion that, with the evidence at our disposal, they do not admit of any certain answer. S. John and S. James, his brother, had a certain priority along with S. Peter during our Lord's lifetime, and, according to S. Clement of Alexandria, they retained that priority after the Ascension ; [1] but it would be

---

[1] See note on p. 120.

difficult to say whether their priority, such as it was, remained to the end, and whether it related only to the twelve, or to other apostles also. Would S. John have taken precedence of S. Paul, or would S. Paul have taken precedence of S. John ? Individual Fathers may perhaps speculate on the matter, but I feel sure that nothing certain has been revealed, and that such questions do not touch the faith.

Our English divines, if they happen to touch on these minor questions, abound each in his own sense. But as regards the more important point of S. Peter's leadership of the apostolic college, at any rate during our Lord's lifetime and during the earlier years of the Church's history, the stream of Anglican teaching has, I should suppose, been quite clear.

Let me give a few examples, which happen to come to hand.

Archbishop Potter of Canterbury (A.D. 1737–1747), in his *Discourse of Church Government* (2nd edit., pp. 75–80), discusses the matter very fully. He says that " some of the apostles were superior to the rest, both in personal merit and abilities, *and in order of place*." He proceeds to prove this by quoting passages from Holy Scripture ; and then states again the conclusion at which he arrives, namely, that " some of the apostles had a pre-eminence above others." Then he goes on to say that " it may be observed farther, that in most places Peter is preferred before all the rest ; whence our Lord often speaks to him, and he replies before, and, as it were, in the name of the rest." Having adduced various passages from the New Testament in proof, he concludes, that " from these and the like passages, it is evident that Peter was the *foreman* of the college of apostles whilst our Lord lived on earth ; and it is plain that he kept the same dignity at least for some time after His Ascension." Then he elaborates this last point out of the earlier part of the Book of the Acts, and, summing up the result of the argument, he says that "it is evident that S. Peter acted as chief of the college of apostles, and so he is constantly described by the primitive writers of the Church, who call him the Head, the President, the Prolocutor, the Chief, the Foreman of the Apostles, with several other titles of distinction." The archbishop goes on to discuss the qualifications of S. Peter, which rendered him fit to be selected to occupy this position of precedence. It is notorious that the Fathers differ very much among themselves on this point ; some like S. Jerome thinking that it was because S. Peter was the eldest,[1] others like Eusebius holding that it was because he was the stronger character, others with greater probability regarding it as the reward of the apostle's great confession. The archbishop says, " Whatever was the true reason of this order, which we will not pretend to determine, since the Scriptures are silent, it is certain that nothing more was founded on it than a mere priority of place ; and that neither Peter nor any other apostle had any power or authority over the rest." This he proceeds to prove by the testimony of Holy Scripture, and then he solidly explains the texts which have been misinterpreted by the Romanists, as if they made in favour of their theory of the papal supremacy. Finally, the archbishop shows how the Church was governed by the apostles after they had ceased to live together at Jerusalem, and had dispersed into different parts of the world.

I have given an account of Archbishop Potter's treatment of this subject at some length, as a specimen. The views of others may be given more succinctly.

Archbishop Bramhall of Armagh (A.D. 1661–1663), in his *Just Vindication of the Church of England* (chap. v., *Works*, ed. 1842, i. 152, 153) says, " All the twelve

---

[1] See p. 392.

apostles were equal in mission, equal in commission, equal in honour, equal in all things, *except priority of order*, without which no society can well subsist." And on p. 154 he speaks " of S. Peter's . . . principality of order." So again in his *Schism Guarded* (chap. i., *Works*, ii. 371), replying to his Romanist adversary, Serjeant, the archbishop says, " If he [Serjeant] had not been a mere novice and altogether ignorant of the tenets of our English Church, he might have known that we have no controversy with S. Peter, nor with any other about the privileges of S. Peter.   Let him be 'first, chief, or prince of the apostles,' in that sense wherein the ancient Fathers styled him so. . . . The learned Bishop of Winchester,[1] (of whom it is no shame for him to learn) might have taught him thus much, not only in his own name, but in the name of the king and Church of England : 'Neither is it questioned among us whether S. Peter had a primacy, but what that primacy was ; and whether it were such an one as the pope doth now challenge to himself, and you challenge to the pope ; but the king[2] doth not deny Peter to have been the prime and prince of the apostles.' "[3]

Bishop Bull, in his reply to Bossuet's queries (*Works*, ed. 1846, ii. 295), cites and adopts the first of the passages which I have just quoted from Bramhall, so that it is clear

---

[1] Bishop Andrewes.   [2] James I.

[3] See Andrewes' *Respons. ad Apolog. Bellarm.*, cap. i., ed. 1851, p. 17. As I hope that what I write may be of some benefit to readers who may not be acquainted with the Latin language, I observe that when Bishop Andrewes speaks of S. Peter as "the *prince* of the apostles," he does not mean to ascribe to him any monarchical or princely jurisdiction over his brethren.   In the Latin the word " princeps" means a person who is *first*, either in time or order. S. Peter is " princeps apostolorum," as being the first in order among them.   The English expression, " prince of the apostles," may easily be misunderstood by less instructed persons. Archbishop Bramhall, translating Bishop Andrewes, and writing for scholars, uses the expression without fear of being misinterpreted.

that he held that S. Peter was invested with a " priority of order " in the college of apostles.

Barrow, in his *Treatise of the Pope's Supremacy* (*Suppos.* i., *Works*, ed. 1818, vol. vi. pp. 48 *ff.*), discusses carefully four different kinds of primacy, which may belong to a person in respect of others. They are (1) a primacy of merit ; (2) a primacy of repute ; (3) a primacy of order ; and (4) a primacy of jurisdiction. He admits that S. Peter, in respect of the original apostles of the circumcision, possessed the first two kinds of primacy ; and he denies that he had any primacy of jurisdiction over any of the apostles either of the circumcision or of the Gentiles. As regards the primacy of order, Barrow is less clear than the other divines to whose opinions I have referred. He thinks that this privilege " may be questioned ; " but at the same time he admits that there are probable arguments which may be brought forward in its favour, and he grants that the Fathers " generally seem to countenance it." He enumerates various acts and words of our Blessed Lord which specially concerned S. Peter, and he concludes that by this manner of proceeding " our Lord may seem to have constituted S. Peter the first in order among the apostles, or sufficiently to have hinted His mind for their direction, admonishing them by His example to render unto him a special deference." He gives a very much larger space to the arguments in favour of the primacy of order than to the arguments against it ; and I can hardly doubt that he personally inclined towards the view that S. Peter had such a primacy, as the more probable, though in his judgment the probability did not amount to a moral certainty.

Having referred to some of the great names of the seventeenth and eighteenth centuries, I will quote the words of a much-respected bishop who has been lately called to his rest, and whose *Exposition of the Thirty-nine Articles* has gone through thirteen editions. Bishop Harold Browne says, " We may readily admit that S. Peter had a certain priority among his brother apostles *assigned to him by our blessed Lord ; *" and this priority he further defines to be a " priority of order," which did not involve " a primacy of power or pre-eminence of jurisdiction." The bishop supports his position with considerable fulness, arguing from Scripture and the Fathers.

I have now quoted Archbishop Potter, Archbishop Bramhall, Bishop Andrewes, Bishop Bull, Dr. Isaac Barrow, and Bishop Harold Browne ; and, with the exception of some slight reserve on the part of Dr. Barrow, they all express very clearly their belief in S. Peter's primacy of order. I have carefully avoided any reference to such writers as Bishop Forbes of Brechin or Dr. Pusey, who might be challenged as representing only one school of theological opinion ; and I should certainly suppose that a view handed on with such a large measure of unanimity by such representative prelates and theologians, agreeing as it does with the consentient witness of the Fathers, may claim to be considered the normal tradition and teaching of the English Church. I say again that I cannot conceive on what grounds Mr. Rivington can have been led to suppose that the negation of S. Peter's primacy of order " is a fundamental· point of Anglican teaching." I am afraid that, if Archbishop Bramhall had been dealing with him, he would have said that he was a " mere novice " and " ignorant of the tenets of our English Church." It is hardly likely that any of my Anglican readers should have fallen into such a curious mistake. If there should be any such, I would urge them to take care lest they also oscillate in this matter from an extreme on the one side to a contrary and far more harmful extreme on the other side.

NOTE D.

On our Lord's words to S. Peter (S. John xxi. 15–17),
"*Feed My lambs;*" "*Tend My sheep;*" "*Feed My
sheep*" (see p. 115).

I PROPOSE in this note to discuss the second great passage,
to which reference is made by the Vatican Council in its
dogmatic decree concerning "the institution of the apostolic
primacy in blessed Peter." It will be remembered that
the Council sets forth, as the scriptural basis of the doctrine
declared and defined in that decree, two utterances of our
Lord to S. Peter, namely, first, the promise made at
Cæsarea Philippi, which begins with the words, "Thou
art Peter, and upon this rock I will build My Church;"
and, secondly, the injunction repeated three times with slight
changes in the words used, when our Lord appeared to
S. Peter and six other disciples on the shore of the Sea of
Tiberias after His resurrection from the dead. On what
the Council calls "the manifest teaching" of these two
passages it builds up its theory that, "when compared with
the other apostles, whether taken separately or collectively,
Peter alone was invested by Christ with a true and proper
primacy of jurisdiction,"[1] and that this primacy "was

---

[1] "Solum Petrum præ cæteris Apostolis, sive seorsum singulis sive
omnibus simul, vero proprioque jurisdictionis primatu fuisse a Christo
instructum" (*Collectio Lacensis*, vii. 483).

conferred upon blessed Peter himself immediately and directly."

I have dealt with the first of these two passages in the third lecture. I now proceed to quote the second passage together with the whole context, as it is translated in the Revised Version : " When they had broken their fast, Jesus saith to Simon Peter, Simon, son of John, lovest thou Me more than these ? He saith unto Him, Yea, Lord ; Thou knowest that I love Thee. He saith unto him, Feed My lambs. He ·saith to him again a second time, Simon, son of John, lovest thou Me ? He saith unto Him, Yea, Lord ; Thou knowest that I love Thee. He saith unto him, Tend My sheep.[1] He saith unto him the third time, Simon, son of John, lovest thou Me ? Peter was grieved because He said unto him the third time, Lovest thou Me ? And he said unto Him, Lord, Thou knowest all things ; Thou knowest that I love·Thee. Jesus saith unto him, Feed My sheep."[2]

All manner of interesting questions suggest themselves to us in connection with this wonderfully beautiful episode ; but for our present purpose the really important problems to be solved are these : Why was this injunction given to S. Peter rather than to the other apostles ? and again, Was any power then and there communicated to S. Peter ? or was it rather that he was authorized and enjoined to use a power previously given ? and once more, Of what sort was the power which our Lord was imparting, or the exercise of which He was enjoining ?

The Roman reply to these questions is this—that our Lord intended to make S. Peter pope, and to give him a

---

[1] In place of "*Tend My sheep*" ($\pi o i \mu a i \nu \epsilon$ $\tau \grave{a}$ $\pi \rho \acute{o} \beta a \tau \acute{a}$ $\mu o \nu$), the Douay version, following the Vulgate, repeats the previous formula, "*Feed My lambs*." Apart from this variation, the Douay differs in this passage in no substantial point from the Revised.

[2] S. John xxi. 15–17.

primacy of jurisdiction over the whole Church, including the apostolic college ; and that this primatial jurisdiction, which was to be transmitted to his successors in the see of Rome, was communicated to him then and there by our Lord's words, "Feed My lambs," and " Feed My sheep." I am not aware that any of the great Fathers of the first five centuries take this view, though the germ of it could doubtless be found in the writings of the popes of the fifth century and of persons closely connected with them.

Setting aside the theories held by what Mr. Gore has called the papal school,[1] there are two views which find favour with the Fathers. They are not necessarily exclusive of each other, and in fact some of the Fathers seem to have held them in combination ; but logically they are quite independent, the one of the other. They agree in this, that they suppose that the right and duty of shepherding and feeding the sheep and the lambs belong to S. Peter as an *apostle*, rather than as the foreman of the apostles. It is his *apostolic* jurisdiction which he is enjoined to use, or which is being committed to him ; and the " sheep " which he is to feed are not his brother shepherds and co-apostles, but rather such members of the

---

[1] It is obvious that, if our Lord really intended by the "*Pasce oves*" to institute a papal monarchy over the Church, in the persons of S. Peter and of his supposed papal successors, then these words are the operative words by which, as De Maistre would say, "the necessary, only, and exclusive foundation of Christianity" was laid. Had that been the case, the great Fathers of the Church would with one voice have dwelt on such a fundamental fact. Unfortunately for the Romanist view, they none of them, when commenting on the text, allude to the supposed fact. They are absolutely unconscious of it. Our Roman friends must not be surprised if, under such circumstances, English Catholics decline altogether to discuss the papal interpretation. It is as much out of court as the Zuinglian interpretation of " *Hoc est Corpus Meum*," or the Socinian interpretation of " *Verbum caro factum est.*"

flock of Christ as are spiritually full-grown, and capable of appreciating "solid food;" while the "lambs" are the babes in Christ, who need to be fed with "spiritual milk."[1] So far the two views agree, but in other points they diverge.

According to the first of these two views, our Lord addresses His injunction to S. Peter because he is the primate-apostle, and therefore the representative or symbol of the whole body of the apostles and of the unity of the Church. The others receive the injunction or the commission, whichever it was, in him, their representative. The Fathers, who take this view, in no way suppose that any primacy of *jurisdiction* over the other apostles is being given to S. Peter ; it is because he is the first *in order* that our Lord addresses him, although what our Lord says applies equally to all the apostles. This is S. Augustine's view.[2]

According to the second view, S. Peter is addressed because of his previous fall. In consequence of that fall he had either lost his apostolic commission, or, at any rate, was doubtful whether he ought to use it ; and he needed either to have it restored to him, or to be encouraged and enjoined to act upon it. This is the view of S. Cyril of Alexandria.[3]

For myself, if it is not impertinent to say so, I have no sort of dogmatic objection to the first of these views. It

---

[1] Compare 1 Cor. ii. 6; iii. 1, 2; Heb. v. 12–14; 1 S. Pet. ii. 2.

[2] See the passage from S. Augustine's 295th sermon, quoted on p. 382.

[3] See the passage from S. Cyril's commentary on S. John xxi. 15–17, quoted on pp. 389, 390. It may be observed that Bishop Moberly, in his *Discourses on the Great Forty Days* (2nd edit., 1846, p. 190), seems to hold in combination both S. Cyril's view and S. Augustine's: he says, " Though his [Peter's] fall was great, greater than that of all who forsook their Lord and fled, yet was his restoration great too, for he was again chosen of [*i.e.* among] them all to be the one to receive, as representing all, the great pastoral commission."

harmonizes thoroughly with Catholic principles of faith
and discipline.   But, exegetically, I venture to think that
the second view is by far the more probable.   I will try
to make this clear.   When we look at the context of the
passage we see an evident allusion to that boasting of
S. Peter which led the way to his fall.   Our Lord had
said to the apostles on the night of the last supper, "All
ye shall be offended in Me this night;" and Peter had
replied, "If all shall be offended in Thee, I will never be
offended."[1]   The boast had been made publicly, and now
our Lord asks publicly the question, "Simon, son of John,
lovest thou Me *more than these?*"   S. Augustine thinks
it probable that the accounts of the boasting, given by
S. Matthew, S. Luke, and S. John,[2] represent three separate occurrences,[3] and, if so, our Lord's thrice-repeated
question would correspond with the threefold boasting;
but, however that may be, the fact that the interrogation
by the Sea of Tiberias contains an allusion to the boast
in the upper room can hardly be denied; and this prepares
us to see a close connection between the threefold injunction, "Feed My lambs," "Tend My sheep," "Feed My
sheep," which follows the three interrogations, and the
threefold denial which followed the boasting.   It was
absolutely necessary, after those terrible denials, that some
public utterance should be made by our Lord certifying
S. Peter and the Church that those denials were not only
forgiven, so far as S. Peter's own condition in the sight
of God was concerned, but that he was at liberty to use,
and in fact bound to use, that apostolic office, which had
been promised to him at Cæsarea Philippi, and the funda-

---

[1] S. Matt. xxvi. 31, 33.

[2] S. Matt. *u.s.*; S. Luke xxii. 33; S. John xiii. 37.

[3] Cf. S. Aug., *De Consens. Evang.*, lib. iii. cap. ii. (*Opp.* ed. Ben.,
1690, tom. iii. pars ii. col. 102).

mental powers of which he had received in common with
the other apostles on the evening of Easter day in the
upper room. S. Peter had then been made an apostle,
but the remembrance of his fall might well have made him
doubt whether he ought to exercise the jurisdiction given
to him. Every student of Church history knows how S.
Jerome, though he was made a priest, never in the whole
course of his life ventured to exercise the powers of his
office. It was of the utmost importance that, in the case
of S. Peter, who was the leader of the apostolic college,
all doubt should be removed, and his right to exercise his
authority be put beyond the reach of question ; and accordingly our Lord granted to him a special authorization, three
times repeated, so as to blot out the effects of his threefold
fall. I think that it might be held, with some show of
probability, that the threefold repetition of the injunction
to feed and tend the Lord's flock implied that the three
denials were so completely done away, that S. Peter was
not only assured of his full and undoubted right to exercise
his apostolic office, but was also restored to the leadership
which had naturally resulted from his precedence in designation to that office. The threefold repetition made it
evident that, notwithstanding his denials, he was not to be
considered to have forfeited his primacy of honour.

I hope that this investigation of the close connection
which binds the episode of the "*Pasce oves*" to the events
of the night in which our Lord was betrayed, will go far
to justify S. Cyril's view, that it was in consequence of
S. Peter's fall that the "*Pasce oves*" was addressed to
him, rather than to any of the other apostles, or to the
apostolic college.

When we consider the words which our Lord used, and
compare them with a parallel passage in one of S. Peter's
own Epistles, we seem to find a confirmation of the view

which has already been suggested, that our Lord's words did not, strictly speaking, convey a commission, but were rather an injunction to use the apostolic commission previously bestowed. For, when S. Peter wrote to the presbyters of the Churches of Asia Minor, and said, " Tend the flock of God, which is among you,"[1] he was not imparting to them the priestly office ; he was enjoining them to exercise the office which they had previously received from the Holy Ghost, when they were ordained.

Before passing on to the patristic interpretation of our Lord's words, I will make one further observation, suggested by the direct consideration of the words themselves. It seems clear that those words do not of themselves imply any grant of jurisdiction to S. Peter over the other apostles. Our Lord does not say, " Act as a shepherd to thy brethren and co-apostles," but " Feed My lambs," and " Tend " and " Feed My sheep." The words evidently have reference to the pastoral office which S. Peter was going to fulfil towards the sheep and lambs of Christ's flock after the Lord Himself had ascended into heaven. Our Lord was accustomed to speak of the future members of His Church as the sheep of His flock. So, for example, in the Gospel of the Good Shepherd, He says, " Other [Gentile] sheep I have, which are not of this [Jewish] fold : them also I must bring, and they shall hear My voice ; and they shall become one flock, one shepherd."[2] Our Lord Himself is " the great Shepherd of the sheep,"[3] and He appoints His ministers to be the under-shepherds, to " take heed unto all the flock," and to " tend the Church of God."[4] That pastoral ministry began with the apostles, who were the first set of under-shepherds, and to each of whom was. given pastoral authority over the whole flock.

[1] 1 S. Pet. v. 2.   [2] S. John x. 16.
[3] Heb. xiii. 20.   [4] Acts xx. 28.

If it were clearly revealed in other parts of Holy Scripture that S. Peter was the supreme under-shepherd, having jurisdiction over the other apostles, then it might be permissible to suppose that such supreme jurisdiction was being communicated to S. Peter by our Lord, when He said, "Feed My sheep," and that consequently on that particular occasion the inferior under-shepherds were numbered among the sheep.[1] But there is no trace in other parts of Holy Scripture of such a supremacy, and therefore there is no reason for numbering the apostolic shepherds among the sheep in the passage which we are considering. The wording of that passage, taken by itself, suggests apostolic, not primatial, jurisdiction.

Gathering up the results of our study of S. John xxi. 15–17, it seems probable that our Lord, by the words, "*Pasce oves Meas*," was not giving a new commission to S. Peter, but was authorizing and enjoining him to use a commission previously bestowed; and it seems clear that that commission was not a commission to be primate, with a rule over the other apostles; but a commission to be an apostle, with a rule over the sheep and lambs belonging to the Church of God. It also seems clear that the reason why this injunction and authorization was needed

---

[1] During the three years of our Lord's ministry in the days of His humiliation, the twelve constituted our Lord's special flock, and He Himself was their visible Shepherd. That was before they received their apostolic commission. That period culminated in the night in which our Lord was betrayed; and, referring to the events of that night, He applied to them all, including S. Peter, the title of sheep. He said, "All ye shall be offended in Me this night: for it is written, I will smite the Shepherd, and the sheep of the flock shall be scattered abroad" (S. Matt. xxvi. 31). But after our Lord's resurrection, in preparation for His departure, He commissioned those disciples to be apostles; and so, while they all, including S. Peter, remained sheep in relation to our Lord, they became shepherds in relation to the Church.

by S. Peter, and was not needed by the others, is to be found in S. Peter's fall, when he denied the Lord.

I proceed now to investigate the interpretations of our Lord's words to S. Peter, which are to be found in the writings of the Fathers. They refer continually to our Lord's injunction to feed the sheep, but when they speak of it in connection with the apostolic age, they assume that all the apostles shared in the commission; or, if S. Peter is specially mentioned, they point out that he is the representative of the Church, or the symbol of her unity, or else they dwell on his fall. They seem to take pains to make it clear that S. Peter had no authority given to him, which was peculiar to himself. And again, when the Fathers speak of our Lord's injunction in connection with post-apostolic times, they dwell on the fact that the bishops, as the successors of the apostles, or as the successors of Peter, have inherited the pastoral commission. A modern Romanist naturally dwells on the *papal* power as guaranteed by the *Pasce oves;* the Fathers, ignoring the papacy,[1] consider that our Lord was instructing or empowering the *episcopate*.

I cannot attempt any exhaustive catena, but I will give specimens of the teaching of both Latin and Greek Fathers.

S. Cyprian, writing to Pope Stephen, says, "Although we [bishops] are many shepherds, yet we feed one flock, and ought to gather together and cherish all the sheep which Christ has acquired by His own Blood and Passion."[2] I quote this passage, although it does not explicitly refer to our Lord's words to S. Peter; but they must have been in S. Cyprian's mind when he wrote. He was writing to the pope, and asking him to help the

---

[1] The papal school of the fifth and later centuries must, of course, be excepted (see pp. 97, 98).

[2] S. Cypr., *Ep.* lxvii. *ad Stephanum* (*Opp.* ed. Ben., p. 116).

Church in Gaul. That was surely a good opportunity for pressing on him the duty of exercising the supreme pastoral office, which is supposed by Romanists to belong to the Roman successors of S. Peter. But instead of that, S. Cyprian puts all bishops on an equality in their pastoral functions, and urges the pope to interfere in Gaul, not as having primatial jurisdiction there, but as belonging to the college of bishops, who all "feed one flock, and ought to gather together and cherish all the sheep" of Christ.[1]

Even the Romanizing interpolator of S. Cyprian's treatise on the *Unity of the Church*, after inserting a reference to the *Pasce oves*, proceeds a few lines lower down to say concerning the apostles, "They all are shepherds, and the flock is shown to be one, which is fed by all the apostles with one-minded concord."[2] The interpolator evidently held that, though for symbolical reasons the words were spoken to S. Peter only, the injunction or commission applied to all the apostles. It is clear that he considered that our Lord was dealing with apostolic, and not with primatial jurisdiction.

S. Augustine is very clear and express. In his treatise, *De Agone Christiano*, he is proving in opposition to the Luciferians that the Church is right in dealing mercifully with penitents. In the course of his argument he says, "Not without cause among all the apostles doth Peter sustain the person of this Church Catholic ; for unto this Church were the keys of the kingdom of heaven given, when they were given unto Peter ; and when it is said unto him, it is said unto all, 'Lovest thou Me ? Feed

---

[1] For a full account of the circumstances under which this letter was written, and for the reason why S. Cyprian asked Pope Stephen to interfere, see pp. 60–65.

[2] S. Cypr., *De Unit. Eccl., Opp.* ed. Ben., p. 195.

My sheep.'"[1]   S. Augustine means that S. Peter, as being the apostle who was the special example of penitence, was fitly chosen to be the representative and first in order among the rulers of the Church, which has ever dealt mercifully with penitents.   He represented the Church when the keys were given to him, so that it was the Church which really received them ; and similarly it was to the Church and to "all" her rulers that our Lord was really speaking when He said, " Feed My sheep."   It was no solitary papal power that was then communicated, but that pastoral authority which belonged first to the apostles, and afterwards to the bishops.

Again, in his forty-seventh homily on S. John's Gospel, S. Augustine says, "Hold ye then, how the Lord Jesus Christ is both Door and Shepherd : Door, by opening Himself ; Shepherd, by entering in through Himself. And indeed, my brethren, that He is Shepherd, He hath given to His members also : thus Peter too is shepherd, and Paul shepherd, and the other apostles shepherds, and good bishops shepherds.   But Door, none of us calleth himself ; this He hath kept proper to Himself, the way by which the sheep enter in."[2]   In S. Augustine's view the pastoral authority is common to all the apostles, and to their successors the bishops.[3]   It does not occur to him

---

[1] S. Aug., *De Agone Christiano,* cap. xxx., *Opp.* ed. Ben., vi. 260. On S. Augustine's teaching about S. Peter as the symbol of the Church, see pp. 99–103.

[2] S. Aug., *in Joh. Evang. tract.* xlvii., *Opp.* ed. Ben., tom. iii. pars ii. col. 608.

[3] I add in a note two more passages from S. Augustine, which bring out with great clearness the thought that what was enjoined on S. Peter in the *Pasce oves* was equally enjoined on all the apostles. In his 296th sermon, preached on the Feast of S. Peter and S. Paul, he discusses at some length our Lord's word, by which He commended His sheep to S. Peter.   Then he adds, " That which was commended to Peter, that which was enjoined on him, not Peter only

to refer to the popes as having a pastoral authority of a higher sort.

It need hardly be added that when, in his homilies on S. John's Gospel, S. Augustine reaches the last chapter, and comments on the *Pasce oves*, he says not a word about any authority in S. Peter over the other apostles, nor about any primatial jurisdiction in the Roman see.   Strange, that when treating expressly of what is supposed by many Ultramontanes to be *the* fundamental proof-text of the papal power, he should so completely ignore an institution which, from their point of view, is "the principal matter of Christianity " ! [1]

Passing to the Greek Fathers, I begin with S. Chrysostom. There are two passages in the treatise which has ever been considered S. Chrysostom's masterpiece,[2] the *De Sacerdotio*, in which he makes clear how he understood the *Pasce oves*. In the first chapter of the second book the saint is showing that the undertaking of the burden of the episcopal office is the greatest evidence of love to Christ.   He naturally bases his argument on S. John xxi. 15–17, and he says, "It was not Christ's intention [by the words, 'Feed My sheep'] to show how much Peter loved Him, because this already appeared in many ways, but how much He Himself loves His Church ; and He desired that we should all learn it, that we also may be very zealous

but also the other apostles heard, kept, observed, and chiefly the Apostle Paul, the partner of his death and of his festival" (*Opp.* S. Aug., ed. Ben., v. 1199).   And in the previous sermon, the 295th, he says, "The Lord commended to Peter himself His sheep to feed. For not he alone among the disciples merited to feed the Lord's sheep: but when Christ speaks to one, unity is commended; and [He speaks] to Peter first (primitus), because among the apostles Peter is first" (*Opp.*, v. 1195).   This last passage exactly expresses S. Augustine's view, as I have described it on p. 374.

[1] See Bellarmine, quoted on p. 95.
[2] Compare Tillemont, xi. 14.

in the same work. For why did God not spare His Son and Only-begotten, but gave Him up, although He was His Only One? That He might reconcile to Himself those who were His enemies, and make them a people for His own possession. And why did He shed forth His Blood? To purchase those sheep whom He committed to Peter and *to his successors*"[1] (τοῖς μετ' ἐκεῖνον). "I follow Mr. Allnatt in translating τοῖς μετ' ἐκεῖνον by "*to his successors*."[2] Those words give the sense very accurately and idiomatically. It is amusing to notice how Mr. Allnatt prints these words in capital letters, evidently imagining that of course S. Peter's successors must be the popes. It is needless to say that S. Chrysostom knew nothing of *papal* successors of S. Peter in his primatial office. According to S. Chrysostom's teaching, the bishops generally were S. Peter's successors, as they were also the successors of the other apostles. The whole argument of the *De Sacerdotio* requires us so to understand the words; and if further proof were needed, it would manifestly appear from the fact that, when S. Chrysostom wrote this treatise, he neither was nor ever had been in communion with the Church of Rome, and in fact he remained outside of that communion for at least sixteen more years, perhaps for as many as twenty-five.[3]

S. Chrysostom's object in the *De Sacerdotio* was to

[1] *Opp.* S. Chrys., ed. Ben., i. 372.

[2] Allnatt's *Cathedra Petri*, 2nd edit., p. 43. Mr. Allnatt's book is a painstaking but very unscholarly *catena* of patristic passages, which, as he supposes, are favourable to the Roman claims. The book may be of great use to any one who has the opportunity of testing the passages by investigating their context and meaning. To other persons such an uncritical performance can only be a snare and a delusion.

[3] The *De Sacerdotio* may have been written as early as A.D. 372. S. Chrysostom was not in communion with Rome until he became Bishop of Constantinople in A.D. 397. Compare pp. 255–257.

comfort and encourage his friend Basil, who had just been consecrated to the episcopate. In the second chapter of the second book he says to Basil, " You are going to be set over all that is God's, and to do those things, in doing which [Christ] said that Peter would be able to outdo the other apostles ; for saith He, 'Peter, lovest thou Me *more than these?* Feed My sheep.' "[1] It is evident from both these passages that S. Chrysostom held that our Lord, in saying, " Feed My sheep," was committing to S. Peter apostolical or episcopal authority. S. Peter's office was the same as Basil's office. Basil, as a bishop, was one of S. Peter's successors. The notion of papal or primatial jurisdiction over the other apostles does not occur to S. Chrysostom.

But, though S. Chrysostom attributes no jurisdiction over the other apostles to S. Peter, he fully recognizes his primacy of order, his leadership ; and as a loyal son of the Church of Antioch, which was accustomed in the fourth century to look on S. Peter as its founder, he often employs his great rhetorical powers in eloquently setting forth that leadership. But it will be found that he knows well how to magnify the primacy of order without suggesting a primacy of jurisdiction. This comes out markedly in his eighty-eighth homily on S. John's Gospel, which also throws light on his interpretation of the *Pasce oves*. S. Chrysostom begins that homily thus : " There are indeed many other things which are able to give us boldness towards God, and to shew us bright and approved, but that which most of all brings good-will from on high is *tender care for our*

---

[1] πᾶσι μέλλων ἐπιστήσεσθαι τοῦ θεοῦ τοῖς ὑπάρχουσι, καὶ ταῦτα πράττων, ἃ καὶ τὸν Πέτρον ποιοῦντα ἔφησε δυνήσεσθαι καὶ τῶν ἀποστόλων ὑπερακοντίσαι τοὺς λοιπούς. Πέτρε γάρ φησι, φιλεῖς με πλεῖον τούτων ; (S. Chrys., *De Sacerd.*, lib. ii. cap. i. § 90, p. 13, ed. Bengel, Lipsiæ, 1872). Mr. Rivington (*Dependence*, p. 18) has quoted the passage, but has mistaken its meaning.

neighbour. Which, therefore, Christ requireth of Peter.
For when their eating was ended, Jesus saith to Simon
Peter, 'Simon, son of Jonas, lovest thou Me more than
these ? He saith unto Him, Yea, Lord, Thou knowest
that I love Thee. He saith unto him, Feed My sheep.'
And why, having passed by the others, doth he speak with
Peter on these matters ? He was the chosen one of the
apostles, the mouth of the disciples, the leader of the band ;
on this account also Paul went up upon a time to inquire
of him rather than of the others." [1]   So far S. Chrysostom
has been speaking of the inculcation of the duty of showing
tender care for our neighbour, which our Lord pressed upon
S. Peter by His injunction, "Feed My sheep," and perhaps also by His question, "Lovest thou Me more than
these ?" S. Chrysostom holds that this lesson was pressed
on S. Peter rather than on any of the other apostles
because he was the leader. Notice how all S. Chrysostom's expressions about S. Peter in his relation to the
other apostles set forth a primacy of honour, and say
nothing about government or jurisdiction. The fervent
preacher then passes on from our Lord's inculcation of the
lesson of love to another aspect of His words. By them,
as he supposes, Christ imparted or rather revived S. Peter's
pastoral commission. The homily proceeds thus : "And
at the same time to show him that he must now be of good
cheer, since the denial was done away, He [our Lord]
putteth into his hands the rule over the brethren ($\tau\grave{\eta}\nu$
$\pi\rho o\sigma\tau a\sigma\acute{\iota}a\nu$ $\tau\hat{\omega}\nu$ $\grave{a}\delta\epsilon\lambda\phi\hat{\omega}\nu$) ; and He bringeth not forward the
denial, nor reproacheth him with what had taken place,
but saith, 'If thou lovest Me, rule over the brethren

---

[1] S. Chrys., *Hom.* lxxxviii. *in Joh. Ev.*, § 1, *Opp.* ed. Ben., viii.
525.   In his commentary on Gal. i. 18 (*Opp.*, x. 677), S. Chrysostom
says that S. Paul went to visit S. Peter, though " he was in no need
of Peter nor of his voice, but was equal in honour with him."

2 D

($\pi\rho o\ddot{\iota}\sigma\tau a\sigma o$ $\tau\hat{\omega}\nu$ $\dot{a}\delta\epsilon\lambda\phi\hat{\omega}\nu$) ; and the warm love which thou didst ever manifest, and concerning which thou didst boast,[1] shew thou now ; and the life which thou saidst thou wouldest lay down for Me, now give for My sheep.'" A few lines lower down S. Chrysostom says, "But He [our Lord] asketh him the third time, and the third time giveth him the same injunction, to shew at what a price He setteth the rule[2] over His own sheep ($\tau\grave{\eta}\nu$ $\pi\rho o\sigma\tau a\sigma i a\nu$ $\tau\hat{\omega}\nu$ $o\grave{\iota}\kappa\acute{\epsilon}\iota\omega\nu$ $\pi\rho o\beta\acute{a}\tau\omega\nu$), and that this especially is a sign of love towards Him." S. Chrysostom repeats over and over again in this passage his view that our Lord, by the words "Feed My sheep," committed to S. Peter "the rule over the brethren," or, in other words, "the rule over His own sheep ;" that is to say, that our Lord gave to S. Peter apostolical authority over the Church. Some Ultramontane writers have tried to make out that "the brethren" here mentioned are the apostles, and that consequently S. Chrysostom held that S. Peter received jurisdiction over the apostles. But this is very far-fetched. It is plain on the surface that "the brethren" and "the sheep" are identical.[3] It is the flock

---

[1] I have translated $\dot{\eta}\gamma a\lambda\lambda\iota\acute{a}\sigma\omega$, "thou didst *boast.*" The word $\dot{a}\gamma a\lambda\lambda\iota\acute{a}o\mu a\iota$ has that sense in the lxx. version of Jerem. xxx. 4 (xlix. 4—Heb.); cf. Isa. xli. 16, 17. Hesychius gives $\gamma a\upsilon\rho\iota\hat{q}$ as one out of two meanings of $\dot{a}\gamma\acute{a}\lambda\lambda\epsilon\tau a\iota$ (cf. Hesych., *Lexic.*, ed. Alberti, 1746 i. 31), and $\dot{a}\gamma a\lambda\lambda\iota\acute{a}o\mu a\iota$ is a late form of $\dot{a}\gamma\acute{a}\lambda\lambda o\mu a\iota$. The more usual meaning of the word is, "*to rejoice.*" The allusion is, of course, to S. Peter's boasts on the night of our Lord's betrayal, which boasts led to his fall.

[2] I have translated $\pi\rho o\ddot{\iota}\sigma\tau a\mu a\iota$, the verb, and $\pi\rho o\sigma\tau a\sigma i a$, the substantive, by the word "*rule.*" It is the rendering usually adopted in the Revised Version of the New Testament, in passages connected with Church offices (*e.g.* Rom. xii. 8; 1 Tim. iii. 4, 5, 12; and v. 17).

[3] The word "brethren" ($\dot{a}\delta\epsilon\lambda\phi o\acute{\iota}$) is very commonly used in Holy Scripture in the sense of *Christians*, e.g. in Acts vi. 3; ix. 30; x. 23; xi. 29; 1 Cor. v. 11; xv. 6; Phil. i. 14, etc., and it continued to be used in the Church in the same sense, as may be seen from the patristic passages cited in Suicer's *Thesaurus*, s.v. $\dot{a}\delta\epsilon\lambda\phi o\acute{s}$. The

of Christian believers that Christ commits to Peter, but of course not to Peter alone. All the apostles shared with him in his rule ($\pi\rho o\sigma\tau a\sigma i a$) over the Church. So S. Cyril of Jerusalem speaks of S. Peter and S. Paul, as being both of them "the rulers of the Church" ($o i\ \tau\hat{\eta}s\ \dot{\epsilon}\kappa\kappa\lambda\eta\sigma i a s\ \pi\rho o\sigma\tau\acute{a}\tau a\iota$);[1] and S. Chrysostom calls S. John "the pillar ($\dot{o}\ \sigma\tau\hat{v}\lambda o s$) of all the Churches throughout the world, who hath the keys of heaven;"[2] and in this eighty-eighth homily on S. John he says that S. Peter and S. John "were about to receive the charge of the world" ($\tau\hat{\eta}s\ o i\kappa o v\mu\acute{\epsilon}v\eta s\ \tau\grave{\eta}v\ \dot{\epsilon}\pi\iota\tau\rho o\pi\acute{\eta}v$).[3] Again, of S. Paul he says that "he had the care, not of one household, but also of cities, and of peoples, and of nations, *and of the whole world.*"[4] Ecumenical jurisdiction belongs to the very essence of the apostolical office.[5] How, then, does S. Chrysostom account for the fact that it was to S. Peter, and not to the others, that our Lord addressed the authoritative words, "Feed My sheep"? He says that our Lord spake those words to S. Peter "to show him that he must now be of good cheer, *since the denial was done away.*" According to to S. Chrysostom's view, the

Dominican Mamachi (*Orig. et Antiq. Christ.*, i. 6, quoted by Mr. Allies in his *Throne of the Fisherman*, p. 73, note 1), says, "Invaluit præterea apud nostros nomen *fratrum*, quod est a Christo servatore in Ecclesiam introductum, itaque deinceps propagatum est, ut non modo ab Apostolis sed etiam a Christianis omnibus usurparetur."

[1] S. Cyr. Hierosol., *Catech.*, vi. xv., *Opp.* ed. Ben., 1720, p. 96.

[2] S. Chrys., *Hom.* i. *in Joh. Ev.*, § 1, *Opp.* ed. Ben., viii. 2.

[3] *Hom.* lxxxviii. § 2, *Opp.* viii. 528.

[4] *Hom.* xxv. *in Ep.* ii. *ad Cor.*, § 2, *Opp.*, x. 614.

[5] S. Cyril of Alexandria, in this commentary on Jacob's benediction of the Patriarch Dan, after saying that "the glorious and admirable choir of the holy apostles are set for the government of believers, and have been by Christ Himself appointed to judge," goes on to observe in reference to these same apostles, "We have had for governors, and have received for *ecumenical judges* ($\kappa\rho\iota\tau\grave{a}s\ o i\kappa o v\mu\epsilon v\iota\kappa o\acute{v}s$), the holy disciples" (S. Cyril. Alex., *Glaphyr. in Gen.*, lib. vii., *Opp.* ed. Aubert., 1638, tom. i. pars ii. pp. 228, 229).

Pasce oves restored to S. Peter the apostolical office, which had been suspended, so far as he was concerned, in consequence of his denial of the Lord.[1]

S. Chrysostom's view of the *Pasce oves*, and of the sort of power which was entrusted by our Lord to S. Peter when He gave him the pastoral commission, has now, I hope, been made clear. But, at the risk of being tedious, I will quote one more passage from this eighty-eighth homily on S. John, because it has been misunderstood, as if it implied that S. Peter had jurisdiction over S. John ; and the misunderstanding, if it were admitted, would affect the interpretation of the whole homily. Commenting on the words, " Then Peter, turning about, seeth the disciple whom Jesus loved following, who also reclined on His breast at supper ; . . . and saith, Lord, and what shall this man do ? "[2] S. Chrysostom says, " Wherefore hath he reminded us of that reclining ? Not without cause or in a chance way, but to shew us what boldness Peter had after the denial. For he who then did not dare to question Jesus, but committed the office to another, this very man was even entrusted with the rule over the brethren " (that is, as we have seen, was restored to his apostolic office), and not only doth not commit to another what relates to himself, but himself now puts a question to his Master concerning another. John is silent, but Peter speaks." S. Chrysostom is not guilty of the absurdity of attempting to prove that S. Peter had jurisdiction over S. John,

---

[1] So in his fifth homily, *De Pœnitentiâ*, S. Chrysostom says, "After that grievous fall (for there is no evil so bad as denial), but yet after so great an evil *He again restored him to his former honour* and entrusted to him the care of the universal Church (τῆς οἰκουμενικῆς ἐκκλησίας) ; and (what is greater than all), He shewed to us that he had more love to the Master than all the apostles, for, saith He, ' Peter, lovest thou Me more than these ? ' " (*Opp.* S. Chrys., ed. Ben., ii. 311).

[2] S. John xxi. 20, 21.

because he put a question to our Lord about S. John. If there were any force in such an argument, it would follow that at the last supper, when S. John questioned our Lord at the request of S. Peter, S. John must have had jurisdiction over S. Peter, which no one has ever supposed. S. Chrysostom's point is that, after the complete forgiveness of S. Peter's denial and his full restoration to the apostolic office, he, to use S. Chrysostom's words, was " of good cheer,"[1] and was filled with holy " boldness." Euthymius Zigabenus, who follows S. Chrysostom point by point in his commentary on this passage,[2] takes exactly the same view of the matter, and evidently understood S. Chrysostom's argument in the way which I have tried to set forth.[3]

But to return to the point of main interest in regard to the *Pasce oves*, namely, the reason which moved our Lord to speak those words to S. Peter rather than to the other apostles. S. Gregory Nazianzen is very explicit. Speaking of S. Peter, he says, " Jesus received him, and by the triple questioning and confession He healed the triple denial."[4]   . . .

But of all the Fathers S. Cyril of Alexandria is perhaps the fullest and the most satisfying in his treatment of this aspect of the subject. Commenting on S. John xxi. 15–17,

---

[1] See p. 385.

[2] Migne's *Patrol. Græc.*, cxxix. 1500.

[3] It may be added, in general confirmation of the view which I have taken of S. Chrysostom's meaning in this homily, that the Benedictines decide that it was preached at Antioch, and therefore at a time when S. Chrysostom was out of communion with Rome (see pp. 256, 257). He cannot possibly have drawn from the *Pasce oves* the deductions which modern Roman Catholics draw from it, or he would not have been content to remain outside the flock, which, on their view, was being tended by the one divinely appointed universal shepherd, the necessary centre of communion.

[4] S. Greg. Naz., *Orat.* xxxix. § xviii., *Opp.* ed. Ben., i. 689.

he says, " When he [Peter] comes, Christ asks him more severely than the others, whether he loves more than them, and this took place three times. Peter assents and confesses that he loves, saying that He [Christ] is the Witness of his inward disposition. At each of his confessions separately he hears that he is charged with the care of the rational sheep. . . . Will not some one say with good reason, Wherefore did He ask the question of Simon only, although the other disciples were standing by ? And what is the meaning of 'Feed My sheep,' and the like ? We say then that Saint Peter had already been appointed (κεχειροτόνητο) to the divine apostolate together with the other disciples : for our Lord Jesus Christ Himself named them apostles, as it is written. But when it fell out that the events connected with the plot of the Jews had come to pass, and in the meanwhile he had somewhat stumbled—for Saint Peter, overwhelmed with excessive terror, thrice denied the Lord—Christ heals the ill effects of what had happened, and demands in various terms the triple confession, setting this, as it were, against that, and providing a correction equivalent to the faults. . . . Therefore by the triple confession of blessed Peter the offence of triple denial was abolished. *But by the Lord's saying, ' Feed My sheep,' a renewal, as it were, of the apostolate already conferred upon him is understood to have taken place, wiping away the intervening reproach of his falls, and destroying utterly the littleness of soul arising from human infirmity.*"[1] Nothing could be clearer or more consistent with the Gospel narrative, except that for myself I think it more probable that the " *Feed My sheep* " was rather an injunction to exercise the apostolate, which had already been renewed, than itself the act by which the renewal took place. But

---

[1] S. Cyril. Alex. *in S. Joann.*, lib. xii. cap. i., ed. Phil. Pusey, 1872, iii. 164–166.

that is a minor point.   The important matter is that S. Cyril
holds that the pastoral office spoken of by our Lord, was
not primatial, but apostolical, and that the whole incident
was necessitated by S. Peter's fall, which had resulted in
S. Peter's apostolate being, so to speak, suspended, on
which account it needed to be renewed.

Reviewing the whole of this discussion, it appears that,
whether we study the passage as it occurs in S. John's
Gospel, or whether we consult the comments on it to be
found in the writings of the great Fathers of the Church,
we find no trace of the papal interpretation.   I verily
believe that S. Leo invented that interpretation, or
rather the germ of it.   Whether he did or not, there is a
consensus of the great Fathers in favour of the view that
S. Peter had authority to feed the sheep and lambs of
Christ's flock, because he was an apostle, and not because
he had any primatial jurisdiction over the other apostles.
In other words, the Anglican view of the passage is the
Catholic view, and the Roman view is an un-Catholic view,
and is in fact a grievous perversion of our Blessed Lord's
meaning.   On investigation, it appears that the whole of
the supposed scriptural basis for the teaching of the
Vatican Council about the pope's jurisdiction[1] collapses.

---

[1] I have not discussed S. Luke xxii. 32, because the Vatican Council
makes no reference to that passage in the first chapter of the Constitution *De Ecclesiâ Christi*, in which it sets forth what it considers to
be the scriptural basis of its doctrine concerning the papal primacy of
jurisdiction.   Later on, in the fourth chapter of the same Constitution,
the Council does quote S. Luke xxii. 32 in connection with its teaching about papal infallibility; but that is a subject, on which in this
book I do not enter (see *Preface*, p. xxvi.).

NOTE E.

On a passage in S. Jerome's treatise against Jovinian
(see p. 175).

THERE is a passage in S. Jerome's treatise against
Jovinian (lib. i. § 26, *Opp.* ed. Vallars., ii. 279) which has
been curiously misunderstood, as if it favoured the Romanist
view of S. Peter's relation to the other apostles, whereas
in truth the passage, taken as a whole, is in thorough
agreement with the ordinary Catholic teaching on that
subject. S. Jerome is proving to Jovinian that S. John
the Evangelist was a *virgin* disciple ; and he says, " If
he was not a virgin, let Jovinian explain why he was more
beloved than the other apostles. But you reply that the
Church is founded on Peter, though that same thing was
done in another place upon all the apostles, and all of them
receive the keys of the kingdom of heaven, and the solidity
of the Church is established equally upon them all ; still
among the twelve one is therefore chosen, that by the
appointment of a head *an occasion of dissension may be
taken away* (schismatis tollatur occasio). But why was not
John chosen, who was a virgin ? Deference was paid to
age, because Peter was the elder, lest one, who was still
a young man and almost a boy, should be given precedence
before men of mature age (progressæ ætatis hominibus
præferretur) ; and lest the good Master, *who felt bound to*

remove from His disciples an occasion of strife (qui occasionem jurgii debuerat auferre discipulis), and who had said to them, 'My peace I give unto you ; peace I leave with you,' and who had also said, 'Whosoever would be great among you, let him be the least of all'—[lest He, I say,] should seem to furnish a cause of grudge against the young man whom He loved. . . . Peter was an apostle, and John was an apostle, the first married, the second a virgin. But *Peter was nothing else than an apostle* (sed Petrus apostolus tantum) ; John was both an apostle, and an evangelist, and a prophet." The Romanists are accustomed to quote a few words out of this passage in order to show that in it S. Jerome taught the doctrine that S. Peter was (and by implication the reigning pope is) the divinely appointed centre and root of unity in the Church. They say that S. Jerome teaches that S. Peter was appointed a head, that "*the occasion of schism might be removed.*" But, if S. Jerome had thought that S. Peter was invested with such a headship as that, his whole argument would have crumbled to pieces. He wants to show the complete equality of the apostles in their relation to the Church. But if one of them had been appointed by our Lord the necessary centre of unity, that equality would have existed no longer. The solidity of the Church would not in that case be "equally established upon them all." S. Jerome, as a matter of fact, attributes to S. Peter a very different kind of headship. It is like the headship of the foreman in a jury, or like the headship of the Duke of Norfolk among our English peers. Such a headship, which is in fact a mere primacy of order, would not affect the equality of the apostles in their relation to the Church. The Romanist mistake has arisen from not noticing that S. Jerome, when he says that our Lord took away an *occasion* of dissension, is referring to the disputes which used to take place among the disciples as to which of them should be greatest. S. Jerome thinks that our Lord gave a primacy of order to one of the twelve that "*an occasion of dissension might be taken away*" (schismatis tollatur occasio); just as he also thinks that "the good Master" chose S. Peter, the elder, rather than S. John, the younger, to be the head, in order that He might remove another "*occasion of strife*" (occasionem jurgii). It was no doubt the word "*schisma*" which caused the mistake. That word is sometimes used in the technical sense of *schism*. But it is also used both in Latin and Greek in the untechnical sense of *dissension*. For example, S. John uses the word σχίσμα in three passages of his Gospel (S. John vii. 43 ; ix. 16 ; x. 19) ; and always in the sense of a *dissension*, or *dispute*, or angry *division of opinion*. In the Vulgate, S. Jerome has rendered the word σχίσμα by "*dissensio*" in S. John vii. 43 and in S. John x. 19 ; but in S. John ix. 16, where the sense is precisely the same, he has used the word "*schisma*." No one would suggest *schism* as the right English translation of S. Jerome's "*schisma*" in S. John ix. 16 ; it there plainly means *dissension ;* and the whole argument requires that a similar meaning should be attributed to it in the treatise against Jovinian. In a letter to Evangelus (*Ep.* cxlvi., *Opp.* ed. Vallars., i. 1076) S. Jerome speaks of one among a body of presbyters being made a bishop "as a preventive against schism" (in schismatis remedium). Here the word "*schismatis*" has undoubtedly its technical meaning, *schism*. The sense of the word varies according to the context. It is worth noticing that S. Jerome wrote his treatise against Jovinian in the year 393, twelve years after the Ecumenical Council of Constantinople, and eight years after his departure from Rome in considerable wrath with the Roman clergy. The admirable teaching on the equality of the apostles, which is contained in this treatise, illustrates Mr. Gore's view that S. Jerome changed his tone about the position and privileges of the Roman bishop after the death of Damasus at the end of the year 384 (see Gore's *Church and the Ministry*, 1st ed., p. 172). Closer acquaintance with the local Roman Church seems to have led S. Jerome to reconsider some of the views which he had expressed in his letters to Damasus, and thus a remedy was provided for the somewhat papalizing tone which he had imbibed in Rome during his catechumenate. S. Jerome's faith was in fact purified, and brought up to the normal level of the faith of the saints.

(396)

NOTE F.

*S. Chrysostom's view of S. Peter's position in connection
with the election of S. Matthias to the apostolate
(see p. 257).*

I HAVE admitted that it is quite possible that S. Chrysostom, though he never connects the primacy of S. Peter with any prerogatives of the see of Rome, may nevertheless have been so filled with veneration for the apostle whom he regarded as the founder of the Church of Antioch, as to be led to speak of him occasionally in an exaggerated way. But the reader must be warned against accepting the account given by Mr. Rivington of S. Chrysostom's views about S. Peter's position in relation to the election of S. Matthias to the apostolate.[1] Mr. Rivington says that "when S. Chrysostom asks the question, 'Might not Peter by himself have elected?' he answers categorically, emphatically, 'Certainly.'" In this passage Mr. Rivington has fallen into two mistakes. He has, in the first place, been misled by the corrupt Benedictine text, which, in the case of S. Chrysostom's Homilies on the Acts, is entirely untrustworthy.[2] But, in the second place, even if it were possible to accept the Benedictine text,[3] Mr. Rivington has

---

[1] *Authority*, p. 73, 2nd ed.

[2] See note 2, on pp. 124, 125.

[3] The passages of S. Chrysostom referred to in this Note occur in his third Homily on the Acts (*Opp.* ed. Ben., ix. 23-25, and in the *Oxford translation*, pp. 37-40).

misunderstood S. Chrysostom's teaching, as there set forth. I will take these two points in their order. The first is perhaps rather a matter of form than of substance. The second is substantial.

1. The Oxford translators, having before them "the old text," that is to say, the genuine text of these Homilies on the Acts, translate the passage, from which Mr. Rivington quotes, as follows : "Then, why did it not rest with Peter to make the election himself? What was the motive? This ; that he might not seem to bestow it of favour. And besides, he was not yet endowed with the Spirit." The question, "Might not Peter by himself have elected?" and the categorical, emphatic answer, "Certainly," are not to be found in the genuine text. There is no trace of them in the New College manuscript ;[1] and evidently there was no trace of them in the Paris manuscripts used by the Oxford translators. But to this it may be answered that even the Oxford translation implies that conceivably Peter might have made the election himself, though in that translation there is no such categorical statement of the fact as appears in the Benedictine text. That is true, but S. Chrysostom's real meaning will be better understood by a consideration of what I have to say about Mr. Rivington's second mistake.

2. Mr. Rivington tells us[2] that "S. Peter called on *the apostles*[3] to elect one in place of Judas, to supply the number of twelve in the apostolic college." This account can hardly be considered accurate. S. Peter was addressing, not "the apostles," but "the brethren,"[4] or, as S.

---

[1] Tom. i. f. 65.   [2] *Authority*, p. 72.   [3] The italics are mine.

[4] Acts i. 15. "In diebus illis exsurgens Petrus in medio fratrum dixit (erat autem turba hominum simul fere centum viginti)"— Vulgate. The Revised Version is in close agreement with the Vulgate.

Chrysostom read in his copy of the Acts, "the disciples," of whom there were about a hundred and twenty present. S. Chrysostom dwells on the fact that some of those who were addressed were women. Commenting on S. Peter's words, "Men and brethren,"[1] he says, "See the dignity of the Church, the angelic condition! No distinction there, *neither male nor female.* I would that the Churches were such now." S. Chrysostom lays the greatest stress on the fact that the choice of the new apostle, or at any rate the selection of the two names, was committed "to the whole body" of the Church. S. Chrysostom nowhere in this passage contrasts S. Peter with the other apostles ; but he contrasts the multitude of brethren, sometimes with S. Peter and sometimes with the whole choir of the apostles. According to the reading of the Benedictine editors, S. Chrysostom, speaking of the apostles, asks the question, "Why of their own selves do they not make the election ? " Thus, so far from saying that "S. Peter called on the apostles to elect," he draws attention to the fact that they did not elect. Further on S. Chrysostom says, " Observe how Peter does everything with the common consent [of the whole body of brethren], nothing autocratically, nor imperiously. And he did not say simply thus : 'Instead of Judas *we* elect this man.'"[2] Notice how S. Chrysostom

---

[1] S. Chrysostom accounts for S. Peter, rather than anybody else, having stood up in the midst of the hundred and twenty to address the others, by three considerations, namely, (1) the ardour of his character; (2) his apostolic office ; "he had been put in trust by Christ with the flock; " (3) "he had precedence in honour" (two of the "*old text*" Paris manuscripts read προτιμότερος, the other one and the New College manuscript, and also the *Catena,* read προτιμώμενος). The reference to the primacy of honour, coming as the climax after the reference to S. Peter's having been put in trust with the flock, fits in with S. Chrysostom's view that the injunction, "Feed My sheep," had to do with apostolic and not with primatial jurisdiction (compare what I have said on pp. 383, 384, 386-388).

[2] The New College manuscript (tom. i. f. 60) here agrees with the

assumes that if S. Peter had announced a name, he would have made the announcement on behalf of the apostolic body, of whom he was the mouthpiece. But he and the other apostles preferred to leave the whole body of the Church to make the election in complete freedom. When once it is perceived that in S. Chrysostom's mind there is no separation between S. Peter and the other apostles in regard to this transaction, all becomes clear. There was on the one side the apostolic college, with S. Peter as its leader and mouthpiece. There was on the other side the multitude of the brethren. S. Peter, as the leader of the apostolic college, might very naturally have made a mental selection of one or more names, and might have submitted it or them to his brother-apostles ; but he preferred to "keep clear of all invidiousness," and "to defer the decision to the whole body " of the Church. That seems to me to be S. Chrysostom's view throughout this somewhat obscure passage.

It is a satisfaction to be able to quote the opinion of the great Bossuet in support of the interpretation, which I have tried to set forth. He is replying to some anonymous writer, who had cited in favour of papal autocracy the very passage which gave rise to this discussion. Bossuet says, "In this passage our anonymous friend dreams that Chrysostom intended to say, that Peter by his own authority was able to settle the whole business, without any consultation with his brethren ; but that is far from the mind of Chrysostom, and from [the practice of] those

Benedictine reading, except that it reads, οὐδὲν ἀρχοντικῶς, instead of οὐδὲν αὐθεντικῶς, οὐδὲ ἀρχικῶς. It is fair to point out that the two passages translated in the text from the Benedictine edition, do not appear in the Oxford translation, and are therefore absent, I suppose, from the "*old text*" Paris manuscripts. However, they at any rate show how S. Chrysostom's meaning was understood by the mediæval concocters of the text, which the Benedictines unfortunately adopted.

times.   Chrysostom meant that it was lawful for Peter,
who was the first of the sacred band, that as he had made
the opening speech about the election, so in that same
speech he might have designated and selected some one, to
whose election the others would afterwards have readily
given their consent.   By such a method of proceeding he
would have been the first, not the sole elector.   But Peter
did not follow this course.   He said indefinitely, ' Of
these must one become a witness with us of the resurrection of Christ.'   Chrysostom therefore draws attention
to the modesty of Peter, who was unwilling to bias the
judgments of the others."[1]   I think that there can be no
doubt that Bossuet's view of S. Chrysostom's meaning is
correct; and that there is no solid ground for the paragraph[2] in which Mr. Rivington triumphs over the
venerable author of the *Roman Question.*

[1] *Def. Decl. Cler. Gall.*, viii. 17, *Œuvres*, xxxii. 627, ed. Versailles,
1817.

[2] *Authority*, pp. 72, 73.

NOTE G.

The 350 Martyrs of Syria Secunda (see p. 294).

I PROPOSE to show in this Note that the 350 martyrs of Syria Secunda, who are commemorated in the Roman Martyrology on July 31, were not in the Roman communion when they died.

As has been stated in the seventh lecture, these martyrs were orthodox monks, who were going on pilgrimage to the sanctuary of S. Simeon Stylites, the wonderful ruins of which still remain at Kuláat es-Simân.[1] While they were on the road they were attacked and murdered by a band of assassins hired by Severus, the Monophysite Patriarch of Antioch, and Peter, the Monophysite Metropolitan of Apamea. From the fact that the Roman Church venerates them as martyrs, and from the letter of their friends to Pope Hormisdas,[2] it is clear that they were murdered on account of their fidelity to the Catholic doctrine of the Incarnation. The date of the martyrdom seems to be A.D. 517, or possibly A.D. 516.

Baronius says that these monks were "Ecclesiæ Romanæ communicantes," and that, having previously been polluted with "the stain of the heretics," they had "joined them-

---

[1] For a description of these ruins, see Mr. George Williams' *Introduction* to Dr. Neale's *History of the Patriarchate of Antioch*, pp. xlix.–lv.

[2] Coleti, v. 593.

selves to the apostolic see."[1]　When he says that they had been previously polluted with "the stain of the heretics," what he means is that they belonged to the orthodox Church of the East, which had been out of communion with Rome for thirty-two or thirty-three years, and which still kept the name of Acacius on its diptychs. But in that Church they had had for their patriarch at Antioch S. Flavian II., and they had enjoyed the communion of S. Macedonius of Constantinople and of S. Elias of Jerusalem, as well as of all that great galaxy of saints which adorned the Eastern Church during that period of its isolation. When Baronius says that before their death they had "joined themselves to the apostolic see," he makes a gratuitous statement, which he does not attempt to prove. He would have probably tried to justify his remark by pointing out that the surviving archimandrites and monks of Syria Secunda wrote a letter to Pope Hormisdas, imploring him to do what he could to succour them in their misery.[2]　But there is no sort of reason for supposing that there had been any previous communication between Syria Secunda and Rome during the whole period of the Acacian troubles, and the letter of the archimandrites which opened communications with Rome was written some time *after the martyrdom of the* 350. Consequently the martyrs themselves died at a time when, according to Baronius, the monks of Syria Secunda were suffering pollution from "the stain of the heretics." It will, I think throw light on the whole matter, and will illustrate the way in which the Eastern Church looked on the question of communion with the see of Rome, if I give an account of these communications between the Syrian monks and the pope.

[1] *Annal. Eccl.*, s.a. 517, tom. vi. p. 694, ed. 1658.
[2] Coleti, v. 598-602.

After the massacre of the 350, the surviving archimandrites and monks sent two of their brethren, John and Sergius, to Constantinople, to claim justice and protection from the emperor. But Anastasius would not hear their petition, and drove them out of the city.[1] When the news of this proceeding reached Syria, the poor monks, who were being persecuted by the heretical patriarch and metropolitan, and who could get no redress from the civil power, determined to write to Hormisdas in distant Rome. There was no influential person in the East to whom they could write. The emperor had driven into exile all the orthodox patriarchs, and had intruded heretics into their sees. Hormisdas alone was living in security under the protection of the Arian king of the Goths, Theodoric. We have only a Latin translation of the letter to Hormisdas. In the salutation they style the pope "universæ orbis terræ patriarchæ," which obviously represents οἰκουμενικῷ πατριάρχῃ (ecumenical patriarch), and they speak of him as "occupying the see of Peter, the chief of the apostles." In the course of their letter they petition (deprecamur) the pope "to arise with fervour and zeal, and to feel a righteous grief for the torn body ('for,' they say, 'thou art the head of all'), and to vindicate the faith which has been despised, and the canons which have been trampled upon, and the Fathers who have been blasphemed, and so great a synod[2] which has been anathematized. To you has been given by God power and authority to bind and to loose. . . . Arise, holy fathers,[3] come and rescue us; be imitators of our Lord, Who came from heaven to earth to seek the wandering sheep; remember Peter the chief of the apostles, whose see you adorn, and Paul the chosen vessel, who, journeying about, gave light to the

---

[1] Coleti, v. 599.   [2] The Synod of Chalcedon.
[3] Evidently addressing all the bishops of the West.

world," etc.　Further on they say, "In this our petition (deprecatione), which stands in lieu of a profession of faith (libelli), we anathematize all those who have been cast out and excommunicated by your apostolic see."　Then they mention specially Nestorius, Eutyches, Dioscorus, Peter Mongus, Peter the Fuller, "and all who defend any one of those heretics."[1]

It should be noticed that the Syrian monks are evidently approaching the Roman see for the first time.　They say that their petition is to stand in lieu of a "*libellus.*"　They knew that Rome would do nothing for them, unless they either explicitly or implicitly anathematized Acacius.　Still they express no sorrow for having been for more than thirty years out of communion with Rome.　They write as those who wished to be admitted into communion with the West, not as those who asked to be received for the first time into fellowship with the Catholic Church.

In February, 518, Hormisdas sent a reply to this letter.　The pope takes a hopeful view of his correspondents' ecclesiastical position.　After giving them some good advice, as to how to behave in times of persecution, he says, "We willingly communicate with you in these teachings.　For the wise Solomon saith, 'Well is he that speaketh in the ears of them that will hear:'[2] for it is indeed a joy to hold converse with willing people, and to urge into the right way those who are not antagonistic.　*For we hold a pledge of your faith, the earnestness professed by your letter, by which, having been separated from*

---

[1] I follow the reading in Baronius (*Annal. Eccl.*, s.a. 517, vi. 696), but Coleti (v. 599) inserts the words, "nihilominus et Acacium, qui fuit Constantinopolitanus episcopus, eorum communicatorem."　I have no opportunity of judging of the manuscript evidence ; but on further consideration, I think that the weight of internal probability inclines towards Coleti's reading.

[2] Ecclus. xxv. 9.

the defilement of transgressors, you are returning to the teachings and commandments of the apostolic see, entering indeed late in the day into the way of truth."[1] Afterwards he goes on to urge them to complete the work of separating themselves from the mud in which the heretics are swallowed up. The pope's letter is addressed to "the priests, deacons, and archimandrites of Syria Secunda, and to other orthodox persons living in any region of the East, and abiding in the communion of the apostolic see."[2] It was through the instrumentality of their letter and of this reply to it, that the Syrian monks were brought into communion with the pope.

But it would be a great mistake to suppose that these Eastern religious, by writing their respectful and complimentary letter to the pope, meant to submit to Rome on any such theory as that only in the Roman communion is the true Church of God to be found. As I have observed before, such a notion never entered the minds of Eastern Catholics. In their dire distress, when their lives were in danger, and all the orthodox patriarchs of the East were in banishment, they had been willing to anathematize Acacius, either explicitly or implicitly, in the hope of getting some sympathy and help from the pope. But five months after the pope's reply had been despatched, we find these same Syrian monks in full communion with the new Patriarch of Constantinople, John the Cappadocian, although he was out of communion with the pope, and was still retaining the name of Acacius on his diptychs. The fact was that Anastasius was dead, and Justin had come to the throne, and the Eastern Church was arising out of the dust. In the summer of the year 518, the archimandrites and monks of Syria Secunda[3] presented a written memorial to the orthodox bishops of their province, in which they gave a

---

[1] Coleti, v. 1116.   [2] Ibid. v. 1112.   [3] Ibid. v. 1217–1225.

detailed account of the crimes of Severus of Antioch and of Peter of Apamea.   In this memorial they describe again the massacre of the 350 martyrs.   The list of names appended to this memorial is substantially the same, so far as it goes, as the list appended to the letter to Hormisdas.[1] The bishops of the province, having received this memorial and other evidence on the subject of the Metropolitan Peter's misdeeds, sent the whole mass of documents,[2] with a letter of their own, to the Patriarch John of Constantinople, and to his "resident synod."[3]   They address John in very respectful terms, calling him, "Father of fathers,[4] archbishop, and ecumenical patriarch."   In the course of their letter the bishops go on to say that "we, instructed by the holy determination of your teachings, anathematize Severus and Peter, the madmen;" and they add, "we, following your example, most blessed ones, deprive them of all honour, dignity, and episcopal power."[5]   Then they ask John to confirm ($\epsilon\pi\iota\kappa\upsilon\rho\hat{\omega}\sigma\alpha\iota$) their acts, and to inform the emperor of them.   It is to be observed that these bishops of Syria Secunda were not headed by their metropolitan ; they were proceeding against him.   They were all suffragan bishops of the province, and they were deposing and excommunicating their intruded patriarch and their intruded metropolitan ; so they might well ask the Patriarch of Constantinople to confirm what they had done.   Anyhow, they were in full communion with John, and therefore out

---

[1] Compare Coleti, tom. v. coll. 599 *ff*. with coll. 1224, 1225.

[2] Coleti, v. 1184–1188.   [3] σύνοδος ἐνδημοῦσα.

[4] Mr. Allnatt (*Cathedra Petri*, 2nd edit., 106, 107) makes a great point of this title having been "given to the pope by the Orientals, from the sixth century downwards."   But this sort of argument loses all its force when one discovers that titles of similar magnificence were also given to the other patriarchs.   If I may venture to say so, Mr. Allnatt is very painstaking, but he appears to me to be curiously undiscriminating.

[5] Coleti, v. 1188.

of communion with Rome ; and it is plain that the
archimandrites and monks who were transmitting their
memorial to the Constantinopolitan patriarch by the hands
of their bishops, had naturally, in the altered state of things,
passed back into the communion of the Eastern Church. The
real reunion of the patriarchate of Antioch with Rome did
not take place until A.D. 521,[1] four years after the martyrdom
of the 350.

[1] See p. 295, note 1.

INDEX.

THE END.

PRINTED BY WILLIAM CLOWES AND SONS, LIMITED, LONDON AND BECCLES.

A Selection of Works

IN

THEOLOGICAL LITERATURE

PUBLISHED BY

Messrs. LONGMANS, GREEN, & CO.

39 Paternoster Row, London, E.C.

Abbey and Overton.—THE ENGLISH CHURCH IN THE EIGHTEENTH CENTURY. By Charles J. Abbey, M.A., Rector of Checkendon, Reading, and John H. Overton, D.D., Canon of Lincoln and Rector of Epworth. *Crown 8vo. 7s. 6d.*

Adams.—SACRED ALLEGORIES. The Shadow of the Cross—The Distant Hills—The Old Man's Home—The King's Messengers. By the Rev. William Adams, M.A. *Crown 8vo. 3s. 6d.*

The four Allegories may be had separately, with Illustrations. *16mo. 1s. each.*

Aids to the Inner Life.

Edited by the Rev. W. H. Hutchings, M.A., Rector of Kirby Misperton, Yorkshire. *Five Vols. 32mo, cloth limp, 6d. each; or cloth extra, 1s. each.*

With red borders, 2s. each. Sold separately.

OF THE IMITATION OF CHRIST. By Thomas à Kempis.

THE CHRISTIAN YEAR.

THE DEVOUT LIFE. By St. Francis de Sales.

THE HIDDEN LIFE OF THE SOUL.

THE SPIRITUAL COMBAT. By Laurence Scupoli.

Barry.—SOME LIGHTS OF SCIENCE ON THE FAITH. Being the Bampton Lectures for 1892. By the Right Rev. Alfred Barry, D.D., Canon of Windsor, formerly Bishop of Sydney, Metropolitan of New South Wales, and Primate of Australia. *8vo. 12s. 6d.*

Bathe.—Works by the Rev. Anthony Bathe, M.A.

A LENT WITH JESUS. A Plain Guide for Churchmen. Containing Readings for Lent and Easter Week, and on the Holy Eucharist. *32mo, 1s.; or in paper cover, 6d.*

AN ADVENT WITH JESUS. *32mo, 1s.; or in paper cover, 6d.*

WHAT I SHOULD BELIEVE. A Simple Manual of Self-Instruction for Church People. *Small 8vo, limp, 1s.; cloth gilt, 2s.*

Bathe and Buckham.—THE CHRISTIAN'S ROAD BOOK: Part I. DEVOTIONS. By the Rev. Anthony Bathe and Rev. F. H. Buckham, *Fcap. 8vo. Sewed, 6d.; limp cloth, 1s.; cloth extra, 1s. 6d.*

Benson.—THE FINAL PASSOVER : A Series of Meditations upon the Passion of our Lord Jesus Christ.   By the Rev. R. M. BENSON, M.A., Student of Christ Church, Oxford.   *Small 8vo.*

Vol. I.—THE REJECTION. 5*s.*
Vol. II.—THE UPPER CHAMBER.
   Part I. 5*s.*
   Part II. 5*s.*

Vol. III.—THE DIVINE EXODUS.
   Parts I. and II. 5*s.* each.
Vol. IV.—THE LIFE BEYOND THE GRAVE. 5*s.*

Bickersteth.—YESTERDAY, TO-DAY, AND FOR EVER : a Poem in Twelve Books.   By EDWARD HENRY BICKERSTETH, D.D., Bishop of Exeter.   *One Shilling Edition, 18mo.   With red borders, 16mo, 2s. 6d.*
   The Crown 8vo Edition (5s.) may still be had.

Blunt.—Works by the Rev. JOHN HENRY BLUNT, D.D.

THE ANNOTATED BOOK OF COMMON PRAYER : Being an Historical, Ritual, and Theological Commentary on the Devotional System of the Church of England. *4to.* 21*s.*

THE COMPENDIOUS EDITION OF THE ANNOTATED BOOK OF COMMON PRAYER : Forming a concise Commentary on the Devotional System of the Church of England. *Crown 8vo.* 10*s. 6d.*

DICTIONARY OF DOCTRINAL AND HISTORICAL THEOLOGY. By various Writers. *Imperial 8vo.* 21*s.*

DICTIONARY OF SECTS, HERESIES, ECCLESIASTICAL PARTIES AND SCHOOLS OF RELIGIOUS THOUGHT.   By various Writers. *Imperial 8vo.* 21*s.*

THE BOOK OF CHURCH LAW.   Being an Exposition of the Legal Rights and Duties of the Parochial Clergy and the Laity of the Church of England.   Revised by Sir WALTER G. F. PHILLIMORE, Bart., D.C.L., and G. EDWARDES JONES, Barrister-at-Law.   *Crown 8vo.* 7*s. 6d.*

A COMPANION TO THE BIBLE : Being a Plain Commentary on Scripture History, to the end of the Apostolic Age.   *Two Vols. small 8vo.   Sold separately.*

THE OLD TESTAMENT. 3*s. 6d.*   THE NEW TESTAMENT. 3*s. 6d.*

HOUSEHOLD THEOLOGY : a Handbook of Religious Information respecting the Holy Bible, the Prayer Book, the Church, etc., etc. *Paper cover, 16mo.* 1*s.*   *Also the Larger Edition,* 3*s. 6d.*

Body.—Works by the Rev. GEORGE BODY, D.D., Canon of Durham.

THE LIFE OF LOVE. A Course of Lent Lectures. *16mo.* 2*s. 6d. 6d.*

THE SCHOOL OF CALVARY ; or, Laws of Christian Life revealed from the Cross. *16mo.* 2*s. 6d.*

THE LIFE OF JUSTIFICATION. *16mo.* 2*s. 6d.*

THE LIFE OF TEMPTATION. *16mo.* 2*s. 6d.*

Boultbee.—A COMMENTARY ON THE THIRTY-NINE ARTICLES OF THE CHURCH OF ENGLAND. By the Rev. T. P. BOULTBEE, formerly Principal of the London College of Divinity, St. John's Hall, Highbury. *Crown 8vo. 6s.*

Bright.—Works by WILLIAM BRIGHT, D.D., Canon of Christ Church, Oxford.

WAYMARKS IN CHURCH HISTORY. *Crown 8vo. 7s. 6d.*

MORALITY IN DOCTRINE. *Crown 8vo. 7s. 6d.*

LESSONS FROM THE LIVES OF THREE GREAT FATHERS: St. Athanasius, St. Chrysostom, and St. Augustine. *Crown 8vo. 6s.*

THE INCARNATION AS A MOTIVE POWER. *Crown 8vo. 6s.*

THE ROMAN SEE IN THE EARLY CHURCH; and other Studies in Church History. *Crown 8vo.*

Bright and Medd.—LIBER PRECUM PUBLICARUM ECCLESIÆ ANGLICANÆ. A GULIELMO BRIGHT, S.T.P., et PETRO GOLDSMITH MEDD, A.M., Latine redditus. *Small 8vo. 7s. 6d.*

Browne.—AN EXPOSITION OF THE THIRTY-NINE ARTICLES, Historical and Doctrinal. By E. H. BROWNE, D.D., formerly Bishop of Winchester. *8vo. 16s.*

Campion and Beamont.—THE PRAYER BOOK INTERLEAVED. With Historical Illustrations and Explanatory Notes arranged parallel to the Text. By W. M. CAMPION, D.D., and W. J. BEAMONT, M.A. *Small 8vo. 7s. 6d.*

Carter.—Works edited by the Rev. T. T. CARTER, M.A., Hon. Canon of Christ Church, Oxford.

THE TREASURY OF DEVOTION: a Manual of Prayer for General and Daily Use. Compiled by a Priest.
18mo. 2s. 6d.; cloth limp, 2s.
Bound with the Book of Common Prayer, 3s. 6d.
Red-Line Edition. *Cloth extra, gilt top.* 18mo, 2s. 6d. *net.*
Large-Type Edition. *Crown 8vo. 3s. 6d.*

THE WAY OF LIFE: A Book of Prayers and Instruction for the Young at School, with a Preparation for Confirmation. Compiled by a Priest, *18mo. 1s. 6d.*

THE PATH OF HOLINESS: a First Book of Prayers, with the Service of the Holy Communion, for the Young. Compiled by a Priest. With Illustrations. *16mo. 1s. 6d.; cloth limp, 1s.*

THE GUIDE TO HEAVEN: a Book of Prayers for every Want. (For the Working Classes.) Compiled by a Priest. *18mo. 1s. 6d.; cloth limp, 1s. Large-Type Edition. Crown 8vo. 1s. 6d.; cloth limp, 1s.*

[continued

Carter.—Works edited by the Rev. T. T. CARTER, M.A., Hon. Canon of Christ Church, Oxford—*continued.*

SELF-RENUNCIATION. 16mo. 2s. 6d.

THE STAR OF CHILDHOOD: a First Book of Prayers and Instruction for Children. Compiled by a Priest. With Illustrations. 16mo. 2s. 6d.

NICHOLAS FERRAR : his Household and his Friends. With Portrait engraved after a Picture by CORNELIUS JANSSEN at Magdalene College, Cambridge. *Crown 8vo.* 6s.

THE LIFE AND TIMES OF JOHN KETTLEWELL. With Details of the History of the Non-Jurors. With Portrait. *Crown 8vo.* 6s.

Conybeare and Howson.—THE LIFE AND EPISTLES OF ST. PAUL. By the Rev. W. J. CONYBEARE, M.A., and the Very Rev. J. S. HOWSON, D.D. With numerous Maps and Illustrations.

LIBRARY EDITION. *Two Vols.* 8vo. 21s.
STUDENTS' EDITION. *One Vol. Crown 8vo.* 6s.
POPULAR EDITION. *One Vol. Crown 8vo.* 3s. 6d.

Creighton.—PERSECUTION AND TOLERANCE : being the Hulsean Lectures preached before the University of Cambridge in 1893-4. By M. CREIGHTON, D.D., Lord Bishop of Peterborough. *Crown 8vo.* 4s. 6d.

Devotional Series, 16mo, Red Borders. *Each 2s. 6d.*

BICKERSTETH'S YESTERDAY, TO-DAY, AND FOR EVER.
CHILCOT'S TREATISE ON EVIL THOUGHTS.
THE CHRISTIAN YEAR.
FRANCIS DE SALES' (ST.) THE DEVOUT LIFE.
HERBERT'S POEMS AND PROVERBS.
KEMPIS' (À) OF THE IMITATION OF CHRIST.
WILSON'S THE LORD'S SUPPER. *Large type.*
*TAYLOR'S (JEREMY) HOLY LIVING.
*———— ———— HOLY DYING.

      * *These two in one Volume.* 5s.

Devotional Series, 18mo, without Red Borders. *Each 1s.*

BICKERSTETH'S YESTERDAY, TO-DAY, AND FOR EVER.
THE CHRISTIAN YEAR.
FRANCIS DE SALES' (ST.) THE DEVOUT LIFE,
HERBERT'S POEMS AND PROVERBS.
KEMPIS (À) OF THE IMITATION OF CHRIST.
WILSON'S THE LORD'S SUPPER, *Large type.*
*TAYLOR'S (JEREMY) HOLY LIVING,
*——— · ——— HOLY DYING.

      * *These two in one Volume.* 2s. 6d.

Diggle.—RELIGIOUS DOUBT : its Nature, Treatment, Causes, Difficulties, Consequences, and Dissolution. By the Rev. JOHN W. DIGGLE, M.A., Vicar of Mossley Hill and Hon. Canon of Liverpool, Author of 'Bishop Fraser's Lancashire Life.' *Crown 8vo. 7s. 6d.*

Edersheim.—Works by ALFRED EDERSHEIM, M.A., D.D., Ph.D., sometime Grinfield Lecturer on the Septuagint, Oxford.

THE LIFE AND TIMES OF JESUS THE MESSIAH. *Two Vols. 8vo. 24s.*

JESUS THE MESSIAH : being an Abridged Edition of 'The Life and Times of Jesus the Messiah.' *Crown 8vo. 7s. 6d.*

PROPHECY AND HISTORY IN RELATION TO THE MESSIAH : The Warburton Lectures, 1880-1884. *8vo. 12s.*

HISTORY OF THE JEWISH NATION AFTER THE DESTRUC-TION OF JERUSALEM UNDER TITUS. Revised by the Rev. HENRY A. WHITE, M.A., Fellow of New College, Oxford. With a Preface by the Rev. WILLIAM SANDAY, D.D., LL.D., Margaret Professor of Divinity and Canon of Christ Church, Oxford. *8vo. 18s.*

Ellicott.—Works by C. J. ELLICOTT, D.D., Bishop of Gloucester and Bristol.

A CRITICAL AND GRAMMATICAL COMMENTARY ON ST. PAUL'S EPISTLES. Greek Text, with a Critical and Grammatical Commentary, and a Revised English Translation. *8vo.*

1 CORINTHIANS. 16s.	PHILIPPIANS, COLOSSIANS, AND
GALATIANS. 8s. 6d.	PHILEMON. 10s. 6d.
EPHESIANS. 8s. 6d.	THESSALONIANS. 7s. 6d.
PASTORAL EPISTLES. 10s. 6d.	

HISTORICAL LECTURES ON THE LIFE OF OUR LORD JESUS CHRIST. *8vo. 12s.*

Epochs of Church History.—Edited by MANDELL CREIGHTON, D.D., LL.D., Bishop of Peterborough. *Fcap. 8vo. 2s. 6d. each.*

THE ENGLISH CHURCH IN OTHER LANDS. By the Rev. H. W. TUCKER, M.A.

THE HISTORY OF THE REFOR-MATION IN ENGLAND. By the Rev. GEO. G. PERRY, M.A.

THE CHURCH OF THE EARLY FATHERS. By the Rev. ALFRED PLUMMER, D.D.

THE EVANGELICAL REVIVAL IN THE EIGHTEENTH CENTURY. By the Rev. J. H. OVERTON, D.D.

THE UNIVERSITY OF OXFORD. By the Hon. G. C. BRODRICK, D.C.L.

THE UNIVERSITY OF CAM-BRIDGE. By J. BASS MULLINGER, M.A.

THE ENGLISH CHURCH IN THE MIDDLE AGES. By the Rev. W. HUNT, M.A.

THE CHURCH AND THE EASTERN EMPIRE. By the Rev. H. F. TOZER, M.A.

THE CHURCH AND THE ROMAN EMPIRE. By the Rev. A. CARR, M.A.

THE CHURCH AND THE PURI-TANS, 1570-1660. By HENRY OFFLEY WAKEMAN, M.A.

HILDEBRAND AND HIS TIMES. By the Rev. W. R. W. STEPHENS, M.A.

THE POPES AND THE HOHEN-STAUFEN. By UGO BALZANI.

THE COUNTER REFORMATION. By ADOLPHUS WILLIAM WARD, Litt. D.

WYCLIFFE AND MOVEMENTS FOR REFORM. By REGINALD L. POOLE, M.A.

THE ARIAN CONTROVERSY. By H. M. GWATKIN, M.A.

Fosbery.—Works edited by the Rev. THOMAS VINCENT FOSBERY, M.A., sometime Vicar of St. Giles's, Reading.

VOICES OF COMFORT. *Cheap Edition. Small 8vo.* 3*s.* 6*d.*
The Larger Edition (7s. 6d.) may still be had.

HYMNS AND POEMS FOR THE SICK AND SUFFERING. In connection with the Service for the Visitation of the Sick. Selected from Various Authors. *Small 8vo.* 3*s.* 6*d.*

Fremantle. — THE WORLD AS THE SUBJECT OF REDEMPTION. Being an attempt to set forth the Functions of the Church as designed to embrace the whole Race of Mankind. (The Bampton Lectures, 1883.) By the Hon. and Rev. W. H. FREMANTLE, M.A., Dean of Ripon. New Edition, Revised, with New Preface. *Crown 8vo.* 7*s.* 6*d.*

Gore.—Works by the Rev. CHARLES GORE, M.A., Canon of Westminster.

THE MINISTRY OF THE CHRISTIAN CHURCH. *8vo.* 10*s.* 6*d.*
ROMAN CATHOLIC CLAIMS. *Crown 8vo.* 3*s.* 6*d.*

Goulburn.—Works by EDWARD MEYRICK GOULBURN, D.D., D.C.L., sometime Dean of Norwich.

THOUGHTS ON PERSONAL RELIGION. *Small 8vo.* 6*s.* 6*d.*
Cheap Edition, 3*s.* 6*d.* ; *Presentation Edition,* 2 *vols. small 8vo,* 10*s.* 6*d.*

THE PURSUIT OF HOLINESS : a Sequel to 'Thoughts on Personal Religion.' *Small 8vo.* 5*s. Cheap Edition.* 3*s.* 6*d.*

THE GOSPEL OF THE CHILDHOOD : a Practical and Devotional Commentary on the Single Incident of our Blessed Lord's Childhood (St. Luke ii. 41 to the end). *Crown 8vo.* 2*s.* 6*d.*

THE COLLECTS OF THE DAY : an Exposition, Critical and Devotional, of the Collects appointed at the Communion. With Preliminary Essays on their Structure, Sources, etc. 2 *vols. Crown 8vo.* 8*s. each.*

THOUGHTS UPON THE LITURGICAL GOSPELS for the Sundays, one for each day in the year. With an Introduction on their Origin, History, the modifications made in them by the Reformers and by the Revisers of the Prayer Book. 2 *vols. Crown 8vo.* 16*s.*

MEDITATIONS UPON THE LITURGICAL GOSPELS for the Minor Festivals of Christ, the two first Week-days of the Easter and Whitsun Festivals, and the Red-letter Saints' Days. *Crown 8vo.* 8*s.* 6*d.*

FAMILY PRAYERS, compiled from various sources (chiefly from Bishop Hamilton's Manual), and arranged on the Liturgical Principle. *Crown 8vo.* 3*s.* 6*d. Cheap Edition.* 16*mo.* 1*s.*

Harrison.—Works by the Rev. ALEXANDER J. HARRISON, B.D., Lecturer of the Christian Evidence Society.

PROBLEMS OF CHRISTIANITY AND SCEPTICISM. *Cr. 8vo. 7s. 6d.*

THE CHURCH IN RELATION TO SCEPTICS : a Conversational Guide to Evidential Work. *Crown 8vo. 3s. 6d.*

THE REPOSE OF FAITH, IN VIEW OF PRESENT DAY DIFFI-CULTIES. *Crown 8vo. 7s. 6d.*

Heurtley.—WHOLESOME WORDS : Sermons on some Important points, of Christian Doctrine, preached before the University of Oxford by the Rev. C. A. HEURTLEY, D.D., late Margaret Professor of Divinity and Canon of Christ Church, Oxford. Edited, with a Prefatory Memoir of the Author, by the Rev. W. INCE, D.D., Canon of Christ Church, and Regius Professor of Divinity, Oxford. *Crown 8vo. 5s.*

Holland.—Works by the Rev. HENRY SCOTT HOLLAND, M.A., Canon and Precentor of St. Paul's.

GOD'S CITY AND THE COMING OF THE KINGDOM : *Crown 8vo. 7s. 6d.*

PLEAS AND CLAIMS FOR CHRIST. *Crown 8vo. 3s. 6d.*

CREED AND CHARACTER : Sermons. *Crown 8vo. 3s. 6d.*

ON BEHALF OF BELIEF. Sermons. *Crown 8vo. 3s. 6d.*

CHRIST OR ECCLESIASTES. Sermons. *Crown 8vo. 2s. 6d.*

LOGIC AND LIFE, with other Sermons. *Crown 8vo. 3s. 6d.*

Hutchings.—SERMON SKETCHES taken from some of the Sunday Lessons throughout the Church's Year. By the Rev. W. H. HUTCHINGS, M.A., Canon of York. *Crown 8vo. 5s.*

Ingram.—HAPPINESS IN THE SPIRITUAL LIFE ; or, 'The Secret of the Lord.' By the Rev. W. C. INGRAM, D.D., Dean of Peterborough. *Crown 8vo. 3s. 6d.*

INHERITANCE OF THE SAINTS ; or, Thoughts on the Communion of Saints and the Life of the World to come. Collected chiefly from English Writers by L. P. With a Preface by the Rev. HENRY SCOTT HOLLAND, M.A. *Crown 8vo. 7s. 6d.*

Jameson.—Works by Mrs. JAMESON.

SACRED AND LEGENDARY ART, containing Legends of the Angels and Archangels, the Evangelists, the Apostles. With 19 Etchings and 187 Woodcuts. *2 vols. 8vo. 20s. net.*

LEGENDS OF THE MONASTIC ORDERS, as represented in the Fine Arts. With 11 Etchings and 88 Woodcuts. *8vo. 10s. net.*

LEGENDS OF THE MADONNA, OR BLESSED VIRGIN MARY. With 27 Etchings and 165 Woodcuts. *8vo. 10s. net.*

THE HISTORY OF OUR LORD, as exemplified in Works of Art. Commenced by the late Mrs. JAMESON ; continued and completed by LADY EASTLAKE. With 31 Etchings and 281 Woodcuts. *2 Vols. 8vo. 20s. net*

Jennings.—ECCLESIA ANGLICANA. A History of the Church of Christ in England from the Earliest to the Present Times. By the Rev. ARTHUR CHARLES JENNINGS, M.A. *Crown 8vo. 7s. 6d.*

Jukes.—Works by ANDREW JUKES.

THE NEW MAN AND THE ETERNAL LIFE. Notes on the Reiterated Amens of the Son of God. *Crown 8vo. 6s.*

THE NAMES OF GOD IN HOLY SCRIPTURE : a Revelation of His Nature and Relationships. *Crown 8vo. 4s. 6d.*

THE TYPES OF GENESIS. *Crown 8vo. 7s. 6d.*

THE SECOND DEATH AND THE RESTITUTION OF ALL THINGS. *Crown 8vo. 3s. 6d.*

THE MYSTERY OF THE KINGDOM. *Crown 8vo. 2s. 6d.*

THE ORDER AND CONNEXION OF THE CHURCH'S TEACH-ING, as set forth in the arrangement of the Epistles and Gospels throughout the Year. *Crown 8vo. 2s. 6d.*

Knox Little.—Works by W. J. KNOX LITTLE, M.A., Canon Residentiary of Worcester, and Vicar of Hoar Cross.

SACERDOTALISM, WHEN RIGHTLY UNDERSTOOD, THE TEACHING OF THE CHURCH OF ENGLAND. *Crown 8vo. 6s.*

SKETCHES IN SUNSHINE AND STORM : a Collection of Mis-cellaneous Essays and Notes of Travel. *Crown 8vo. 7s. 6d.*

THE CHRISTIAN HOME. *Crown 8vo. 3s. 6d.*

THE HOPES AND DECISIONS OF THE PASSION OF OUR MOST HOLY REDEEMER. *Crown 8vo. 2s. 6d.*

CHARACTERISTICS AND MOTIVES OF THE CHRISTIAN LIFE. Ten Sermons preached in Manchester Cathedral, in Lent and Advent. *Crown 8vo. 2s. 6d.*

SERMONS PREACHED FOR THE MOST PART IN MANCHES-TER. *Crown 8vo. 3s. 6d.*

THE MYSTERY OF THE PASSION OF OUR MOST HOLY REDEEMER. *Crown 8vo. 2s. 6d.*

THE WITNESS OF THE PASSION OF OUR MOST HOLY REDEEMER. *Crown 8vo. 2s. 6d.*

[continued.

Knox Little.—Works by W. J. KNOX LITTLE, M.A., Canon Residentiary of Worcester, and Vicar of Hoar Cross.—*continued.*

THE LIGHT OF LIFE. Sermons preached on Various Occasions. *Crown 8vo. 3s. 6d.*

SUNLIGHT AND SHADOW IN THE CHRISTIAN LIFE. Sermons preached for the most part in America. *Crown 8vo. 3s. 6d.*

Lear.—Works by, and Edited by, H. L. SIDNEY LEAR.

FOR DAYS AND YEARS. A book containing a Text, Short Reading, and Hymn for Every Day in the Church's Year. *16mo. 2s. 6d. Also a Cheap Edition, 32mo. 1s.; or cloth gilt, 1s. 6d.; or with red borders, 2s. 6d.*

FIVE MINUTES. Daily Readings of Poetry. *16mo. 3s. 6d. Also a Cheap Edition, 32mo. 1s.; or cloth gilt, 1s. 6d.*

WEARINESS. A Book for the Languid and Lonely. *Large Type. Small 8vo. 5s.*

THE LIGHT OF THE CONSCIENCE. *16mo. 2s. 6d. 32mo. 1s.; cloth limp, 6d.*

CHRISTIAN BIOGRAPHIES. *Nine Vols. Crown 8vo. 3s. 6d. each.*

MADAME LOUISE DE FRANCE, Daughter of Louis XV., known also as the Mother Térèse de St. Augustin.

A DOMINICAN ARTIST: a Sketch of the Life of the Rev. Père Besson, of the Order of St. Dominic.

HENRI PERREYVE. By PÈRE GRATRY.

ST. FRANCIS DE SALES, Bishop and Prince of Geneva.

THE REVIVAL OF PRIESTLY LIFE IN THE SEVENTEENTH CENTURY IN FRANCE.

A CHRISTIAN PAINTER OF THE NINETEENTH CENTURY.

BOSSUET AND HIS CONTEMPORARIES.

FÉNELON, ARCHBISHOP OF CAMBRAI.

HENRI DOMINIQUE LACORDAIRE.

DEVOTIONAL WORKS. Edited by H. L. SIDNEY LEAR. *New and Uniform Editions. Nine Vols. 16mo. 2s. 6d. each.*

FÉNELON'S SPIRITUAL LETTERS TO MEN.

FÉNELON'S SPIRITUAL LETTERS TO WOMEN.

A SELECTION FROM THE SPIRITUAL LETTERS OF ST. FRANCIS DE SALES.

THE SPIRIT OF ST. FRANCIS DE SALES.

THE HIDDEN LIFE OF THE SOUL.

THE LIGHT OF THE CONSCIENCE.

SELF-RENUNCIATION. From the French.

ST. FRANCIS DE SALES' OF THE LOVE OF GOD.

SELECTIONS FROM PASCAL'S 'THOUGHTS.'

Liddon.—Works by HENRY PARRY LIDDON, D.D., D.C.L.,LL.D., late Canon Residentiary and Chancellor of St. Paul's.

LIFE OF EDWARD BOUVERIE PUSEY, D.D. By HENRY PARRY LIDDON, D.D., D.C.L., LL.D. Edited and prepared for publication by the Rev. J. O. JOHNSTON, M.A., Principal of the Theological College, and Vicar of Cuddesdon, Oxford; and the Rev. ROBERT J. WILSON, D.D., Warden of Keble College. *With Portraits and Illustrations. Four Vols. 8vo. Vols. I. and II., 36s. Vol. III., 18s.*

CLERICAL LIFE AND WORK: Sermons. *Crown 8vo. 5s.*

ESSAYS AND ADDRESSES : Lectures on Buddhism—Lectures on the Life of St. Paul—Papers on Dante. *Crown 8vo. 5s.*

EXPLANATORY ANALYSIS OF PAUL'S EPISTLE TO THE ROMANS. *8vo. 14s.*

SERMONS ON OLD TESTAMENT SUBJECTS. *Crown 8vo. 5s.*

SERMONS ON SOME WORDS OF CHRIST. *Crown 8vo. 5s.*

THE DIVINITY OF OUR LORD AND SAVIOUR JESUS CHRIST. Being the Bampton Lectures for 1866. *Crown 8vo. 5s.*

ADVENT IN ST. PAUL'S. Sermons bearing chiefly on the Two Comings of our Lord. *Two Vols. Crown 8vo. 3s. 6d. each. Cheap Edition in one Volume. Crown 8vo. 5s.*

CHRISTMASTIDE IN ST. PAUL'S. Sermons bearing chiefly on the Birth of our Lord and the End of the Year. *Crown 8vo. 5s.*

PASSIONTIDE SERMONS. *Crown 8vo. 5s.*

EASTER IN ST. PAUL'S. Sermons bearing chiefly on the Resurrection of our Lord. *Two Vols. Crown 8vo. 3s. 6d. each. Cheap Edition in one Volume. Crown 8vo. 5s.*

SERMONS PREACHED BEFORE THE UNIVERSITY OF OXFORD. *Two Vols. Crown 8vo. 3s. 6d. each. Cheap Edition in one Volume. Crown 8vo. 5s.*

THE MAGNIFICAT. Sermons in St. Paul's. *Crown 8vo. 2s. 6d.*

SOME ELEMENTS OF RELIGION. Lent Lectures. *Small 8vo. 2s. 6d. ; or in paper cover, 1s. 6d.*

The Crown 8vo Edition (5s.) may still be had.

SELECTIONS FROM THE WRITINGS OF H. P. LIDDON, D.D. *Crown 8vo. 3s. 6d.*

MAXIMS AND GLEANINGS FROM THE WRITINGS OF H. P. LIDDON, D.D. Selected and arranged by C. M. S. *Crown 16mo. 1s.*

DR. LIDDON'S TOUR IN EGYPT AND PALESTINE IN 1886. Being Letters descriptive of the Tour, written by his Sister, Mrs. KING. *Crown 8vo. 5s.*

Luckock.—Works by HERBERT MORTIMER LUCKOCK, D.D., Dean of Lichfield.

THE HISTORY OF MARRIAGE, JEWISH AND CHRISTIAN, IN RELATION TO DIVORCE AND CERTAIN FORBIDDEN DEGREES. *New and Enlarged Edition. Crown 8vo. 6s.*

AFTER DEATH. An Examination of the Testimony of Primitive Times respecting the State of the Faithful Dead, and their Relationship to the Living. *Crown 8vo. 3s. 6d.*

THE INTERMEDIATE STATE BETWEEN DEATH AND JUDGMENT. Being a Sequel to *After Death. Crown 8vo. 3s. 6d.*

FOOTPRINTS OF THE SON OF MAN, as traced by St. Mark. Being Eighty Portions for Private Study, Family Reading, and Instructions in Church. *Crown 8vo. 3s. 6d.*

THE DIVINE LITURGY. Being the Order for Holy Communion, Historically, Doctrinally, and devotionally set forth, in Fifty Portions. *Crown 8vo. 3s. 6d.*

STUDIES IN THE HISTORY OF THE BOOK OF COMMON PRAYER. The Anglican Reform—The Puritan Innovations—The Elizabethan Reaction—The Caroline Settlement. With Appendices. *Crown 8vo. 3s. 6d.*

THE BISHOPS IN THE TOWER. A Record of Stirring Events affecting the Church and Nonconformists from the Restoration to the Revolution. *Crown 8vo. 3s. 6d.*

LYRA GERMANICA. Hymns translated from the German by CATHERINE WINKWORTH. *Small 8vo. 5s.*

MacColl.—Works by the Rev. MALCOLM MACCOLL, M.A., Canon Residentary of Ripon.

CHRISTIANITY IN RELATION TO SCIENCE AND MORALS. *Crown 8vo. 6s.*

LIFE HERE AND HEREAFTER : Sermons. *Crown 8vo. 7s. 6d.*

Mason.—Works by A. J. MASON, D.D., Lady Margaret Professor of Divinity in the University of Cambridge.

THE FAITH OF THE GOSPEL. A Manual of Christian Doctrine. *Crown 8vo. 3s. 6d.*

THE RELATION OF CONFIRMATION TO BAPTISM. As taught in Holy Scripture and the Fathers. *Crown 8vo. 7s. 6d.*

Mercier.—OUR MOTHER CHURCH : Being Simple Talk on High Topics. By Mrs. JEROME MERCIER. *Small 8vo. 3s. 6d.*

Milne.—THE DOCTRINE AND PRACTICE OF THE EUCHARIST as deduced from Scripture and the Ancient Liturgies. By J. R. MILNE, Vicar of Rougham, Norfolk. *Crown 8vo. 3s. 6d.*

Mortimer.—Works by the Rev. ALFRED G. MORTIMER, D.D., Rector of St. Mark's, Philadelphia.

HELPS TO MEDITATION : Sketches for Every Day in the Year. With an Introduction by the Right Rev. the BISHOP OF SPRINGFIELD.
VOL. I.—ADVENT to TRINITY. *8vo. 7s. 6d.*
VOL. II.—TRINITY to ADVENT. *8vo. 7s. 6d.*

SERMONS IN MINIATURE FOR EXTEMPORE PREACHERS : Sketches for Every Sunday and Holy Day of the Christian Year. *Crown 8vo. 6s.*

NOTES ON THE SEVEN PENETENTIAL PSALMS, chiefly from Patristic Sources. *Fcp. 8vo. 3s. 6d.*

STORIES FROM GENESIS : Sermons for Children. *Crown 8vo. 4s.*

LEARN OF JESUS CHRIST TO DIE : Addresses on the Words of our Lord from the Cross, taken as Teaching the Way of Preparation for Death. *16mo. 2s.*

THE LAWS OF HAPPINESS ; or, The Beatitudes as teaching our Duty to God, Self, and our Neighbour. *18mo. 2s.*

THE LAWS OF PENITENCE : Addresses on the Words of our Lord from the Cross. *18mo. 1s. 6d.*

Mozley.—Works by J. B. MOZLEY, D.D., late Canon of Christ Church, and Regius Professor of Divinity at Oxford.

ESSAYS, HISTORICAL AND THEOLOGICAL. *Two Vols. 8vo. 24s.*

EIGHT LECTURES ON MIRACLES. Being the Bampton Lectures for 1865. *Crown 8vo. 3s. 6d.*

RULING IDEAS IN EARLY AGES AND THEIR RELATION TO OLD TESTAMENT FAITH. Lectures delivered to Graduates of the University of Oxford. *8vo. 10s. 6d.*

SERMONS PREACHED BEFORE THE UNIVERSITY OF OXFORD, and on Various Occasions. *Crown 8vo. 3s. 6d.*

SERMONS, PAROCHIAL AND OCCASIONAL. *Crown 8vo. 3s. 6d.*

A REVIEW OF THE BAPTISMAL CONTROVERSY. *Crown 8vo. 3s. 6d.*

Newbolt.—Works by the Rev. W. C. E. NEWBOLT, M.A., Canon and Chancellor of St. Paul's Cathedral, Select Preacher at Oxford, and Examining Chaplain to the Lord Bishop of Ely.

COUNSELS OF FAITH AND PRACTICE : being Sermons preached on various occasions. *New and Enlarged Edition. Crown 8vo. 5s.*

SPECULUM SACERDOTUM ; or, the Divine Model of the Priestly Life. *Crown 8vo. 7s. 6d.*

THE FRUIT OF THE SPIRIT. Being Ten Addresses bearing on the Spiritual Life. *Crown 8vo. 2s. 6d.*

THE MAN OF GOD. Being Six Addresses delivered during Lent a the Primary Ordination of the Right Rev. the Lord Alwyne Compton, D.D., Bishop of Ely. *Small 8vo. 1s. 6d.*

THE PRAYER BOOK : Its Voice and Teaching. Being Spiritual Addresses bearing on the Book of Common Prayer. *Crown 8vo. 2s. 6d.*

Newman.—Works by JOHN HENRY NEWMAN, B.D., sometime Vicar of St. Mary's, Oxford.

PAROCHIAL AND PLAIN SERMONS. *Eight Vols. Cabinet Edition. Crown 8vo. 5s. each. Cheaper Edition. 3s. 6d. each.*

SELECTION, ADAPTED TO THE SEASONS OF THE ECCLE-SIASTICAL YEAR, from the 'Parochial and Plain Sermons,' *Cabinet Edition. Crown 8vo. 5s. Cheaper Edition. 3s. 6d.*

FIFTEEN SERMONS PREACHED BEFORE THE UNIVERSITY OF OXFORD *Cabinet Edition. Crown 8vo. 5s. Cheaper Edition. 3s. 6d.*

SERMONS BEARING UPON SUBJECTS OF THE DAY. *Cabinet Edition. Crown 8vo. 5s. Cheaper Edition. Crown 8vo. 3s. 6d.*

LECTURES ON THE DOCTRINE OF JUSTIFICATION. *Cabinet Edition. Crown 8vo. 5s. Cheaper Edition. 3s. 6d.*

₌ *A Complete List of Cardinal Newman's Works can be had on Application.*

Norris.—RUDIMENTS OF THEOLOGY: a First Book for Students. By JOHN PILKINGTON NORRIS, D.D. late Archdeacon of Bristol, and Canon Residentiary of Bristol Cathedral. *Cr. 8vo. 3s. 6d.*

Osborne.—Works by EDWARD OSBORNE, Mission Priest of the Society of St. John the Evangelist, Cowley, Oxford.

THE CHILDREN'S SAVIOUR. Instructions to Children on the Life of Our Lord and Saviour Jesus Christ. *Illustrated. 16mo. 2s. 6d.*

THE SAVIOUR KING. Instructions to Children on Old Testament Types and Illustrations of the Life of Christ. *Illustrated. 16mo. 2s. 6d.*

THE CHILDREN'S FAITH. Instructions to Children on the Apostles' Creed. *Illustrated. 16mo. 2s. 6d.*

Overton.—THE ENGLISH CHURCH IN THE NINE-TEENTH CENTURY, 1800-1833. By the Rev. JOHN H. OVERTON, D.D., Canon of Lincoln, Rector of Epworth, Doncaster, and Rural Dean of the Isle of Axholme. *8vo. 14s.*

Oxenden.—Works by the Right Rev. ASHTON OXENDEN, formerly Bishop of Montreal.

PLAIN SERMONS, to which is prefixed a Memorial Portrait. *Crown 8vo. 5s.*

THE HISTORY OF MY LIFE: An Autobiography. *Crown 8vo. 5s.*

PEACE AND ITS HINDRANCES. *Crown 8vo. 1s. sewed; 2s. cloth.*

THE PATHWAY OF SAFETY; or, Counsel to the Awakened. *Fcap. 8vo, large type. 2s. 6d. Cheap Edition. Small type, limp, 1s.*

THE EARNEST COMMUNICANT. *New Red Rubric Edition. 32mo, cloth. 2s. Common Edition. 32mo. 1s.*

OUR CHURCH AND HER SERVICES. *Fcap. 8vo. 2s. 6d.*

[continued

Oxenden.—Works by the Right Rev. ASHTON OXENDEN formerly Bishop of Montreal—*continued.*

FAMILY PRAYERS FOR FOUR WEEKS. First Series. *Fcap. 8vo.* 2s. 6d. Second Series. *Fcap. 8vo.* 2s. 6d.

LARGE TYPE EDITION. Two Series in one Volume. *Crown 8vo.* 6s.

COTTAGE SERMONS; or, Plain Words to the Poor. *Fcap. 8vo.* 2s. 6d.

THOUGHTS FOR HOLY WEEK. *16mo, cloth.* 1s. 6d.

DECISION. *18mo.* 1s. 6d.

THE HOME BEYOND; or, A Happy Old Age. *Fcap. 8vo.* 1s. 6d.

THE LABOURING MAN'S BOOK. *18mo, large type, cloth.* 1s. 6d.

Paget.—Works by FRANCIS PAGET, D.D., Dean of Christ Church.

STUDIES IN THE CHRISTIAN CHARACTER: Sermons. With an Introductory Essay. *Crown 8vo.* 6s. 6d.

THE SPIRIT OF DISCIPLINE: Sermons. *Crown 8vo.* 6s. 6d.

FACULTIES AND DIFFICULTIES FOR BELIEF AND DIS-BELIEF. *Crown 8vo.* 6s. 6d.

THE HALLOWING OF WORK. Addresses given at Eton, January 16-18, 1888. *Small 8vo.* 2s.

PRACTICAL REFLECTIONS. By a CLERGYMAN. With Prefaces by H. P. LIDDON, D.D., D.C.L., and the BISHOP OF LINCOLN. *Crown 8vo.*

THE BOOK OF GENESIS. 4s. 6d.	THE HOLY GOSPELS. 4s. 6d.
THE PSALMS. 5s.	ACTS TO REVELATIONS. 6s.
ISAIAH. 4s. 6d.	

PRIEST (THE) TO THE ALTAR; or, Aids to the Devout Celebration of Holy Communion, chiefly after the Ancient English Use of Sarum. *Royal 8vo.* 12s.

Prynne.—THE TRUTH AND REALITY OF THE EUCHARISTIC SACRIFICE, Proved from Holy Scripture, the Teaching of the Primitive Church, and the Book of Common Prayer. By the Rev. GEORGE RUNDLE PRYNNE, M.A. *Crown 8vo.* 3s. 6d.

Puller.—THE PRIMITIVE SAINTS AND THE SEE OF ROME. By F. W. PULLER, M.A., Mission Priest of the Society of St. John Evangelist, Cowley, Oxford. *Crown 8vo.* 7s. 6d.

Pusey.—LIFE OF EDWARD BOUVERIE PUSEY, D.D. By HENRY PARRY LIDDON, D.D., D.C.L., LL.D. Edited and prepared for publication by the Rev. J. O. JOHNSTON, M.A., Principal of the Theological College, Vicar of Cuddesdon, Oxford, and the Rev. ROBERT J. WILSON, D.D., Warden of Keble College. *With Portraits and Illustrations. Four Vols.* 8vo. *Vols. I. and II.,* 36s. *Vol. III.,* 18s.

Pusey.—Works by the Rev. E. B. PUSEY, D.D.

PRIVATE PRAYERS. With Preface by H. P. LIDDON, D.D. *32mo.* 1s.

SELECTIONS FROM THE WRITINGS OF EDWARD BOUVERIE PUSEY, D.D. *Crown 8vo.* 2s. 6d.

Randolph.—LAW OF SINAI : being Devotional Addresses on the Ten Commandments delivered to Ordinands. By B. W. RANDOLPH, M.A., Principal of the Theological College and Hon. Canon of Ely. *Crown 8vo. 3s. 6d.*

Sanday.—Works by W. SANDAY, D.D., Margaret Professor of Divinity in the University of Oxford.

INSPIRATION : Eight Lectures on the Early History and Origin of the Doctrine of Biblical Inspiration. Being the Bampton Lectures for 1893. *Crown. 7s. 6d.*

THE ORACLES OF GOD : Nine Lectures on the Nature and Extent of Biblical Inspiration and the Special Significance of the Old Testament Scriptures at the Present Time. *Crown 8vo. 4s.*

TWO PRESENT-DAY QUESTIONS. I. Biblical Criticism. II. The Social Movement. Sermons preached before the University of Cambridge. *Crown 8vo. 2s. 6d.*

Seebohm.—THE OXFORD REFORMERS—JOHN COLET, ERASMUS, AND THOMAS MORE : A History of their Fellow-Work. By FREDERICK SEEBOHM. *8vo. 14s.*

Williams.—Works by the Rev. ISAAC WILLIAMS, B.D.

A DEVOTIONAL COMMENTARY ON THE GOSPEL NARRATIVE, *Eight Vols. Crown 8vo. 5s. each. Sold Separately.*

THOUGHTS ON THE STUDY OF THE HOLY GOSPELS.

A HARMONY OF THE FOUR GOSPELS.
OUR LORD'S NATIVITY.
OUR LORD'S MINISTRY (Second Year).
OUR LORD'S MINISTRY (Third Year).
THE HOLY WEEK.
OUR LORD'S PASSION.
OUR LORD'S RESURRECTION.

FEMALE CHARACTERS OF HOLY SCRIPTURE. A Series of Sermons, *Crown 8vo. 5s.*

THE CHARACTERS OF THE OLD TESTAMENT. *Crown 8vo. 5s.*

THE APOCALYPSE. With Notes and Reflections. *Crown 8vo. 5s.*

SERMONS ON THE EPISTLES AND GOSPELS FOR THE SUNDAYS AND HOLY DAYS. *Two Vols. Crown 8vo. 5s. each.*

PLAIN SERMONS ON CATECHISM. *Two Vols. Cr. 8vo. 5s. each.*

SELECTIONS FROM ISAAC WILLIAMS' WRITINGS. *Cr. 8vo. 3s. 6d.*

THE AUTOBIOGRAPHY OF ISAAC WILLIAMS, B.D., Author of several of the ' Tracts for the Times.' Edited by the Venerable Sir GEORGE PREVOST, as throwing further light on the history of the Oxford Movement. *Crown 8vo. 5s.*

Wordsworth.—Works by the late CHRISTOPHER WORDSWORTH, D.D., Bishop of Lincoln.

THE HOLY BIBLE (the Old Testament). With Notes, Introductions, and Index. *Imperial 8vo.*

Vol. I. THE PENTATEUCH. 25*s.* Vol. II. JOSHUA TO SAMUEL. 15*s.* Vol. III. KINGS to ESTHER. 15*s.* Vol. IV. JOB TO SONG OF SOLOMON. 25*s.* Vol. V. ISAIAH TO EZEKIEL. 25*s.* Vol. VI. DANIEL, MINOR PROPHETS, and Index. 15*s.*

Also supplied in 12 Parts. Sold separately.

THE NEW TESTAMENT, in the Original Greek. With Notes, Introductions, and Indices. *Imperial 8vo.*

Vol. I. GOSPELS AND ACTS OF THE APOSTLES. 23*s.* Vol. II. EPISTLES, APOCALYPSE, and Indices. 37*s.*

Also supplied in 4 Parts. Sold separately.

LECTURES ON INSPIRATION OF THE BIBLE. *Small 8vo.* 1*s.* 6*d. cloth.* 1*s. sewed.*

A CHURCH HISTORY TO A.D. 451. *Four Vols. Crown 8vo.*

Vol. I. TO THE COUNCIL OF NICÆA, A.D. 325. 8*s.* 6*d.* Vol. II. FROM THE COUNCIL OF NICÆA TO THAT OF CONSTANTINOPLE. 6*s.* Vol. III. CONTINUATION. 6*s.* Vol. IV. CONCLUSION, TO THE COUNCIL OF CHALCEDON, A.D. 451. 6*s.*

THEOPHILUS ANGLICANUS: a Manual of Instruction on the Church and the Anglican Branch of it. *12mo.* 2*s.* 6*d.*

ELEMENTS OF INSTRUCTION ON THE CHURCH. *16mo.* 1*s. cloth.* 6*d. sewed.*

ST. HIPPOLYTUS AND THE CHURCH OF ROME. *Cr. 8vo.* 7*s.* 6*d.*

ON UNION WITH ROME. *Small 8vo.* 1*s.* 6*d.* Sewed, 1*s.*

THE HOLY YEAR : Original Hymns. *16mo.* 2*s.* 6*d. and 1s. Limp, 6d.*

  ,,   ,, With Music. Edited by W. H. MONK. *Square 8vo.* 4*s.* 6*d.*

GUIDES AND GOADS. (An English Edition of 'Ethica et Spiritualia.') *32mo.* 1*s.* 6*d.*

MISCELLANIES, Literary and Religious. *Three Vols. 8vo.* 36*s.*

ON THE INTERMEDIATE STATE OF THE SOUL AFTER DEATH. *32mo.* 1*s.*

Younghusband.—Works by FRANCES YOUNGHUSBAND.

THE STORY OF OUR LORD, told in Simple Language for Children. With 25 Illustrations on Wood from Pictures by the Old Masters, and numerous Ornamental Borders, Initial Letters, etc., from Longmans' New Testament. *Crown 8vo.* 2*s.* 6*d.*

THE STORY OF GENESIS, told in Simple Language for Children. With Frontispiece. *Crown 8vo.* 2*s.* 6*d.*

THE STORY OF THE EXODUS, told in Simple Language for Children. With Map and 29 Illustrations. *Crown 8vo.* 2*s.* 6*d.*

Printed by T. and A. CONSTABLE, Printers to Her Majesty, at the Edinburgh University Press.

10,000/1/96

www.ingramcontent.com/pod-product-compliance
Lightning Source LLC
Chambersburg PA
CBHW052337110726
47901CB00005B/1264